THE MUSIC OF TIME

Also by John Burnside

Poetry collections

The Hoop (1988)
Common Knowledge (1991)
Feast Days (1992)
The Myth of the Twin (1994)
Swimming in the Flood (1995)
Penguin Modern Poets (1996)
A Normal Skin (1997)
The Asylum Dance (2000)
The Light Trap (2002)
A Poet's Polemic (2003)
The Good Neighbour (2005)
Selected Poems (2006)
Gift Songs (2007)
The Hunt in the Forest (2009)
Black Cat Bone (2011)
All One Breath (2014)
Still Life with Feeding Snake (2017)

Fiction

The Dumb House (1997)
The Mercy Boys (1999)
Burning Elvis (2000)
The Locust Room (2001)
Living Nowhere (2003)
The Devil's Footprints (2007)
Glister (2008)
A Summer of Drowning (2011)
Something Like Happy (2013)
Ashland & Vine (2017)
Havergey (2017)

Non-Fiction

Wild Reckoning with Maurice
Riordan (2004)
A Lie About My Father (2006)
Wallace Stevens: poems (2008)
Waking up in Toytown (2010)
I Put a Spell on You (2014)
On Henry Miller (2018)

THE MUSIC
OF TIME

POETRY IN THE
TWENTIETH CENTURY

JOHN BURNSIDE

Princeton University Press
Princeton and Oxford

Requests for permission to reproduce material from this work should be sent to *permissions@press.princeton.edu*

First published in a slightly different form in Great Britain in 2019 by
Profile Books Ltd
29 Cloth Fair, London ECIA 7NN

Published in the United States and Canada by
Princeton University Press
41 William Street, Princeton, New Jersey 08540

press.princeton.edu

ISBN 978-0-691-20155-9
ISBN (e-book) 978-0-691-20156-6
Library of Congress Control Number 2019949624

Jacket design by Richard Green

This book has been composed in Dante

Printed on acid-free paper. ∞

Printed in the United States of America

10 9 8 7 6 5 4 3 2 1

In memory of Lucie Brock-Broido

CONTENTS

And yet sometimes
The wheel turns of its own weight, the rusty
Pump pumps over your sweating face the clear
Water, cold, so cold! you cup your hands
And gulp from them the dailiness of life.

Randall Jarrell

All poetry translations are by the author
unless otherwise stated.

A NOTE TO THE READER

SINCE WORK BEGAN ON this book, five years ago, the original project – a personal history of twentieth century poetry – has changed considerably; so much so that, when talking about it, I find myself resorting to John Donne's 'simply perfectest' definition, that 'can by no way be express'd but negatives'. In this manner, I can say that *The Music of Time* is not a literary history, or even a survey, in the usual sense; nor is it a textbook or primer on how to read certain poets. I would even add that, while it is tempting to describe these vagabond and occasionally digressive chapters as a personal meditation on a life spent reading and writing poetry, and leave it at that, I would be doing an injustice to an underlying, if occasionally elusive current that I hope will finally emerge from these pages, a current whose central ideas are gradually revealed using the somewhat unconventional methods of investigation (lyrical, imaginative, anti-reductive) that they propose.

In short, my approach has been to step outside the more academic analyses of literature, and write about poetry responsively, which is to say, to discuss poems and ideas of poetry as they inform, not just 'the life of the mind' but also my own day-to-day existence. For this is where poetry works best, in what Randall Jarrell calls 'the dailiness of life' – and what the poets discussed here have achieved, in the face of societal violence, rapid change, environmental degradation and the mechanisation of almost everything, is a continuing, if sometimes minority, culture in which an appreciation of the everyday, and of the 'irrational' (beauty, for example, or the sense of wonder) provides, not only a counter to overly mechanistic, procedural thinking, but also a basis for what might be described as a science of *belonging*. Returning to Donne's expression by negatives, I am happy to admit that this book is digressive and idiosyncratic, and it is by no means as inclusive as I would have liked (a second volume might include some thoughts on French and Polish poetry, both regretfully omitted here, as well as work from China, Canada, Ghana, Australia – the list goes on). Nevertheless, I dare to hope that these, and its many other flaws, may be partly offset by the experimental nature of the approach, and the audacity of an argument that proposes, not only that poetry is not a minority or elitist art, but is, in some form or another, the central pillar of any nurturing culture. Or, to paraphrase Stephen Spender, the struggle of any society – against external powers, and sometimes with itself – is a struggle for the conditions in which the writing and reading of poetry are not only possible, but also prized.

INTRODUCTION

[…] it has been shown, as well as the narrow limits assigned them would permit, that what is called poetry, in a restricted sense, has a common source with all other forms of order and of beauty, according to which the materials of human life are susceptible of being arranged, and which is poetry in an universal sense.

Percy Bysshe Shelley

AS A YOUNG MAN in the 1910s, the poet and travel writer Osip Mandelstam joined the Acmeist group, a loose affiliation of writers who met regularly at St Petersburg's Stray Dog Café until the authorities closed it down in 1915. The group's founders, Nikolay Gumilev and Sergei Gorodetsky, set as their programme a rejection of the decadence and excess of the Symbolist Movement, with its exclusivist mystique rooted in the music of Wagner, Nietzschean philosophy and the writings of Fyodor Tyutchev, whose finest work, 'Silentium', was a key influence:

How can a heart expression find?
How should another know your mind?
Will he discern what quickens you?
A thought once uttered is untrue.
Dimmed is the fountainhead when stirred:
drink at the source and speak no word.

Live in your inner self alone
within your soul a world has grown,
the magic of veiled thoughts that might
be blinded by the outer light,
drowned in the noise of day, unheard ...
take in their song and speak no word.[1]

This mood of mystical withdrawal from the public realm, compounded with the sometimes wilful obscurity of second-wave Symbolists such as Vyacheslav Ivanov and Andrei Bely, provoked Gumilev and his friends (the group included such future luminaries as Mikhail Kuzmin, Anna Akhmatova and Georgiy Ivanov) to propose a new poetic art, based on clarity of expression and a new foregrounding of the image as subject, that invites comparison both with the poetic philosophy of Ezra Pound and T. E. Hulme, and with the William Carlos Williams of 'The Red Wheelbarrow'. Like many such groups, however, the Acmeists were something of an odd mix, aligning Gumilev's high rhetoric and penchant for exoticism with the tight, near-Minimalist work collected in Mandelstam's first volume, *Stone* (first published in 1913), and Akhmatova's elegant and economical love lyrics. Mandelstam was never entirely comfortable with the group, and eventually he set out on his own path, but before he did so, he wrote a manifesto-like document, *The Morning of Acmeism*, in which he declared: 'To exist is the artist's greatest pride. He desires no other paradise than existence [...] Love the existence of the thing more than the thing itself and your own existence more than yourself: that is Acmeism's highest commandment.' It is a remark that he is reported to have made at public meetings on several occasions, however, that most resonates for us now. Asked to define the essence of Acmeism, Mandelstam's response summed up everything he believed about this new, post-Symbolist, philosophically engaged aesthetic: Acmeism, he said, was 'homesickness for a world culture'. That may have pleased at least some of his audience, but it was anathema to the new Bolshevik regime – and most of Acmeism's principal adherents soon fell to the Bolshevik

Terror. (Gumilev, who made no attempt to conceal his contempt for the Bolsheviks, was executed in 1921; Ivanov went into exile, where he waged a long-running dispute with Nabokov; Anna Akhmatova survived, but the regime punished her indirectly by persecuting her son with Gumilev, Lev Nikolayevich, who would spend the best part of eighteen years, off and on, in Stalin's labour camps.)

Mandelstam, meanwhile, quickly attracted the attention of the NKVD and, though it has been claimed that he was protected, briefly, by Stalin himself (who had started out as an aspiring poet), he suffered a series of exiles and imprisonments before finally vanishing in the 1930s into a Soviet labour camp, where he is presumed to have died. A few years before that, from yet another period of exile in Voronezh, he would write a poignant rider to that youthful expression of love for the mere fact of existence, a love that transcends even the attachment to self. 'My desire', he said, 'is not to speak about myself but to track down the age, the noise and the germination of time. My memory is inimical to all that is personal.'[2] It was a sentiment that he had expressed in various forms throughout his brutally truncated career, perhaps most elegantly in the 1923 poem 'The Age':

> To free the age from its confinement,
> To instigate a brand new world,
> The discordant, tangled days
> Must be linked, as with a flute.*

Sadly, the new world that Mandelstam had in mind was as different from Stalin's as it was possible to be. Yet that image of the flute remains and, occurring as it does in lines by a poet who, in 1914, could capture the song of 'orioles in the woods' in a string of singing vowel sounds,[†] it seems not overly fanciful to imagine

---

* Translation by Marc Adler.

† Есть иволги в лесах, и гласных долгота
В тонических стихах единственная мера,
Но только раз в году бывает разлита

that we can hear that flute still, weaving the tangled days together, transforming the noise of time into a kind of music.

As the grinding wheels of the Industrial Revolution transmogrified into the ever-shifting cityscapes of modernity, the noise of time would be made manifest in any number of ways, of which the First World War and the Bolshevik Revolution were among the most extreme. Anna Akhmatova captured it from the Russian perspective in a poem that marked the outbreak of war with Germany, 'In Memoriam, July 19, 1914':

> The hushed road burst in colors then, a soaring
> Lament rose, ringing silver like a bell.
> And so I covered up my face, imploring
> God to destroy me before battle fell.
>
> And from my memory the shadows vanished
> Of songs and passions – burdens I'd not need.[3]

Here, Akhmatova seems to be saying, the preoccupations of her youth (poetry, love, music) would no longer be required, as new burdens were imposed on a desperate people. Those earlier burdens had been light, part of the dailiness of life – and they had been of her own choosing. Now, the pressure was to come from outside, and it would not be optional.

Meanwhile, the chaos being wrought by war, revolution and the rise of fascism would give rise to similar sensations of helplessness and inevitability elsewhere. All of a sudden, history, once conceivable as an ordered narrative, was transformed, in Walter Benjamin's vision, into tragic allegory:

В природе длительность, как в метрике Гомера.

Как бы цезурою зияет этот день:
Уже с утра покой и трудные длинно́ты,
Волы на пастбище, и золотая лень
Из тростника извлечь богатство целой ноты.

The Angel of History must look just so. His face is turned towards the past. Where we see the appearance of a chain of events, he sees one single catastrophe, which unceasingly piles rubble on top of rubble and hurls it before his feet. He would like to pause for a moment so fair as to awaken the dead and to piece together what has been smashed. But a storm is blowing from Paradise, it has caught itself up in his wings and is so strong that the Angel can no longer close them. The storm drives him irresistibly into the future, to which his back is turned, while the rubble-heap before him grows sky-high. That which we call progress is this storm.[4]

Elsewhere still, as the cacophony persisted and grew, conservative writers and artists tried to draw together the wisps of an acceptable canon, in hopes of securing some fragments they might shore against their ruin. That fear of cultural collapse was to continue well into the century; here, for example, the English artist-writer Wyndham Lewis recalls his own formulation of a highly Eurocentric canon in his autobiographical sketch *Rude Assignment*:

Darwin, Voltaire, Newton, Raphael, Dante, Epictetus, Aristotle, Sophocles, Plato, Pythagoras: all shedding their light upon the same wide, well-lit Greco-Roman highway, with the same kind of sane and steady ray – one need only mention these to recognize that it was at least excusable to be concerned about the threat of extinction to that tradition.

For a difficult period, it seemed clear that the response of art to the pandemonium of modernity would be entirely defensive, the proposal of a self-defeating museum culture, with values defined by a polite coterie of patrons and trustees who could not see beyond their own social class and culture (or, for that matter, gender and race).

This conservative retreat to higher ground was not universal, however. In fact, many poets relished the challenges of modernity and regarded the winds of historical change as advantageous to the creation of new ways of seeing, breaking the limits that had been imposed by the class and societal boundaries that men like Wyndham Lewis thought so essential to the continuance of a laudable culture. William Carlos Williams, a keen socialist who spoke out against the poverty and degradation he saw as a general practitioner in Rutherford, New Jersey, spoke of a new 'American idiom' that would allow poets in the United States to break away from received European forms (as a previous generation of innovative prose writers, such as Melville and Hawthorne, had done in fiction, creating a new kind of novel as they went), while an intrepid band of mostly self-educated working-class writers came to feel sufficiently liberated by social change to write and publish in areas and outlets they had rarely been able to access in the past. As they did so, they were eager to offer the social critiques that had been suppressed for so long; here, for example, Clifford Chatterley's prejudice against working people is allowed to speak for itself, in D. H. Lawrence's *Lady Chatterley's Lover*:

> And don't fall into errors: in your sense of the word, they are not men. They are animals you don't understand, and never could. Don't thrust your illusions on other people. The masses were always the same, and will always be the same. Nero's slaves were extremely little different from our colliers or the Ford motor-car workmen. I mean Nero's mine slaves and his field slaves. It is the masses: they are the unchangeable.

And here is Langston Hughes, in a poem simply entitled 'Question', subjecting race relations in America to a new kind of scrutiny:

> When the old junk man Death
> Comes to gather up our bodies
> And toss them into the sack of oblivion,
> I wonder if he will find
> The corpse of a white multi-millionaire
> Worth more pennies of eternity,
> Than the black torso of
> A Negro cotton-picker?[5]

At the same time, all across Europe and the Americas, those who could entertain notions of tradition that were more fluid than those espoused by the old guard started to assimilate the changes and to respond imaginatively (as opposed to merely reacting). Thus, while he could be accused of the benefit of hindsight, the poet Eugenio Montale was only summarising a lifelong commitment to intellectual integrity when he described (and carefully qualified) this response in his Nobel speech of 1975: 'I have always knocked at the door of that wonderful and terrible enigma which is life', he said, going on to add: 'I have been judged to be a pessimist, but what abyss of ignorance and low egoism is not hidden in one who thinks that Man is the god of himself and that his future can only be triumphant?'

But how had time come to be so noisy in the first place? There had always been wars; there had always been poverty and prejudice. What had been lacking, however, was the intense regulation of day-to-day life that the *measurement* – and, eventually, the industrialisation – of time imposed.

The first human communities had calculated time, on one level, by looking up to the sun and the moon and, on another, by observing the changes in the natural world as they happened, sometimes in minute detail. Even later, when time was measured by human-made devices, the images that governed the hours and days were organic: the flow of water in a clepsydra, the movement of a shadow across the face of a sundial, sand trickling steadily through the neck of an hourglass. The first mechanical clocks did not appear in Europe until late in the thirteenth century, and for a long time they were too large to be located anywhere but in churches and other public spaces. The first pocket watches appeared in the sixteenth century; the first mechanical alarm clock was patented by the French inventor Antoine Redier in 1847. By that time, rumblings from the Efficiency Movement were being heard in the halls of industrial power, and by the 1880s the new system of scientific management began introducing such 'improvements' in labour practices as Frederick Winslow Taylor's time-and-motion studies. So it was that humanity's experience of measured time progressed from water flowing through a clay funnel to the steady ticking of town hall clocks and, finally, to the digitisation of everything – and as that process continued, our analogues for time and space became more and more remote from the physical world. Alongside the noise of time as manifested in war and the industrialisation of the land, we came to inhabit a world of infinite temporal subdivisions, a lifetime of shift-work and comfort breaks, of upload times and nanoseconds. Now, for too many, the daily round is a long monotone dictated by the mobile phone and the online schedule, a condition of voluntary servitude that allows us, by 'checking in' continuously, to verify the validity of our existence. It is interesting, then, to think that Montale, who so valued the fabric of daily life, should have summarised this condition so perfectly as far back as 1962, when he remarked, in a mood of darkest irony:

> It is not true that man is too mechanised, the fact is that he is not mechanised enough. If, one day, he is absorbed and interpenetrated entirely by the universal mechanical order, ideas of freedom and its lack will lose all meaning, for this new man will no longer feel any need to question himself about his destiny, while words like philosophy and art will be forgotten, as the human being (if we can still call him by that name) will come to attain that functional contentment that is the only happiness of which he is capable.[6]

This conclusion was not reached impulsively, or without a long history of evidence, however; what we know most surely about modernity is that it exponentially hastened an industrialisation process that began with the appearance of the Albion flour mills in Lambeth that William Blake so prophetically decried in 'Jerusalem'. Soon Marx and Engels were adding to the prophetic choir, declaring (in *The Communist Manifesto* of 1848): 'All that is solid melts into air, all that is holy is profaned.' The only valid response to all this noise, however, was not pessimism – an accusation that, in the end, Montale quietly refuted – but that highly singular kind of hope that only flourishes in the absence of optimism. And while this will sound contradictory, it is, nevertheless, significant – for optimism has never been a very sound position from which to work, strategically; it usually operates by blinding us to the real parameters of hope, which only come clear when, as Marianne Moore notes in 'The Hero', we have 'to go slow':

> tired but hopeful –
> hope not being hope
> until all ground for hope has
> vanished; and lenient, looking
> upon a fellow creature's error with the
> feelings of a mother – a
> woman or a cat.[7]

The twin heroic attributes of which Moore speaks – hope *in extremis* and a form of leniency that is not indulgent so much as informed by a radical responsibility towards our fellow creatures – are the two attributes that strike me as most interesting in the poetry I have chosen, from a wide range of possibilities, to explore in this book.

These poets, to whom I have had sometimes repeated recourse, are rarely optimistic, but they are, nevertheless, creatures of hope, and this is what makes even the least political of them actively dissident, in the best sense of the word. For, unlike optimism, hope is always an act of courage, even when it is contradicted by every rule of logic. Add to this that optimism is a personal concern, while hope is general – and truly inclusive. Optimism speaks of the individual or her kin; hope speaks for the species as a whole.

That said, I have no wish to take issue with Dylan Thomas when he refuses to accept that 'poets must have positions – other than upright'.* I agree that what matters most in a poem is its music and how it refreshes the language, strengthening it against the abuses of the unscrupulous and the careless, and allowing it to retain its ability to enchant, to invoke and to particularise in ways that mere denotation, or the sometimes reductive language employed by salesmen, politicians and Gradgrindly industrialists, all too often curtails. The first task, the first impulse, of the poet is an effort at a very specific kind of speech – and, as T. S. Eliot says, in 'Little Gidding': 'Since our concern was speech [...] speech impelled us/ To purify the dialect of the tribe.' Unlike the usual linguistic resources we draw on to describe and delimit and so navigate our environment, that particular form of speech is able to draw on intuition and invocation and all the other as yet unnamed faculties that scientific orthodoxy deems frivolous or unreliable. As Shelley argues, in *A Defence of Poetry*:

> Poetry, as has been said, differs in this respect from logic, that it is not subject to the control of the active powers of the mind, and that its birth and recurrence have no necessary connection with the consciousness or will. It is presumptuous to determine that these are the necessary conditions of all mental causation, when mental effects are experienced unsusceptible of being referred to them.

Nevertheless, even poets whose most pressing engagement is with the language are still, by that very token, engaged. To purify the dialect, to enrich the language, to resist those who would let speech slide into mere gossip or drivelling, is also political. To imagine otherwise is to be self-deceived.

---

* Indeed, discussing the position of Welsh poets in particular during a 1946 radio broadcast, he made what, for many, is so decisive an argument that only the most determinedly ideological reader would seriously dispute him: 'It's the poetry, written in the language which is most natural to the poet, that counts, not his continent, country, island, race, class, or political persuasion.'

Hope is of the essence, then, for all poets. We might even say that to make a poem at all is an act of hope. Yet while it is one thing to diagnose the damage done to the land, or to the language, by the noise of time (and by its quieter, more monotonous undertones), it is another to find, if not solutions, then some means by which to re-interpret all this noise and so make of it a kind of music. For many, in fact, this will seem an unreasonable task, requiring not so much mental fight and informed hope as an out-and-out miracle. That may be true – but if this book is to be anything more than a history of twentieth century poetry that even the most casual observer will see as unashamedly partial (in both senses of the word), I feel it must at least try to offer some kind of response to the challenge posed by the American anarchist poet and publisher Lawrence Ferlinghetti when he said that 'the state of the world calls out for poetry to save it'. This will seem absurd to many. How can poetry, a neglected, even derided art, save anything? According to some observers, it can't even save itself from creeping Bowdlerisation and gimmickry. But then, as any musician knows, you can play a tune badly and the music remains unharmed. For every arts page feature that proclaims the death of poetry, a new poem emerges, miraculously, into a supposedly indifferent world. Whenever an oddly gleeful-sounding piece claims that 'Poetry is going extinct, government data show', pointing out that poetry is now less popular than jazz, 'singing with others' and even knitting, I pick out another journal from the news-stand and read the latest offering from Robert Wrigley, or Jorie Graham, or I chance upon a poet I have never read before, someone from Chad or Ecuador who is rediscovering a buried tradition and, in so doing, renewing mine – and I remind myself that, while it would be easy to get upset by all this flummery, we have to remember that it is a calculated distraction, just more noise to add to the general cacophony.

With all these distractions playing out in the public sphere, then, this book is intended to examine the different ways in which poets have responded to the noise of time, loud or insinuating, global or local, farcical or tragic. As we have seen, many erected elaborate but essentially rearguard defences against what they perceived as impending catastrophe, and that is understandable. Yet the writers who have most interested me have been those who made it their project to transform the cacophony into some kind of new and more inclusive music – and, in doing so, created new harmonies, new forms and new ways of seeing. And though poetry as a discipline needs no external, and certainly no *societal* justification (any more than astronomy, dance or singing with others does), I will argue that, as music-making is a way of making sense of noise, of giving noise order, so poetry is a way of ordering experience, of giving a meaningful order to lived time – and that that process of ordering could be summed up in a phrase from the Old Irish, a phrase that is first found in a tale of the Fianna-Finn, who, during a break from hunting, begin to debate what might constitute 'the finest music in the world'. One man says it is 'The cuckoo calling from the tree that is highest in the hedge', while others jump in to suggest 'the top of music is the ring of a spear on a shield', 'the belling of a stag across water', 'the song of a lark' and 'the laugh of a gleeful girl'. Finally, they turn to their chief, Fionn, and ask him what he would choose, to which he replies: 'The music of what happens ... that is the finest music in the world.'

The music of what happens. What better way of talking about the life of home and circumstance and local region that, so far, is the only alternative to conflict that we have discovered (for, let a person learn to value what is at hand, and he or she is less likely to go out looking to steal from others)? Another way of expressing this idea might be Randall Jarrell's notion of 'the dailiness of life' as a deep source of cool, life-giving water that we cannot necessarily summon at will but receive by grace, when the wheel of this world turns 'of its own weight'. This dailiness of life comes under a variety of different rubrics by way of different cultures and different poets, but there is a consistency, in their emphasis on the everyday as a meaningful alternative to conflict, that runs across the board. What matters is the music of what happens (the given, the natural, the everyday, the free) as an expression of a quality not only of, but also *in*, life.

When I began work on this book, I wanted to write something like a defence of poetry, in the spirit, if not exactly the letter, of Shelley's essay of that name, which appeared not quite two hundred years ago, an elegant and justly renowned treatise on the power poetry has to purge 'from our inward sight the film of familiarity which obscures from us the wonder of our being'. Back in 1821, Shelley composed his *Defence* as 'an antidote' to *The Four Ages of Poetry*, in which his friend Thomas Love Peacock rather wittily opined that 'in whatever degree poetry is cultivated, it must necessarily be to the neglect of some branch of useful study: and it is a lamentable spectacle to see minds, capable of better things, running to seed in the specious indolence of these empty aimless mockeries of intellectual exertion.' As if this were not enough, he went on to assert that

> mathematicians, astronomers, chemists, moralists, meta-physicians, historians, politicians, and political economists [...] have built into the upper air of intelligence a pyramid, from the summit of which they see the modern Parnassus far beneath them, and [...] smile at the little ambition and the cir-cumscribed perceptions with which the drivellers and moun-tebanks upon it are contending for the poetical palm and the critical chair.

Shelley's response to all this was to claim, famously:

> It is impossible to read the compositions of the most celebrated writers of the present day without being startled with the electric life which burns within their words. They measure the circumference and sound the depths of human nature with a comprehensive and all-penetrating spirit, and they are themselves perhaps the most sincerely astonished at its manifestations; for it is less their spirit than the spirit of the age. Poets are the hierophants of an unapprehended inspiration; the mirrors of the gigantic shadows which futurity casts upon the present; the words which express what they understand not; the trumpets which sing to battle, and feel not what they

inspire; the influence which is moved not, but moves. Poets are the unacknowledged legislators of the world.

Is Shelley right? Or are the crafters of verse and metaphors wasting time that could be better employed serving technology? Can poetry save the world, as Ferlinghetti suggests? This will sound quixotic, but I have to say, not only that it can, but that it *does*. Poetry saves the world every day. It is how we declare our love for things and for the other animals; it is how we remember, in spite of a constant diet of 'hard' science, that the 'invisible' informs the visible in ways beyond our direct telling; and it is how we nurture hope, cradling it in words and music as a hand cradles a flame against the wind. It is how we define ourselves as something more than a mechanical being for whom 'the chief good and market of his time / Be but to sleep and feed' (and make money). This is what we are; this is what we do. We make culture. It doesn't matter if it's poetry or baseball or German Expressionism, but some kind of magic is what we are here to perpetrate. For the most part, we do the other things (the money stuff, the daily round of chores and obligations, the rendering unto Caesar) so that we can have some kind of poetry in our lives and, no matter how powerful or rich or privileged they are, we pity those who either do not have it or who possess it as an acquired thing, a badge of authority or status, a gaudy ornament or a mere entertainment. Poetry is how we give shape to our griefs, the better to see and measure and, in time, heal them, winding them, along with our quotidian pleasures and our reasons for joy, into the fabric of history, both personal and common, folding each individual experience of place and time into the shared music of what happens.

GHOSTLY MUSIC IN THE AIR

For all the history of grief
An empty doorway and a maple leaf.

For love
The leaning grasses and two lights above the sea – [1]

Archibald MacLeish

THERE IS A LONG MOMENT, before a summer storm breaks over Berlin, when everything is still. An eerie darkness hangs above the streets and cafés, not unlike the darkness in a theatre before the lights go up, and the city falls quiet for miles. We feel it, my son and I, as we take shelter at the Rathaus Schöneberg U-Bahn station: a hush that extends all the way from Dahlem Dorf to Bernau and out over the stork-haunted ponds and asparagus fields of Brandenburg, a hush that includes everything until, finally, the first lightning illumines the grey air and the rain comes lashing down. Few European cities do a summer storm as well as Berlin, and almost everyone here is a connoisseur: none more so than the elderly man with a cart full of groceries at the foot of the U-Bahn stairs, whose face breaks into a delighted, conspiratorial grin at the first roll of thunder. He has heard Lucas speaking to me in English, so he turns and says, with just the right level of theatricality, '*Donner!* Thunder!' We can see from his face that he wants to share this drama with us, as guests of his city: for him, as an old-time Berliner, it may be the best hospitality he can offer.

Then the sky lights up again and we know the storm is right above our heads, which means that we will be standing here for some time – time enough, as it happens, for the old man, who tells us his name is Ernst, to recall the historic day, fifty years earlier, when an American president stood in front of the Rathaus and declared himself a citizen of Berlin. I feel a faint rush of gratitude to him for this: we had come here for reasons of homework, to get a sense of the place and try to imagine the scene on 26 June 1963, when John F. Kennedy made his famous *Ich bin ein Berliner* speech. Luckily for us, this old man, in his perfect, 1950s cinema English, tells a great story.

For Lucas, who is studying at the Berlin British School, Ernst is a gift from heaven on this wet summer's day. He knows his facts, but he also furnishes his account with the authority and vividness of an eyewitness. He has learned much of Kennedy's speech by heart and impresses us by reciting key lines: 'Two thousand years ago, the proudest boast in the world was *civis romanus sum*. Today, the proudest boast is *Ich bin ein Berliner*.' He even claims to remember the storms of 'Black Friday', when supply planes from the Combined Task Force stacked up dangerously over Tempelhof as they delivered supplies to the besieged city after the Soviet blockade was imposed. I try to calculate how old he is; if he is seventy now, say, he would have been five years old in 1948, and I wonder if he is telling us something he saw, or a story he heard long ago, when the real witnesses were still alive. The next moment, however, I realise that, in the current context, it doesn't actually matter. His stories are true, for him and for whomsoever he has shared them with down the years – and now they are true for us.

Finally, when the rain slows, we help him carry his shopping up the steep steps of the U-Bahn exit, then head off to John F. Kennedy Platz itself. The weather is against us, however. Some of the traders from the weekly flea market are sheltering in the doorway of the Rathaus, smoking cigarettes and staring out across the square, but most are packing up early, saving what they can of their bric-à-brac and war memorabilia for another day. Even the cafés are closing, and another downpour seems imminent ('too much water', one waiter says). So, after taking a moment to stare at the Rathaus, we turn and go back the way we came. The air is darkening again and, just as we reach the U-Bahn, the sky opens once more and a new storm flickers across the city. Homework is done with, for today at least, so we get back on the train and head over to Neu-Westend for coffee and cakes at the Viennese café on Steubenplatz.

While Lucas's engagement with John F. Kennedy was mostly academic, my own reason for being in Schöneberg on that rainy afternoon was personal. Because the first strong influences that guided me as a poet were American, I have always had a particular fascination with the relationship between poets and the political system of the United States – and on the political side it was Kennedy who most dramatically raised the bar when it came to poetry's influence on policy and national culture, first when he chose Robert Frost to 'say' a poem at his inauguration ceremony in 1960, and then, perhaps more importantly, in the words he spoke at the old poet's memorial service, two years later – words that inspired me, as a younger writer, with hope that my chosen craft really could play a direct role in political life:

> Robert Frost coupled poetry and power, for he saw poetry as the means of saving power from itself. When power leads man towards arrogance, poetry reminds him of his limitations. When power narrows the areas of man's concern, poetry reminds him of the richness and diversity of his existence. When power corrupts, poetry cleanses. For art establishes the basic human truth which must serve as the touchstone of our judgment.

In the end, Kennedy's willingness at least to consider drawing on the wisdom of poets was short-lived (as we shall see later, it evaporated after Frost's ill-fated meeting with Nikita Khrushchev in

1962), and subsequent US presidents have been highly reluctant to involve poets in public life or policymaking. (In fact, only two, Bill Clinton and Barack Obama, have invited poets to speak at their inauguration.) Since that brief era – a time to which an optimistic Frost initially referred as '*a golden age of poetry and power*' – many readers would tend to agree that poetry as an art form has come to be regarded as marginal and ineffective, in the English-speaking world, at least. Those who are happiest with this view of poetry are apt to quote Auden's supposed adage 'poetry makes nothing happen' or, worse, to misquote Adorno, whose notorious remarks about the supposed 'barbarity' of writing poetry after Auschwitz have been so gleefully misunderstood.* That idea is very much of its time (and, it almost goes without saying, grossly Eurocentric in its assertion that the Holocaust represents a global high-water mark in horror, compared with, say, the slave trade).

By contrast, however, Auden's supposed dismissal of poetry as a political force merits further examination. It comes from one of his finest works, 'In Memory of W. B. Yeats', written in 1939 as Europe descended into a second world war, and not long before Auden left Britain to live in the United States. Taken in isolation, and out of context, it is not hard to see the single phrase – 'poetry makes nothing happen' – as a bald contention that poets have no role in social change, and so make it seem that Auden rejected,

---

* Adorno's original remark, taken from an essay published in 1955, was: 'The critique of culture is confronted with the last stage in the dialectic of culture and barbarism: to write a poem after Auschwitz is barbaric, and that corrodes also the knowledge which expresses why it has become impossible to write poetry today.' Only the central phrase, 'to write a poem after Auschwitz is barbaric', was generally cited by other commentators who quoted the essay, however, leading to a gross oversimplification of his argument. He did try to clarify his position on a number of occasions. For example: 'I would readily concede that, just as I said that after Auschwitz one could not write poems – by which I meant to point to the hollowness of the resurrected culture of that time – it could equally well be said, on the other hand, that one must write poems, in keeping with Hegel's statement in his *Aesthetics* that as long as there is an awareness of suffering among human beings there must also be art as the objective form of that awareness.'

gently, but with sharp irony, not only Shelley's claim that poets are 'the unacknowledged legislators of the world', but also Yeats's own role as poet-senator of the newly independent Irish state. To leave it at that, however, would be to succumb to a fundamental misunderstanding of how poetry actually works, both on the individual imagination and in the social sphere. Meanwhile, it should go without saying that, if we would obtain a clearer, and more textured, understanding of Auden's position, then we must study the poem as a whole, and not quote individual phrases out of context.

'In Memory of W. B. Yeats' was written in the winter of 1939, not long after Yeats's death. It works with the conventions of pastoral elegy, but subverts them in various ways: for example, the poem opens not with a bucolic scene of natural beauty,* as one might expect (and there are definitely no shepherds), but with a bitterly cold and decidedly urban landscape:

> He disappeared in the dead of winter:
> The brooks were frozen, the airports almost deserted,
> And snow disfigured the public statues.

With the poet gone (and not just gone but 'disappeared', as if he had performed some magic trick), the poem goes on to imagine his

>   last afternoon as himself,
> An afternoon of nurses and rumours;
> The provinces of his body revolted,
> The squares of his mind were empty,
> Silence invaded the suburbs,
> The current of his feeling failed.[2]

With a judicious dash of irony Auden now envisions the moment

---

* As in the opening of Milton's 'Lycidas' (1637), with its laurels, myrtle and 'ivy never sere', or Gray's 'Elegy Written in a Country Churchyard' (1750), which opens with 'lowing herds' and moves on to a variety of rustic features, an 'ivy-mantled tow'r', 'rugged elms' and a 'yew-tree's shade'.

of Yeats's death as a city at the height of some kind of inverted revolution. For the poet who, whatever else his readers might know of him, is eternally associated with the IRA fighters of 'Easter 1916' –

> I write it out in a verse –
> MacDonagh and MacBride
> And Connolly and Pearse
> Now and in time to be,
> Wherever green is worn,
> Are changed, changed utterly:
> A terrible beauty is born[3]

– death is seen as an uprising that begins in 'the provinces', then enters into the suburbs and the city squares to impose the kind of eerie stillness that comes after violent conflict. The overall effect is to render the poem's subject both larger than life and eerily disembodied – and this leads immediately to a vision of what happens to a poet in death, his works 'scattered among a hundred cities / And wholly given over to unfamiliar affections', his words 'modified in the guts of the living'. Now, Auden says, Yeats has become his admirers. He no longer exists as a living creature, but his poems (and his public image) remain:

> But in the importance and noise of to-morrow
> When the brokers are roaring like beasts on the floor of the
>   Bourse,
> And the poor have the sufferings to which they are fairly
>   accustomed,
> And each in the cell of himself is almost convinced of his
>   freedom,
> A few thousand will think of this day
> As one thinks of a day when one did something slightly unusual.

It is, we cannot help but feel, rather a spare vision of posterity, but a posterity nonetheless. Yeats the man is dead, but the poet lives on and is remembered, as one remembers a day that is ever so slightly out of the ordinary, with a kind of mild curiosity.

Traditionally, the classical elegy comprises three more or less distinct stages: first, the utterance of a lament, in which the speaker gives voice to sorrow at the loss of the one who has died; this is followed by a hymn of praise for the deceased, in which the subject is often idealised or sentimentalised; finally, the poem closes on a note of solace.* With this expectation in mind, then, the opening of the second section of Auden's poem comes as a surprise:

> You were silly like us; your gift survived it all:
> The parish of rich women, physical decay,
> Yourself. Mad Ireland hurt you into poetry.

Silly. Not the obvious word choice for a paean. Nevertheless, coming at this exact point in the poem, the word 'silly' is a brilliant stroke, a near-magical surprise. Even outside an elegy, we seldom refer to the recent dead as *silly*, and to say so of someone like Yeats – a senator, a Nobel laureate, an international figure – seems even more egregious. But Yeats *was* silly – not least in his late-life flirtation with fascism. However, as Auden says, he was silly *like us*, which is to say, when he was snobbish, or self-aggrandising or sentimental, he was nevertheless well intentioned, as we assume ourselves to be, a man acting in good faith, just as we act in good faith, a poet and public figure failing to the best of his ability in hopes of, as Samuel Beckett says, failing better. The word 'silly' mocks real character flaws, but it does so kindly; it is not an accusation but an explanation and a partial exculpation. We use it in the spirit that Marianne Moore identifies in 'The Hero', which is to say 'lenient, looking/ upon a fellow creature's error with the/

---

*One of the finest examples of this third stage comes in Shelley's 'Adonais: An Elegy on the Death of John Keats': 'The massy earth and spherèd skies are riven!/ I am borne darkly, fearfully, afar;/ Whilst, burning through the inmost veil of Heaven,/ The soul of Adonais, like a star,/ Beacons from the abode where the Eternal are.'

feelings of a mother' – and here, in place of the usual, conventional praise, Auden calls Yeats 'silly' the way a mother might a child, acknowledging the error, but gently, and with affection. And in the end, how silly Yeats may have been is of little consequence: his gift survives everything, even himself.

In the most obvious ways, however, that gift had little or no effect on history, even though the poetry is scattered across a hundred cities. Yeats may have lived and died, but 'Ireland has her madness and her weather still'; nothing has changed, nothing has been accomplished, or not in any permanent sense, at least. And here we come to the much-quoted and controversial statement that, coming from a formerly engaged poet speaking about another, sounds – or can be made to sound – like an admission of failure:

> For poetry makes nothing happen: it survives
> In the valley of its making where executives
> Would never want to tamper, flows on south
> From ranches of isolation and the busy griefs,
> Raw towns that we believe and die in; it survives,
> A way of happening, a mouth.

This passage is extraordinary; there is so much going on in these six lines. Oddly, however, it is the most quoted assertion – that poetry makes nothing happen – that is the least challenging, in spite of the fact that, far too often, the debate concerning the socio-political role of poetry has so often foundered on this confusion between function and value. That poetry makes nothing happen can, in fact, be taken as a given, a truism even; after all, it would be naïve to expect a poem, or even an entire career in poetry, to change the world. If poetry had this kind of simple public function, war would have ended long ago, racism would be a mere rumour and we would all live in gardens full of daffodils and apple blossom. What Auden is really saying is that this isn't how it works.

What he says next, however, is key. For what poetry does, first, is to *survive* – not in some dogged but enfeebled fashion, hanging on, though barely noticed, in an indifferent world, but *actively*, on its own terms – that is, 'in the valley of its making' (here Auden refers back to previous lines, where wolves 'ran on through the evergreen forests' and the 'peasant river was untempted by the fashionable quays'). The poem's place is in something that resembles wild nature, away from fashionable concerns and current affairs, where the executives have no interest. (Is it not odd how petty he makes these executives look, without using a single term of opprobrium? They are, it would seem, too unimaginative to know what is going on outside their self-imposed limits.) Like that peasant river, poetry flows on, through and away from 'the busy griefs' and the 'raw towns that we believe and die in', its business is more fundamental, its true nature more elemental than any executive can imagine. It is, at root, 'a way of happening, a mouth'.

The invocation of 'a mouth' here is perhaps the most surprising, even shocking, element of the poem. At first it seems stark, even clumsy, until we remember that the mouth is integral to everything that we do to live: we eat and drink and breathe with our mouths, it is the mouth that tastes, and it is through the mouth that we speak. A baby's first instinct is to seek the breast with its mouth, and anyone who has raised a family knows that, at a formative age, up until as late as three years old, toddlers put every new thing straight into their mouths, because that is how they first get to know things. We smile, laugh and kiss with our mouths – and, of course, poetry is in its origins an oral art form, an *effort at speech* that, when it fails, leaves us socially and morally bereft, as William Meredith says:

Error from Babel mutters in the places,
Cities apart, where now we word our failures:
Hatred and guilt have left us without language
that might have led to discourse.[4]

Discourse may not succeed – but to make no effort at speech at all is certain failure.

The most significant term in Auden's lines, however, is the designation 'A way of happening'. This suggests that we can think of poetry as a *modus vivendi*: not just words on a page, or some kind of performance, but as a way of being, a provider of context, an independent, non-oppositional, entirely autonomous state. As a way of happening, poetry does not engage with the executives on their terms but takes its own sweet course, reframing the old questions in new ways, redrawing the maps the better to reflect the terrain, qualifying the rational and the public with intuition and a lived attentiveness to the mysteries. A poem is not a piece of art created to entertain a public or to please a patron; it makes itself, using the mouth of the poet as a means to utterance. It is, in short, how the music of what happens gives voice to itself.

The poem now enters its third and final stage, where solace is offered, on the one hand, and the soul of the Adonais figure is allowed to depart for the Eternal. Here Auden employs a simple, almost songlike technique, using a lilting trochaic tetrameter and an easy *aabb* rhyme scheme, to set against a world that is descending (here we recall that the poem was written in 1939) into a 'nightmare of the dark', calling not on the 'Irish vessel' W. B. Yeats, a personage now dead and buried, and 'emptied of its poetry' but to the poet (addressed only as 'poet') to teach us the essential virtues that poetry can call forth:

> Follow, poet, follow right
> To the bottom of the night,
> With your unconstraining voice
> Still persuade us to rejoice;
>
> With the farming of a verse
> Make a vineyard of the curse,
> Sing of human unsuccess
> In a rapture of distress;

In the deserts of the heart
Let the healing fountain start,
In the prison of his days
Teach the free man how to praise.

Here the poem comes to a quiet yet triumphant end – and as it does so, we discover that, far from suggesting that poetry is impotent to make things happen in the public sphere, Auden is making a space for the reader to see that poetry is capable of so much more than that. What he is telling us is that the poet is not a foot soldier in some predictable societal battle but an independent agent who, with craft and humility, can resonate – chime in, as it were – with the music of what happens.

Having said all this, I would still make the claim that poetry has a significant role in our communal life, in that it causes us to attend not only to the poem itself but also to the world around us – and this is important in the public as well as the private sphere. Poetry *as a discipline* heightens the attention of both poet and reader. This act of paying due attention is in itself a political act, for it enhances both our appreciative and our critical abilities, which are key to defining a position in a societal sphere in which both these faculties are currently at risk.* However, as the media and educational authorities downplay the humanities in general, and literature in particular, what emerges is a more malleable populace.

---

* That risk, initially fostered in the modern age by PR and advertising campaigns, political spin and a strong anti-intellectual bias in the media and public institutions, has been further heightened by the growth of social media, infotainment and internet-based disinformation programmes ('fake news'). For instance, according to the National Literacy Trust: 'The final report from the Commission on Fake News and the Teaching of Critical Literacy Skills in Schools, published on 13 June 2018, found that only 2% of children and young people in the UK have the critical literacy skills they need to tell if a news story is real or fake. It also found that almost two-thirds of teachers believe fake news is harming children's well-being by increasing levels of anxiety, damaging their self-esteem and skewing their world view.'

To clarify, I want to cite another American writer – the novelist Jonathan Franzen – writing from the heart of the US imperium at a time when faith in writing as a political force had diminished considerably:

> The writer leads, he [*sic*] doesn't follow. The dynamic lives in the writer's mind, not in the size of the audience [...] Writing is a form of personal freedom. It frees us from the mass identity we see in the making all around us. In the end, writers will write not to be outlaw heroes of some underculture but mainly to serve themselves, to survive as individuals [...] If serious reading dwindles to near nothingness, it will probably mean that the thing we're talking about when we use the word 'identity' has reached an end.[5]

From this lucid passage we begin not only to see what writing is for, but also to identify those forces that a literary discipline opposes. The creation of that mass identity (what Franzen elsewhere calls 'cultural totalitarianism') is the key problem of our times.* The proponents of cultural totalitarianism – the corporate and political institutions and individuals who rely for their prosperity on mass-market consumerism – are the ones who *really* want to 'change the world', if only to reduce the diversity of our interests (since diversity runs counter to the apparatus of monoculture and mass production). This enterprise – in effect, the simplification of a rich and complex reality to the point at which any snake-oil salesman can package it – adds increasingly greater urgency to what Franzen defines as 'the problem of preserving individuality and complexity in a noisy and distracting mass

---

* 'The American writer today faces a cultural totalitarianism analogous to the political totalitarianism with which two generations of Eastern bloc writers had to contend. To ignore it is to court nostalgia. To engage with it, however, is to risk writing fiction that makes the same point over and over: technological consumerism is an infernal machine, technological consumerism is an infernal machine.' Jonathan Franzen, 'Why Bother?', in *How To Be Alone* (New York: Farrar, Straus and Giroux, 2002).

culture'.* Depending on the constituency, the results are various: from cynicism through a stoical pursuit of seemingly outmoded values to a variety of alternative fundamentalisms, all accompanied by a worrying rise in the incidence of part-time vampirism and a mysterious increase in the market share of books by celebrity chefs. None of these seems immediately worthy of applause. On the other hand, the poet may seek to upset the apple cart by insisting on precise observation and a playful and serious attentiveness to the dailiness of life that refuses to relinquish everyday pleasures for an array of sleekly manufactured virtual substitutes (the best things in life being, as we know, free – for now at least).

The plain fact is, then, that poetry does not seek to 'change the world' in the usual sense. On the contrary, it aims in every possible way to reaffirm the world that we actually inhabit, in all its vital, messy, beautiful, tragic reality. It is not so much the case that poetry makes nothing happen as that it attempts to reveal what is already happening, to offer a context to events and so propose a means by which the noise of time can be re-experienced as the music of what happens. So it is that, while Kennedy's avocation of poetry as a counter to the arrogance of power may well have been mostly rhetorical (a way of enhancing his reputation as a cultivated Commander-in-Chief), I refuse to surrender the expectations implicit in his words that once provoked in me, as a newly practising poet, a sense of vocation and a possible purpose that, at the very least, challenges Auden's supposed dictum. As a poet, I have always felt that it was incumbent on me to take Kennedy's words at face value.

At the same time I would contend that, in a subtler way, all poetry is political, because it insists on the centrality of the imagination in daily life and on the necessity of rejecting the misuse of language practised by politicians, advertisers and the sorts of

---

* Astutely, Northrop Frye saw all this coming long ago: 'We are being swallowed up by the popular culture of the United States,' he observed, 'but then the Americans are being swallowed up by it too. It's just as much a threat to American culture as it is to ours.'

people who think that by calling a civilian massacre 'collateral damage' they can disguise its criminal nature. By now it seems clear that, in this sense, all poetry has an active socio-political function that, in various ways, can be seen as *dissident*. What that means will vary from place to place and from age to age, but since the beginning of the Industrial Revolution the background societal noise – a huge part of Mandelstam's 'noise of time' – is always the same. It is the noise of the Industrial Revolution and its fallout, the noise of Allen Ginsberg's 'Death-Scandal of Capital Politics' as it scythes down our forests and poisons our oceans. It is the martial clamour that lies behind Robert Lowell's Sunday-morning vision of 'man thinning out his kind [...] the blind/ swipe of the pruner and his knife/ busy about the tree of life'.[6] One of poetry's tasks, or at least one of its potential powers, is to transform the noise of its own time into a music that, in a no doubt overused but still powerful phrase, 'speaks truth to power' while at the same time working to restore a natural order to our building, dwelling and thinking and a natural rhythm to our speech. Poetry's varied political, philosophical and social aims and impacts will be examined in more detail later, but for now I want to ask, in general terms, what might constitute a dissident poetry in the current climate.

The dictionary defines 'dissident' thus: 'Disagreeing (in opinion, character, etc.) at variance, different. One who disagrees, a dissentient.' The roots of the modern meaning lie in religious debate, and this, I would suggest, is the most useful way of seeing dissidence in poetic culture. A suspicion of the prescribed jargon and euphemisms; a disdain for the rhetoric of PR and advertising and a determined attempt to replace it with a new form of prayer: celebration of the dailiness of life, respect for other lives and unsentimental wonder. A quiet yet dogged *Non serviam* on every level, from aesthetics to politics: from the books we read to the food we eat, from how we speak in public places to the most private recesses of our imaginations. This role, the role of dissident in the widest sense, has always been the privilege of the poet, from Shelley's unacknowledged legislator to Robert Lowell reading the aforementioned 'Waking Early Sunday Morning' on the steps of the Pentagon to protest the Vietnam War. We see it in Victor Jara's defence of the democratically elected Allende government in the years before the US-backed coup in Chile (a defence that would cost him his life), and we see it in Yevgeni Yevtushenko's protest against Soviet anti-Semitism, 'Babi Yar'. Yet we also see it in tender and conscientious poems about the natural world, the other animals, everyday life and love in its various forms.

'What are poets for in our brave new millennium?' asks Jonathan Bate in his study of poetry and ecology, *Song of the Earth*:

> Could it be to remind the next few generations that it is we who have the power to determine whether the earth will sing or be silent? As earth's own poetry, symbolized for Keats in the grasshopper and the cricket, is drowned ever deeper – not merely by bulldozers in the forest, but more insidiously by the ubiquitous susurrus of cyberspace – so there will be an ever greater need to retain a place in culture, in the work of human imagining, for the song that names the earth.[7]

It is, perhaps, one of the most unfortunate of ironies that, just as poetry began to respond to the demands of modernity, the discipline itself started to be dismissed in some quarters as elitist, inward-looking and marginal. From Eliot's time till now, opponents have claimed that poetry has become too difficult or too self-referential for the non-specialist reader. From the other side of the divide, for someone from a far from rarefied social background whose entire life has been enriched by the reading of poetry – for someone, that is, like me – this seems an odd position to adopt. What use is a poetry that is instant, like a microwave dinner or packet mashed potato? Poetry that is so 'accessible' that we know what obvious sociological or comic point it is making even before we reach the last line? I am not advancing a case for obscurity here, or for those works concocted from dictionaries and arcane research so as to sound clever and unusual. I expect poetry to yield some kind of fruit; I expect to be nourished not just intellectually but emotionally and, on occasion, in the spirit – but I also know that it can take time for any difficult idea or method of enquiry to gain wider understanding in any discipline. At the time of his death, the general public knew almost nothing about Alan Turing's work on computing; now he is a cultural icon. How many people, even today, are aware of the importance of the work of Claude Shannon or George Boole or, for that matter, James Clerk Maxwell, in bringing them the latest electronic gewgaw?

The truth is that contemporary poetry will often seem difficult in its own era, only to become common currency in the next. What poets are doing to the language now will have a real and enriching impact on how our children and grandchildren think, speak and imagine, just as the more difficult poetry that our grandparents may not have understood in their day has subsequently had on us. It is also worth saying that, even when we do not 'understand' a poem in full, it is worth engaging with it nevertheless, for its music and for the associations it provokes, sometimes quite unexpectedly, in the imagination. As the late writer and musician Ivor Cutler once remarked to me about a poem he had just discovered, 'I don't know if I understand it, but I read it often, for the sound.' While poetry can be difficult – what worthwhile pursuit is not? – it is also infinitely rewarding. Most importantly of all, in an age of environmental threat, when not just the land and its diversity but even our grasp on non-virtual reality and the deep satisfactions of quotidian life have become endangered, poetry has the power to make each of us think anew about the natural order and our place within it, to recognise and appreciate the living world's complexities and to become, in Seamus Heaney's words 'one of the venerators'. As this book progresses, through discussions of animal poetry, philosophical poetry, love poetry and poetry about the ordinary pleasures and griefs of daily life, I hope it will demonstrate that, far from making our lives more difficult and confusing, even the most complicated poetry enriches our world, making it more vivid, more manifold and more our own.

It was mid-evening, on that rainy Berlin day, by the time Lucas and I arrived at our apartment in Halensee to make dinner. All along the pavements the great plane trees dripped water shot through with coloured light from the shop windows on Kurfürsten-damm; streams of spent blossom and dusty water poured into the drains and gutters; in the apartment blocks the lights were going on, families and friends sitting down to eat together – that most sacred ritual, even if the blue eye of the TV screen still watches, impassively, from its designated corner. As always, at this time of day, somebody was playing a piano in what I pictured as a narrow room high above everything on the corner of Sandbacherstrasse. On Storkwinkel, our home street, the fence lines were scented with the usual mix of dust and cabbages and burnt sugar, but something was different here too. Cars often get bottled in on this narrow street, and we often come home on foot to find them tilted at all angles, waiting to manoeuvre in or out of the gaps in the shifting mêlée, but when I saw the blue lights flashing on the walls of the building opposite, I understood that this wasn't the usual evening traffic jam. Nor was I particularly surprised to see that, three doors down from us, parked on the kerb between two great lime trees, an ambulance was waiting while a pair of paramedics brought out our neighbour, a Middle Eastern woman with whom we exchanged halting, ungrammatical greetings, in a language that was non-native to us all, whenever we happened to pass on the street. I knew this woman had been ill, and I had heard from another neighbour that it was serious. Of course, we did not loiter: for pity's sake, as much as propriety, I hurried my son inside and, with one backward glance at the tableau of lights and shadows and wet boughs, I closed the front door behind us.

It was a glance, nothing more – but it was enough to strip so much bare in my life at that moment and to pose so many con-tradictory feelings that, for an hour or so, I was lost. That glance had provoked in me an aesthetic response that was both legiti-mate (there was real beauty in the tableau, and I can see it still, in my mind's eye) and inappropriate (a neighbour was critically ill, perhaps dying), as well as the inevitable concern for what my teenage son would make of the event itself or, worse, of any sign of that aesthetic response he might catch in my face. Even more inevitably, I experienced a powerful surge of angst about what would happen to both my young sons in the event of my own demise. Of course, we made our way upstairs to our own apartment and, of course, we glanced out of the window now and then, to see what was going on while dinner cooked, so life, as it must, did go on – but all that time I was aware of an unspoken question, in my own head, and in my son's, a question I could not convincingly answer (for it makes no difference at all to say to a child, or to anyone else who cares, that I have no fear of death, even if I would rather avoid the actual tedium of dying). Besides, it wasn't a simple question; it was composed, I knew, of several parts, some of them unsayable, at least in that moment. Is our neighbour going to die? An easy one: I didn't know. Will you die soon? Same answer, though less easy. From there on in, however, all the queries would be about grief, about what it will feel like and how it can be avoided or healed, and about loss, which is, indubitably, part of the natural order and therefore, in my own more detached moments, something I can come to terms with. But I cannot impose that detachment on Lucas, and I cannot make him into the philosopher that he is not now and may never be. Were he a little older, I might offer some solace, with the poignant and enigmatic closing lines of William Matthews's poem 'The Buddy Bolden Cylinder' –

> There's more than one
> kind of ghostly music in the air, all
> of them like the wind: you can't see it
> but you can see the leaves shiver in place
> as if they'd like to turn their insides out.[8]

– but he isn't older, he's a young teenager, and I know that (like Webster in T. S. Eliot's 'Whispers of Immortality') he will be 'much possessed by death' before he sleeps tonight, and that it will not be our neighbour's impending demise that will haunt him. Besides, I have been reading William Matthews for almost forty years, and even after all that time, there is nothing I can say to a young boy, or even to myself, to explain in full why those lines make so much difference to how I see death and loss and the entirely inexplicable sense I share with Wordsworth, that everything is renewed, one way or another:

> Rolled round in earth's diurnal course,
> With rocks, and stones, and trees.

What I do know is that Matthews's poem exists and that with some luck, or possibly because now and again my son actually listened to some of my more extravagant encomiums of that great poet, he will remember the source, go to it himself and drink. That, more than anything, is what poetry does. It nourishes us, it contributes to our grieving and healing processes, it gives focus to our loves and to our fears, allowing us to sing them, at the back of our minds, in a deliberate and disciplined transformation of noise into music, of grief into acceptance, of anger at pointless destruction into a determination to save at least something of what remains. Poetry makes so much happen, in fact, that I am at a loss to count the ways and, though Frost's golden age of poetry and power may never come, no other art form has done so much to establish 'the basic human truth which must serve as the touchstone of our judgment'.

EVERYONE SANG

When it is peace, then we may view again
With new won eyes each other's truer form
And wonder.[1]

Charles Hamilton Sorley

IT'S A BLUSTERY AUTUMN DAY in Scarborough, late enough in the afternoon for my taxi driver to be worried about the build-up of traffic. Nevertheless, he gamely strikes up a conversation, in spite of the fact that neither of us is visibly interested in the social niceties. He being Yorkshire, me being Scots, and both of us being male, this customer relations gambit seems doomed from the start, but then he asks what I do for a living, and when I tell him, he studies me with something close to interest in the rear-view mirror. 'Ah,' he says. 'You'll be here for the poet then.'

'The poet?' I say. I'm here to visit an old friend that I haven't seen in some time.

He grimaces. 'Aye. The poet,' he says. 'What's his name?'

I have no clue, but I hazard a guess, for the sake of our new acquaintanceship, a guess based on an unlikely rumour that, tired of London and weary with the cloying *tendresse* of his lover, Paul Verlaine, the seventeen-year-old Arthur Rimbaud had ventured up to Scarborough to take the waters, back in the early 1870s. 'Do you mean Arthur Rimbaud?' I say. I pronounce Arthur the English way so as not to seem pretentious.

He looks at me through the mirror for a long moment, then his face brightens as he remembers that I am Scottish and don't really speak the language. 'Aye,' he says. 'That's the one.' He shakes his head in wonder at the scope of my literary knowledge. 'Wilfred Owen.'

'Ah,' I say, nodding gravely.

'That's why you're at the Clifton,' he adds. It is a statement, not a question. 'Because that's where he stayed when he was here.'

I nod some more, feeling a little foolish.

'I hear they keep his room just the way he left it,' the driver says. We are now passing Peasholm Park, heading down towards the North Bay. 'All his books. All the little knick-knacks.' He considers for a moment, and now, it seems, he is talking to himself. 'Just the way he left it,' he says again, with an almost imperceptible shake of the head, as if someone had just told him that it was possible to stop time.

As it happened, I had been unaware of Owen's visits to Scarborough when I made my reservation at the Clifton Hotel. In fact, as a working-class Scot, obliged in my teens to recite passages from the war poets at my Catholic comprehensive, I had always been rather mistrustful of that company of doomed youth – or rather, of the nostalgia that had grown up around them. Those fearless public-school boys and rowing blues had struck me as absurdly glamorous, even when they were being cut down by enemy fire. Nevertheless, with the driver's story fresh in my head and out of some kind of professional obligation, I asked about Owen while checking in, intrigued by the idea of his untouched room. Unfortunately, the young man at reception had never heard of him (he seemed to think that this Mr Owen was another guest for whom I wanted to leave a message), and after a brief but annoyingly muddled conversation I headed off to my room in a surprisingly bad humour. The mood lifted, however, when I found, on a small table in the hallway, a neat pile of freshly printed leaflets, the cover adorned by a familiar, yet oddly generic portrait of the man himself. The leaflet was titled

FREE TRAIL GUIDE

WALK IN THE FOOTSTEPS

OF WILFRED OWEN

IN SCARBOROUGH

and, inside, the unnamed author gave a potted history of Owen's life – more specifically, of the two periods he spent in the town (where he had re-joined his regiment after some months of treatment for shell shock at the Craiglockhart Hydropathic Institute in Edinburgh), as well as a couple of poems: the inevitable 'Dulce et decorum est', of course, but also (for me, the more interesting) 'Miners', composed in this very hotel on the occasion of the Minnie Pit disaster of 12 January 1918, in which 155 colliers died. Here Owen's speaker is sitting by the hearth, listening to the flames licking the coals, which he fancies as having grown 'wistful of a former earth':

> I listened for a tale of leaves
> And smothered ferns,
> Frond-forests, and the low sly lives
> Before the fauns.
>
> My fire might show steam-phantoms simmer
> From Time's old cauldron,
> Before the birds made nests in summer,
> Or men had children.

Owen had been something of an amateur geologist in happier times, and he was fond of the young miners he encountered at the front (a number of the men of D Company, Second Battalion, Manchester Regiment, were of Lancashire mining stock). Written in response to a newspaper account, the poem poignantly brings together that knowledge of deep time and a spontaneous sense of compassion for the casualties of Minnie (the most grievous mining disaster in the history of the Staffordshire collieries). Soon, however, memories of the war intrude –

> I thought of all that worked dark pits
> Of war, and died
> Digging the rock where Death reputes
> Peace lies indeed.
>
> Comforted years will sit soft-chaired,
> In rooms of amber;
> The years will stretch their hands, well-cheered
> By our life's ember

– until, at the poem's close, the lost miners and the war dead are conflated in one great underground charnel house of forgotten men who perished for different reasons, but to serve the same end: the comfort and warmth of those lucky few who stay at home. In the last stanza Owen's use of the quatrain is extended to six lines: it is as if the poem was meant to end at 'crooned', but spilled over into the additional content, a bitter afterthought spoken in a mood of resignation to the fact that, for all their sacrifice, it is entirely expected that such men shall be consigned to oblivion:

> The centuries will burn rich loads
> With which we groaned,
> Whose warmth shall lull their dreaming lids,
> While songs are crooned;
> But they will not dream of us poor lads,
> Left in the ground.*

---

* This is reminiscent, for me, of the final lines of George Seferis's poem 'Argonauts' (from the sequence *Mythistorema*, of 1935), in which Jason's 'good companions', their extraordinary journeys done with, are lost to history:

> The companions died one by one,
> with lowered eyes. Their oars
> mark the place where they sleep on the shore.
>
> No one remembers them. Justice

(trans. Edmund Keeley)

The remainder of the leaflet comprised an annotated map, showing the places Owen would have visited when off-duty: the route he would have followed, for example, when he went to take tea with the Sitwells (who had a house at Woodend, near the Pavilion), the wide sweep of the North Promenade, where swifts and other birds still nest among the dunes, and the churchyard of St Mary's, where Anne Brontë is buried. The real find here, however, is 'Miners', a poem I have not read in many years – and a reminder that there is much more to Owen's poetry than is usually advertised. Over the next several days, while my friend and I stroll around the town, inadvertently tracing the poet's foot-steps, my mind keeps coming back to that poem, and to a ques-tion that had troubled me as a young reader, a question I could barely frame then and still cannot get quite clear in my mind. It has something to do with a notion that, by calling Owen and his comrades 'war poets', we commit a real error, one that risks blinding us to the work as a whole – and I cannot help thinking that, if the poets who died in the First World War were here now, they might demur at the label, just as Elizabeth Bishop did when, unwilling to be classified as a 'woman poet', she refused to be included in women-only anthologies. In many cases (and, perhaps most poignantly, Owen's) we cannot know what these young men would have gone on to write had they lived; it is inviting to specu-late that at least some of them would have moved beyond the War Poet label – not to mention the sometimes dubious myth-making that surrounds it.

For reasons that were left unexplained at the time, and which still trouble me now, the first poems I was given to read were 'about' war. As a twelve-year-old, I assumed my teachers were right in assuming that their male charges were more disposed to battle-field heroics than, say, to romantic love. (It is possible that the education system has made no greater error than this casual erad-ication of the natural tenderness of boys, though some would argue that the system knows exactly what it is doing.) So it was that we studied literature in which the horrors, and even the futility of war might be depicted, but our guided readings never went quite so far as to suggest that peace was an absolute good while war was to be avoided under any circumstances. The message was overtly pacifist, but the underlying currents were equivocal. Every shrill, demented choir of wailing shells was matched by the six hundred, riding bravely into the Valley of Death, to do and die and, should the times require it, be emulated. Every expression of contempt for the 'incompetent swine' behind the front lines was outweighed by some *beau geste* of desperate heroism.* Even with Jesus peering over their shoulders, our elders could reserve for a later date the expediency that war, however repellent, was sometimes necessary and, when it was, good men were obliged to dig deep and find an unaccustomed ferocity in their hearts.

Gradually, however, as the 1960s slowly caught up to my industrial Midlands backwater, the scales began to tip towards a tacit dismissal of the First World War poets, not only for pacifist but also for class reasons. No matter how well they depicted the pity and sorrow of that conflict, the poets themselves were still touched with the silvery, almost cinematic glow of unearned luck; even in death they were darkly privileged, oddly clean amid all the squalor.† Those deaths were tragic, but it was *their* tragedy, not

---

* From Siegfried Sassoon's 'The General':

'Good-morning; good-morning!' the General said
When we met him last week on our way to the line.
Now the soldiers he smiled at are most of 'em dead,
And we're cursing his staff for incompetent swine.
'He's a cheery old card,' grunted Harry to Jack
As they slogged up to Arras with rifle and pack.

But he did for them both by his plan of attack.

† In a letter to a friend, the composer William Denis Browne describes the last hours of Rupert Brooke, who died of septicaemia en route to the Dardanelles in April 1915: 'At 4 o'clock he became weaker, and at 4.46 he died, with the sun shining all round his cabin, and the cool sea-breeze blowing through the door and the shaded windows. No one could have wished for a quieter or a

ours. For me, the pivotal moment came when, called upon to recite Rupert Brooke's 'The Soldier' at a Remembrance Day assembly, I tried instead to read 'Does It Matter?' by Siegfried Sassoon, managing to get as far as the lines

> Does it matter? – losing your sight?
> There's such splendid work for the blind;
> And people will always be kind[2]

before I was interrupted by the kindly music teacher, who tried to pass my petty rebellion off as a bookmarking error.

It might seem odd now that, more than Owen, more than my fellow Scot Charles Hamilton Sorley, the writer my working-class teen self was most drawn to among the First World War poets was the wealthy and undeniably snobbish Siegfried Sassoon, but there was something about his approach – the bitterness, the pungency, the satiric bite, reminiscent of Swift – that caught my attention from the first. It was purely a matter of taste and background, I know, but I much preferred Sassoon's work to Owen's poetry of pity, as seen in 'Dulce et decorum est' or 'Anthem for Doomed Youth'* – and when I read the same poet's 'Futility' I feel something had been diminished to create the effect in lines like:

---

calmer end than in that lovely bay, shielded by the mountains and fragrant with sage and thyme.' This is a strangely beautiful *mise en scène*, but it sounds a little at odds with the known symptoms of septicaemia, which include fever, confusion, nausea and vomiting, florid skin rash and shock.

* Though I cannot agree with W. B. Yeats, who, after omitting Owen from the 1936 edition of *The Oxford Book of Modern Verse*, wrote to a friend:

> When I excluded Wilfred Owen, whom I consider unworthy of the poets' corner of a country newspaper, I did not know I was excluding a revered sandwich-board man of the revolution and that some body has put his worst and most famous poem (Dulce et Decorum Est) in a glass-case in the British Museum – however if I had known it I would have excluded him just the same. He is all blood, dirt and sucked sugar stick (look at the selection in Faber's Anthology – he calls poets 'bards', a girl a 'maid', and talks about 'Titanic wars'). There is every excuse for him but none for those who like him.

If anything might rouse him now
The kind old sun will know.

There was no irony, here, large enough to accommodate the futility recognised in the title, while the rhetoric of

Was it for this the clay grew tall?
– O what made fatuous sunbeams toil
To break earth's sleep at all?[3]

stuck in my craw. I can admit now to a certain youthful arrogance, but I couldn't help suspecting that it wasn't for this hackneyed, borderline sentimental vision that the clay grew tall, just as I suspected not only that sunbeams did not toil but also that life emerged, grew and decayed on a schedule that had nothing whatsoever to do with the vanity of human wishes. For me, all too often, Owen's dramatis personae were smaller than life. By contrast, reading Robert Lowell's 'For the Union Dead', I recognised a larger truth in the portrait given there of Colonel Robert Gould Shaw (the white commander of the all-black 54th Massachusetts regiment) killed at Fort Wagner, near Charleston, South Carolina, in 1863, whom the poet describes as having an

angry wrenlike vigilance,
a greyhound's gentle tautness;
he seems to wince at pleasure,
and suffocate for privacy.

He is out of bounds now.
He rejoices in man's lovely,
peculiar power to choose life and die.

That was a different war, of course: a struggle that, like the Second World War, could lay claim to a moral purpose. The main problem for a non-English working-class reader was the simplistic but rather persuasive argument that, from the point of view of the mass of people, the First World War had been a cynical dispute between two sets of imperial powers over resources and colonial dominion – and nobody came to see this, and to express it with such raw power, as Sassoon did, not just in his poetry but also in his public life. Here, for example, is his much-publicised 'A Soldier's Declaration', written on 15 June 1917 and published in the *Bradford Pioneer*, decrying the mismanagement of the war and the consequent suffering of the men at the front:

> I am making this statement as an act of wilful defiance of military authority, because I believe that the war is being deliberately prolonged by those who have the power to end it.
>
> I am a soldier, convinced that I am acting on behalf of soldiers. I believe that this war, upon which I entered as a war of defence and liberation, has now become a war of aggression and conquest. I believe that the purposes for which I and my fellow soldiers entered upon this war should have been so clearly stated as to have made it impossible to change them, and that, had this been done, the objects which actuated us would now be attainable by negotiation.
>
> I have seen and endured the sufferings of the troops, and I can no longer be a party to prolong these sufferings for ends which I believe to be evil and unjust.
>
> I am not protesting against the conduct of the war, but against the political errors and insecurities for which the fighting men are being sacrificed.
>
> On behalf of those who are suffering now I make this protest against the deception which is being practised on them; also I believe that I may help to destroy the callous complacence with which the majority of those at home regard the continuance of agonies which they do not share, and which they have not sufficient imagination to realise.

Sassoon took a personal risk by making this declaration, and it was only the timely intervention of well-connected friends such as Robert Graves that prevented his being court-martialled. Instead, he was sent to Craiglockhart, where new methods in treating shell shock were being developed. Here he continued to create a poetry that, while paying tribute to the bravery and camaraderie of his fellow soldiers, also exposed the arrogance and disdain for other lives among the powers-that-be – and, like Swift, he was prepared both to be forthright in his judgements and to apportion blame. Here he is in 'Base Details' lambasting those who daily fed Owen's doomed youth to the cannons without a moment's remorse:

> If I were fierce, and bald, and short of breath
> I'd live with scarlet Majors at the Base,
> And speed glum heroes up the line to death.
> You'd see me with my puffy petulant face,
> Guzzling and gulping in the best hotel,
> Reading the Roll of Honour. 'Poor young chap,'
> I'd say – 'I used to know his father well;
> Yes, we've lost heavily in this last scrap.'
> And when the war is done and youth stone dead,
> I'd toddle safely home and die – in bed.[4]

Is this a better poem, technically, than 'Futility'? I would argue yes and no. The verse form Sassoon chooses to use is regular, almost plodding and obvious (see how artlessly the punchline is set up, for example), but that isn't because he is not capable of something more elaborate. On the contrary, form is matched to the capabilities of its subject – that is, to the 'scarlet Major' back at base, whose grasp of literary style is unlikely to be any more sophisticated than his understanding of battlefield strategy. As one who had begun the war as a genuine instance of the scholar-warrior, for whom honour and personal responsibility were paramount, Sassoon rightly despised these men – and his contempt for them is expressed not just in what he says about them but in the way he spells it out, in the most basic and predictable form possible, so that they might understand.

Sassoon does not confine his critique to incompetent senior officers and hypocritical politicians, however. He also takes aim not only at the 'smug faced crowds [...] Who cheer when soldier lads march by', or the cant of churchmen spouting hackneyed non-sense about the enemy as Antichrist, but also at the banal gossip he finds 'On Reading the War Diary of a Defunct Ambassador':

> The world can read the rumours that you gleaned
> From various Fronts; the well-known Names you met;
> Each conference you attended and convened;
> And (at appropriate moments) what you ate.
> Thus (if the world's acute) it can derive
> Your self, exact, uncensored, and alive.
>
> The world will find no pity in your pages;
> No exercise of spirit worthy of mention;
> Only a public-funeral grief-convention;
> And all the circumspection of the ages.
> But I, for one, am grateful, overjoyed,
> And unindignant that your punctual pen
> Should have been so constructively employed
> In manifesting to unprivileged men
> The visionless officialized fatuity
> That once kept Europe safe for Perpetuity.[5]

He also finds time to expose the hypocrisy of the women at home who perpetuate the unrealistic mythology of war, ready to support anyone who is suitably heroic or, if wounded, suitably gracious about it.

> You love us when we're heroes, home on leave,
> Or wounded in a mentionable place.
> You worship decorations; you believe
> That chivalry redeems the war's disgrace.
> You make us shells. You listen with delight,
> By tales of dirt and danger fondly thrilled.
> You crown our distant ardours while we fight,
> And mourn our laurelled memories when we're killed.
> You can't believe that British troops 'retire'
> When hell's last horror breaks them, and they run,
> Trampling the terrible corpses – blind with blood.[6]

It is an area where other poets, even those who are most critical of the system, fear to tread – and it comes almost as a shock when we notice the bitter ambiguity of the fifth line's 'You make us shells', or the disdain the speaker shows for those who 'worship decorations' and wilfully blind themselves to the horrors of war in their determination to perpetuate a myth of romantic chivalry. It is hard not to be reminded, here, of e. e. cummings,* whose mordant 'my sweet old etcetera' similarly exposes the easy heroism of those patriots privileged enough not to have to witness the carnage at first hand:

> my sister
>
> Isabel created hundreds
> (and
> hundreds) of socks not to
> mention fleaproof earwarmers
>
> etcetera wristers etcetera, my
> mother hoped that
>
> i would die etcetera
> bravely of course my father used
> to become hoarse talking about how it was
> a privilege and if only he
> could[7]

There is, however, more to Sassoon than a satirical gift worthy of Swift – and the poem of his that I most love, 'Everyone Sang', might not be a war poem at all. It might even be that rare thing, a peace poem. It begins, much as a flash mob does, with an unexplained outburst, in which the most powerful element is the impromptu choir's improbable, even miraculous, synchronicity:

---

* A pacifist, cummings volunteered for the Norton-Harjes Ambulance Service and served for some time in France before being detained on a charge of espionage and held at the Dépôt de Triage at La Ferté-Macé, an experience that provided the basis for his autobiographical novel of 1922, *The Enormous Room*.

Everyone suddenly burst out singing.

This is an astonishing, arresting moment, and we might be tempted to charge Sassoon with having a personal epiphany here. But there is no Romantic ego at the centre of this experience; instead, the speaker, who is throughout a spectator at the spontaneous chorus, is

> filled with such delight
> As prisoned birds must find in freedom,
> Winging wildly across the white
> Orchards and dark-green fields

and the image Sassoon chooses to convey that sudden sense of freedom is, like the singing, a *communal* one – not a single bird that rises, suddenly liberated, into a blue sky (like Picasso's symbolic and entirely hypothetical dove, say), but an entire flock of flesh-and-blood and hollow-boned creatures. The underlying suggestion, it seems to me, is that all must be able to fly free for freedom to be considered freedom. What should also be noted is that the image does not stay; the freed birds do not linger to act as emblems or signs for the speaker's emotional state, they just fly

> on – on – and out of sight

as real, mortal birds would. In short, having been freed, they vanish into their own world, becoming invisible in ours. Rather elegantly, the poet teases us with the expectation that the liberation will be accomplished in one movement, leaving the birds to stand for something in the human realm, in the way he plays with the rhythm here:

> As prisoned birds must find in freedom,
> Winging wildly across the white
> Orchards and dark-green fields; on – on – and out of sight.[8]

We at once hear and see how everything runs regularly here, up till 'white', with a satisfyingly predictable series of rhymes, rhythms and end-stops to the lines, and mentally we relax into the pattern, only for it to stagger forward with the enjambment at 'orchards' and the egregious extension of the line so that it inevitably tails away and into the distance, just as the freed birds would do. This has several effects, but to my mind the most powerful is the way it emphasises the nature – and extent – of the blossom in the picture, creating with the merest poetic brushstroke an English landscape worthy of Samuel Palmer or Stanley Spencer. With the introduction of the word 'white', the listener might have expected nothing but an abstract image (an empty sky, say, or a field of snow), but it is the blossom that is white, and the poem chooses to insist on that point, thus enhancing the contrast with the 'dark-green fields'.

Now 'everyone' sings. And who is this everyone? A group of soldiers celebrating the announcement of the Armistice? An entire village back home or even England itself, raising its voice in hope, now that the horror of years is drifting away? In a real sense, it does not matter – in another it is, and should be, all of these things; for one unguarded moment, what matters is the spontaneity of the people, matched by a powerful sense of common cause:

> Everyone's voice was suddenly lifted;
> And beauty came like the setting sun.

The poem is a wonderful, seemingly simple (indeed, brilliantly artless-seeming) expression of an important truth, one often overlooked by the 'executives' of Auden's Yeats memorial: the enduring fact that community cannot be constructed, but can only emerge spontaneously from events, and when it does, even though the heart is still 'shaken with tears', and horror only drifts gradually away, what results, even if it lasts only a short time, is a birdlike freedom for everyone –

> O, but Everyone
> Was a bird.

And the song is open to everyone because it *is* wordless – not a jingoistic recruiting song or a wail of national angst, or even one of those suspect anthems in which well-meaning Romantics call for universal brotherhood – and so is both purely musical and eternal for the only reason anything can be eternal: because it can never be finished –

and the song was wordless; the singing will never be done.

Where, in 'Mattina', his celebrated two-line response to a different kind of lull in the conflict, the Italian poet Giuseppe Ungaretti retains absolute technical and psychological control (see the next chapter), Sassoon allows the emotion to spill over, stretching his lyric form to breaking point and, in the process, extending and strengthening it. But the emotion that almost bursts the dam here does not come across as staged, or personal; it is *shared* – it is a *response* in the old, quasi-religious sense, and it happens at the very cusp of participation. (One feels, without being told as much, that, having put down his burden of tears and horrors, the speaker is just about to join this chorus, perhaps for the first time.) However, it is the overall sense of participation that matters, even more than the individual liberation, in making this a great poem of peace, rather than a momentary and entirely personal epiphany that does little to challenge the mortal fascination of war.

In many ways, the poetry written by those who served in the First World War offers a definitive high point of war poetry in English. Nothing comparable had been created before 1914; certainly, no similar phenomenon can be found in the Second World War (where, it could be argued, the cinema became the dominant art form in depicting conflict). There is no doubt that something extraordinary, something that was mythically much more than the sum of its parts, came together out of the individual work of poets such as Owen, Sassoon, Sorley, Ivor Gurney, Robert Graves and Isaac Rosenberg (the list goes on).

For some readers, however, our continuing fascination with that period is somewhat troubling. Is it possible to set aside its more dubious links with jingoism, nostalgia and the sometimes subliminal preparedness for future military adventures that the mythology of war fosters? Surely we need no reminder of the horrors that men like Sassoon and Owen endured, or of the human and environmental damage done by industrial-scale warfare – and with each glut of anti-war anthologies that appear whenever a new conflict erupts, it becomes more and more clear that no amount of war poetry, or even of informed analysis about the underlying motives for military action (usually resources), can end the carnage, should the powers-that-be wish to pursue it. Some might even feel that, as consumers of those contested resources, we are all complicit in such wars.

Nevertheless, we continue to read the war poetry of a century past, for we cannot escape the notion that it has something valuable to offer. For me, the abiding power of work like Sassoon's is its portrayal of the profound fellowship that arises among people who, having endured the unthinkable together, witness in one another a grace that goes beyond pity, even beyond compassion, to postulate something more radical than either – and, given form and music in poetry, this grace offers, in turn, a context, a way of happening, a brave if not wholly rational intuition that, in spite of the gross waste of life and limb, a lesson with a more general application can be learned. Much has been made of the homo-erotic element of that fellowship, and we could argue at length about the relative importance of *eros* and *agape* in the work of the First World War poets, but there is no reason for one to occlude the other. When I read Sassoon, recalling the 'ashen grey / Masks of the lads who once were keen and kind and gay', or lying in his bed, unable to sleep, half-dreaming the

> ghost of remembered chords
> Which still can make such radiance in my dream
> That I can watch the marching of my soldiers,
> And count their faces; faces; sunlit faces

until, finally, drifting away, he finds a landscape of peace again:

> the herons, and the hounds …
> September in the darkness; and the world
> I've known; all fading past me into peace[9]

I feel that I am being inducted into a vision that goes beyond mere epiphany, a vision in which the life of the land is, or can be, continuous with that of those who dwell in it. That vision transcends tribe and nation; it recognises all of humanity as deserving of equal respect, as revealed in the startling conclusion of 'Reconciliation', shown here in full:

> When you are standing at your hero's grave,
> Or near some homeless village where he died,
> Remember, through your heart's rekindling pride,
> The German soldiers who were loyal and brave.
>
> Men fought like brutes; and hideous things were done;
> And you have nourished hatred, harsh and blind.
> But in that Golgotha perhaps you'll find
> The mothers of the men who killed your son.[10]

It is this vision that transcends the impulse to Romantic epiphany, on the one hand, and the appeal to pity, on the other, both of which seem to me to get the best war poetry wrong. On the one hand, epiphany is a kind of diversion or, worse, delusion. On the other, appeals to pity, or to compassion – for whom? The dead? They no longer feel. For the witnesses? – risk even more untenable errors. What survival – what privilege in any and all its forms – calls us to is radical responsibility, a condition that, in a development of the philosophy of Emmanuel Levinas, health law and bioethics specialist Lois Shepherd sets out in a paper published in *St. John's Law Review* in 2012:

> We are either terribly naive or, worse, unthinkingly presump-
> tuous, if we think that we know how the other person feels or
> that we even transitorily or vicariously experience or share in
> the suffering of the other person. Too often, what seems like
> sharing is actually presuming, presuming that we can know
> what another experiences when we are not that person and
> when we may never have experienced anything similar.

And she continues:

> If we look no further than compassion to determine our
> duties to one another, then we seek no more than contract.
> We assume that everyone is equal and has the equal ability to
> enter into contracts for his benefit. No one has a greater claim;
> no one has a greater responsibility. By contrast, an ethics of
> radical responsibility […] means that whether or not I feel com-
> passion for the other person I have a responsibility for another's
> suffering. Responsibility does not have the voluntary nature of
> compassion.[11]

This is a truly radical analysis and, though it does Shepherd's
work an injustice to cherry-pick extracts in this way (and out of
context also, as she is not discussing war here), what lies at the
heart of her argument (that it is not pity, or even compassion, but
this radical responsibility that must guide us in our dealings with
others) is strangely akin to the moral predicament of a poet like
Sassoon who, having witnessed the fellowship of men in battle,
can never forget 'the Battalion in the mud'. Later in life, when he
had converted to Catholicism and become something of a recluse
at Heytesbury, Sassoon seems to have come to understand this
predicament in terms similar to those of Levinas himself (who
famously proclaimed that 'responsibility is actually love') and to
resolve that predicament in 'A Chord', a late poem published in
the privately printed collection *The Tasking* (1954) and, arguably,

one of the finest religious poems of the twentieth century:*

> On stillness came a chord,
> While I, the instrument,
> Knew long-withheld reward:
> Gradual the glory went;
> Vibrating, on and on,
> Toward harmony unheard,
> Till dark where sanctus shone;
> Lost, once a living word.
>
> But in me yet abode
> The given grace though gone;
> The love, the lifted load,
> The answered orison.[12]

This is a fitting postscript to the career of a poet too much possessed by war, for it ends on what, for Sassoon, seems to have mattered most: the response, the answer, that, even if it has no remedy or earthly solace to offer, makes of the mere act of attending to, of listening to and responding to the other, a vital first step in the long and difficult process of healing.

---

*And a work that bears comparison with that of Henry Vaughan, whom Sassoon greatly admired, and whom he memorialised in the poem 'At the Grave of Henry Vaughan', after visiting the poet's tomb at Llansantffraed in 1923.

L'INFINITO

> e mi sovvien l'eterno,
> E le morte stagioni, e la presente
> E viva, e il suon di lei. Così tra questa
> Immensità s'annega il pensier mio:
> E il naufragar m'è dolce in questo mare.[1]

Giacomo Leopardi

IF THERE IS ONE REAL PROBLEM with much Romantic landscape paint-ing (Caspar David Friedrich's *Wanderer above the Sea of Fog*, say, or his *Monk by the Seashore*), it is that the solitary figure is seen from the outside (in a suitable pose, unavoidably) and so becomes an essential element of the picture's narrative. The viewer of the painting does not perceive the landscape from the Byronic fig-ure's point of view, but sees *him* as the defining figure *of* that land-scape – as an ego, a protagonist and so, almost inevitably, a hero. There is nothing intrinsically wrong with this: many Romantic poets create the same, or very similar, scenarios. For example, Wordsworth's 'Lines Written a Few Miles above Tintern Abbey' begins thus:

> Five years have past; five summers, with the length
> Of five long winters! and again I hear
> These waters, rolling from their mountain-springs
> With a soft inland murmur

setting the scene strictly in its temporal relation to the speaker; so much so that, in a poem of 160 lines, the first person pronoun appears twenty-five times. In poems of this kind the reader does not look out at *the land* as a subject of enquiry; rather, she views *a human speaker* (subject) looking out at the land (object), and this distinction makes all the difference. Again, there is nothing wrong with this approach, as one of many possible stances. Nevertheless, it is hard not to feel that, even if, as F. R. Leavis suggests, Wordsworth had 'a wisdom to communicate', it was a wisdom he brought *to* the scene, not something he discovered when he got there. Whatever wisdom the poem offers originates with him and, as sincere as it may have been, it is also to some extent a pose. (Leavis uses the word 'wisdom' here because he cannot help but agree with Matthew Arnold, who astutely observes that, for Wordsworth, his 'poetry is the reality' while 'his philosophy […] is the illusion'.) Again, this is not to point out a flaw in Wordsworth's method (in fact, Arnold was a huge admirer, happy at times to set this self-designated priest of nature on a par with Shakespeare); it is only to say that he comes to the natural world with an artistic and moral agenda, rather than an open spirit of enquiry. He has, in the end, come to say:

> How exquisitely the individual Mind
> (And the progressive powers perhaps no less
> Of the whole species) to the external World
> Is fitted: – and how exquisitely, too –
> Theme this but little heard of among Men –
> The external World is fitted to the Mind;
> And the creation (by no lower name
> Can it be called) which they with blended might
> Accomplish: – this is our high argument.

Whether the individual Mind and the external World are so exquisitely fitted to one another is arguable, but what matters here, for me, is the memory Wordsworth evokes of my days as a devout Catholic child, come to the altar to try to figure out what to make of the Holy Ghost (an obsession for my twelve-year-old self) only to find the priest, clad in his sumptuous robes, always there between me and the source, *telling* me what to make of it. To go to the natural world armed with preconceived notions of what can be learned there is not a successful strategy for producing either truth or insight. The 'truth' of 'Nature' is always an artificial construct, whether it is manifest in the shape of some Noble Savage figure such as the famous Leech Gatherer or made apparent by way of a moralised element of a pleasing landscape that, even if it is not steeped in 'romantic *Weltschmerz*' is nevertheless absurdly idealised.* It is not *out there*; rather, we bring it with us. And, as the American poet William Matthews points out, to surrender oneself to nature is more difficult that one might imagine:

> Here's what I think:

> the soul in the woods is not alone.
> All he came there to leave behind
> is in him, like a garrison

> in a conquered city. When he goes
> back to it, and goes gratefully
> because it's nearly time for dinner,

> he will be entering himself,
> though when he faced the woods,
> from the road, that's what he thought then, too.[2]

Which is to say that, whether he is a monkish wanderer in a sea

---

* *Weltschmerz* is a condition, or pose, of Romantic melancholy or world-weariness. The term was coined by the German Romantic writer Jean Paul (1763–1825), a flavour of whose work can be found in this oft-quoted remark from his 'biographical' novel of 1795, *Hesperus, oder 45 Hundsposttage*: 'Der lange Schlaf des Todes schließt unsere Narben zu, und der kurze des Lebens unsere Wunden' ('The long sleep of death closes our scars, and the short of life our wounds'). Leo Marx describes it as 'a state of feeling thought to be basically subversive yet in most cases, like "beat" rebelliousness today, adolescent and harmless'.

of Teutonic fog or a sprightly youth out for an extended consti-
tutional in the Wye Valley, the Romantic figure seems to come
to 'Nature' already knowing what he will find there. He cannot,
or perhaps chooses not to, see past the blinkers of his Romantic worldview. As the culture moved into the twentieth century,
however, it seemed like a contrivance for the poet to go out into
the natural world armed with a given 'wisdom'. With the advent
of poets such as Eugenio Montale or Rainer Maria Rilke (to name
only two), going out to face the woods, or the sea, or the horizon,
was to be exposed to an unsayable beauty that is, as Rilke warns
in the *Duino Elegies*:

> nothing but the beginning of terror
> which we are barely able to endure, and it amazes us so,
> because it serenely disdains to destroy us.[3]

Interestingly, the poet whose work most effectively foreshadows
this condition of existential terror in the face of the unsayable
world is Giacomo Leopardi, a slightly younger contemporary of
Jean Paul and a truly melancholic figure who is often regarded,
mistakenly, as a typical *Weltschmerz* poet. This comes as no surprise: the congenitally deformed child of minor aristocrats, Leopardi was born in the Papal States in 1798 and, having endured a
lifetime of romantic disappointments, indifferent parenting and
a chronic shortage of money, died of cholera in Naples in 1837. In
that relatively short life, however, he wrote several philosophical
commentaries (on despair, of which he was something of a connoisseur), a couple of plays (tragedies, it goes without saying) and
some of the finest poetry ever written. His themes would be considered 'dark' or 'gloomy' today: lost or unrequited love, death,
the duplicity of the natural world:

> O nature, o nature,
> why do you not then fulfil

the promises you make? Why do you deceive
your children so?

O natura, o natura,
Perché non rendi poi
Quel che prometti allor? perché di tanto
Inganni i figli tuoi?[4]

However, any suspicion that this was some kind of literary pose might be called into question by the sheer relish with which he lays out his philosophy, particularly in his most important prose work, *Zibaldone di pensieri*, in which, at times, he foreshadows the nihilism of Nietzsche:

The truth, that a thing may be good, and another bad, that is to say good and bad, is believed to be naturally absolute, whereas they are in fact relative.

La verità, che una cosa sia buona, che un'altra sia cattiva, vale a dire il bene e il male, si credono naturalmente assoluti, e non sono altro che relativi.

Yet, as dark as all this might sound, what comes across in Leopardi is the sheer sense of his intellectual duty to say how things were in the world, as he encountered them. A person of noble mind, Leopardi thought, was obliged to tell the truth about what he or she saw; better to say what is true than settle for a comfortable illusion or, worse, forgetting. Yet, however dark the place to which his investigations might lead him, his melancholy goes beyond the pose of the world-weary Romantics; lyrical and open to existential extremes, Leopardi is, at the same time, a realist in his examination of the given world.

It is, therefore, fascinating to read a poem like 'L'infinito', a sonnet that has been dated to 1819, when Leopardi would have been around twenty. It begins with lines that betray a real tenderness for a specific place in the countryside around his home in the dismal Papal States town of Recanati:

Always dear to me was this lonely hill,
And this hedge, that obscures the view
of the far horizon.

Sempre caro mi fu quest'ermo colle,
È questa siepe, che da tanta parte
Dell'ultimo orizzonte il guardo esclude.

This could be the opening of any number of landscape poems in the bucolic manner. However, it is not long before the speaker's imagination runs away with him, conjuring up the endless spaces and inhuman silences that lie just beyond that screening hedge, until his heart gives way to something that resembles fear (though, to my mind, the line invites us to doubt: either it is not fear, as such, that the speaker feels or it is not fear alone but fear admixed with something else). He continues:

And as I listen to
the wind gusting through these branches,
I begin to compare this voice
To that infinite silence: and the eternal comes to mind,
And all seasons past, and the present
Living season.

E come il vento
Odo stormir tra queste piante, io quello
Infinito silenzio a questa voce
Vo comparando: e mi sovvien l'eterno,
E le morte stagioni, e la presente
e viva.[5]

By this point we have a sense of the poet, alone in the natural world, listening to what is there, bringing nothing to the scene that is not there, a near-cousin, perhaps, to Wallace Stevens's listener in 'The Snow Man', who hears

the sound of the land
Full of the same wind
That is blowing in the same bare place

For the listener, who listens in the snow[6]

– and surely, for both these listeners, standing alone in the wind, the question of what is there and what the mind makes of it is salient in a way that it is not in the work of the Romantic solitary, for whom the subject of the drama is himself – *his* solitude, *his* loneliness, *his* sense of place and the wisdom *he* brings to it.

In the same way, coming to the land empty-handed (as it were), Leopardi's speaker is given a similar key. What he wins is not understanding, nor is it respite in the usual sense, but it is an apprehension of the land as subject, a presence that he cannot shape either as picturesque or as dramatic backdrop to his own philosophy. Yet just as there is tenderness in the opening, a strange pleasure is implied in the final line, where to be shipwrecked in the infinite is 'sweet', for a moment at least:

Thus, in this
immensity my thought is drowned:
And it is sweet to founder (to be shipwrecked) in such a sea.

Così tra questa
Immensità s'annega il pensier mio:
E il naufragar m'è dolce in questo mare.

Here, at last, is a poetry that treats the witnessed world as a subject and, in creating this, Leopardi offers his reader an experience of what Mandelstam called 'genuine piety before the three dimensions of space'. Later, those who claimed him as a predecessor would confront the infinite, more or less self-consciously, with this poem playing, inevitably, at the back of their minds. The results would be interestingly varied.

On 26 January 1917, at Santa Maria la Longa, a soldier on the Austrian front composed what may well be the shortest poem in the history of literature, 'Mattina' ('Morning'):

M'illumino
D'immenso.[7]

In this hermetic piece, almost impossible to translate into English,* Giuseppe Ungaretti said he wanted to try to reconcile, or fuse, 'the individual, that which is finite, with the immense – we might say, the infinite, or even, in a particular sense, the sublime – finding in the light the principle and the possibility of such a fusion'. Yet, though there are significant differences here, I cannot help seeing this project as echoing, in some way, Wordsworth's notion of an exquisite fitting of the individual Mind to the external World, and it is not long before I begin to feel, if not suspicious, then a little uneasy. What is going on here? What sort of 'fusion' is the poet proposing?

The poem's brevity invites us to fill in the blanks, in much the same way as a stage direction (a cryptic one, especially) invites us to make a mental picture of the scene. In fact, it could be called the 'Exit, pursued by a bear' of Modernist poetry. My own picture begins quite literally: a man hunkers in a muddy trench, in the aftermath of a ferocious battle, looking up at the first light of morning. I know this, though there is nothing in the poem to lead me to such an image – and this is the first problem I have, reading this text. Here, though the poet provides no clues as to the where, when (other than the time of day) or why, context is everything. I have to ask myself whether, if I were to imagine this scene outside that context – as, say, the vision of a drunkard or drug user – I would respond to it differently. I do not see the battle, I do not undergo, however indirectly, what the speaker of the poem has undergone, I do not feel the relief as morning finds me, so I am compelled to take on trust what has been distilled – or possibly

---

* We might say: 'I illuminate myself/ With the immense', though this completely lacks the music and the nuance of the original.

reduced – to a single utterance. This utterance is not directed at me, however; it is the outcome of a specific, and to the bystander, exclusive experience. When I compare 'Mattina' to another short poem, Stephen Crane's untitled

I was in the darkness;
I could not see my words
Nor the wishes of my heart.
Then suddenly there was a great light –

'Let me into the darkness again'[8]

for which I have no context at all, it is hard not to feel that even this stark utterance, coming from someone of whom nothing is or can be known for certain, still offers me entry to a process of some kind. There are steps I can identify, a history about which I can hypothesise. Ungaretti does not even offer this, however. His utterance is essentially mystical. Yet it does not unfold in isolation, and, though it lays no claim to anything other than extreme experience, it belongs to a tradition.

When 'Mattina' first appeared in print, it would not have taken a particularly alert reader to notice that Ungaretti's vision harks back to the *immensità* of Leopardi's 'L'infinito', but, while noting the similarities between the two poems, it is also worth paying attention to the contrasts: at the centre of the world, though noticeable mainly by its absence in Leopardi's case, the self stands alone: ego, the Romantic I, the lyric agent. One looks out into the given world, and what can be inferred to lie within or behind it, and tries to reconcile the sublime with his individual being, while the other turns inward – in the manner of Modernist epiphany* –

---

*I have tended here, perhaps unfairly, to be a little unforgiving of the literary epiphany as such. Of course, epiphanies, like everything else, come in a variety of forms, but I do not think it entirely wrong to treat them all with suspicion. With more time and leisure, it might be interesting to go into the differences between what might be called the 'heroic' and other types of epiphany: affirmative (which differs significantly from the heroic, though it may flourish in the same hedgerow), negative, minor etc.

to give stark utterance to his sense of immensity. One finds himself sweetly shipwrecked; the other – what? Illumined, sublime, possibly heroic? The poem is too hermetic to know, though we can say that Ungaretti, while horrified by the cruelty of the war, would later align himself with Mussolini and the fascist cause. Perhaps that is not significant, but a cursory analysis of the poem already suggests that the heroic stance may not have been far from Ungaretti's mind. After all, he begins with the reflexive 'M'illumino', which can be read ambiguously: *illuminare* means to light up, illuminate or enlighten. '*M'illumino*' can and does mean that the speaker is lit up or enlightened by the immense, but that reflexive, while not grammatically salient, puts the self – the Romantic 'I' – centre-stage, and deftly hints at agency. Where is the illumination's origin? Immensity? Or the I? Both? It is a question worth asking, though an answer is not easy to come by, unless we look away, triangulate, as it were, with other works.

In our own time, Ungaretti's poem poses a serious question: which is, put crudely: is the very idea of a fusion of the finite self with the infinite sublime not intrinsically inimical to a necessary separation of self and world, a separation that allows both for humility and for a sense of wonder at the vastness that we inhabit? In Leopardi, the sense of the infinite seems to be summed up by Kant's postulate that 'the sublime is limitless, so that the mind in the presence of the sublime, attempting to imagine what it cannot, has pain in the failure but pleasure in contemplating the immensity of the attempt'. This honouring of the sublime (this *admittance of wonder*) seems to me to be at the very heart of Leopardi's vision, in which the self, the Romantic 'I', dissolves into the experience of 'attempting to imagine what it cannot'. Everything is given over to the world as Other. In Leopardi, this surrender can be breathtaking; I must confess, however, that I do not find it in Ungaretti. What stands out, instead, is the continuation, by other means, of the Romantic 'I' in its most heroic terms. That 'I' has two main modes of relating to immensity: it feels humbled or diminished, on the one hand, or exalted and heroic, even defiantly so, on the other. Yet these poses are, at best, childish. The universe isn't there to make any one human feel like a speck of dust, on the one hand, or singled out, on the other, by the limelight of the stars. The universe isn't there *for us*; it is simply there – and we are here, neither too small nor too large but to scale, as the dinosaurs were to scale, in their time, as people and elephants and the praying mantis are to scale now. At times the given world pulls us up short and gives us pause, offering a moment's sense of wonder that can be miraculously affirmative but need not always be so. In fact, it could be argued that, for the sake of our ontological health, we need to make ourselves aware, from time to time, of the space that

> is distinguished from the world and imposes itself as such, empty and without limits. The discovery is hailed by the poet as a 'miracle', [that is] as an acquisition of truth opposed to the 'habitual illusion', but is also experienced as a terrifying vertigo …

> lo spazio si distingue dal mondo e s'impone in quanto tale, vuoto e senza limiti. La scoperta è salutata dal poeta con favore, come 'miracolo', come acquisizione di verità contrapposta all' 'inganno consueto', ma anche sofferta come vertigine spaventosa …*

This is not to say that I do not find Ungaretti's poem effective, or affecting. Quite the contrary. My problem is that, in my own time, that is in the light of the current state of affairs, it is not something for which I can find very much use. In a real sense, 'Mattina' is a poem that belongs to the literary past, while Leopardi's 'L'Infinito' remains as urgent today as it was two hundred years ago.

Five words. This is the power of language: just five words – in my case, 'Le néant hante l'être' ('Nothingness haunts being') – can change the way a person thinks, possibly for ever. There I was,

---

*In the words of Italo Calvino; see below.

sitting in the college library on a sunny day, looking out at the gardens beyond, then going back to my book, only to break off and look out again, hoping my friend Louise would go by on her old Hercules bicycle, her basket full of good things from Arjuna or Basil's Bakery. There was an exam coming and, though I cannot remember ever being that diligent, something or other was forcing me to stay there, unable to quit my reading unless the world offered some kind of exit. Louise would cycle up, the sun glinting on her hair and on the handlebars of the Hercules and, looking up at me with a quizzical expression, as if to say, what in hell are you doing, would silently mouth the shibboleth, the single word that would release me from my labours. *Grantchester*. Which meant picnic, river, larks, possibly cold wine and the dog fox gone to ground. It was, after all, a Friday, and I had cause to feel hopeful. But nobody sauntered or cycled or otherwise happened along and I turned to a new page and read that line of Jean-Paul Sartre, who would have been quite blind by then, chain-smoking in a Paris café and thinking about Flaubert, it being Maytime and all. *Nothingness haunts being* – just three words in translation, though rather less elegant in the expression. To be fair, I wasn't any kind of a Jean-Paul Sartre buff (I was too easily bored, back then, by questions relating to existence and essence), but there was a whiff of the real, the ghostly real at that, to this passing remark. At the same time, there was something else there too – a clue, a hint. A suggestion of how things really are, rather than how they seem according to the conventions of time and space by which we are obliged to live, all the time knowing that they are, indeed, conventions. Everyone was a mystic in 1976 (well, everyone but me and Jean-Paul Sartre); devotees of Bhagwan Shree Rajneesh bounced to and fro in the spring sunshine in orange shirts and deep-red corduroys, practitioners of TM sat out on Parker's Piece or in small bedsit rooms above bicycle shops, practising their mantras – even I had my Eastern philosophical side, expressed as a devotion to Dao De Ching and the more manageable Zen koan. *Nothingness haunts being* said something to me about the nature of the world. I just didn't know what it was, until I read the poem 'Forse un mattino' from *Ossi di seppia*, by Eugenio Montale.

It might be, one morning, walking in dry, glassy air,
I will turn around – with a drunkard's terror –
to see the miracle:
the nothing at my back, the void behind me.

Then, as on a screen, trees houses hills
will gather again for the usual illusion.
But it will be too late, and I'll walk on in silence,
amongst men who don't look back, cradling my secret.

Forse un mattino andando in un'aria di vetro,
arida, rivolgendomi, vedrò compirsi il miracolo:
il nulla alle mie spalle, il vuoto dietro
di me, con un terrore di ubriaco.

Poi come s'uno schermo, s'accamperanno di gitto
alberi case colli per l'inganno consueto.
Ma sarà troppo tardi; ed io me n'andrò zitto
tra gli uomini che non si voltano, col mio segreto.[9]

The philosophical origins of the 'negative epiphany' – the immediate, even urgent experience of nothingness that this poem actualises – are not difficult to find. Kierkegaard comes to mind, and the speaker's existential crisis is paralleled elsewhere in the first third of the twentieth century in everyone from Kafka to Gödel. Yet it is important to note that this poem is about something more than mere existential angst. It could be argued, in fact, that the lyrical embodiment of the crisis that Montale offers here is one of the century's most significant achievements (on a par with Heisenberg's uncertainly principle, or Gödel's Incompleteness Theorems), by recognising a new depth and texture to our experience of modernity that both exposes and transcends the kind of quasi-heroic, self-illuminating epiphany captured by Ungaretti. On one level Montale seems to suggest that, if we attempt to resist such moments of self-abandonment, then the nothing that haunts being will overwhelm us. Yet this is not the end of the matter, for the void, the *nothing*, that this poem unveils is referred to as *a miracle*, and the speaker who moves on from that moment, among men who do not look back to see that nothingness, has been both blessed and cursed with a secret. *His* secret. For his one moment of terror – the kind of terror that comes of Dionysian intoxication – he has been in the presence of the sublime, not just attempting to imagine what his mind cannot but also aware that he cannot share that moment, or even talk about it, with his fellows. By now his idea of order has been overturned, but he has come to see that it was a false order in the first place. At the same time he is aware that what he has seen is miraculous, and while he may experience pain in the failure to understand it, there remains a vestige not so much of pleasure as of terrible, unseemly privilege in having had this encounter with the sublime. This is step one of a larger process, a peek behind the existential curtain, as it were, at a void that may be terrible but which, if viewed in the right light (and as many Eastern thinkers have seen it), may also be experienced as the creative ground of being itself. Nothingness haunts being – yes, but being takes that void as its origin.

Perhaps the final word on this should go to Italo Calvino, who, in his discussion of this poem mentioned earlier, recognises Montale's philosophical as well as his poetic achievement in opening the door to a new way of thinking about space, selfhood and being. Noting that 'the void' and 'nothingness' are 'at my back', he points out that what Montale offers the reader is not 'an indeterminate sensation of dissolution' but 'the construction of a cognitive model that is not easy to refute and that is capable of co-existing in our minds with other more or less empirical models'. By this, he means that the sense of nothingness is not just a philosophical idea: it is a fact of life. We are defined, literally, by the space (that is, by the absence of self) that surrounds us, a space that is strange, alien and ungovernable. The central paradox in this is that, while that space around us is divided into 'a visual field that lies before our eyes and an invisible field that lies behind us', it is the visible field that must be considered 'as an illusion' and emptiness that must be considered 'the true substance of the world'. Finally, citing 'a legend of the Wisconsin and Minnesota

lumbermen reported by Borges in his *Book of Imaginary Beings*',
Calvino proposes a narrative parallel to Montale's poetic vision:

> There is an animal that is called the Hidebehind that is always
> behind you, follows you everywhere, in the forest, when you
> go for wood; you turn around but no matter how fast you are,
> the Hidebehind is faster still and has already moved behind you;
> you will never know how it does so, but it is still there. Borges
> does not mention his sources (it may well be his own invention),
> but this would not detract from his hypothesis, which I would
> describe as genetic, categorical. We could say that the man in
> Montale's poem is the one who managed to turn around and
> catch the Hidebehind out: and what he sees is more frightening
> than any animal: it is nothing.*

It would be wrong to suggest that any single poem is, by itself,
a turning point in the history of human perception, but 'Forse

---

*It is worth citing the full passage here, in the original:

Il 'vuoto' e il 'nulla' sono 'alle mie spalle', 'dietro di me'. Il punto
fondamentale del poemetto è questo. Non è una indeterminata
sensazione di dissoluzione: è la costruzione d'un modello conoscitivo
che non è facile da smentire e che può coesistere in noi con altri modelli
più o meno empirici. L'ipotesi può essere enunciata in termini molto
semplici e rigorosi: data la bipartizione dello spazio che ci circonda
in un campo visuale davanti ai nostri occhi e un campo invisibile
alle nostre spalle, si definisce il primo come schermo d'inganni e il
secondo come un vuoto che è la vera sostanza del mondo … La stessa
problematica, in positivo (o in negativo, insomma con segno cambiato)
la ritrovo in una leggenda dei boscaioli del Wisconsin e del Minnesota
riportata da Borges nella sua Zoologia fantastica. C'è un animale
che si chiama hidebehind e che sta sempre alle tue spalle, ti segue
dappertutto, nella foresta, quando vai per legna; ti volti ma per quanto
tu sia svelto lo hidebehind è più svelto ancora e si è già spostato dietro
di te; non saprai mai com'è fatto ma è sempre lì. Borges non cita le sue
fonti e può tarsi che questa leggenda se la sia inventata lui; ma ciò non
toglierebbe nulla alla sua forza d'ipotesi che direi genetica, categoriale.
Potremmo dire che l'uomo di Montale è quello che è riuscito a voltarsi
e a vedere com'è fatto lo hidebehind: ed è più spaventoso di qualsiasi
animale, è il nulla.

un mattino' comes close. For, just as Gödel's theorems or the *Tractatus Logico-Philosophicus* of Wittgenstein exposed the limits of traditional logic, so Montale's vision exposed the failure of the Romantic pose to encompass the complexities of the human experience, face to face with the mysterious spaces around us. He did not claim that these spaces were easy to explain or to navigate, but his work continued to insist, in the face of war, rejection and Italy's descent into fascism, that it is always better to live with a difficult truth than to accommodate an easy, but treacherous, lie.

EINEN REINEN VORGANG

Not that you could withstand
God's voice: far from it. But listen to the breath,
the unbroken message that creates itself from the silence.[1]

Rainer Maria Rilke

ON A WARM JULY MORNING in the Swiss Valais, my younger son and I are walking the trail that runs from the bottom of the Rhône Valley and up through the ancient villages of Raron and Saint-Germain to the old railway station at Ausserberg. After a recent illness, I have been advised to take it easy and stick to the lower slopes, so we are following the old irrigation ditches that bring fresh, icy water from the mountains down to the pastures and vineyards below – in this particular instance, via the Niwärch and Görperi *bisses*, elegant, human-made water-runs constructed in the fourteenth century and still in use today. To begin with, the path is easy going, but after a while I start to tire and, as noon approaches, we are forced to go slow, gradually accepting the need to pace ourselves and fortified, in the midday heat, by the scent of the cold meltwater, which is the very spirit of the glacier itself. The great *bisses*, and the silvery stone-built channels they feed, are a real blessing in this weather; every now and then we drop to our knees to plunge a hand into the chill current, so cold, so clear. It's like plugging in to some ancient, energising force, as we scoop the water up and splash it on our faces – and this is half the pleasure of walking anywhere around these parts, this contrast between the hot and the cold, the earth and the sun, the still and the flowing. The *bisses* do the same work that drainage and irrigation systems do throughout the world, but there is also something holy about them, something unique in the care with which they have been constructed, the water at this lower level pouring, more often than not, over natural stone, cut and laid to guide it more efficiently but allowing it, here and there, to spill out into the lush pasture, clear cold water spending through viridian leaves of grass.

Just below us, on a rocky outcrop, sits the Burgkirche of Raron, one of a series of extraordinary buildings (churches, town houses and daring bridges over terrifying precipices) designed by the gifted sixteenth-century architect Ulrich Ruffiner. On its own merits, the church is well worth a visit, though it is not what remains of the fine murals, or the intricate wood carvings, that draws thousands of visitors every year, but the last resting place of the poet Rainer Maria Rilke, a writer all too frequently misunderstood, by admirers and detractors alike, as 'metaphysical', 'mystical' or even conventionally religious. Such designations are ironic when applied to a man who, in an early work, addresses the divinity as 'Du, nachbar, Gott' and wrote, in a letter sent to a young friend towards the end of his life:

> I have never drawn distinct boundaries between body, mind and spirit: each has given active service to the other and each has been precious to me ... so it would be a very strange and novel thing to do if I were now to confront my sickly, failing body with a definitive religious principle.[2]

That Rilke loved the things of this world, that he valued the physical as much as the spiritual and saw no meaningful division between the two, is borne out by the headstone that marks the grave, a simple slab of local stone set in its own diminutive walled garden and inscribed only with his name and three lines of verse –

Rose, oh reiner Widerspruch, Lust,
Niemandes Schlaf zu sein unter soviel
Lidern

– which translate (inelegantly) as 'Rose, oh pure contradiction, Joy, to be nobody's sleep under so many eyelids'. These lines, like the burial site, were chosen by Rilke himself, and, aware of his love of roses, a handful of local people have tried, year after year, to establish rose bushes around the grave, only to see them die every winter when the snow comes. Finally, they gave in to circumstance and planted ivy, though in summer people bring bedding plants, and, occasionally they leave bouquets of the lush, velvety rose varieties that Rilke loved so much.

This love of roses is enshrined in the legend of his death, told here by William H. Gass:

> The myth concerning the onset of his illness was, even among his myths, the most remarkable. To honor a visitor, the Egyptian beauty Nimet Eloui, Rilke gathered some roses from his garden. While doing so, he pricked his hand on a thorn. This small wound failed to heal, grew rapidly worse, soon his entire arm was swollen, and his other arm became affected as well. According to the preferred story, this was the way Rilke's disease announced itself, although Ralph Freedman, his judicious and most recent biographer, puts that melancholy event more than a year earlier.[3]

As Freedman suggests, the story is indeed apocryphal; Rilke actually died of an uncommon form of leukaemia and the end came in the middle of winter, not a rose in sight, on 29 December 1926, less than a month after his fifty-first birthday. Wearied by a lifetime of travelling, and with no fixed abode (always the guest, he immortalised in his work the castles and villas of those who took him in along the way), the finest German-language poet of his era had come to this French-speaking corner of the Swiss Alps to rest, and to make a small garden of his own in the tiny hamlet of Muzot, just above Sierre. It was a wise choice, for his work at least. In the space of two years he settled happily into his adopted homeland and at last found the peace and inward composure to complete the *Duino Elegies*, a work he had begun ten years earlier as a guest of Princess Marie von Thurn und Taxis at her castle retreat near Trieste, in what must have seemed a different world. He also created a number of poem sequences (written in French) that are as elegant and philosophically rewarding as any he composed in his native language. One of those sequences was, unsurprisingly, given over to roses:

> One rose, alone, it is all roses
> and this one, the irreplaceable,
> the perfect, the supple vocable
> framed by the text of things.
>
> Without her, how could we speak
> of our hopes
> and of the tender intervals
> in the continuum of parting.
>
> Une rose seule, c'est toutes les roses
> et celle-ci : l'irremplaçable,
> le parfait, le souple vocable
> encadré par le texte des choses.
>
> Comment jamais dire sans elle
> ce que furent nos espérances,
> et les tendres intermittences
> dans la partance continuelle.[4]

But who was this weary world-traveller, a bohemian in the eyes of the stolid citizens of Le Valais, who nevertheless found the closest thing to a home of his own in what is still a fairly quiet backwater? So much has been written about Rilke, yet he remains an enigma, a poet considered by many to be the finest of his era, who nevertheless remarked of himself in an early poem:

He is not drawn to victories;
he grows by being defeated
by greater and greater things.

Die Siege laden ihn nicht ein;
Sein Wachstum ist: Der Tiefbesiegte
Von immer Größerem zu sein.[5]

The truth is, it behoves us to be wary of investing too much in a poet's biography, especially as regards the political details.* As to the personal life – the marriage, the family, the friendships, the betrayals, not to mention all the sins and delights that flesh is heir to – we can never have anything more than a partial account. Of Rilke we can say, as all the old biographies used to say, that our subject (and here it is usual to give the name in full) René Karl Wilhelm Johann Josef Maria Rilke was born on 4 December 1875, into an unhappy middle-class Prague household. His mother, having lost a daughter two years earlier, dressed the boy up in girl's clothes until he went to school; his father, invalided out of the army before he could secure a commission, attempted, disastrously, to live out his failed ambitions through his sickly, deeply unmartial son. After several thoroughly miserable years in military academies, followed by spells at Prague and Munich universities (where his studies were once again disrupted by chronic illness), Rilke published his first poetry collection, *Leben und Lieder*, in 1894. Further publications followed; but it was a bad case of romantic love, rather than any literary ambitions, that would change the

---

* For instance, we can take note of the fact that, towards the end of his life, Rilke wrote letters to an acquaintance praising Mussolini and welcoming the advent of Italian fascism, just as we cannot quite dismiss Conor Cruise O'Brien's contention that (again, in his later years) 'Yeats the man was as near to being a Fascist as the conditions of his country permitted'; however, it should also be noted that Yeats expressed support for the Spanish Republic and, after a brief flirtation, rejected the Irish Blueshirts, while Rilke took real risks to support the Bavarian Soviet, stating: 'In 1918, in the moment of collapse Germany could have shamed and moved the world through an act of deep truthfulness and reversal. Then I hoped for a moment.'

course of his life, setting him on the path of compulsive wanderer and perennial outsider until he was overtaken by an early death.

It is difficult, now, to know for certain how the young Rilke felt *personally* (as opposed to philosophically) about love and marriage. In his letters and other writings love is a solemn affair, a mental and spiritual discipline, with frivolity, on the one hand, and practicality, on the other, frowned upon. For him, marriage was a contract between two souls that went far beyond anything that the customary vows required. Later, he would write that,

> [t]he demands which the difficult work of love makes upon our development are more than life-size, and as beginners we are not up to them. But if we nevertheless hold out and take this love upon us as burden and apprenticeship, instead of losing ourselves in all the light and frivolous play [...] then a little progress and alleviation will perhaps be perceptible to those who come after.

Meanwhile, his vision of married life is almost shocking – and certainly goes beyond anything that a conventional bridegroom might ask of himself, or of his bemused bride:

> The point of marriage is not to create a quick commonality by tearing down all boundaries; on the contrary, a good marriage is one in which each partner appoints the other to be the guardian of his solitude, and thus they show each other the greatest possible trust. A merging of two people is an impossibility, and where it seems to exist, it is a hemming-in, a mutual consent that robs one or both parties of their fullest freedom and development. But once the realization is accepted that even between the closest people infinite distances exist, a marvellous living side-by-side can grow up for them, if they succeed in loving the expanse between them, which gives them the possibility of always seeing each other as a whole and before an immense sky.[6]

There is a kind of absurd beauty to this idealism, though it is hard to imagine any of Rilke's precepts working in practice. With the possible exception of D. H. Lawrence, no other writer of that time was so vitally aware of the immense gap between the ideal and the contingent in matters of the heart – and at the same time, so ready to bridge it. For many, Rilke's ideal of married life is comparable only to sainthood in its demands and its intensity; nevertheless, in the summer of 1900, during a stay at the rural artists' colony in Worpswede, Germany, he fell in love with, and declared his wish to marry, the painter Paula Becker (who, rather inconveniently, was already promised to another artist, named Otto Modersohn*). When Paula insisted on staying true to her betrothed, Rilke immediately attached himself to her best friend, the sculptress Clara Westhoff, whom he married in 1901. The couple had a daughter, Ruth, the following year, but it soon became clear that they could not remain together. Family life, as it happened, was far too much of a distraction from their artistic ambitions – and so Rilke left (though he did not one-sidedly abandon Clara, as at least one biographer has suggested; she was just as wrapped up in her work as her husband, while Ruth seems to have been well cared for by her maternal grandparents).

From that point on, Rilke travelled extensively, staying here and there across Europe, usually for only brief periods.[†] It is hard to think of any writer who has been more dependent on the kindness, if not of strangers, then at least of admirers and acquaintances. His last five years, spent in various parts of Switzerland, were among his happiest and most productive, and he was looking forward to creating the rose garden that he had always dreamed of when he fell ill once again. He died at the Val-Mont

---

* She did, indeed, go ahead with the wedding, thus becoming the highly regarded painter Paula Modersohn-Becker we remember today – and we have to admit that the name has a certain ring to it. Certainly it trumps Paula Rilke-Becker, which sounds like a child sneezing and hiccoughing at the same time.

† Paula Modersohn-Becker died in 1907, after giving birth to her first child. A year earlier Rilke had sat for her in Paris, where he was working as Rodin's assistant: her portrait shows a dark-eyed man in a stiff, high collar, looking much older than his thirty-one years.

sanatorium on 29 December 1926. No one can say, now, whether he would have remained at Muzot or if he could have been happy there in the longer term. Certainly, the place inspired hope, as he reveals in a letter to a young woman he had befriended in 1919. After describing his dismay at having to leave his former residence near Zurich (he seems apprehensive at the prospect of going off again on one of his interminable European journeys, 'to flit about like a ghost'), the mood changes, and he goes on to describe what he sees as his salvation:

> By way of giving myself a farewell treat I journeyed over to Wallis which is the grandest of all the Swiss Cantons (though to my mind it scarcely seems to be part of Switzerland any more). I had discovered it a year previously, and again, as when I first saw it, it gave the impression of a vast, lost world, its landscapes huge yet at the same time graceful, very much as how I remember Provence and, in certain aspects, even Spain. And it was here that, by the strangest coincidence, I found a *manoir* that had not been lived in permanently for hundreds of years. It has been a long struggle (and it is not over yet) but I can, at least, claim some success in that I now live in an old castle keep where I have made myself snug for the winter. Getting Muzot under control was no small matter and without the assistance of a Swiss friend all efforts to overcome its daunting obstacles would have continued to fail. As you can see, my dwelling (admittedly there is only me and a housekeeper here) is no bigger than your own. The small photograph I enclose does not show it quite as it is today and must have been taken before 1900. That was when there was a change of ownership and the old manor underwent a thorough restoration. Fortunately, not much was altered and nothing was spoiled; it was really done only to halt decay. A small garden was added and the plants stand rather dramatically in groups all round the walls, like defenders.[7]

Sadly, work on the garden would be interrupted on several

occasions. This letter was dated 27 December 1921, and though he remained officially domiciled at Muzot until the end of his life, chronic illness would frequently oblige him to move, either to the hospital at Valmont or to stay elsewhere with any friend who was available to look after him. Nevertheless, a small rose plot did appear at Muzot in due course (Rilke's first English biographer, E. M. Butler, describes them as 'clad in pink silk boudoir-gowns and red summer dresses, like carefully tended and cherished, fragrant and fragile hothouse blooms'), and it is satisfying to think that, as Rilke prepared to enter 'into absolute and passionate presence with all that is here', each and every one of them, irreplaceable and perfect, offered a *tendre intermittence* in the long continuum of parting.

As important as they were to him, however, roses were elements of an outward aesthetic, something if not akin then at least not alien to the pose (*Haltung*) that each of us, not only the artist, adopts, to a greater or less degree, in order to live in the open.* This pose, or attitude, may come about without our knowing why, or it may in itself be a work of artifice, but it is inevitable. The apparent alternative – 'being natural' – is an act of deception, both of the self and of the other, and, as Wilde points out, is 'such a very difficult pose to keep up'. For Rilke, the pose associated with the rose is best expressed in these lines from the eighth of the *Duino Elegies*:

---

* By this I mean the presentation of an outward version of one's inner life, as opposed to the inner life itself. To be understood as a counter to 'being natural', which Oscar Wilde called 'the most irritating pose I know', this variety of the pose is based on an acceptance that, to paraphrase Wilde, the inner life, the source of the art, is too important a thing ever to talk seriously about it or even, indeed, to let it be seen. See the 'Eighth Elegy', from the *Duino Elegies*, below.

Who has turned us around, thus, that
no matter what we do, we assume the pose
of the one who is (forever) about to depart?

Wer hat uns also umgedreht, daß wir,
was wir auch tun, in jener Haltung sind
von einem, welcher fortgeht?[8]

However, as central as the rose may be, the most frequent and powerful image in the major works is that of the angel – so it would seem fitting that Rilke, of all poets, should be buried in the yard of a church that boasts vivid murals of the angelic hosts going about their work. In the winter of 1926, however, the good Christian folk of Raron didn't see it that way: Rilke was not a local and, what with the gossip about his bohemian life, his Paris manners and the steady stream of glamorous visitors, it would have been clear to them that their neighbour from Muzot was not a God-fearing man in any common sense of the word. This, at least, is the official story; today, though, some of the local people, especially the women, point out that, as much as he loved the Valais itself, Rilke had on several occasions been audibly critical of the inherent sexism of a society in which wives and daughters did most of the work while the men reaped all the rewards.

Still, this supposedly bohemian poet had not chosen Raron as his grave site to win the approbation of the local *religieux*, or to be closer to the Christian God he had grown up with and away from. He may have been drawn to the beauty of the mountain landscape, but he rarely ascended those peaks, preferring the valley and the lower slopes. A favourite place was the Forêt de Finges, just a few miles west of Raron, where he could look upwards in all directions and see the snow-capped peaks from the safe refuge of a wide marshland inhabited by bee-eaters and hoopoes, a site renowned throughout Europe for the profusion and diversity of its butterflies. 'Outside is a day of inexhaustible splendour', he wrote to a friend in 1921. 'This valley inhabited by hills – it provides ever-new twists and impulses, as if it were still the movement of creation that energised its changing aspects. We have discovered the forests – full of small lakes, blue, green, nearly black. What country delivers such detail, painted on such a large canvas? It is like the final movement of a Beethoven symphony.'[9] From the Burgkirche at Raron, just as at Finges, one looks up and, inevitably, one sees the mountains. It was looking up, rather than looking down, that gave Rilke the power to renew his vision. His mind reached for the stony peaks, but his heart belonged to the valley.

As for the angels of the church at Raron – solid and sensible, mere ushers escorting the souls of the dead to their appointed places in the afterlife – they are nowhere near as colourful as the harlequinade of exotic birds that flit along the banks of the Rhône. That this stolid Burgkirche's main wall painting is a Last Judgement comes as no surprise; J. L. Carr has it right in his novel *A Month in the Country* (1980), when the shell-shocked art restorer, recently returned from the First World War's trenches, says of the mural he is uncovering in the local church, that

> it was bound to be a Judgement because they always got the plum spots where parishioners couldn't avoid seeing the God-awful things that would happen to them if they didn't fork out their tithes or marry the girls they'd got with child. It would be St Michael weighing souls against Sin, Christ in Majesty refereeing and, down below, the Fire that flameth evermore.

I have seen many such provincial Judgements and, no matter how colourful or dramatic, I still think of this kind of work as the most dismal use of the angel as an image. But then, the angels here are mere bit-players, little more than extras. What matters is the agony of the damned, the relief of the saved and the stolid face of God, hovering above it all, apparently unperturbed.* The impulse behind these works is not spiritual, or even individual,

---

*It is one of the occasional sly pleasures of this genre that, now and then, the painter shows that relief in just a little too much detail – so much so that one wonders whether the pardoned wretch might have been an acquaintance of his. Dante was not alone in securing his enemies a good seat in Hell.

but societal. A well-painted Judgement probably translated into a full tithe barn. As with the Nativity, and the various Assumptions, Ascensions and Resurrections, the angels are only there for show.

The sole exception to all this is the Annunciation scene. In this particular tableau of Western art, a single human figure finds herself face to face with the unsayable, with what Rilke calls 'the unbroken message that creates itself from the silence'. Reading the *Duino Elegies*, as with the great Annunciation paintings, we are invited to experience an event that, to any rational person, would seem wholly absurd, an event in which the angel is not only *real* but appears, squarely and incontrovertibly, in the midst of the everyday. In a space that is, momentarily, set apart from the normal course of events, Rilke's angels emerge not from the poem, or from the individuated mind of the poet, but from the world itself, the way the Annunciation angel emerges from the collaborative geometry of Botticelli's *Cestello Annunciation*, or how it appears all at once, as if from the very fabric of the garden, in Lorenzo Lotto's *Recanati Annunciation* of 1534, scaring the cat with the urgency of an unforeseen yet entirely fleshly presence.* Of course, every scrap of reasoned thinking that any rational being can muster cries out that angels are apparitions, illusions, objects of superstition and, most importantly, *creatures of another world* – which is all very well until this logical impossibility appears, vivid as fire in the noon air, or, as Rilke puts it:

> Every Angel is terrifying.
> And so I check myself and suppress the cry
> of a darkened sobbing. Ah, who then can
> we use? Not Angels: not humans,
> and the resourceful animals can tell
> that we are not entirely at home
> in the interpreted world.

---

* Lotto's angel is, in fact, powerfully physical, its hair streaming, Maenad-like in the divine wind, its eyes intent, the green of its wings as dark as the *viriditas* so prized by Hildegard von Bingen.

Ein jeder Engel ist schrecklich.
Und so verhalt ich mich denn und verschlucke den Lockruf
dunkelen Schluchzens. Ach, wen vermögen
wir denn zu brauchen? Engel nicht, Menschen nicht,
und die findigen Tiere merken es schon,
daß wir nicht sehr verläßlich zu Haus sind
in der gedeuteten Welt.

Of course, we are able to endure 'the interpreted world', the
world of phenomena, but we do not feel altogether at home
there, because we sense what is behind, or within, or beyond the
surfaces of that world; and though the 'other' reality is beyond
our capacity for description, and cannot even be named, we sense
it as a beauty that

> is nothing but
the beginning of a terror that we can scarcely endure,
and we admire it so, because it serenely disdains
to destroy us.

> ist nichts
als des Schrecklichen Anfang, den wir noch gerade ertragen,
und wir bewundern es so, weil es gelassen verschmäht,
uns zu zerstören.

None of this is intended to suggest that the angels of the *Duino
Elegies* are *true* in the narrowly literal way that the faithful might
have chosen to see them in the Burgkirche's Judgement scene. On
the contrary: the congregation's choice is a matter of faith, for
which no evidence is required. Rilke's angels, however, are *all* evidence. Encountering them, here, in this world, we have no need
to believe, because we are overwhelmed by their incontrovertible
reality – and unless we accept that reality, we will never be able
to negotiate a path through the angelic world, a path that leads,
as the *Elegies* unfold, to the imaginary gardens with real toads in
them that Marianne Moore proposed. It may be difficult to accept
the idea that, when we use the word 'real' here, we are not just

talking about a figure of speech. Nor are we proposing that the angels are entirely poetic devices. They exist in the *Elegies* to give form to an experience that is a necessary and unavoidable part of being in the world: the sense that there is something beyond rational description, 'behind, or within, or beyond the surfaces of that world'. If we read the poem as Rilke intended, the angels must be conceived of as real – which is to say, indelibly *present*. They may not have been there at first, when the poem began to be said, but they are there *now*. This is what we mean when we speak of *poiesis*,* a faculty that includes not only the celebrated imaginative achievements of artists and poets but also the ways in which we all make our world habitable from day to day, in the flow of the dailiness of life.

This being so, the idea of *poiesis*, set alongside the discovery of the power of such faculties as intuition, and apprehension, raises questions about what we are talking about when we talk about science. The twentieth century was a period of enormous scientific breakthroughs, but Rilke's poetry tacitly counsels against seeing science as the only possible answer to questions about what we know and what can learn about the world. There was a tendency in the twentieth century to see scientists as 'rational' in their thinking, and so (by definition, so to speak) non-spiritual. This has not always been the case: for example, Edward Williams Morley (who in 1887, together with Arthur A. Michelson, conducted the series of experiments on the speed of light in

---

*From the Greek, meaning 'bringing forth'. See Heidegger, in *The Question Concerning Technology*: 'It is of utmost importance that we think bringing-forth in its full scope and at the same time in the sense in which the Greeks thought it. Not only handicraft manufacture, not only artistic and poetical bringing into appearance and concrete imagery, is a bringing-forth, *poiesis*. *Physis*, also, the arising of something from out of itself, is a bringing-forth, *poiesis*. *Physis* is indeed *poiesis* in the highest sense. For what presences by means of *physis* has the bursting open belonging to bringing-forth, e.g., the bursting of a blossom into bloom.' The same view of the poem as comparable to an organic event such as the blossoming of a flower, or the emergence of a butterfly from its cocoon, can be found in César Vallejo's definition of the poem as 'a vital entity' (*una entidad vital*).

'the luminiferous aether' that paved the way for Einstein's relativity theory*) was also a preacher and had begun his education in a seminary; J. J. Thomson, the Nobel prize-winner who discovered the electron, was a regular communicant in the Anglican Church; Guglielmo Marconi, a Nobel laureate in physics in 1909, was a devout Catholic. The list goes on – even Einstein himself, though never orthodox in his beliefs, responded in guarded, but revealing, language to a query from the writer and biographer George Sylvester Viereck in 1930:

> We see a universe marvellously arranged, obeying certain laws, but we understand the laws only dimly. Our limited minds cannot grasp the mysterious force that sways the constellations. I am fascinated by Spinoza's Pantheism [...] Spinoza is the greatest of modern philosophers, because he is the first philosopher who deals with the soul and the body as one, not as two separate things.

Perhaps the most interesting scientist to attempt a reconciliation between 'rational' science and other modes of experiencing the world was the Quaker cosmologist Arthur Stanley Eddington, whose experimental work during the solar eclipse of 29 May 1919 confirmed relativity theory. Eddington is a fascinating figure. A champion of relativity at a time when it was generally misunderstood (and in Britain, in particular, treated with some hostility as a 'German' idea), he was nevertheless a proponent of the then radical doctrine of indeterminism,[†] which positioned itself in direct contradiction to Einstein's view that 'God does not play dice with the universe'. With his appreciation that human beings

---

* The Michelson–Morley experiment, notorious as the most famous failed experiment in history, had a huge impact on physics, as it suggested that the stationary ether did not exist, thus throwing many assumptions about light and about the nature of space into question.

† Very briefly, the idea that physical events do not necessarily have a determining cause, but happen randomly (whatever 'randomly' might mean).

have a range of faculties for navigating reality,* Eddington offers a vision of the world in which the use of methods 'transcending the methods of physics' is seen as valid and not as superstitious, or tainted by the supernatural, though these methods can be seen as allocating some kind of truth value to the real, if temporarily inexplicable and so apparently irrational, powers embodied in the *Duino Elegies* by Rilke's angels. In fact, reading Eddington, we may be reminded of the now famous letter Emily Dickinson wrote to Thomas Wentworth Higginson in 1863:

> I was thinking to-day, as I noticed, that the 'Supernatural' was only the Natural disclosed.
>
> Not 'Revelation' 't is that waits,
> But our unfurnished eyes.

It should be emphasised that neither Dickinson nor Eddington is choosing to adopt an unscientific, or irrational, position in their observations of the world. As Einstein says, we 'cannot grasp the mysterious force that sways the constellations' – or not by means of reason alone. However, the rational faculty – the process of observing the world through our five senses and processing that data using strict logical methods – is not the only faculty that human beings possess. In a poem probably written in the early 1860s (poem 668 of the Thomas H. Johnson edition of her works), Dickinson explores what we can know of the world around us (i.e., nature), first through sight –

> 'Nature' is what we see –
> The Hill – the Afternoon –
> Squirrel – Eclipse – the Bumble bee –
> Nay – Nature is Heaven –

then by way of auditory stimuli –

---

* Some may baulk at words such as 'spiritual' as against 'mental'; for the moment, the terminology seems to me less important than accepting that scientific method is not the only game in town.

Nature is what we hear –
The Bobolink – the Sea –
Thunder – the Cricket –
Nay – Nature is Harmony.[10]

We note, here, that the final line in each of these sensory investigations moves from the raw data to an abstract quality (Heaven, Harmony) which depends for its existence on the active interpretation of the observing mind; there is no such thing, in nature, as heaven, or harmony – we *find* these qualities there. Whether they exist as such is debatable. Biologists often remark on the ubiquity of the Fibonacci sequence in natural phenomena, from the arrangement of leaves on an agave plant to the chambers of a nautilus shell – but is it there because it is *there*, or because we see it there? The last four lines of Dickinson's nature poem proposes a possible answer to this question:

Nature is what we know –
Yet have no art to say –
So impotent Our Wisdom is
To her Simplicity.

Here it is another faculty, one that does not depend on sensory observation governed by logical method, that allows us fully to apprehend the natural world. Knowing is not only a matter of scientific enquiry; it involves some other faculty – intuition, we might say, or apprehension – that traditional science is obliged, for rigour's sake, either to dismiss or discount. This knowing without being able to explain what (or why) we know, this apprehension, this faculty of intuition is outside the realm of logic – where, as Wittgenstein says, 'what we cannot speak about we must pass over in silence' – but it is of the essence of poetic enquiry. Reading poets such as Rilke and Dickinson, it once again becomes clear that, where they work from an *intuited* reality, they are not being superstitious or talking about 'the supernatural'. Hamlet's contention – that 'There are more things in heaven and earth, Horatio,/ Than are dreamt of in your philosophy' – has become an out-and-out cliché, but it is, nevertheless, an important point. The vital thing to remember with any method is that its usefulness vanishes as soon as we forget its limits. To return to Wittgenstein:

> My propositions serve as elucidations in the following way: anyone who understands me eventually recognizes them as nonsensical, when he has used them – as steps – to climb up beyond them. (He must, so to speak, throw away the ladder after he has climbed up it.)
>
> He must transcend these propositions, and then he will see the world aright. What we cannot speak about we must pass over in silence.*

Again, at the risk of repeating myself, I think it is important to say that, when Wittgenstein points to 'what we cannot speak about', he is drawing a limit to *thought*, and specifically rational thought, not *perception*. I feel that this is important because it is easy to forget that one of this philosopher's principal achievements, in this early stage of his work at least, is in drawing such a limit. That act, that setting of limits, creates a space for other forms of experience (let us call them *apprehensions*, for want of a better term) to prosper. As we know, Wittgenstein capped this exercise in setting limits to what logic could achieve by suggesting that 'philosophy ought really to be written only as a form of poetry'. The form of poetry he had in mind was probably not very specific, though it is worth noting that in 1913, when he was engaged in divesting himself of a considerable inherited fortune, one of the poets to benefit from his generosity was Rilke. It would be interesting to know if, around a decade later, Wittgenstein read

---

*The translation here is by D. F. Pears and B. F. McGuiness. The original reads: 'Meine Sätze erläutern dadurch, dass sie der, welcher mich versteht, am Ende als unsinnig erkennt, wenn er durch sie – auf ihnen – über sie hinausgestiegen ist. (Er muss sozusagen die Leiter wegwerfen, nachdem er auf ihr hinaufgestiegen ist.) Er muss diese Sätze überwinden, dann sieht er die Welt richtig. Wovon man nicht sprechen kann, darüber muss man schweigen.' Wittgenstein, *Tractatus Logico-Philosophicus*.

the ninth of the *Duino Elegies*, arguably the most accomplished philosophical poem of the last century – a philosophical poem, in fact, that in many ways echoes, or perhaps composes its own variations on, some of his own most urgent concerns. In its attention to the use of language as a means both to praise and to self-definition, the miraculous nature of being and the celebration of the here and now as against some other, 'higher' realm of being, it is a work that Wittgenstein would surely have approved. At just over eighty lines in length it is, arguably, the culmination of an extraordinary lifetime's work and, though too long to analyse in detail here, it is rewarding to pick out some of the threads of Rilke's poetic thinking, as it is so perfectly distilled here.

The poem begins with an surprising question: why, when we could have been something else (laurel trees, say), did we have to be created human? Is it because humans are capable of happiness? Wonder? Or perhaps 'Exercise of the heart'? No, the poet says, the laurel could have done these things. We are here

> because being here is a lot, and because
> what is here, this fleeting world, seems to need us

> weil Hiersein viel ist, und weil uns scheinbar
> alles das Hiesige braucht, dieses Schwindende

– which in itself is puzzling, because we are the most fleeting things of all, we who live only once and pass away. Nevertheless:

> this
> having been once, even if only once,
> to have been of this earth, seems to be irrevocable.

> dieses
> ein Mal gewesen zu sein, wenn auch nur ein Mal:
> irdisch gewesen zu sein, scheint nicht widerrufbar.

What Rilke is saying here is that what makes us unique is that we live as mortals on this earth, and care for it, and this in itself is a something – a privilege? a duty? – that cannot be taken from us.

Readers of Heidegger might relate these lines to his contention, in his long essay of 1951, *Building Dwelling Thinking*, that dwelling is 'a staying with things', that 'mortals nurse and nurture the things that grow, and specially construct things that do not grow. Cultivating and construction are building in the narrower sense. Dwelling [on the other hand] is, as this keeping, a *building*.'[11]

From this Rilke moves on through a discourse on what he calls the long experience (or practice, or, one might say, learning) of love (*der Liebe lange Erfahrung*) to a beautiful passage about language and the joy of naming:

> Are we perhaps here
> to say: house, bridge, fountain, gate, pitcher,
> fruit tree, window – at most, pillar, tower?
> But to say them, you understand –
> to say them in a way that even the things
> themselves never thought to be so intimately.

> Sind wir vielleicht hier, um zu sagen: Haus,
> Brücke, Brunnen, Tor, Krug, Obstbaum, Fenster, –
> höchstens: Säule, Turm … aber zu sagen, verstehs,
> oh zu sagen so, wie selber die Dinge niemals
> innig meinten zu sein.

Language is the means by which, between the hammer blows that assault us, the heart sustains itself ('Zwischen den Hämmern besteht unser Herz'); language, in the service of naming (which, in many spiritual traditions, is in itself a form of invocation), language as praise is the purpose and home [*Heimat*] of mortals.

Now the angel is invoked once again, for it is to him that this praise must be recounted – but in an astonishing and graceful twist on the very idea of the angel as a representative of the supernatural, calling us to some higher reality Rilke advises:

> Praise this world to the Angel, not the unutterable:
> don't try to show off with high sounding words: in the
>   cosmos,

to which he is so fully attuned, you are a mere novice.
Show him some simple thing, shaped from generation to
    generation,
something that is there to hand and in plain sight.
Tell him the things of this world. He will be all the more
    astonished.

Preise dem Engel die Welt, nicht die unsägliche, ihm
kannst du nicht großtun mit herrlich Erfühltem; im Weltall,
wo er fühlender fühlt, bist du ein Neuling. Drum zeig
ihm das Einfache, das, von Geschlecht zu Geschlechtern
    gestaltet,
als ein Unsriges lebt, neben der Hand und im Blick.
Sag ihm die Dinge. Er wird staunender stehn.

In short, when the angel summons us to the moment of annunciation, it is the quotidian reality, the dailiness of life that mortals
offer up in praise.

The poem continues now with a further delineation of our
responsibility to 'the things', a responsibility to make them ours
through praise, and to preserve them, in Heidegger's sense of preserving as staying with, or keeping. Finally, in some of the most
beautiful closing lines in all of poetry, Rilke sets out a kind of song
of praise to the earth,

Earth, is this not what you want, to arise
invisibly in us? Is it not your desire to become
invisible some day? Earth! Invisible!
If it is not this transformation, what is your most pressing
    mandate?
Beloved Earth, I wish it …
Nameless, I am pledged to you from afar.
You were always true, and your most sacred idea
is that death is a trusted friend.

See: I live. Whence? Neither childhood nor the future
decreases … Yet my heart overflows with Being.

Erde, ist es nicht dies, was du willst: unsichtbar
in uns erstehn? – Ist es dein Traum nicht,
einmal unsichtbar zu sein? – Erde! unsichtbar!
Was, wenn Verwandlung nicht, ist dein drängender Auftrag?
Erde, du liebe, ich will …
Namenlos bin ich zu dir entschlossen, von weit her.
Immer warst du im Recht, und dein heiliger Einfall
ist der vertrauliche Tod.

Siehe, ich lebe. Woraus? Weder Kindheit noch Zukunft
werden weniger … Überzähliges Dasein
entspringt mir im Herzen.

It was our last night in Raron. Unable to work, or even to read, in the heat of the apartment, I called my son away from his video game and we went out walking while it was still almost light. I was aware that I had been a little inward over the last few days, preoccupied with all the things a sick man thinks of when he is with his child, and I suppose I wanted to say something, to make some explanation – but, of course, there was nothing to say, or nothing that could be taken as explanatory, at least. We cannot make our children – we cannot *make* anyone – understand anything, especially when it is something that we can barely put into words for ourselves, but if I could make this child know anything, it would be what several years of reading, and abandoning, and finally returning to the *Duino Elegies* can teach even the most haphazard of readers. It is there, expressed in surprisingly simple language, in the thick of the late elegies:

A time
for everything, but only once. Once and no more. And we too,
only once. Never again. But to have been here
this once, even if only once:
to have been *earthly*, this cannot be revoked

Ein Mal
jedes, nur ein Mal. Ein Mal und nicht mehr. Und wir auch
ein Mal. Nie wieder. Aber dieses
ein Mal gewesen zu sein, wenn auch nur ein Mal:
irdisch gewesen zu sein, scheint nicht widerrufbar

and you do not have to be a sick parent, fretting about time and
mortality, to know that being there is *everything*. Nor do you have
to be very smart, emotionally, lyrically, to know that, if the understanding that is bound up in these lines could be passed along
freely, from one to another, it would be the finest gift a father
could give to his son. But it can't be done, of course. We each have
to learn, according to our own natures, what is of the essence, and
what is a passing distraction.

We had walked down to the river, for the cooler air over the
milky, glaciated water; now, at midnight, barely a feather of
a breeze touched our faces as we climbed back up the hill past
the Burgerhof and along Unterdorf, the pour of Alpine water
running under our feet from the *bisse* system on the mountain
slopes above, the water ice-cold and rapid, zigzagging down from
the high mountains, our shadows dancing about us in the angular
Caligari light from the way-lamp at the corner of Oberdorfsgasse.
I guess that we had been walking around for too long, or long
enough, at least, for me to be getting fanciful, while Gil kept pace
with me steadily, his father's keeper during this period of recu-
peration, but I couldn't help thinking that Rilke would have liked
the juxtaposition: the ephemeral dance of our mortal shadows on
the ancient stone walls and this constant, elemental flow of cold
glacier water under our feet that, for some, is the very origin – the
source – of warm-blooded witness.

THE GRIEF THAT DOES NOT SPEAK

Give sorrow words. The grief that does not speak
Whispers the o'erfraught heart and bids it break.

Shakespeare, Macbeth

ALREADY WE HAVE SEEN that one of the major poetic enterprises of the twentieth century was the attempt to 'give sorrow words' at times when the noise of time came close to overwhelming the poet, her closest kin or the community as a whole. Rilke's *Duino Elegies* offer what might be the most powerful of such efforts at speech in a difficult era; other poets, however, took different and sometimes surprising approaches to the elegy as a form, and commemoration as a discipline. One of the most audacious, and sometimes puzzling, of these works is an elegy entitled *New Year's*, written by Marina Tsvetaeva, a poem composed between December 1926 and February 1927 in one of her many temporary homes in exile (in this case, Paris, where she was obliged to endure terrible poverty).

The subject of this poem is Rainer Maria Rilke, with whom Tsvetaeva had been exchanging letters since the previous May. That correspondence had grown more intimate during the months that led up to Rilke's death – news she received, as the first section of the poem records, when an acquaintance suggested that she should 'do a piece' about the great poet's passing.

Tsvetaeva rejected this idea, but soon began work on her own elegy for the century's supreme elegist, whose genius in the form so depended on his abilities as a poet of praise. Some years earlier, in a letter directed to the Belgian poet Émile Verhaeren, Rilke had remarked: 'My friend said one day: "Give us those masters who celebrate the here-below"' ('Mon ami a dit un jour: "Donnez-nous des maîtres qui célèbrent l'Ici-Bas"').

And in a very early poem Rilke says:

> There is nothing too small, but my tenderness paints
> it large on a background of gold,
> and I prize it, not knowing whose soul at the sight,
> released, may unfold.

> Nichts ist mir zu klein und ich lieb es trotzdem
> und mal es auf Goldgrund und groß.
> und halte es hoch, und ich weiß nicht wem
> löst es die Seele los.[1]

Reading these lines, I cannot help but think of the Magnificat, the Canticle of Mary, which begins with her response to the angel at the moment of the Annunciation: 'My soul doth magnify the Lord' (from *magnificare*, meaning 'to extol, or praise'). Nobody understood better than Rilke the dynamic by which the soul that magnifies the unsayable other is itself magnified – so much so that it is a cause of wonder, even to the angel of the Annunciation:

> You are in no way closer to God than we are;
> we all live far [from him].
> But it is wonderful
> how your hands
> have been blessed.
> …
> I am the day, I am the dew,
> but you are the tree.

Du bist nicht näher an Gott als wir;
wir sind ihm alle weit.
Aber wunderbar sind dir
die Hände benedeit.
…
ich bin der Tag, ich bin der Tau,
du aber bist der Baum.[2]

But our love for the perishable things of this world (for the roses, for the fleeting scents, for the light reflected in a casement window) drives us to consider the lilies and, with them, our own perishability. It was inevitable, then, that this poet of *l'ici-bas* would have felt compelled to envisage his own death – not in the form of an elegy but as a philosophical enquiry. In 'The Death of the Poet', from the 1907 *New Poems* collection, Rilke sets up an almost formal enquiry into the question of what it would be like not to be – or rather, to exist no more in the form to which he is accustomed. The result is both an affirmation of absence and a picture of healing transformation through absorption into the whole of creation:

Those who saw him live did not know
how much he was one with all this [the land];
for this: these depths, these meadows
and these waters were his face.

O, his face was this entire expanse,
that, even now, would go to him and court him;
and his mask, which is now lifeless,
is tender and open like the interior
of a fruit that spoils, [left open to] the air.

Die, so ihn leben sahen, wußten nicht,
wie sehr er Eines war mit allem diesen;
denn Dieses: diese Tiefen, diese Wiesen
und diese Wasser waren sein Gesicht.

O sein Gesicht war diese ganze Weite,
die jetzt noch zu ihm will und um ihn wirbt;
und seine Maske, die nun bang verstirbt,
ist zart und offen wie die Innenseite
von einer Frucht, die an der Luft verdirbt.

He echoed this notion of transformation in a poem he sent to
Tsvetaeva in July 1926, just months before he died:

O, The losses into the All, Marina, the ever falling stars!
We add nothing, wherever we throw ourselves,
to no matter what star! Every thing is already part of the All.
Thus, nothing that falls can diminish the sacred number.
All that is forsaken descends into the origin and heals.
…
Waves, Marina, we are Ocean! Depths, Marina, we are
   Heaven.
Earth, Marina, like larks in our thousand springtimes, we are
   Earth,
ascending in boisterous song to the Invisible.

O Die Verluste ins All, Marina, die stürzenden Sterne!
Wir vermehren es nicht, wohin wir uns werfen, zu welchem
Sterne hinzu! Im Ganzen ist immer schon alles gezählt.
So auch, wer fällt, vermindert die heilige Zahl nicht.
Jeder verzichtende Sturz stürzt in den Ursprung und heilt.
…
Wellen, Marina, wir Meer! Tiefen, Marina, wir Himmel.
Erde, Marina, wir Erde, wir tausendmal Frühling, wie
   Lerchen,
die ein ausbrechendes Lied in die Unsichtbarkeit wirft.[3]

Tsvetaeva's response, when it came, was to be quite different in
tenor, however. We might even say that, in this exchange between
two poets – the first a last letter from a dying man, the second a
response to one now dead – we can see the end of one age and
the beginning of another, as the babble of modernity drowns out

the music of the falling stars and what begins as the healing work of elegy – of finding in the poem's transformation of noise into music, and so creating a 'way of happening' for grief – descends into an oddly hesitant and fractured exercise in irony, evasion and magical thinking in which the speaker, too badly wounded to seek anything from the stars, simply resolves to defy them.

Meanwhile, the wishful picture of the afterlife that she conjures up for Rilke's soul to continue living and writing in veers from a resonant emptiness, like Aeolus' tower of the winds, to a child's vision of heaven not unlike the earthly paradise depicted in *Des Knaben Wunderhorn*, a compendium of nineteenth-century German folk stories collected by the Romantic poets Achim von Arnim and Clemens Brentano, and made famous by Mahler's song-cycle of the same name. Here, in a lush, sensual lyric ('Das himmlische Leben') the children sing of the afterlife as an earthly paradise, in which – this being a children's poem – food and play are to the fore:

> There goes Saint Peter running
> with his net and his bait
> to the heavenly pond.
> Saint Martha must be the cook.
>
> There is just no music on earth
> that can compare to ours.
> Even the eleven thousand virgins
> venture to dance,
> and Saint Ursula herself has to laugh.
>
> Dort läuft schon Sankt Peter
> Mit Netz und mit Köder
> Zum himmlischen Weiher hinein.
> Sankt Martha die Köchin muß sein.
>
> Kein' Musik ist ja nicht auf Erden,
> Die uns'rer verglichen kann werden.
> Elftausend Jungfrauen

Zu tanzen sich trauen!
Sankt Ursula selbst dazu lacht!

In this vision of a perfect existence in the hereafter, there is no sense of possible transformation or of rebirth; what is required is a garden of earthly delights in which spiritual transfiguration is of no consequence. All that matters, in fact, is that nothing changes. And just as the children in this afterlife continue to do what they did on earth – to play, to sing, to eat – so, in *New Year's: An Elegy for Rilke*, Tsvetaeva pictures Rilke going about his usual business of searching for rhymes and writing letters (to her, of course):

How are you writing, in your new place?
But if you are – your poems are: for you yourself are –
Poetry! How is your writing, in that good life,
With no table for your elbow, no brow for your hand,
Your cupped hand.
Send me some news of yourself,
in your usual, undecipherable scrawl!
Rainer, how do you find the new rhymes?
But, to decline the word Rhyme
Properly – what's Death – if not
A whole new series of Rhyme?

This insistence on seeing the dead continue with their normal routines in the next world, coupled with Tsvetaeva's earlier refusal – on two occasions – to use the word 'death' directly in speaking of her subject is like the response of a child to news it does not wish to absorb:

Shall I tell you how I learned of your –?
No earthquake, no avalanche,
A man walked in – someone – (you
Are who I adored). – A sad story.
– In the *News* and the *Daily*. –Would you write something?
Where? In the mountains. (A window onto fir branches,
A sheet.) – You haven't seen the newspapers?

And again, a few lines later, she asks:

> Shall I tell you what I did on learning of …
> Shh … a slip of my tongue. Out of habit.
> When I was always the one to put *life* and *death* in italics
> As if they were the most idle gossip.[4]

Such circumlocution allows the speaker of the poem to deny the bitter fact that the beloved is, in fact, dead, but at the same time it undermines the main task of elegy, which is *transformation*. In a remarkable essay on this poem Joseph Brodsky notes how the first line rises tonally, giving 'the sensation of a pure voice soaring upward and, as it were, renouncing (relinquishing) itself' – and we can just detect this here, and in the lines that follow, even as we recognise that this tone is impossible to sustain. Brodsky then goes on to point out a single, overarching quality that separates Tsvetaeva from other poets of her time:

> Tsvetaeva's poetry differs from the production of her contemporaries by virtue of a certain *a priori* tragic note, by a hidden – in a verse – wail. Given that, it should be kept in mind that this note started to sound in the voice of Tsvetaeva not as a result of firsthand tragic experience but as by-product of her working with language, in particular as a result of her experiments with folklore.[5]

Tsvetaeva's biography is, without doubt, a catalogue of painful, tragic experiences. After a rather privileged upbringing, the Revolution plunged her into stark poverty. One of her daughters was to die of starvation in a state orphanage during the Great Famine, while Tsvetaeva herself spent many years in exile in Prague and Paris. Her husband, Sergei Efron, and another daughter were arrested on their return to Russia, and Efron was eventually executed in 1941.* Nevertheless, Brodsky is right in saying that the

---

* She herself committed suicide a few months later; it was rumoured that the NKVD had tried to 'turn' her as an informant and that she saw death as her only escape and, possibly, the only way to protect her son, Georgy.

development of her unique voice *preceded* these events. One of her earliest, and best-known, poems is pessimistic about humanity in the most matter-of-fact way:

> I know the truth – give up all other truths!
> No need for people anywhere on earth to struggle.
> Look – it is evening, look, it is nearly night:
> what do you speak of, poets, lovers, generals?
>
> The wind is level now, the earth is wet with dew,
> the storm of stars in the sky will turn to quiet.
> And soon all of us will sleep under the earth, we
> who never let each other sleep above it.[6]

The stark contrast of sleep 'under the earth' and the vision of Rilke in heaven is telling. If the purpose of the elegy is to effect a transformation of the dead, then, as we have seen, the deceased must first be acknowledged *as* dead, and so capable of becoming so much a part of the natural order that he or she can be reconstituted, as it were, *in* nature – as here in Milton's *Lycidas*, where the subject of the elegy sinks into the ocean to be transformed there:

> Weep no more, woeful shepherds, weep no more,
> For Lycidas, your sorrow, is not dead,
> Sunk though he be beneath the wat'ry floor;
> So sinks the day-star in the ocean bed,
> And yet anon repairs his drooping head,
> And tricks his beams, and with new spangled ore
> Flames in the forehead of the morning sky:
> So Lycidas sunk low, but mounted high
> Through the dear might of him that walk'd the waves.

Tsvetaeva cannot acknowledge Rilke's death, however – and this is what makes *New Year's* such a heart-breaking poem. Instead of being allowed to become part of the fabric of nature, the subject of her poem is preserved for ever in an artificial paradise. From that initial, unsustainable rush of the 'pure voice soaring upward' to the final promise to meet again, we are faced with a willed reversal of the tradition of elegy – a tradition in which the dead are necessarily *relinquished* to be 'Rolled round in earth's diurnal course, / With rocks, and stones, and trees'. Rather than release the Beloved once and for all, Tsvetaeva attempts to dismiss her own grief by renouncing, or at least delegitimising, herself ('Nothing ever worked out between us ... nothing to suit our capacity or stature'):

> From my barren suburb – I wish you
> Happy new place, Rainer, world, Rainer!
> To the furthermost point of proof –
> Happy new eye, Rainer, ear, Rainer!
>
> Anything would have been an obstacle
> To you: a passion, a friendship.
> Happy new sound, my dear Echo!
> Happy new echoes, dear Sound!

When I read the words from *Macbeth* that opened this chapter – 'Give sorrow words. The grief that does not speak / Whispers the o'erfraught heart and bids it break' – I am inclined to believe that, in some previous time before what Adam Curtis has called 'the century of the self', people who suffered serious hurt were able to give some kind of voice to their grief and, by doing so, begin to work on the slow process of healing. In actuality, I cannot know if this is the case; what does seem clear, however, is that in more recent times the passage from grief (passive suffering) to mourning (an active attempt at healing) has all too often been ill defined and so left unaccomplished. We have lost the outward and communal rites for mourning, or rather, we perform them blindly, without entering into them fully. Again, it was Shakespeare who recognised the problems that can arise from this process of internalisation, as we can see from *Richard II*:

> 'Tis very true, my grief lies all within;
> And these external manners of laments

Are merely shadows to the unseen grief
That swells with silence in the tortured soul.

We sometimes forget the essentially public nature of elegy: it gives external, communal, expression to private sorrow, at the loss not only of a deceased beloved but also of the time and place that was shared with that individual. Perhaps more than any other art form, the elegiac poem is capable of recognising how grievously we feel this sense of loss, as time dribbles through our fingers and we try to explain that we don't want to hold on to happiness or beauty for ever; we just want to see, and hear and feel it as it happens, without distractions, without interruptions and without having someone else come along and explain it away. This sense of the lost moment – that dies even as it unfolds – might consist of 'something with a girl in summer', as Robert Lowell puts it, or just the snow that fell steadily through the rings of streetlight on my way to work this morning, whitening and widening my world, suspending time. Of course, it is truly poignant, and most of us feel it deeply, that we cannot stop time. But then, this is not a matter for grief, for it is natural. What is unnatural is to exist in a constant state of interruption, of being, as Eliot points out in 'Burnt Norton':

Distracted from distraction by distraction
Filled with fancies and empty of meaning
Tumid apathy with no concentration
Men and bits of paper, whirled by the cold wind
That blows before and after time.[7]

Faced with the passing of time, the elegiac poem, which itself unfolds and so dissipates in time, makes due ceremony of the dailiness of life – that is, of the eternal quality of the here and now. It forages, uses what it can, scavenges. That doesn't mean it cannot be baroque; on the contrary, the baroque might be all the imagination can find to convey its intent. An intent that is, of course, more musical than semantic. Poetry is essential to mourning in that it helps us not only to name but to inventory the causes of our grief, and so to acknowledge what has been lost. It finds words for the ceremony. But where we cannot locate and give utterance to the pain, it surely follows that we cannot heal it. What characterised the twentieth century, for too many, was an inability to see what ailed them. For others, however, the losses were too wildly gratuitous, ever to assimilate – and surely Tsvetaeva, of all people, perennial exile, wife of a murdered husband and mother of slaughtered children, can be counted in that number.

In the last section of his famously 'difficult' poem 'The Owl in the Sarcophagus' (written after the death of his friend Henry Church in April 1947), Wallace Stevens raises an interesting – and troubling – question about modern elegy:

> This is the mythology of modern death
> And these, in their mufflings, monsters of elegy,
> Of their own marvel made, of pity made,
>
> Compounded and compounded, life by life,
> These are death's own supremest images,
> The pure perfections of parental space,
>
> The children of a desire that is the will,
> Even of death, the beings of the mind
> In the light-bound space of the mind, the floreate flare …
>
> It is a child that sings itself to sleep,
> The mind, among the creatures that it makes,
> The people, those by which it lives and dies.[8]

It is not easy to paraphrase this passage – and it shouldn't be – but, as I read it, Stevens seems to be suggesting that, for the mourner, what is lost in the death of another is a being 'of the mind', a creature the mind invents, as it were, in the pursuit of its own existence. On one level this could be read as an acceptance that, as Kant notes in *A Critique of Pure Reason*: 'it remains completely unknown to us what the objects may be by themselves and apart from the receptivity of our senses. We know nothing but our manner of perceiving them.' Yet I cannot help but think there is more to it than that. That idea of our mental image of the other as a 'creature' – not one created by a God, or nature, but a product of an individual mind peopling its own 'light-bound space' – is unsettling, even painful to acknowledge. It is hard not to be reminded of Judith Butler's remarks after the events of 9/11:

> When we lose certain people, or when we are dispossessed from a place, or a community, we may simply feel that we are undergoing something temporary, that mourning will be over and some restoration of prior order will be achieved. But maybe when we undergo what we do, something about who we are is revealed, something that delineates the ties we have to others, that shows us that these ties constitute what we are, ties or bonds that compose us. It is not as if an 'I' exists independently over here and then simply loses a 'you' over there, especially if the attachment to 'you' is part of what composes who 'I' am. If I lose you, under these conditions, then I not only mourn the loss, but I become inscrutable to myself. Who 'am' I, without you? When we lose some of these ties by which we are constituted, we do not know who we are or what to do. On one level, I think I have lost 'you' only to discover that 'I' have gone missing as well.[9]

What these observations suggest is that, when we lose something, it is not just that the 'outside' world is being diminished but that the inner – the world of the I – is becoming less orderly, its vital structures beginning to break down until the mind's only option is to sing itself to sleep. At the same time, faced with the impulse to cling to the dead and, in the words of American poet Carol Muske-Dukes, to 'insist on the desire of the lost to remember us, / to recognize the shape of our small flames' we cannot find rest. Butler goes on to add:

Let's face it. We're undone by each other. And if we're not, we're missing something. This seems so clearly the case with grief, *but it can be so only because it was already the case with desire.* One does not always stay intact. One may want to, or manage to for a while, but despite one's best efforts, one is undone, in the face of the other, by the touch, by the scent, by the feel, by the prospect of the touch, by the memory of the feel. [my italics]

This seems to me a key point. We try to manage grief as we try to manage desire, in the hope of avoiding the possible loss of self, which is to say, the loss of a vital sense that one is 'intact' and able to function as a separate and autonomous individual. Both grief and desire rob us of that autonomy, for each magnifies what had begun, in everyday perception, as the natural dependence on the other, making of it something monstrous and unmanageable. For Marina Tsvetaeva, possessed as she was of the '*a priori* tragic note' that Brodsky finds in her work, the great temptation was to preserve the integrity of the self by surrendering it before any assault was possible, just as she preserved her poems by surrendering, from the very first, any pretensions to an informed readership in her own time.* Her clearest expression of this idea of necessary renunciation comes in the poem 'To Steal …', from 1923:

And perhaps, the finest victory
Over time and gravity –
Is to pass, without leaving a trace,
Is to pass, without leaving a shadow

On the walls … Finer perhaps – to exact
By refusal? To erase myself from mirrors?

(Translated by Mary Jane White)[10]

---

*In a poem of 1913 she says: 'All my unread pages/ / lie scattered in dusty bookshops/ where nobody picks them up/ to this day. Like expensive wines,/ your time will come, my lines.' (Translated by Elaine Feinstein.)

This refusal – this self-abnegation – would seem costly to many; certainly it would involve relinquishing not only the sense of self but also one's artistic gifts:

> Like: Lermontov moving through the Caucasus
> To steal, without disturbing the rock-faces.

> And perhaps – the finest amusement
> Given the finger of Sebastian Bach
> Would be not to trouble the organ's echo?*

Death would not be enough to gain this strange, negative freedom; what is needed is to vanish altogether and leave no trace:

> To collapse, leaving no dust
> For the urn … Finer perhaps – to exact
> By fraud? To write myself out of the latitudes?
> Like: Time moving through an ocean
> To steal, without disturbing the waters …†

It seems that, from her early days, Tsvetaeva learned that pain was to be expected and that, as she says in the poem 'Bus', from the mid-1930s:

> Happiness? Far away … North of here.
> Somewhere else. Some other time.
> Happiness? Even the scent is cold.
> I looked for it once, on all fours.

---

*During a particularly ugly incident in his superfluous-man novel *A Hero of Our Time*, Lermontov's anti-hero, Pechorin, steals a horse, then frames another man for the crime, leading to a murder. However, he is not indifferent to his actions or their consequences; it is just that, as he notes in his journal: 'I sometimes despise myself. Is not that the reason why I despise others also? I have grown incapable of noble impulses; I am afraid of appearing ridiculous to myself.'

† Translation by Mary Jane White.

When I was four years old
looking for a clover with four leaves.
What do these numbers matter?
Happiness? Cows feed on it.[11]

What Tsvetaeva does in *New Year's* is to dodge the necessary elegy and instead compose what Brodsky aptly calls a 'love lyric' – though we should remember that it is a love lyric to a man she has never met, to the idea of a man, a 'being of the mind', and – to the extent that it is an elegy at all – the poem is the enactment of a mourning process for a lover that the speaker never had. That this makes it painfully beautiful few would contest; however, it does not make the necessary step into the healing process that – shaped and directed by the elegiac form – mourning eventually becomes. As for the speaker of Philip Larkin's poem 'Wants', the cost of rational pessimism (which is not as rational as it seems, since the future cannot be predicted with any certainty) is the loss of that opportunity for healing and for growth that mourning offers:

Beneath it all, the desire for oblivion runs:
Despite the artful tensions of the calendar,
The life insurance, the tabled fertility rites,
The costly aversion of the eyes away from death –
Beneath it all, the desire for oblivion runs.[12]

THE POWER OF THE VISIBLE

it is a privilege to see so
much confusion[1]

Marianne Moore

WHEN I THINK OF MY CHILDHOOD HOME, I can recover only a few visual memories and almost zero facts. I remember public events in the abstract, formal and colourless, like the italicised dates in an old calendar: Easter weekend, the summer holidays, the last day of school before Christmas and, of course, Christmas itself. In principle, I remember various birthdays, two weddings, a handful of bereavements, but I cannot summon up the specifics – or none that I trust as more than anecdotal. Nevertheless, I have a strong sense of a home-place; it's just that the bulk of what I do recall is atmosphere, texture, scent. The sensed rather than the seen. The felt, more than the known. I am still haunted by a week-on-week sense of hymn tunes and folding chairs, of frosts and thaws and the warmth of the milkman's dray-horse standing in the snow at the end of our lane. When, like every other child at St Bride's Catholic Primary School, I wrote my address in my Douay Bible, it was this atmosphere, this labyrinth of warm and cold, of sweet and sour, of coal dust and frozen milk shot through with needles of ice that I intended to set down in words when I wrote:

17 Blackburn Drive
Cowdenbeath
Fife
Scotland
Great Britain
Europe
Earth
The Solar System
The Milky Way

and not what I understood, from history and geography classes, to be the true facts (which is to say, the important details) of my day-to-day existence, because there were no true facts save that fabric of sense-data, and nothing was important, other than the smell and feel and seasons of the place from which I came – a place to which I would always belong, even if I were one day to realise my wildest dreams and follow in the footsteps of Livingstone and Stanley in 'darkest Africa'.

There was, however, one exception to this vague and impressionistic history, and that was the very specific memory of the Russian cosmonaut Valentina Tereshkova – or rather, the *thought* of her as she travelled through space, looking down at the earth through a tiny window, a woman from Yaroslavl with hair the same colour and style as my Aunt Margaret's, guiding her *Vostok 6* forty-eight times around the planet during the summer of 1963. I remember wondering if she had gone to the hairdresser's the day before the launch, as my aunt would certainly have done, just to make sure she looked presentable for the cameras when they counted down to lift-off. This was important to the people I grew up with: to be *presentable*, in their persons and in their homes. Not beautiful, or elegant, and certainly not stylish (which might have betrayed aspirations beyond their means), but presentable. There were many ways to make this happen: you could *tidy* (a more or less constant process of low-level maintenance that was done as one went along) or you could *tidy up* (a serious and systematic exercise, for days when visitors came) or, when time was of the essence and a general impression would suffice, you could *tidy round*. Certain purchases were frowned on as potential sources of *clutter*, which, by definition, could not be kept tidy. Pets were not encouraged, for the same reason. Any accumulation of pretty much anything not only looked untidy but might also *attract vermin*, a prospect that filled the women in my family with a profound horror. I have no sense, now, of what my mother and aunts thought of Valentina Tereshkova, or whether they took any notice of her at all, but I, for one, could only imagine her home-place as supremely tidy and, through an effort of will, vermin-free. (And I knew this would have taken considerable effort, because my Uncle John had told me once that, in atheist, non-Catholic Russia, they had rats the size of Jack Russell terriers; how he knew this, I have no idea.) Valentina Tereshkova's house would be spick and span, however: not one salt cellar or Soviet knick-knack out of place, the dishes wiped and put away, the books she had accumulated during her ten years of night classes lined up on their shelves in alphabetical order – and when she returned from her triumphant space voyage, I knew that she would remember every single thing that she had seen, before, during and after that flight, but that none of it would mean as much to her as that home-place.

I knew all this because the one thing I really understood back then, understood intuitively and so without a doubt, was that if I could only achieve an orderly life (not just tidiness, not mere pre-sentability, but the true *order* of home), I would be gifted with a perfect, almost cinematic memory, an ability to slow time, or even to stop it long enough to hold one magical moment up to the light and *know* it – not through a glass, darkly, but even as I was known. At the same time I knew that, whenever Valentina Tereshkova looked back at Planet Earth from her little box in space, she always located herself by picturing, in all that mass of ocean and land, the place from which she had come, the home town, the village, the spire of her church, the black-and-white collie dog barking in her neighbour's yard. As long as that home-place existed, you didn't have to remember anything; it was all there, a lived repository of time. That such a place existed made all that cold, featureless space around us the space in which, with just one flick of a dial, Valentina Tereshkova could have been lost for ever – and when, after three days in that limbo, she came home, I felt not just relieved but strangely vindicated, as if it had been my own home, my own sense of gravity and my own native place that had been in jeopardy.*

It is no accident that the name Dürer is the first word of Marianne Moore's poem 'The Steeple-Jack', first published in the summer of 1932 and, arguably, one of the landmark works of Modernist writing. For one thing, the name Dürer alone (as what these days would no doubt be called a 'tag') suggests a mental climate in which certain values – a sense of perspective, an attention to detail and a reverence for the phenomena of this world for their own sake – are fundamental. While side-stepping mere literalism, and both too early and too spiritually alert to succumb to reductionism, Dürer was a realist of the best kind, an artist who wanted to experience, and to depict, the world as it is, not as he, or his church, or some artistic fad, would prefer it to be. Of course he would have enjoyed living in a place that had

> eight stranded whales
> to look at; with the sweet sea air coming into your house
> on a fine day, from water etched
> with waves as formal as the scales
> on a fish

just as he would have noticed, and approved, the way local builders had learned from their natural surroundings when constructing

---

*To the Catholic boy I was then, the fact that she spent three days in the void was not, of course, insignificant.

> the antique
> sugar-bowl shaped summer-house of
> interlacing slats[2]

– the human-made thing echoing the wave forms of the sea, and the morphology of fishes. As we know from his diaries, Dürer was prepared to go a long way to see the real thing, when he could:

> *Antwerp, 22 November – 3 December 1520*
> At Zierikzee, in Zeeland, a whale has been stranded by a high tide and a gale of wind. It is much more than 100 fathoms long, and no man living in Zeeland has seen one even a third as long as this is. The fish cannot get off the land; the people would gladly see it gone, as they fear the great stink, for it is so large that they say it could not be cut in pieces and the blubber boiled down in half a year.

Some days later, he continues:

> *9 December*
> Early on Monday we started again by ship and went by the Veere and Zierikzee and tried to get sight of the great fish, but the tide had carried him off again.

After quoting the above passages in his biography (published in 1905) of this most individual of painters, T. Sturge Moore notes that 'the object of the whole expedition was, doubtless, that Dürer might see and sketch the whale', going on to repeat the well-known story of the artist's near-death, while out whale-watching:

> In the Netherlands, Dürer's curiosity to see a whale nearly resulted in his own shipwreck, and indirectly produced the malady which finally killed him. But Dürer's curiosity was really most scientific where it was most artistic; in his portraits, in his studies of plants and birds and the noses of stags, or the slumber of lions.

Of course, the whales in 'The Steeple-Jack' serve as reminders of the history of the New England coastal towns, where whaling was for many years the main industry, but the syntax makes it clear that they are not the main focus of the poem. Moore's strategy depends very much on her reader's knowing a fair amount about Dürer's artistic method and philosophy, but she does not hesitate to take that knowledge for granted. Unlike some of her contemporaries, she is optimistic about 'the culture', though she accepts that the nature of its art might change with time – and I have always been encouraged by the idea that Moore appears to trust in the power of imaginative making, *poiesis*, to continue (and to renew itself) on its own momentum, independently from any social class or elite group. This, I think, arises from a fundamental conviction that the ability to recognise Dürer's value-set is based not on educational or class background but on innate imaginative and intellectual character.

What I most want to emphasise, however, is that, by beginning her poem with the artist's name, Moore is invoking Dürer's determination to see the universe as it is, rather than as we are told it must be: to see it, that is, for himself, and not simply to accept the authority of contemporary experts, or churchmen, or those systematisers who bend the given world to fit their own pet theories of what is real.* It is the same impulse that informs an underlying

---

* This is not to say that the making of truthful art depends solely on direct observation; no matter what is being depicted, there will always be an element of artifice and, as Kant notes: 'imagination is a necessary ingredient of perception itself'. As with any other artist, Dürer's work springs from his imagination, but it is an imagination fed by attentiveness to the real world, to experience, and not to authority. On occasions when Dürer was unable to make direct observation of his subject, as in the famous *Rhinoceros* woodcut, he did his best to become informed about it (in this case, through letters and a sketch made by someone who had seen the animal). Though we can point to inaccuracies in the woodcut, what is most interesting is how accurate the representation actually is, especially when we compare it with other works of the time, such as that of Giovanni Giacomo Penni, who reproduced an image of the Lisbon rhinoceros, in his book *Forma & Natura & Costumi de lo Rinocerothe stato condutto importogallo dal Capitanio de larmata del Re & altre belle cose condutte dalle insule nouamente trouate* ('The Shape, the Nature and the Way of the Rhinoceros brought by the Captain of the Portuguese King's Armada and other beautiful things brought from the new insulars'), which

change of emphasis in the seventeenth century, when, as the age of (relatively) independent artisanship heralded by Dürer becomes a reality, many Northern (i.e., non-Catholic) painters are no longer content to expend all their energies on religious works and instead apply themselves to the reflective surfaces of an oyster-shell or the glistening skin of a lemon. (The spiritual forerunner of much of this is, in fact, Dürer's own *The Large Turf*, painted in Nuremberg in 1503, a work whose attention to detail allows us clearly to identify a number of plants specifically, including cock's-foot, creeping bent, smooth meadow grass, daisy, dandelion, germander speedwell, greater plantain, hound's-tongue and yarrow.) This realism, this honouring of the thing itself, this *specificity*, is continued in the work of the still-life painters, as they reproduce the blemish on a fallen plum as carefully as the striation of some – at that time exotic and glamorous – turk's-cap tulip.

However, the invocation of Dürer's practice, informed as it was by the conviction that close observation of nature should be the starting-point of our imaginative engagement with the world, is only half of what the poet is up to here. Notice how, as she insinuates this constellation of expectations around the artist's name, Moore also introduces the poem's principal concern, which is: what makes place *place*, rather than just another *space*?* At first,

---

pre-dated Dürer's work. It was, nevertheless, rare for Dürer to rely on second-hand material; in this case, as a self-employed artist with an eye to making a profit, he probably acted quickly to take advantage of a good business opportunity. The woodcut would become one of his most popular items, running to several editions.

* I am reminded here of the Chinese-American geographer Yi-Fu Tuan, whose book *Space and Place: The Perspective of Experience* (1977) offers a fascinating account of the play between our ideas of 'space' and 'place':

> In experience, the meaning of space often merges with that of place. 'Space' is more abstract than 'place'. What begins as undifferentiated space becomes place as we get to know it better and endow it with value. Architects talk about the spatial qualities of place; they can equally well speak of the locational (place) qualities of space. The ideas 'space' and 'place' require each other for definition. From the security and stability of place we are aware of the openness, freedom, and threat

even though she takes a panoramic view of the town,* it might seem that she has not given herself much to work with, for what follows, as we have noted, is a description of a quiet, very 'ordinary' New England coastal settlement, whose only visible inhabitants are a student named Ambrose and the local steeplejack, C. J. Poole, who is, at present, working on gilding the star atop the church steeple (clues abound throughout the poem that the speaker is, like Ambrose's books, 'non-native'), a place that, apparently, 'could not be dangerous' – and therefore, by implication, must be a little dull. But is it?

If we take another look at the poem, we find that the answers are many, and they relate to the balance of order and 'confusion' that the poem rehearses – a balance, a meaningful tension, that necessarily informs everyday life. We enact this tension on a daily

---

of space, and vice versa. Furthermore, if we think of space as that which allows movement, then place is pause; each pause in movement makes it possible for location to be transformed into place.

And he continues:

People tend to suppress that which they cannot express. If an experience resists ready communication, a common response among activists ('doers') is to deem it private – even idiosyncratic – and hence unimportant. In the large literature on environmental quality, relatively few works attempt to understand how people feel about space and place, to take into account the different modes of experience (sensorimotor, tactile, visual, conceptual), and to interpret space and place as images of complex – often ambivalent – feelings. Professional planners, with their urgent need to act, move too quickly to models and inventories. The layman accepts too readily from charismatic planners and propagandists the environmental slogans he may have picked up through the media; the rich experiential data on which these abstractions depend are easily forgotten. Yet it is possible to articulate subtle human experiences. Artists have tried – often with success. In works of literature as well as in humanistic psychology, philosophy, anthropology and geography, intricate worlds of human experience are recorded.

* A God's-eye view, even; though I, for one, cannot help remembering the work of Carleton Watkins, whose commercial photographs of industrial and railroad towns transformed landscape photography.

basis, even though we are not always conscious of the work we are performing. Yet every time we *imaginatively* experience place as place, and not as an agglomeration of objects and intervening spaces, we are involved in an act of making, a *poiesis*. This act of making is, in fact, dramatised in the poem, as the speaker (and, following the speaker's voice as it travels across the panoramic scene, the listener or reader) makes order of what is before them. For place is not a given, it must be made, invested with meaning and history, constantly renewed. Places have resonance, tenor, complex networks of relationship and interanimation, while spaces are imaginatively empty and inert and are thus more susceptible to exploitation, invasion and abuse.

Yet, as vital as this imaginative process is, the two poles of the creative tension that leads to the order of place are presented in 'The Steeple-Jack' in an almost throwaway manner. The first pole is represented by 'an elegance of which / the source is not bravado' that informs the design of the aforementioned 'antique / sugar-bowl shaped summer-house / of interlacing slats', as well as the commendable restraint (we should not forget that Moore was a lifelong Presbyterian) mingled with astute craft implied by:

> church portico has four fluted
> columns, each a single piece of stone, made
> modester by white-wash.

The other pole is represented by a necessary wildness in nature that we find everywhere, even in this safe little town, a 'confusion' that it is a privilege to experience, even as the mind seeks to discover its underlying order. Here Moore uses the list, or inventory, as her method of discovery:

> You can see a twenty-five
> pound lobster; and fishnets arranged
> to dry. The

> whirlwind fife and drum of the storm bends the salt
> marsh grass, disturbs stars in the sky and the

star on the steeple; it is a privilege to see so
much confusion. Disguised by what
    might seem the opposite, the sea-
side flowers and

trees are favored by the fog so that you have
    the tropics at first hand: the trumpet-vine,
fox-glove, giant snap-dragon, a salpiglossis that has
spots and stripes; morning-glories, gourds,
    or moon-vines trained on fishing-twine
at the back

door; cat-tails, flags, blueberries and spiderwort,
    striped grass, lichens, sunflowers, asters, daisies –
the yellow and the crab-claw blue ones with green bracts –
   toad-plant,
petunias, ferns; pink lilies, blue
    ones, tigers; poppies; black sweet-peas.

It is a privilege to witness so much confusion, not just because
it is a pleasure to look at a local riot of colour and texture but
also because it offers the opportunity to make a list like the one
the poem's speaker creates from the prospect before her. In fact,
the real privilege is to draw order *from* the confusion, rather than
imposing a pre-existing template on the environment. To identify,
to name, to see connections, to make distinctions – this is one
privilege of language. The other, as Spinoza notes, in *Ethics, Dem-
onstrated in Geometrical Order* (1677), is to take stock of the universal natural order:

> Nothing comes to pass in nature, which can be set down to
> a flaw therein; for nature is always the same, and everywhere
> one and the same in her efficacy and power of action; that is,
> nature's laws and ordinances, whereby all things come to pass
> and change from one form to another, are everywhere and
> always the same; so that there should be one and the same

method of understanding the nature of all things whatsoever, namely, through nature's universal laws and rules.

Confusion is to be celebrated, even as it is made habitable by our interventions: looked at with an awareness of inherent, rather than imposed, order, the coastal town depicted in the poem is a habitable place in the fullest meaning of the term – which is to say that it has a native culture, trade with other cultures, a built environment appropriate to the terrain, a set of fundamental and incontrovertible values expressed in an elegant, economical architecture and, as the poem ends, a confidence in the midst of confusion that is not presumptuous, a 'solid/pointed star, which on a steeple/stands for hope'.

There is so much more to say about this poem (especially its form), but I want to conclude with a brief discussion of the 'solid-pointed star' and what it stands for. 'The Steeple-Jack' was originally published (in the summer 1932 edition of *Poetry*) as one element in a sequence entitled 'Part of a Novel, Part of a Poem, Part of a Play' (the sequence structure was later discarded when the three component poems were published in the *Collected Poems* of 1951). Considering what was happening in the wider political sphere – the Depression, social inequality and the growth of fascism in Europe – we could imagine a lesser poet giving way to the temptation to ironise that invocation of 'hope' with which Moore concludes this, the first part of her triptych. But that would have been to ironise, and so risk dismissing, the idea of home itself. However, as has been noted, Moore goes on to explore, in the following poems, what hope is, and in so doing she offers, via the figure of a certain kind of hero, one of the finest definitions that anyone could wish for:

>   tired but hopeful –
> hope not being hope
> until all ground for hope has
> vanished.

On one level, we might argue that to say this is to state the obvious. Just as we do not require faith where there is clear evidence of a phenomenon, so we do not require hope if there are clear grounds to feel optimistic. In the same way, if home already existed, we would not need to imagine it by drawing order from the seeming confusion we find in the world about us. But home is not simply *there* as a given. As the Gospel says (Luke 9:58): 'Foxes have holes, and birds of the air have nests; but the Son of man hath not where to lay his head.' As I have already suggested, home is a process of imaginative making that begins with the given – nature, space – and ends with a dwelling place. That sense of place as a locus of dwelling comes into being when, as Yi-Fu Tuan notes, we 'endow it with value' – a process that requires both attentiveness to what is there and the active exercise of the imagination to counteract what Moore (in 'He Digesteth Harde Yron') calls 'unsolicitude'. I read this as being similar in spirit to Stephen Crane's notion of 'the unconcern of the universe' – that is, while we must make a dwelling place and attempt to survive in this world, nature owes us no solicitude, and the universe is indifferent to the hopes and wishes of its denizens:

> The power of the visible
> is the invisible; as even where
> no tree of freedom grows,
> so-called brute courage knows.
> Heroism is exhausting, yet
> it contradicts a greed that did not wisely spare
> the harmless solitaire
>
> or great auk in its grandeur;
> unsolicitude having swallowed up
> all giant birds.[3]

Throughout her work Marianne Moore engages with the 'unsolicitude' that swallows up not only giant birds but also place, hope, faith, home. As she does so, she constructs a worldview that is founded on hope without grounds for hope, a sense of dwelling predicated on the sheer force of a vigilant imagination and the intuition of an order that, even when it cannot be altogether grasped by a human subject, it is still a privilege to witness.

In his wonderfully uncategorisable book *The Message in the Bottle: How Queer Man Is, How Queer Language Is, and What the One Has to Do with the Other* (1975) Walker Percy describes the typical behaviour of a tourist coming to the Grand Canyon for the first time:

> Seeing the canyon is made even more difficult by what the sightseer does when the moment arrives, when sovereign knower confronts the thing to be known. Instead of looking at it, he photographs it. There is no confrontation at all. At the end of forty years of preformulation and with the Grand Canyon yawning at his feet, what does he do? He waives his right of seeing and knowing and records symbols for the next forty years. For him there is no present; there is only the past of what has been formulated and seen and the future of what has been formulated and not seen. The present is surrendered to the past and the future.

The present is surrendered – as is the music of what happened; for, camera in hand, we tend to look, first, for scenes, or images, or features that *can* be photographed and, second, for views that resemble views we have already seen, views that conform to some notion of Grand Canyon picturesque (as opposed to, say, Yosemite or Niagara picturesque). In short, we bring our expectations to the place, and are so busy verifying those pre-formulated ideas that we miss what is actually there. The nature writer Barry Lopez noticed this danger on his first visit to the Canyon, this time with reference to the bird life:

> I had come to the canyon with expectations. I wanted to see snowy egrets flying against the black schist at dusk; I saw bluewinged teal against the green waters at dawn. I had wanted to hear thunder rolling in the thousand-foot depths; I heard the

guttural caw of four ravens ... what any of us had come to see
or do fell away. We found ourselves at each turn with what we
had not imagined.[4]

Even in more familiar terrain there is a danger of wandering
blindly through a prefabricated world, seeing only what we expect
to see, locked into the assumption that there is nothing behind the
patterns we impose on the world. In one of the finest landscape
poems ever written in America, A. R. Ammons describes his daily
walk around part of Corson's Inlet, a beautiful stretch of coast on
the New Jersey shore (it is now a state park), taking care to focus,
from the beginning, on what is actually present and not what he
expects, or hopes, to see. This recalls Keats's pledge to seeing the
thing as a subject extended to an entire landscape – to a terrain –
and not just the individual phenomena (birds, plants, dunes) that
can be witnessed on the walk.* What Ammons is out to convey
is as complete an *inventio* of the scene, on that particular day, as
it is possible to get and, in so doing, to make an experimental,
though ultimately doomed, attempt to decipher what he calls 'the
Overall'. What he also wants to do is eliminate from his mind the
human order he begins by automatically imposing on the scene,
an order that is born of urban development, and so is inevitably
geometrical:

> I went for a walk over the dunes again this morning
> to the sea,
> then turned right along
>   the surf
>   rounded a naked headland

That 'turned right' is revealing, but the poem's speaker has done
this walk before, and he is patient, waiting for the moment when
he is:

---

* See Keats's letter to John Hamilton Reynolds, February 1818: 'Poetry should
be great and unobtrusive, a thing which enters into one's soul, and does not
startle it or amaze it with itself – but with its subject.'

> released from forms
> from the perpendiculars,
>   straight lines, blocks, boxes, binds
> of thought
> into the hues, shadings, rises, flowing bends and blends
>   of sight.

From here on in, with a flagrant wave, rather than a mere nod, to Walt Whitman, the speaker attempts to bring his work – that is, his thinking, which is also, at this point, Ammons' compositional process – into line with the natural order:

> I allow myself eddies of meaning:
> yield to a direction of significance
> running
> like a stream through the geography of my work:
>   you can find
> in my sayings
>   swerves of action
>   like the inlet's cutting edge.[5]

He is seeking to attune himself to what is there, to make of his mind a mirror that will not only reflect but encompass the scene – because he knows that there is something here that is more than the sum of its parts, an entire system in which each thing inter-animates every other thing, a system that, with each new event, will shift in response to the wind, to a flight of birds and even to a subtle change in the direction of his walk. That is the Overall – the first of two huge abstract entities that, even as he reaches for it, the speaker knows he cannot capture:

> but Overall is beyond me: is the sum of these events
> I cannot draw, the ledger I cannot keep, the accounting
> beyond the account.

If we had not guessed it by now, it is clear, in this encounter with the Overall, that this poem, this walk, is a form of play, a serious game that, as much as anything, is a philosophical exercise not just in brushing away the linear paraphernalia of the human-made world, but also in keeping eyes and ears open, and, as Emily Dickinson might say, the soul ajar:

> in nature there are few sharp lines: there are areas of
> primrose
>> more or less dispersed;
> disorderly orders of bayberry; between the rows
> of dunes,
> irregular swamps of reeds,
> though not reeds alone, but grass, bayberry, yarrow, all …
> predominantly reeds.

Again the speaker permits himself a nod to Whitman's expansive, open, ever-experimenting 'I' –

> I have reached no conclusions, have erected no boundaries,
> shutting out and shutting in, separating inside
>> from outside: I have
>> drawn no lines

– before allowing the first recognition of time – of constant flux – to come to the fore:

> manifold events of sand
> change the dune's shape that will not be the same shape
> tomorrow,
>
> so I am willing to go along, to accept
> the becoming
> thought, to stake off no beginnings or ends, establish
>> no walls
>
> by transitions the land falls from grassy dunes to creek
> to undercreek: but there are no lines, though
>> change in that transition is clear
>> as any sharpness: but 'sharpness' spread out,
> allowed to occur over a wider range
> than mental lines can keep.

Now the inlet is perceived as an ever-shifting *Gestalt*: the walker is part of it, as witness and participant, and out there, on the rock and on the sands, life depends on it:

> the moon was full last night: today, low tide was low:
> black shoals of mussels exposed to the risk
> of air
> and, earlier, of sun,
> waved in and out with the waterline, waterline inexact,
> caught always in the event of change:
> > a young mottled gull stood free on the shoals
> > and ate
> to vomiting: another gull, squawking possession, cracked a
> > crab,
> picked out the entrails, swallowed the soft-shelled legs, a
> > ruddy
> turnstone running in to snatch leftover bits.

One thinks of Rachel Carson here: not the better-known Carson of *Silent Spring*, but the marine-biologist nature writer of the 1940s and '50s who did so much to shape the way Americans looked at the natural world, and at the foreshore in particular. Here she is, in 1941, in her debut book, *Under the Sea Wind*:

> In the morning the sanderlings, moving down to the surf line to feed in the first light, found the inlet beach littered with dead squids. The sanderlings did not linger on this part of the beach, for although it was very early in the morning many large birds had gathered and were quarreling over the squids. They were herring gulls, bound from the Gulf Coast to Nova Scotia. They had been long delayed by stormy weather and they were ravenous. A dozen black-headed laughing gulls came and hovered, mewing, over the beach, dangling their feet as though to alight, but the herring gulls drove them away with fierce screaming and jabs of their bills.

What stands out in Carson's work – and in the best of several of her near-contemporaries, such as Loren Eiseley and Edwin Way

Teale – is an acknowledgement of the harshness and jeopardy of the environment, alongside a refusal ever to succumb to the simplistic nature-red-in-tooth-and-claw philosophy that reduces animal life to a near-mechanical round of hunting, feeding and mating. She sees play, she sees the everyday miracles of survival and, most of all, she attests to the richness of animal life, a life that is not mere 'behaviour'. Ammons' walker sees these things too – the risk, the beauty, the excitement of the chase:

> risk is full: every living thing in
> siege: the demand is life, to keep life: the small
> white blacklegged egret, how beautiful, quietly stalks and
>   spears
>   the shallows, darts to shore
>   to stab – what? I couldn't
>   see against the black mudflats – a frightened
>   fiddler crab?

Up to this point, except for minor hints here and there, this scene has been seasonless – now, however, the walker tells us that it is autumn: that is, another level of change. And with that change there comes one of the more remarkable sights in nature –

>   thousands of tree swallows
>   gathering for flight:
>   an order held
>   in constant change: a congregation
> rich with entropy: nevertheless, separable, noticeable
> as one event,
>   not chaos: preparations for
> flight from winter

– an example of collective intelligence that has probably held humans rapt on the shore of this ocean for millennia: not chaos, in the old sense of that word, but emergent order, a constant play of bodies in the air proposing

the possibility of rule as the sum of rulelessness:
the 'field' of action
with moving, incalculable center.

Everywhere the walker looks now, he sees order: 'order tight with shape', 'pulsations of order', 'larger orders', 'the working in and out, together and against, of millions of events'

> so that I make
> no form of
> formlessness.

Again, he is echoing Whitman – the Whitman of 'Poem of the Road', clearly, but also of 'Poem of the Many in One' – yet the walker is necessarily a part of this circus of emergent events, simply by being there: if he walks in one direction, then 'the swallows could take flight', with the result that

> some other fields of bayberry
> could enter fall
> berryless

– a reminder that the human subject is, always, active in the drama, part of the play – though a token of his partial separation from the other creatures is that the outcome of his actions appears, more often than not, as part of a series of unintended consequences. This is where Ammons introduces his other big abstraction – Scope, with a capital S – a condition to which the animals and birds are privy, in their various niches, hunting and being hunted, flowing with the tide and the movements of the weather. However, because he has no designated place in the *Gestalt*, as the other creatures do, Scope eludes the walker's grasp, so that

> there is no finality of vision,
> that I have perceived nothing completely,
> that tomorrow a new walk is a new walk.

Nothing is ever finished, reality is always open-ended, shifting, in flux. Individual elements come into being and die away so that the Overall can continue – and the walker's achievement is to see that his inability to grasp Scope is a matter of freedom, not constraint. This recognition is a philosophical achievement in itself, for it allows the walker to be at home in this place without having to master or control it. Various traditions, from Buddhism to Heideggerian philosophy, have named this condition; we might call it, for simplicity's sake, right dwelling. Like the birds, or the crabs, the walker is, for a time, a denizen of Corson's Inlet. What the poem celebrates is that, for as long as that time lasts, he is able to dwell there as naturally as they do.

A VERY YOUNG POLICEMAN EXPLODING

A poem should not *mean*
But be.[1]

Archibald MacLeish

HART CRANE'S 'THE WINE MENAGERIE' was published in 1926 as part of his debut collection, *White Buildings*. It was one of the first poems I read outside the classroom, and I remember the exhilaration of that experience still, because I did not understand a word of it. It was 1971, Jim Morrison had recently been found dead in his Paris hotel room and I had just been expelled from school, which didn't actually matter because I was still trying to get my head round Miles Davis's *Bitches Brew*, a project infinitely more urgent than planning for a career. Everyone I knew who was reading at all was reading Sylvia Plath, and I was still struggling to divest myself of a whole gamut of received ideas about poetry, the worst of which was that it was there to be understood, like a Bible verse, or a problem in logic.* Imagine my surprise, then, when I read the opening to this strange text:

---

* The Bible verse reference may not be so far from the truth, as even my generation had gained much of its supposed literary-interpretative skills trying to figure out what God was trying to tell us in the sometimes murky pages of the Old Testament. Might it be that our most basic error about poetry – that it is there to be 'understood' – is rooted in a middle-school confusion of literature and theology?

Invariably when wine redeems the sight,
Narrowing the mustard scansions of the eyes,
A leopard ranging always in the brow
Asserts a vision in the slumbering gaze.[2]

'Mustard scansions'? Did that mean something? Anything? In literal terms, I didn't think so – and I have to admit that, back then, and in a somewhat different way now, I rather wanted a poem to *mean* as much as I wanted it to *be*, Archibald MacLeish notwithstanding. I believed that the making of a poem depended on establishing a vital relationship between music and meaning – as the Duchess advises Alice: 'Take care of the sense and the sounds will take care of themselves' (and vice versa). To put it another way, I was of the view that the music creates meaning but, at the same time, the meaning creates music.* So, though I had no idea what 'mustard scansions' might be, I did not reject them outright. I sensed that they had a meaning, in the world of poetic rather than syllogistic reasoning, and I set them aside for further consideration. Meanwhile, like Dante at the opening of the *Commedia*, I was both attracted to, and wary of, the leopard – its restless, 'ranging' energy, its promise of a 'vision', its reputation as the most deceptive and predatory of the larger cats.

So it was that, right from the start, I was *with* the speaker of the poem – only I didn't know where I was until the next stanza:

Then glozening decanters that reflect the street
Wear me in crescents on their bellies. Slow
Applause flows into liquid cynosures:
– I am conscripted to their shadows' glow.

Now it became clear: the speaker is in a bar – and, given the date, it

---

* Perhaps it would have helped, back then, to think in terms of *resonance*, rather than meaning, which too easily gets tangled up with conventional ideas of logic and public significance. Resonance conveys the idea of meaning at some level (though not necessarily logical, in the usual sense) and, at the same time, the affective power of music, not only on the listening ear but on the mind and body as a whole.

would have to be a speakeasy-type establishment, with all the associations that carries – and he is surrounded by the 'glozening' of the wine decanters, his face reflected in the dark glass. Clearly, he has already imbibed enough for his sight to have been redeemed, awakened from its slumber into vision, or preparedness, at least, for some vision that the leopard, ever present but inactive in the duller and soberer spells of the daily routine, is about to usher in. This heightening of the senses extends to the speaker's hearing – the sound of the slowly poured wine has come to resemble applause, drawing him in, 'conscripted' to a dim theatre of shadow and light.

The visionary drinker is not alone, however. Looking up, he sees a couple engaged in some private and apparently squalid drama of their own: the woman's smile is compared to 'forceps', the man is perspiring freely: 'Percussive sweat … spreading to his hair' (need it 'make sense', logically, that 'percussive', when it creates exactly the effect that Crane requires?), while into the leopard's wild, visionary Eden, a serpent – signal of jealousy and possessiveness – makes its (inevitable?) trespass. Almost immediately, however, as if to heighten the confusion and randomness of the data coming from outside the drinker's impending vision, the minor drama is interrupted by the arrival of an 'urchin', come in out of the snow – a gust of cool air in what had come to seem a hothouse – to nudge a canister across the bar. On a first reading, I had no idea what was going on here. Later, however, remembering the fact that this poem would have been composed under Prohibition, and knowing that, under the Volstead Act, wine could be sold for home consumption if used 'for sacramental purposes' (in fact, during Prohibition, the consumption of wine rose by 100 per cent), it began to come clear;* but the historical detail matters

---

* A few pages earlier in *White Buildings*, in a poem entitled 'Lachrymae Christi', Crane treats us to a highly sensual and sadomasochistic fantasia on one of those sacramental wines, in which the Christ-figure is exhorted, as he converges with the wild Dionysus, to 'Lift up in lilac-emerald breath the grail/ Of earth again' – an extraordinary piece of writing that conflates the raising of the 'grail'-like chalice at the moment of transubstantiation with the pagan energy of the Dionysian mysteries.

less than the introduction of another interruption, drawing the poet ever further into a bizarre, or possibly Dionysian, vision of his surroundings, culminating in the line 'Between black tusks the roses shine!'

I confess that, logically speaking, I have no idea what this line means. It does strike me, however, as both violent and sensual – or rather, as indicative of the twin possibilities of violence (some sort of goring?) and sex – especially as it modulates into the next stanza and beyond, with its vision of sexual transformation and romantic encounter:

> New thresholds, new anatomies! Wine talons
> Build freedom up about me and distill
> This competence – to travel in a tear
> Sparkling alone, within another's will.
>
> Until my blood dreams a receptive smile
> Wherein new purities are snared

This is a powerful moment, one of Crane's great *aperçus*, in which he captures perfectly the condition of the drinker who, catching sight of what the usual cliché might call 'a face across a crowded room' is half-aware, even then, that this romance is something dreamed up by the blood, another wishful inevitability, given the drunken subject's longing for that 'receptive smile'. A gay man whose friends were highly critical of his more or less open, masochistic sexuality, Crane fell in love often; and more often than not, during his drunken nights in Manhattan or cruising in the shadows of the Brooklyn Bridge, he fell in love with inappropriate people in inappropriate places. Days later, he would recount terrible stories to friends about the physical assaults and abuse to which he had been subjected after imagining he had detected 'a receptive smile' in the face of a stranger. That self-destructive sexual impulse was admixed with a deeply romantic, even idealistic, vision of loving selfhood, a vision we can see clearly in the first poem in *White Buildings*, the extraordinary, crystal-clear 'Legend', in which the optimism of the first hours of an evening – of going out, of being open to everything, indifferent to fear or danger – is reimagined with an extraordinary tenderness:

> As silent as a mirror is believed
> Realities plunge in silence by …
>
> I am not ready for repentance;
> Nor to match regrets. For the moth
> Bends no more than the still
> Imploring flame.

This may be so, the flame may implore as passionately as the moth, but its heat still burns. Crane's speaker knows this, but he continues –

> It is to be learned –
> This cleaving and this burning,
> But only by the one who
> Spends out himself again.[3]

– and there is no denying the masochism of this pose, the essential masochism of the romantic who, were it possible to enter the flame unharmed, would probably decline the passage.

Returning to 'The Wine Menagerie', we now find that the speaker, having caught only a fleeting glimpse of 'New thresholds, new anatomies', has almost completely lost the thread of the vision that the leopard had promised in the first flush of intoxication, the tawdry interruptions of the ordinary world flooding in to take its place:

> Alas, – these frozen billows of your skill!
> Invent new dominoes of love and bile …
> Ruddy the tooth implicit of this world
> Has followed you.

The tooth may well remind us of the Edenic serpent, emblem of jealousy and deceit, but Crane compounds the Biblical imagery with references to two male figures, one from the Old Testament, the other from the New, both of whom are beheaded by (or at the behest of) a woman. The first is Holofernes, general to the Assyrian king Nebuchadnezzar, who is killed by Judith (in *Purgatorio*, it is interesting to note, Dante places Holofernes among those whose chief sin is Pride, and he shows us the great general's mutilated body). The second head belongs to John the Baptist, who rebuked Herod for lusting after his brother's widow, Herodias. Grotesquely, these two severed heads float by – and then 'their whispering begins', advising the poem's protagonist to 'fold your exile on your back again', a signal that the leopard's vision has long ago dissipated.

But then, was it ever to be relied on? We remember that the leopard is the first of the three animals that block Dante's way at the opening of *The Divine Comedy*, driving him back to 'where the sun is silent'; we also remember that this same leopard is associated, in medieval symbolism, with trickery and guile, and this association is extended in the final, bathetic image of the poem, which invokes the clumsy, Chaplinesque puppet Petrushka, from Stravinsky's ballet of the same name, composed in 1911. The tale itself, drawn from traditional Russian puppet stories, is both grotesque and tragic: Petrushka is in love with a beautiful ballerina, but she rejects him, at the instigation of a manipulative magician (also known as The Charlatan) who serves both as controller and frightened victim of the masquerade he has contrived. This masquerade begins when a crowd of drunken revellers arrives, at the start of the show, looking for entertainment; it ends – though only for a few hours – as Petrushka's ghost walks away from the scene of his betrayal, knowing that he is condemned to repeat the pantomime the following day, when the drunken revellers return.

From all of the above, it is clear that only a partial 'understanding' of a poem like 'The Wine Menagerie' can ever be reached. We search for clues, for landmark references and images, then we light out for the territory. In a letter Crane composed in 1926 to Harriet Monroe, after she criticised this very poem for its illogicality, Crane laid out the basis and the justification for his method:

as a poet, I may very possibly be more interested in the so-called illogical impingements of the connotations of words on the consciousness (and their combinations and interplay in metaphor on this basis) than I am interested in the preservation of their logically rigid significations at the cost of limiting my subject matter and the perceptions involved in the poem.

This strikes us as non-controversial today, but it seems that it had to be stated then. Reading these lines, I cannot help recalling Marianne Moore's contention, in the early version of the poem 'Poetry':

> Hands that can grasp, eyes
> that can dilate, hair that can rise
>   if it must, these things are important not because a

> high sounding interpretation can be put upon them but
>   because they are
>   useful.[4]

For Moore, a 'high-sounding interpretation' is not what the poet is after; what she wants is an immediate, even visceral, response that cannot be faked, a response that will lead to further reading, further resonance – and Crane is after a similarly immediate experience:

> This may sound as though I merely fancied juggling words and images until I found something novel, or esoteric; but the process is much more predetermined and objectified than that. The nuances and feeling and observation in a poem may well call for certain liberties which you claim the poet has no right to take. I am simply making the claim that the poet does have that authority, and that to deny it is to limit the scope of the medium so considerably as to outlaw some of the richest genius of the past.

And he goes on to speak of those other faculties – which do not replace 'the purely rationalistic' but are capable of making sense of the world in ways that logic is not equipped to do:

> Its paradox, of course, is that its apparent illogic operates so logically in conjunction with its context in the poem as to establish its claim to another logic, quite independent of the original definition of the word or phrase or image thus employed. It implies (this inflection of language) a previous or prepared receptivity to its stimulus on the part of the reader. The reader's sensibility simply responds by identifying this inflection of experience with some event in his own history or perceptions – or rejects it altogether. The logic of metaphor is so organically entrenched in pure sensibility that it can't be thoroughly traced or explained outside of historical sciences, like philology and anthropology. This 'pseudo-statement', as I. A. Richards calls it in an admirable essay touching our contentions in last July's *Criterion*, demands completely other faculties of recognition than the pure rationalistic associations permit.[5]

This really is an extraordinary document, arguably the most disarming apologia ever written by a writer in defence of their art – and while Crane did not always live up to his own standards, his significance as a poet is, or should be, beyond doubt.* That he wrote much of his *oeuvre* while actually drunk makes his achievement even more remarkable.† Yet, drunk or not, his method

---

*Gerald Stern: 'Crane is always with me, and whatever I wrote, short poem or long, strange or unstrange – his voice, his tone, his sense of form, his respect for life, his love of the word, his vision have affected me. But I don't want – in any way – to exploit or appropriate this amazing poet whom I am, after all, so different from, he who may be, finally, the great poet – in English – of the twentieth century.'

†Gradually he would fall silent, and a little later he disappeared. In lulls that began to interrupt the laughter, now Hart was gone, we would hear a new hubbub through the walls of his room – the phonograph playing a Cuban rumba, the typewriter clacking simultaneously; then the phonograph would run down and the typewriter stop while Hart

demonstrates that, when it comes to writing or reading great poetry, we cannot rely on logic and 'meaning' alone; we must be ready to deploy *all* of our faculties. Perhaps Randall Jarrell summarises it best when he says, 'if sometimes we are bogged down in lines full of "corybulous", "hypogeum", "plangent", "irrefragably", "glozening", "tellurian", "conclamant", sometimes we are caught up in the soaring rapture of something unprecedented, absolutely individual.'

Hart Crane wrote two full collections in his short life. Dismayed by the loss of his family fortune in the crash of 1929 – an inheritance he had been counting on to make a new life for himself – and falling in an ever-accelerating spiral of alcoholism and self-lacerating sexual behaviour, he committed suicide by leaping from the steamship *Orizaba* on the voyage home to New York from Mexico, where, according to his old friend Waldo Frank, 'he was invaded subtly by a cult of death old as the Aztecs, ruthless as the sea. There was in Mexico also the will to be free of this death and of the beauty that flowers in death.' Perhaps: the simple truth, however, is that Crane had probably just borne too much for one lifetime. Some months before he set sail, he sat for the Mexican artist David Alfaro Siqueiros, who was obliged to ask his subject to close his eyes for the portrait. When asked why, later, Siqueiros said that he could not have painted Crane with his eyes open, for there was 'too much pain in them'.

The pain that Siqueiros saw in Hart Crane's eyes doubtless had its origins in his family circumstances and in the insults and injuries

---

changed the record, perhaps to a torch song, perhaps to Ravel's Bolero. An hour later ... he would appear in the kitchen or on the croquet court, his face brick-red, his eyes burning, his already iron-gray hair bristling straight up from his skull ... In his hands would be two or three sheets of typewritten manuscript, with words crossed out and new lines scrawled in. 'R-read that,' he would say. 'Isn't that the greatest poem ever written?

Malcolm Cowley, *Exile's Return*

imposed daily by a society deeply hostile to his sexual orientation, but it is not beyond the bounds of possibility that it was also provoked by the sheer frustration of not being heard as a poet. The 'misunderstood artist' is, of course, a perennial cliché, but the fact remains that it can be emotionally damaging to engage for days, or weeks, in seeking out ways of giving voice to a new music, only for the established culture to reject it – or, worse still, ignore it altogether. Add to this the incomprehension of colleagues and friends and it is not difficult to see that, living as Crane did, with little to no emotional support system, the personal life of such an uncompromising artist must have been lonely and racked with doubt. No one who has seen the filmed interview where William S. Burroughs is obliged to stand by and listen as his brother Mortimer casually disparages his finest works will readily forget the hurt that appears, however briefly, in the face of the man whom the film critic Roger Ebert described as 'one of the most pathetic figures in modern literature [...] who walks around with something wounded inside, something that hurts so much that his spirit simply shut down'.

Nevertheless, as Randall Jarrell notes, in his essay 'The Obscurity of the Poet', the problem of incomprehension is complicated:

> When I was asked to talk about the Obscurity of the Modern Poet I was delighted, for I have suffered from this obscurity all my life. But then I realized that I was being asked to talk not about the fact that people don't read poetry, but about the fact that most of them wouldn't understand it if they did: about the difficulty, not the neglect, of contemporary poetry. And yet it is not just modern poetry, but poetry, that is today obscure.

He continues:

> Since most people know about the modern poet only that he is obscure – i.e., that he is difficult, i.e., that he is neglected – they naturally make a causal connection between the two meanings of the word, and decide that he is unread *because* he is difficult. Some of the time this is true: the poet seems difficult because

he is not read, because the reader is not accustomed to reading his or any other poetry.

Yet, while it may be both true and useful to point out that so much poetry is considered 'obscure' simply because so few readers are willing to engage with it, this is of little comfort to the poet – and it remains a loss to the reader because, as Jarrell says later in the same essay, 'Art matters not merely because it is the most magnificent ornament and the most nearly unfailing occupation of our lives, but because it is life itself.' True, there are those who, avoiding the challenge of difficult art, content themselves with what Goethe calls 'technical facility accompanied by triteness', but this, surely, is no more rewarding than cheating at solitaire.

This is not to say that poets are never wilfully, or stupidly, obscure. The trick, for the reader (and for the critic, of course), is to be alert enough to the gap between difficulty and obscurity to discern one from the other. Coleridge says that, '[a]n author is obscure when his conceptions are dim and imperfect, and his language incorrect, inappropriate, or involved' – and while this observation covers a multitude of sins, it also reveals an important truth about the ways in which seemingly direct, and thus popular, poetry sometimes fails. For, while the language of certain poems may not be 'involved' or 'incorrect', their dim and imperfect conceptions readily give them away. This can easily be illustrated by looking at a work such as 'Shopping for Meat in Winter', by Oscar Williams, a poet whom Randall Jarrell loved to mock:

The sun like incense fumes on the smoky glass,
The street frets with people, the winter wind
Throws knives, prices dangle from shoppers' mouths
While the grim vegetables, on parade, bring to mind

The great countryside bathed in golden sleep,
The trees, the bees, the soft peace everywhere –
I think of the cow's tail, how all summer long
It beat the shapes of harps into the air.

These lines are not semantically or syntactically difficult, as in some of Hart Crane's earliest works, where we see an ambitious observer in his chosen field searching for ways to express something beyond the usual limits of his time's speech. True, the language is sloppy, the similes unpersuasive, the music forced (mainly through grating rhymes, but also through the use of clichés like 'golden sleep' and 'soft peace everywhere'). The main difficulty, however, lies in the poem's 'conceptions' (to use Coleridge's term). The sheer laziness of thought displayed here, the crude mental shorthand of received idea backed up against received idea ('the trees, the bees' – what, no birds?), the utter verbiage of a line like 'The sun like incense fumes on the smoky glass' (do we really need 'incense', 'fumes' and 'smoky' to get Williams' drift?) make this poem an easy read at first sight, difficult for all the wrong reasons. In short, we understand it; we just cannot *see* it. The poet's desire for clever and convoluted gesture blinds us to the scene itself.

Dylan Thomas (whose work was championed by Oscar Williams in the US) was very much aware of the danger of drifting, unwittingly, into obscurity in the search for new ways of seeing and saying. Unlike Crane and Burroughs, however, he seems to have remained defiant in the face of his critics. Partly, this was the result of an unashamed self-awareness; not only was he able to acknowledge that he was capable of work that ended up 'overweighted, overviolent, or daft'; not only was he capable of looking back at early work and seeing its limits (he claimed not to recall 'the first impulse that pumped and shoved most of the earlier poems along [...] with their vehement beat-pounding black and green rhythms like those of a very young policeman exploding'), but he was also painfully aware of the risks a poet takes in espousing difficulty when he also wishes to be appreciated by the widest possible readership. 'Go on thinking that you don't need to be read,' he once remarked, 'and you'll find that it may become quite true: no one will feel the need to read [your work] because it is written for yourself alone; and the public won't feel any impulse to gate crash such a private party.' Nevertheless, when he was sure of what he was about, Thomas refused to be cowed by the expectations – or the limitations – of others. During a radio programme in which he introduced and recited recent work, he remarked of the poem 'If my head hurt a hair's foot' that

> The next poem tells of a mother and her child who is about to be born. It is not a narrative, nor an argument, but a series of conflicting images which move through pity and violence to an unreconciled acceptance of suffering: the mother's and the child's. This poem has been called obscure. I refuse to believe that it is obscurer than pity, violence, or suffering. But being a poem, not a lifetime, it is more compressed.

This, in essence, is the conundrum faced by all exploratory poets. On the one hand, they know that there is a fine line between difficulty and obscurity and that the attempt at capturing complexity will often be taken by less careful readers as obfuscation; on the other, they would not be pursuing their craft honestly if they did not seek out the difficult, the complex and the paradoxical and then try, within the limits of a given grammar, to express such insights as musically as possible. Even when the brickbats fly, or the accolades pile up, nobody can ever be altogether sure of how successful a poem has been on its own terms – because in poetry real success is not measured by brickbats or accolades. Of course, it is pleasant when the prizes come, and annoying when the critics are more than usually dense (as in this anonymous review from *The London Critic*, on the publication, in 1855, of *Leaves of Grass*: 'Walt Whitman is as unacquainted with art as a hog is with mathematics. His poems – we must call them so for convenience – twelve in number, are innocent of rhythm, and resemble nothing so much as the war-cry of the Red Indians. Indeed, Walt Whitman has had near and ample opportunities of studying the vociferations of a few amiable savages'). As Jarrell says, the risks of obscurity – in both senses of the word – are constant, but that should not be an obstacle for the poet in his or her pursuit of difficulty. In fact, the higher the risks, the more miraculous the possible outcome, as Dylan Thomas knew in his bones, even as he confessed to his misadventures with exploding policemen.

One of Thomas's finest works is 'Poem in October', which was written in 1944 during a walk around Laugharne, the poet's South Wales home, on his thirtieth birthday – or as he himself puts it, his 'thirtieth year to heaven' (heaven would claim him less than a decade later, after a drunken ramble through New York that has gone down as the most famous binge in literary history). Like 'The Steeple-Jack' or 'Corson's Inlet', the poem draws on the land, rather than on a picturesque landscape, for its power – which is to say, on the *fact* of the land, on what is given to the senses on this particular day, along with what is remembered from others. Immediately, all the senses are engaged, and the sense of a terrain teeming with life is clear:

> Woke to my hearing from harbour and neighbour wood
> > And the mussel pooled and the heron
> > > Priested shore
> > The morning beckon
> With water praying and call of seagull and rook
> And the knock of sailing boats on the net webbed wall.

Intent on an early start, the poet sets forth while the town is still sleeping – and I think we get just a hint of the sense, developed later, that this part of the day, when others are abed, is the best. At the very least, there are no distractions, no noise from the human world to drown out the

> > > water–
> Birds and the birds of the winged trees flying my name
> > Above the farms and the white horses.[6]

The reference to the poet's name here is apropos for several reasons: the name of the Welsh hero, or in pagan times the divinity, Dylan eil Ton, means Son of the Wave (or sometimes, Dylan eil Mor, Son of the Sea). He features in *The Mabinogion*, and in a lament of *Taliesin* – and in both cases what comes to the fore is the story of his untimely death and the calling-out of the waves for vengeance; or, as one scholar puts it:

> The waves lament his death, and, as they dash against the shore, seek to avenge it. His grave is 'where the wave makes a sullen sound', but popular belief identifies him with the waves, and their noise as they press into the Conwy is his dying groan. Not only is he Eil Ton, 'son of the wave', but also Eil Mor, 'son of the sea'. He is thus a local sea-god, and like Manannan iden-tified with the waves, and yet separate from them, since they mourn his death. The Mabinogi gives us the débris of myths explaining how an anthropomorphic sea-god was connected with the goddess Arianrhod and slain by a god Govannon.[7]

So it is that, on his birthday, walking abroad 'in a shower of all my days' through the blessed realm of his home ground, full of mem-ories and images from childhood, the poet is also aware of death, as the creatures of the seashore call out his name, echoing the waves of mythic times – and it is here, between birth and death, that he crosses the invisible line in the land that, in the fairy tales and myths, marks the division between the human world and the mythic:

> High tide and the heron dived when I took the road
> Over the border

At the same time he notes that, the moment he passes from this world to the other,

> the gates
> Of the town closed as the town awoke.

There is no sound here, yet the image of gates suggests noise – a clanging, perhaps – and it is important that, as the land, itself pagan, opens to the walker, the human world, a world of conven-tion and religious strictures, closes behind him. As soon as it does, the land surges into a teeming life that is both of the present – that is, this day of the poet's birthday – and preserved in the indelible past:

> A springful of larks in a rolling
> Cloud and the roadside bushes brimming with whistling
> Blackbirds and the sun of October
> Summery
> On the hill's shoulder,
> Here were fond climates and sweet singers suddenly
> Come in the morning where I wandered and listened
> To the rain wringing
> Wind blow cold
> In the wood faraway under me.

Now that we have moved into the past, Thomas cannot resist characterising the powers-that-be of the societal world – a world that is far away under him in the rain and the cold wind – as 'the sea wet church the size of a snail' and the castle 'Brown as owls', the church's spires transformed to 'horns through mist', offering a picture of some lost gastropod fumbling blindly onward. Though some might argue that this reads too much into the line, it takes only a moment's reflection to recall Thomas's distaste for organised religion: see, for example, the passage in *A Child's Christmas in Wales* where, as the narrator reminisces about scouring 'the swatched town for the news of the little world' on Christmas mornings, the men and women come 'wading or scooping back from chapel, with taproom noses and wind-bussed cheeks, all albinos, huddled their stiff black jarring feathers against the irreligious snow'. This is not to say that Thomas himself was not, as Richard Burton describes him, 'a terribly compassionate man and a deeply religious one', but his individual, unorthodox religious sense, a sense that included a pagan awareness of 'the force that through the green fuse drives the flower' and the unity of all living things, made him only the more aware, and the more contemptuous, of Chapel hypocrisy. The basis of his earthly and essentially pagan sensibility, here, is the snow – which is doggedly irreligious – and the close and holy darkness of the night, as well as the land and the sea, from which, like his divine namesake, he claimed, more seriously than many imagined, to have come.*

Meanwhile, in contrast to the snail-like church and the castle, the mythic land the poet now occupies – a private domain suspended between the present and the past – is colourful and full of music:

> But all the gardens
> Of spring and summer were blooming in the tall tales
> Beyond the border and under the lark full cloud.

This seems fit ground to 'marvel' his birthday away – but now the weather turns around, 'away from the blithe country', and just for a moment the mood of the poem changes. It is as though a shadow had passed across the sun in the present time, and the poet is obliged to invent a world in which to stand, using a patchwork of impressions from memory. What results is a kind of miraculous summer:

> And down the other air and the blue altered sky
> Streamed again a wonder of summer
> With apples
> Pears and red currants.

However, there may be something not quite right about this 'summer'. It is a 'wonder', yes, and this shows in the fact that the apples and redcurrants are shown together – which in Thomas's time, and even now, would have been a strange sight, considering redcurrants flower and fruit in late June, into July, while even

---

* The phrase 'close and holy' comes from *A Child's Christmas in Wales*: 'Looking through my bedroom window, out into the moonlight and the unending smoke-coloured snow, I could see the lights in the windows of all the other houses on our hill and hear the music rising from them up the long, steady falling night. I turned the gas down, I got into bed. I said some words to the close and holy darkness, and then I slept.'

an apple variety like 'Stark's Earliest' which, as its name implies, fruits sooner than most, would only be available for picking by the end of July and into August. All of this may seem finicky, but the eerie conjunction suggests a rather odd, possibly fairy-tale quality: in short, this is a 'summer' supplied by memory and imagination, a composite season of unheard melodies whose sweetness is unearthly. Further evidence of this shift is given in the lines that follow, where the speaker remembers the 'parables' and 'legends' of a mother's storytelling:

> And I saw in the turning so clearly a child's
> Forgotten mornings when he walked with his mother
>   Through the parables
>   Of sun light
>   And the legends of the green chapels
>
>   And the twice told fields of infancy.

Now the speaker is almost overwhelmed with a sense of loss, and of the elusive – and possibly illusory – nature of personal history, even as he achieves a kind of unity with the boy he once was:

> That his tears burned my cheeks and his heart moved in mine.
>   These were the woods the river and sea
>   Where a boy
>   In the listening
> Summertime of the dead whispered the truth of his joy
> To the trees and the stones and the fish in the tide.

Nevertheless, what Thomas calls 'the mystery' sings 'alive' in that part-remembered, part-imagined world – alive enough, he thinks, for him to be able to try once more to marvel his birthday away. But no: once again, the weather turns around, and the vision is replaced by yet another, in which the true:

>   Joy of the long dead child sang burning
>   In the sun.

The child this thirty-year-old man was is now long gone – and here it is hard not to think of the ending of 'Fern Hill', another poem in which the speaker's remembered child-self is magnified, almost beatified, blithely enjoying the kind of pagan energy and *joie de vivre* that may be found in the old Celtic tales, only to end in a ravelling of vigorous new life and death into one eternal moment. This eternal moment, in which the poet, like all life, is both 'green' and 'dying', is an occasion for song:

> Oh as I was young and easy in the mercy of his means,
>> Time held me green and dying
>> Though I sang in my chains like the sea.[8]

We are bound to pause here: this child is, it emerges, the child of a sea spirit, as well as a mortal creature, but even he can see that, like birds, beasts, flowers and humans, the sea itself is chained to the fundamental laws of nature. And yet, within that given order, it is the child's instinctive singing that matters, the singing that, elemental in its own way as the sea itself, outlasts the grasp of (linear) time, the end of summer, the loss of childhood. When we remember the year in which 'Poem in October' was written (1944), we recall that Dylan, a man Richard Burton described as 'doomed' by 'the incredible tragedies that go on ... the viciousness and murder', had also borne agonised witness to the events of the Second World War in his 'Refusal to Mourn the Death, by Fire, of a Child in London':

> murder
> The mankind of her going with a grave truth
> Nor blaspheme down the stations of the breath
> With any further
> Elegy of innocence and youth.[9]

This response led William Empson to say, famously, that:

> obscurity in a writer may be due, not to concentration, but to a refusal to speak out. This poem tells us that Dylan Thomas isn't going to say something. I take it that the child was killed

in an air raid, and that Dylan Thomas won't say so because he is refusing to be distracted by thoughts about the war from thoughts about the child herself or about death in general.

Empson adds:

> his is a refusal to integrate perceptions of the dead girl into a coherent, 'logical' whole which is necessarily inadequate to its object, and to use this misrepresented experience or fate of another person to achieve a false poetic resolution.

Yes! This is exactly what Thomas is doing and, I believe (though I am not certain) that Empson has seen the paradox that lies at the heart of Thomas's genius: whether called to an effort at speech by horror, compassion, memory, unsayable grief or a reverence for the natural world that reaches back into the bright repositories of pagan life, he will not be betrayed into going further than his inspiration takes him. It is true that Thomas refuses to say *certain* things in 'Refusal', just as he refuses to say *other* things in other poems – sometimes deliberately calling attention to that refusal. The most notable example of this strategy of silence is the steady repetition of the phrase 'And I am dumb' throughout 'The Force That Through the Green Fuse Drives the Flower':

> The force that through the green fuse drives the flower
> Drives my green age; that blasts the roots of trees
> Is my destroyer.
> And I am dumb to tell the crooked rose
> My youth is bent by the same wintry fever.
>
> The force that drives the water through the rocks
> Drives my red blood; that dries the mouthing streams
> Turns mine to wax.
> And I am dumb to mouth unto my veins
> How at the mountain spring the same mouth sucks.[10]

Of course he is 'dumb' here, but he has said what can be said in the poem's first lines and this is also what *needs* to be said, this momentous fact of a natural order that both includes us, alongside all other things, as creaturely, unrepeatable instances of life and, at the same time, allows us to wither away in time, so that other plants and creatures might come into equally forceful being. What Thomas is saying, in short, is that he is capable of utterance, but will not descend to mere exegesis. He will not bend the given world into some logical, or merely pleasing, shape; he will not seek an easy resolution, poetic or otherwise; he refuses to make the poems more accessible, or more pleasing as surfaces. As 'Poem in October' moves towards its conclusion, we see him standing, like Dante, between childhood and death, in a time of such violence that even the autumn leaves become as blood on the lanes of the town below, and he does all that he can do, under the circumstances: he carries on giving utterance, as well as he can, to whatever 'truth' his heart has learned:

> It was my thirtieth
> Year to heaven stood there then in the summer noon
> Though the town below lay leaved with October blood.
> O may my heart's truth
> Still be sung
> On this high hill in a year's turning.

Throughout his career, even as his work was treasured by a wider public, Dylan Thomas drew the wrath, first, of self-styled traditionalists and, later, of The Movement (or rather, of poetry's mid-century Robespierre, Robert Conquest, who loudly decried the 'extremities and excesses' of Thomas and others).* Even

---

* A favourable review of Thomas's *Eighteen Poems* in the *Sunday Times* by Edith Sitwell provoked a landslide of angry letters which make for entertaining, and instructive, reading now. One correspondent, a Mr Kenneth Hare, reminded readers that, all appearances to the contrary, 'these are not the verses of a young gentleman from the Congo who, eschewing cannibalism and Hoodoo, is cramming English with a tutor, but those of a native of this island. What do they mean?' Hare continued: 'I concede that poetry will never appeal to the plain "man in the street". It should, however, do so to the man in Intellectual

today, it could be argued that Thomas's reputation has not fully recovered from the attacks launched on his work during the 1950s. Meanwhile, Hart Crane has never won the wider readership he deserves: labelled from the start as difficult and obscure, he seems doomed to be confined to academia. This is a real pity, but it says more about the way poetry is taught, and how it is represented in the media, than it does about these poets' work. Perhaps the last word on this, however, belongs to another Thomas reviewer, the critic John Graddon, who, writing in *Poetry Review* in 1953, offered an assessment that could be applied not only to Thomas and Crane but to any number of poets whose work remains neglected because the public has been educated into prejudices and limits that are altogether unjustified. 'It is the reader soaked in the traditional style,' Graddon writes, 'who finds [Thomas] the more incomprehensible. Perhaps the reason is that the traditionalist brings into play [...] only that compartment of his mind labelled "Poetry" [while] the uninitiated relate to him by association and *comparison with personal experience*.' This observation is not only astute; it should also go without saying. When we shed our schoolroom approach to the poem and experience it fully, with all our faculties, rather than searching for its 'meaning' as if it were an instruction manual or a shopping list, we shall begin to appreciate fully an art form that is, in Randall Jarrell's words, 'life itself'.

---

or Beautiful Street. I venture to prophesy that posterity will willingly let the work of our obscurantists die, despite the protests of the critics of Cryptic Street, Recondite Alley, and Mystification Boulevard.'

AN OLD CHAOS OF THE SUN

Here, now, we forget each other and ourselves.
We feel the obscurity of an order, a whole,
A knowledge, that which arranged the rendezvous.[1]

Wallace Stevens

WHEN A POET LIKE WALLACE STEVENS makes a direct statement, we pay attention. Under normal circumstances Stevens is circumspect, his theses tentative and much qualified, and when his lifelong quarry – the idea of order – is finally expressed, it is as a 'fiction', in which, faced with a cosmos that is beyond comprehension, the lone imagination is obliged to construct some provisional sense of being-at-home in that cosmos by a supreme mental effort. There are times, however (as here, in Canto IV of 'Thirteen Ways of Looking at a Blackbird'), when he spells out what looks like one element of a credo:

A man and a woman
Are one.
A man and a woman and a blackbird
Are one.

On first acquaintance, this statement seems unequivocal. Man, woman, bird, all of creation, it seems, are one – and at first sight this inclusiveness is all. We are all one. Not just humans: everything. And, as can be seen if we look carefully to the natural order, we are all equal players in the narrative of being: all of us, from a flea to the prime minister. There are no natural hierarchies, there is no higher or lower. What is, is, according to its own nature, but in a shared world – and we hurry to assume that this is, or should be, the basis of any idea of order. This oneness.

However, if we begin at the beginning, we see that the unified field in which 'Thirteen Ways of Looking at a Blackbird' unfolds – canto by brief, haiku-like canto – is the outcome of a specific landscape, a snowy stillness conjured up in the opening lines of the poem in which almost nothing moves:

Among twenty snowy mountains,
The only moving thing
Was the eye of the blackbird.

This is the closest we can come to perfect stasis in this world; to go further, we would have to enter an ideal realm (like that pictured in Keats's 'Ode on a Grecian Urn', say, of which, more below). However, immediately after that fourth canto, in which the oneness of creation is so uncompromisingly stated, the speaker of the poem is teased by a doubt that at first sight seems playful, even whimsical, but which is in fact crucial:

I do not know which to prefer,
The beauty of inflections
Or the beauty of innuendoes,
The blackbird whistling
Or just after.[2]

Here, if we take inflection to mean what is audible, an actual sound in which some movement or shift in pitch expresses some nuance of perception or feeling openly (dictionary: 'change in the quality of the voice, often showing an emotion'), while considering innuendo to be a matter not of utterance but of suggestion (and even of a suggestion based on a withholding of utterance), we may well feel the poem is in danger of stumbling into the kind of Platonic sensibility that Keats allows to muddy the waters in

'Ode on a Grecian Urn':

> Heard melodies are sweet, but those unheard
>> Are sweeter; therefore, ye soft pipes, play on;
> Not to the sensual ear, but, more endear'd,
>> Pipe to the spirit ditties of no tone.

Stevens remains sure-footed, however; for, while the sweetness of the unheard melody in Keats depends on the absolute stasis of the pictured scene, the 'still unravish'd bride of quietness', and while Stevens's snowy landscape is even colder than the Grecian urn's 'Cold Pastoral', its brief stasis is nevertheless disrupted by the audible call – and by the moving eye – of the blackbird. So it is that, although his speaker cannot decide between the live music of the blackbird whistling or the charged silence 'just after', the poem has already moved beyond the realm of static ideal. Later still, in Canto IX, when the speaker notices that

> When the blackbird flew out of sight,
> It marked the edge
> Of one of many circles

we see that the undivided white space of the earlier vision has been irrevocably broken. That the inhabitants of that space are one (which is to say, we all exist in a condition of interdependence) is not disputed, but now the field of vision is divided into discrete areas, first by the circle that the bird delimits when it flies out of sight, and then by the 'many circles' that this rupture implies. It is as if Stevens had tossed a stone into the still waters of his poem and set off an endless ripple effect. Now, while man, woman and blackbird remain one, in the sense of occupying the same space and the same natural order, each sits at the centre of its own circle, its own narrative of presence and absence. We are all here, together, we may even say that we are all one, but the very fact that we exist as identifiable and discrete entities – 'man', 'woman', 'blackbird' – also means that we are separate within our own circles, each of us making up our own 'small part of the pantomime'. It is this paradox that sits at the centre of Stevens's *oeuvre*, an *oeuvre* that, in part at least, documents a lifelong quest to articulate a poetic order – and so some kind of tangible meaning – in what, because of the limits of our understanding, we are obliged to perceive as a fragmented and inchoate cosmos. It may well be – indeed, it seems indisputable – that there is an order to nature that is larger than anything we can imagine, but it is not *our* order. Our order has to be won by an almost heroic process of perception and imaginative apprehension.

In the revised version of his early masterpiece 'Sunday Morning' (published in *Harmonium* in 1923) Stevens creates what he later called 'simply an expression of paganism', in which a woman takes time off on the Sabbath to enjoy 'coffee and oranges in a sunny chair' instead of attending church. It is a pleasant interlude in which, enjoying this interval of unlooked-for leisure, the woman blithely rejects the Christian teaching in which she was raised, in favour of the pleasures to be found in this earthly kingdom. At the same time, however, haunted by the 'need of some imperishable bliss', she cannot quite come to terms with the mutability of this world; all the while claiming to be

> content when wakened birds,
> Before they fly, test the reality
> Of misty fields, by their sweet questionings

she nevertheless turns to wondering, 'when the birds are gone, and their warm fields/ Return no more, where, then, is paradise?' This debate, at times leisurely, at times more urgent, plays out in her mind for several stanzas, until the poem concludes with a passage that is at once beautiful and unsettling:

> She hears, upon that water without sound,
> A voice that cries, 'The tomb in Palestine
> Is not the porch of spirits lingering.
> It is the grave of Jesus, where he lay.'

We live in an old chaos of the sun,
Or old dependency of day and night,
Or island solitude, unsponsored, free,
Of that wide water, inescapable.
Deer walk upon our mountains, and the quail
Whistle about us their spontaneous cries;
Sweet berries ripen in the wilderness;
And, in the isolation of the sky,
At evening, casual flocks of pigeons make
Ambiguous undulations as they sink,
Downward to darkness, on extended wings.[3]

Here the woman is obliged to recognise, finally, that the tomb to which Jesus was consigned is not a gateway to some other reality, or to the resurrection of the dead; it is simply the grave in which a broken man was laid out as all the dead are laid out, with no hope of return. If she is to pass beyond her Christian upbringing and come to terms with the here and now, she will have to accept this fact, just as she must accept that, while the natural world may resemble Eden in some ways, its mortal and sometimes capricious fauna are not there to please her, and the world in which she lives is not governed by some divine order but is simply 'an old chaos of the sun'. Unlike the dove that descends from heaven in the Gospel of Matthew,* casual flocks of pigeons make 'ambiguous undulations' as they sink into the darkness.

The philosopher James P. Carse gives this vision fuller expression when he points out that: 'Nature is the realm of the unspeakable. It has no voice of its own, and nothing to say. We experience the unspeakability of nature as its utter indifference to human culture.' Stevens would probably have agreed. Philosophically, he seems to accept from the first that a *model* of order could be found in the physical world, but this neutral, indifferent order offers no habitation as such; like Heidegger, we might say, Stevens felt

---

* Matthew 3:16: 'And Jesus, when he was baptised, went up straightway out of the water: and, lo, the heavens were opened unto him, and he saw the Spirit of God descending like a dove, and lighting upon him.'

that humans are somehow thrown, or have fallen, into a world in which they are essentially homeless and therefore obliged to construct a possible dwelling place by an imaginative and philosophical leap of vision. In other words, he understood that nature expresses a fundamental order, but that order is not specific, or favourable, to human beings. Intellectually, it is possible to observe and appreciate the mathematical order of nature, but that order offers no security, no guarantees, no lasting comfort – and in what was to become Stevens's most famous poem, 'The Snow Man', he insisted that, like some inanimate, emotionless snowman standing out in the cold, 'One must have a mind of winter' and 'have been cold a long time':

> To behold the junipers shagged with ice,
> The spruces rough in the distant glitter
>
> Of the January sun; and not to think
> Of any misery in the sound of the wind.

That is, one would have to be *humanly* cold and unfeeling (a mere simulacrum of humanity, in fact, as the snowman is) *to be able* to regard this icy landscape and not think of *some* misery 'In the sound of a few leaves', even though one knows that this sound is a fundamental part of the natural order that governs everything: that it is, in short,

> the sound of the land
> Full of the same wind.

That the land is both indifferent to us and eternally mutable, that nature is, in fact, the very source of all mutability and cannot be relied on to provide reliable sanctuary, is a long-established philosophical truth – among 'civilised' people, at least. In fact, reading 'The Snow Man', it is hard not to think of these lines from Edmund Spenser's *Mutabilitie Cantos*, published in 1609:

> What Man that sees the ever-whirling Wheel
> Of Change, the which all mortal things doth sway,

But that thereby doth find, and plainly feel,
How MUTABILITY in them doth play
Her cruel Sports, to many Mens decay?

That cold wind, signal of nature's indifference to our wants and needs, blows where it will, as Jesus says in the third chapter of *The Gospel according to John*:

The wind bloweth where it listeth, and thou hearest the sound thereof, but canst not tell whence it cometh, and whither it goeth.

And we have to remember that, just as the wind blows *out there*, in the cold world, among the trees, so it is also

blowing in the same bare place

For the listener, who listens in the snow,
And, nothing himself, beholds
Nothing that is not there and the nothing that is.

This conclusion, especially the last line, is both famous and frequently quoted, with various interpretations offered as to the meaning of the three 'nothings'. My own view is that the second 'nothing' speaks of the poet's sacred duty to observe, and to speak of, only what is evident to imaginative perception, resisting any temptation to impose on the scene objects, ideas or mental phenomena that are 'not there', while the final 'nothing' denotes an unknowable void at the heart of existence – i.e., Sartre's 'nothingness [that] haunts being'. However, the 'nothing' that really gives us pause is the first one: the 'nothing himself' of the listener (and it is important to note here that, while the poem began and continued with *visual* images of snow and frozen trees, this changes as it moves towards its logical end, when the hypothetical protagonist of the poem becomes a *listener*, and listening is an activity that demands more attention than the relatively passive acts of looking and hearing). The onlooker, the person who only sees and hears, is merely present, receiving the given world as it comes to him. The listener, however, is on a quest, all attention, search-ing for something that is not necessarily vouchsafed him. Might it be, in fact, that this is how he becomes 'nothing' – by surrendering everything to the act of listening, of attending to and apprehend-ing the natural order? This is one possible perspective. Or is it that, by surrendering himself to the work of listening, and so becom-ing one element of the snowstorm, he is gradually absorbed into the land itself, and so becomes 'nothing' in the human arena – at which point he is able to 'behold' the natural realm? Or is it possible that Stevens, while admitting the beauty of the natural order, also knows that, when it comes to our need for warmth and secure dwelling, nature offers us nothing and that we are – or rather, *might as well be* – 'nothing' when we come face to face with that wild order?

In the end, we can read the finer detail of this conclusion in any number of ways, but the overall sense seems incontrovert-ible: if one (the use of the impersonal pronoun is important here) does not possess a mind of winter, if one is, in fact, human, then one must endure the 'misery', if not of homelessness, as such, then of an inevitable and creaturely condition of mutability and insecurity that is intrinsic to a felt existence. In short, humans are also creatures, and the natural world is both our doom and our destiny: if we can inhabit it, that world will give us shelter, even if only on a temporary and provisional basis; if we fail to enter into the natural world imaginatively – if we do not listen actively to the music of what happens, thus mistaking it for mere noise – we will remain homeless.

Yet while we can talk about the natural order in holistic terms, while we can accept that the given is the basic ground of our being, this does not help us live in the way we would choose to live, day to day. We recognise, of course, that human order is artificial (as a house or a coat or, for that matter, a name is), but that does not make it any less real, or any less needful. Unless a man possesses a mind of winter, he requires warmth in order to live – by which we mean not only a good fire but also a sense that there is 'something more' to life than the sound of the wind crying in the land. Meaning. Purpose. Commonality. Throughout his writing life Stevens seems to wrestle with what that something more was: certainly, it involved the sense of a human order, but there was more to it than that. For a long time he seems to have hoped to reconcile, as it were, the natural and the human, by the creation of a 'supreme fiction' in which the two, while distinct, contrive to overlap – and when he speaks of the supreme or necessary fiction, what we take him to be saying is that it is the task and fate of each person to find a way to live an orderly life, somewhere between the apparent indifference of nature and the burden of societal expectations. Often, this vision of *human* order is predicated on light: faced with the all-encompassing and neutral darkness, we build small citadels of light, with lanterns, with candles, with whatever else comes to hand. For example, in 'Final Soliloquy of the Interior Paramour', a poem that actually begins with the word 'light' (used as an imperative, no less), Stevens offers a response that sits as a perfect complementarity to 'The Snow Man';* however, where that poem stressed the passivity of the human subject in the face of the given, 'Final Soliloquy of the Interior Paramour' is full of active verbs (lighting, resting, thinking, collecting, forgetting, feeling, saying and finally making):

Light the first light of evening, as in a room
In which we rest and, for small reason, think
The world imagined is the ultimate good.

This is, therefore, the intensest rendezvous.
It is in that thought that we collect ourselves,
Out of all the indifferences, into one thing:

---

*By 'complementarity' we mean exactly that, like the *yin* and *yang* of Daoist philosophy, and not merely an opposite.

Within a single thing, a single shawl
Wrapped tightly round us, since we are poor, a warmth,
A light, a power, the miraculous influence.

'We are poor' here cannot help but remind us of the Beatitudes (see Matthew 5:1, 'Blessed are the poor in spirit: for theirs is the kingdom of heaven'), and it requires a certain awareness of poverty to appreciate how 'a warmth/A light, a power' may at times constitute something 'miraculous'. Indeed, if we have seen the world of 'The Snow Man', we know that to possess any sense of home 'out of all the indifferences' is indeed miraculous. As the poem continues, Stevens demands of its subjects (and who the 'we' of this poem might be is an interesting question) not that they become 'nothing', as in 'The Snow Man', but that they 'forget' themselves in order to gain a sense of some overarching whole,* an order that, for the moment, is capable of being felt, even if obscurely:

Here, now, we forget each other and ourselves.
We feel the obscurity of an order, a whole,
A knowledge, that which arranged the rendezvous,

Within its vital boundary, in the mind.
We say God and the imagination are one …

Stevens's suggestion that 'We say God and the imagination are one' is a way of referring back to the Beatitudes: for when the human imagination is able to see the world truly, when we employ the imagination to its fullest, the kingdom of heaven is not only at hand; it becomes *ours*, both to inhabit and to make, in an active sense, as an echo of the divine making, *in principio*:

How high that highest candle lights the dark.

---

*It is interesting to conjecture as to how close this might be to A. R. Ammons's sense of the Overall that is 'beyond me: is the sum of these events/ I cannot draw, the ledger I cannot keep, the accounting/ beyond the account'. See the discussion of 'Corson's Inlet', p. 121.

Out of this same light, out of the central mind,
We make a dwelling in the evening air,
In which being there together is enough.

'The Snow Man' is an early poem in Stevens's writing career; 'Final Soliloquy of the Interior Paramour' was composed towards the end of his life. What separates them is a matter not so much of technique as of philosophical, or even grammatical, perspective: 'The Snow Man' speaks of the abstract 'one' – that is, of the individual as the subject of an ontological or epistemological thought experiment – while the later poem speaks from the position of a 'we', and so embraces a communal experience of light in the darkness, and of the making of a dwelling place. On the road from one to the other, Stevens took some alarming excursions (in which he was capable of exhibiting moments of casual racism, and the kind of sexism that could dismiss a woman's idea of happiness as somehow inferior to a man's*). At the same time, he began to engage with the basic givens of the kingdom that is at hand (space, darkness, night, light, home) with a real urgency that he was self-aware enough to mask with elegance and careful allusion. Finally, he created (if that is the right word) this elegant conceit of the 'interior paramour', a figure or device that begins to appear in poems from the 1930s, but which is only given its proper title in the late work. That the interior paramour is a variation on the Romantic Beloved seems clear, though again, Stevens is careful to distinguish between his idea of 'Romantic' and that of others.† 'When people speak of the romantic', he says, in a letter written in 1935,

---

* One wishes poems such as 'Like Decorations in a Nigger Cemetery' could simply disappear from our libraries, as if written in invisible ink, but they must be read and critiqued, not only because they are central to a period of our literary history but also because they show that, in a culture founded on racism and sexual inequality, even a mind as fine as Stevens's was capable of entertaining and giving voice to such nonsense.

† Or perhaps we could invoke here the Sufi concept of the Beloved. See Rumi:

A man went to the door of the Beloved and knocked. A voice asked:

they do so in what the French commonly call a pejorative sense. But poetry is essentially romantic, only the romantic of poetry must be something constantly new and, therefore, just the opposite of what is spoken of as the romantic. Without this new romantic, one gets nowhere; with it, the most casual things take on transcendence.

In that same year he composed 'Restatement of Romance', a poem that in many ways foreshadows 'Final Soliloquy', announcing the arrival of a poet who is intent on finding new ways to appreciate the most basic facts of life. Again his subject is darkness and light and how, in addition to the given shifts of night and random illumination, we cast upon one another a possibly brief, but nevertheless visible 'pale light' of our own.

> The night knows nothing of the chants of night.
> It is what it is as I am what I am:
> And in perceiving this I best perceive myself
>
> And you. Only we two may interchange
> Each in the other what each has to give.
> Only we two are one, not you and night,
>
> Nor night and I, but you and I, alone,
> So much alone, so deeply by ourselves,
> So far beyond the casual solitudes,
>
> That night is only the background of our selves,
> Supremely true each to its separate self,
> In the pale light that each upon the other throws.[4]

'Who is there?' He answered: 'It is I.'

The voice said: 'There is no room here for me and thee.' The door was shut.

After a year of solitude and deprivation this man returned to the door of the Beloved.

He knocked. A voice from within asked: 'Who is there?'

The man said: 'It is Thou.' The door was opened for him.

Here Stevens has reached the point of recognition that, for every light source – every candle, every lantern crossing a frosty yard, every brazier burning at a city crossroads – there is not just another person but a narrative centre, a fellow conspirator in the imagining of an inhabitable world. However, there is no attempt to draw from this vision the conclusion that we are 'all one' or 'connected' in anything other than the most basic ways, and it would be a real mistake to see Stevens's vision of shared world-making as warm and fuzzy in the manner of lesser poets. We are together, here, but we are also separate, and though, at its best, what we imagine can be made hospitable to all communally, we are still 'so deeply by ourselves, / So far beyond the casual solitudes' that each of us can only be *supremely* true in isolation, 'each to its separate self', even as we work in parallel to find meaning in a seemingly indifferent world.

Stevens created his vision of order while living the life of a well-paid insurance executive in suburban Connecticut – though even in those circumstances, that vision was not only hard-won, forged over decades by mental effort in a world that offered no obvious solace, but also could not be accounted as entirely solid, the imagined home constructed from a neutral cosmos never quite secure. However, this poetic enterprise was hardly conducted in extremity. For that we must turn to another, admittedly lesser but nonetheless exemplary, poet who, stripped of all the certainties of his own highly privileged youth and deprived of any other ground on which to build 'a dwelling in the evening air', was obliged to conjure a home of sorts from the shadowy depths of a prison cell in Hitler's Germany. To do so, this scientifically trained son of a senior government figure would use his understanding of the cosmos itself to construct his final poetic vision, as he waited, over a period of several months, to be executed for crimes against the homeland that he loved.

WELTENTON

Wir kennen kaum den kleinsten Teil davon:
Gesetz ist Wunder, Zahl ist Weltenton.

Albrecht Haushofer[1]

IMAGINE YOU COME ACROSS an old-fashioned cinema, perched on
the corner of a small *Platz* in Berlin. You go in, mostly to get out of
the rain, barely noticing what is on the programme, just wanting
to be warm and dry and alone for a couple of hours in that But-
terkist and velour dream you remember from childhood mati-
nees. You take off your coat and set it on the next seat – there's no
one else here, just the dim wall lights and the red velvet curtain
and the ivory-coloured EXIT signs above the doors – and it brings
back an odd memory of that word you loved as a child, EXIT, NO
EXIT, EXIT STAGE RIGHT, EXIT PURSUED BY A BEAR … This is the stuff
that goes through your head in the idle moments: scraps of nonsense, wordplay, child's play. Odd, then, that this is where poetry
seems to begin too – single words or phrases, or just a rhythm
sliding from one train of thought to another, nothing to do with
reason, or philosophy or the intensely meant moral or political
ideas that, surely, poetry is supposed to 'be about'. But no, making
a poem is more like beachcombing than some considered, professional practice; there is nothing deliberate there to explain, you
just begin to feel it and then, gradually, things – images, words,
echoes – begin to cohere.

Now that you are sitting comfortably, the house lights dim and the screen brightens. No ads, no trailers, just the main feature, in black and white, the true story (or so you have been led to believe) of a Resistance fighter, set in Germany during the Second World War. The central character, Albrecht Haushofer, is played by Leslie Howard.* When the film opens, he is standing by an old-fashioned casement window in an upper room, looking out at a winter landscape – we see farmland in Bavaria, leafless orchard trees, thick flakes of snow falling across the yard – and he is saying something, quietly, almost inaudibly, so we have to strain to make out the words:

schuldig bin ich
Anders als Ihr denkt ...

Which, as a wavering subtitle at the foot of the screen explains, means 'I am guilty, but not in the way you suppose', or something to that effect. Finally, Howard begins to speak in English as the camera pans away and we see the first of a series of memories:

I should have accepted my duty,
I should have acted sooner,
I should have called evil by its true name,
Yes, I sounded a warning,
But it's clear, now, that it wasn't enough,
And today I know what I was guilty of.

One flashback scene follows another as the voice continues, the scriptwriter taking ever more egregious liberties with a speech that had begun as Albrecht Haushofer's confession poem 'Guilt'. As it continues, scraps from T. S. Eliot – 'Ridiculous the waste sad time / Stretching before and after' – and Ezra Pound – 'Here error is all in the not done, / All in the diffidence that faltered' – are none too subtly woven in, to remind us that this is Hollywood, not Babelsberg. Gradually we begin to put together, in pictures

---

* The archetypal English gentleman, he was born Leslie Howard Steiner, in 1893, to a British mother and a Hungarian father.

and scraps of dialogue, a lifetime of significant moments from schooldays and newsreels and idyllic summer afternoons in this very place, the apple blossom blowing from the trees in a gust of wind, everything falling together to create the biography of a privileged and highly intelligent young man, a life full of hope and promise and a deep love of Homeland. And then the Nazis come to power.

A disaster, of course, which the soundtrack underlines; but this young man is a brilliant polymath, son of the esteemed State Geographer, Karl Haushofer, and so a potentially valuable asset to the new government. In fact, though partly Jewish on the mother's side, the entire family prospers for a time under the protection of Rudolf Hess. The father even rises to become a near-insider, the trusted architect of Hitler's *Lebensraum* plan,* while Albrecht is appointed to a leading government position in the Foreign Office and enjoys some success as a playwright. Nevertheless, life is not always easy: the two men, father and son, having supported Hitler's rivals in the 1920s and early '30s, must walk a political tightrope daily, working from the inside in the vain hope of tempering the worst excesses of the regime until, finally, when all hope of mediation is gone, Albrecht joins the Resistance.

Here the ironies come thick and fast. Though he is not directly involved in Stauffenberg's 20 July plot to assassinate Hitler, Haushofer, like Dietrich Bonhoeffer and many others who had survived thus far, is incriminated by association and now, in desperation, has fled to the family home in Bavaria. This is his *Heimat*, a regional locus that, as for so many Germans, has a power over

---

* After some time spent in the Pacific region, Karl Haushofer based his specific and highly toxic geopolitical theories on the success of Japanese expansionism in the first decade of the century. Established on 'a mixture of sound observations and hazy theories, geopolitics was based on the works of the German geographer Friedrich Ratzel, who compared the state to a biological organism, and on the less scientific theories of the Swedish political scientist Rudolf Kjellen, who took Ratzel's metaphor literally and viewed the state as an actual organism with a natural right to growth and to *Lebensraum* ("living space")' (*Encyclopaedia Britannica*).

his imagination that is close to sacred. That word, *Heimat*, is hard for non-Germans to understand fully. It is not just home; it is the source, the homeland, or, as literary editor Frederick Studemann observed, in a *Financial Times* review:

> *Heimat* is one of those German words that is almost beyond translation. A dictionary [...] will typically give you a simple answer: home, place of origin or subsequent association. In truth, it is so much more. Drawing deeply on landscape and culture, music and smell, the word, along with all its associations, evokes an almost visceral response, sparking feelings of longing and security, loss and melancholia. It goes to the gut. It is, in that charged term of our times, ultimately about identity.

Haushofer, a geographer by education who has travelled widely, seemed to develop a stronger sense of *Heimat* the further he ranged outwards from Germany – a not infrequent experience for habitual travellers. Bavaria is in his blood, in his soul; it feeds his imagination in ways that no exotic land could. Why he goes there now, however, is a mystery, for it is the first place the authorities will look for him, and he probably knows that he cannot rely on support from his family.* Surely he is aware that he is not safe and, in fact, as the camera returns to show his face, the winter light illuminating him coldly from beyond the casement, we hear the sounds of army vehicles pulling up in the courtyard, first one, then another, followed by the all too familiar clump of jackboots on the stairs … A moment later, the arresting officer arrives – perhaps he is a stock Erich von Stroheim lookalike, with a ridiculous duelling scar, or maybe he is George Sanders,[†] a smooth

---

* Later, in fact, when asked to use his influence with Hitler to get Albrecht released from prison, his father is alleged to have replied: 'Why should I do that? He has betrayed his country and his people and deserves no help from me.'

† An archetypal Englishman with a touch of the villain when needed, born in St Petersburg in 1906. Perhaps his finest role is as Major Quive-Smith, Walter Pidgeon's Nazi tormentor, in Fritz Lang's film *Man Hunt* (1941).

English man-about-town type who could turn in a sardonic, politely sadistic foreign villain if required. The two exchange courtesies, reminiscing about their student days in Heidelberg or Oxford, or some London club they frequented before the war, then Howard/Haushofer is taken away, to be 'interrogated', tortured and finally conveyed to the prison at Moabit, Berlin, where he will wait almost a year to die, all the while composing a series of carefully crafted sonnets reflecting on his imprisonment, his life and a philosophy that, at a time when his sense of home has been stripped from him, becomes a new vision of dwelling in which the lost *Heimat* is replaced, imaginatively, by the hum of the cosmos itself.

I visited Moabit prison on a warm summer's day in 2015. By then, only part of the old Prussian gaol remained, and that had become a kind of glorified remand centre, with a constantly shifting population of men waiting to be moved elsewhere, or possibly released, depending on the vagaries of the judicial process. Some of the prisoners I met there would remain at Moabit for a few days, or a couple of weeks at most; others would stay for months, trapped in some bend in the system, waiting vainly for news; one or two would be discharged the next morning. As the room settled (I had got through the many gates and doors on the pretext of giving a talk on 'the writer's craft'), I took a good look around. A few betrayed signs of the first-timer's dismay that I had seen in prisons before, and I felt for these feckless creatures who, over the last few days, or possibly the last couple of hours, had begun to understand that careless acts – often performed in a blur of alcohol or drugs – could have truly dire consequences. I did my best not to remember my own more feckless days (I had no wish to succumb to some 'there but for the grace of' cycle of thinking) and I hoped, quite sincerely, that the newcomers would keep up their façade and bluff it out till somebody else came to take their places. There are few things the state does that are crueller than

incarcerating a scrawny first-time offender in a prison full of seasoned veterans and I wonder that any government calling itself
'civilised' still permits it.

By the time I had made my way into the heart of the prison
facility, I could see that the Moabit of today was very different
from the brutal Nazi gaol of the 1940s. As the guard who had
showed me around earlier had dutifully explained, a large part of
the building had been demolished after the war. Now, the cells,
though still spartan, were more comfortably appointed than in
Haushofer's time, and other features – recreation areas, and a
small but pleasant garden – set the facility much in line with other
prisons. The guillotine chamber, recorded in footage made during
the Nazi era, was long gone (it was, in fact, destroyed during an
Allied air attack in 1943), and if it was still there, my brief tour
did not include the wide, frighteningly clinical room, fitted with
a reinforced hinged beam, where the condemned appear to have
been hanged on loops of tensile wire. Even during the 1940s, most
executions had taken place not in Moabit but at the neighbouring
and even more brutal gaol at Plötzensee, where several leading
members of the German Resistance were put to death, by guillotine if they were lucky (until the mid-1930s beheadings had
still been carried out in the open yard, using an axe). Today the
warders are serious, by the book, but (as far as my limited experience allows me to conclude) well intentioned towards the visiting writers' scheme of which I am a part. They do not provoke
compassion, or pity; they are men doing a job of work in a highly
professional manner. Haushofer's warders, however, were different: 'good chaps' ('brave Burschen') of farming blood, torn from
the relative security of their home villages to serve a regime that
they neither supported nor understood. We should remember,
here, that by the time Haushofer got to meet these men, the war
had been going badly for some time and the ordinary guards, with
none of the power, experience or ruthlessness of the stereotypi-
cal SS/Gestapo-type Nazi, would soon be left painfully exposed
and vulnerable when the regime finally collapsed. Yet, in spite of
the fact that they are his gaolers, Haushofer's compassion for the

guards is genuine: young men from areas that had been devastated by war, they too have acquired a tragic sense of *Heimat* and of the terrible fate that has transformed them, like their charges, into prisoners, waiting for the Russians to come down upon them, as Byron puts it, 'like the wolf on the fold'. Already aware of what is to come, the political sophisticate Haushofer knows that they are suffering this fate for no other reason than that, in a desperate time, they had fallen into the hands of a demagogue – and he wonders when they will awaken and see what has been done to them. Tomorrow? Some time later? Never? By means of this train of argument, he almost reverses the position: as things stand, both he and his captors may be prisoners, but he, at least, understands the process that has brought them both to disaster.

Considering the circumstances in which they were written, it would be foolish, and unfair, to expect all of the poems in the posthumously published *Moabit Sonnets* to be of a consistently high standard. What is surprising, however, is how powerful many of these sonnets are. The human and intellectual qualities of this man – his sense of humour, his wit, his philosophical depth, his sense of *Heimat* and of history – come across in poem after poem, and if he sometimes appears to lapse into something close to sentimentality, that should come as no surprise. Several of the poems are deeply personal, yet Haushofer makes them accessible to a general reader, time and again, by transforming himself – the speaker, the actual prisoner in his dismal Moabit cell – into a kind of Everyman. Take the twenty-fifth sonnet, 'Honig' ('Honey'). The surface is simple, but this is a delicate, poignant poem that, even if it does flirt with sentimentality, gets away with it rather elegantly, simply by keeping the verse spare and honest. It begins:

> When I was driven from my native land,
> All I had left to get me through the journey
> Was something I'd saved for later – a jar of honey!
> If nothing else, that much of home remained.

Nachdem sie aus der Heimat mich getrieben
auf meiner langen Flucht und bittren Fahrt
ein Glas mit Honig hab ich mir gespart –
so viel an Heimat ist mir nun geblieben.

Though it has been suggested that he enjoyed some minor privileges that other prisoners were not permitted, none of my researches into Haushofer's life at Moabit confirms the existence of this jar of honey. I suspect it was a product of his imagination, an imaginary device that, in its compact form, contained everything he needed to bring his home-place to mind:

I open it, now and then, for the stored bouquet
Of a thousand blossoms, yes, from a thousand trees,
And bees spill, like a multicoloured breeze
To light this world of grey, and grey on grey.

Ich öffne's nur: dann steigt ein Duft empor
von tausend Blüten, ja von tausend Bäumen,
und Bienen summen wie aus bunten Träumen
aus allen grauen Ecken rings hervor.

The interior of Moabit is grey, yes, and the land outside would have ben cold and still under a Prussian winter, from the dark alleys around the prison itself to the darker, leafless woods at Tegel – and that vision would have stood in sharp contrast to the gold of the Bavarian *Heimat*, with its lush woods and orchards, where Haushofer had been so happy as a child. In the endless summer of that remembered childhood, the Hausbergen (the Home Mountains) would have been clearly visible from the centre of Munich, and even in the city a warm breeze from the south would have come streaming through the Englische Garten, where every tree and shrub would have been animate with birdsong. Now, however, all across Germany, it is winter, both meteorological and metaphorical, the entire land dead and silent, as if to echo David Gascoyne's prophetic 'Snow in Europe', composed at Christmastime, in 1938, just months after the appeasement at Munich. Offering a bitterly ironic response to Neville Chamberlain's infamous 'peace with honour' speech, in which Chamberlain advised his listeners 'to go home and sleep quietly in your beds', Gascoyne's poem creates a hushed, inert landscape in which the 'dense dreams' of all of Europe and the 'glimpsed flash / Of a new golden era' are instantaneously erased by the 'white weight that fell last night / And made their continent a blank'. Then, having established that deadly white landscape, in which

> The Ural and Jura now rejoin
> The furthest Arctic's desolation. All is one;
> Sheer monotone: plain, mountain; country, town

Gascoyne continues:

> The warring flags hang colourless a while;
> Now midnight's icy zero feigns a truce
> Between the signs and seasons, and fades out
> All shots and cries. But when the great thaw comes,
> How red shall be the melting snow, how loud the drums![2]

It is unlikely that Haushofer knew this poem, yet it is not surprising that he, like Gascoyne, chose to compare the spread of totalitarianism across Europe with the imagery of a cold, deathly winter that, perhaps for both, had its generative seed in Byron's dream poem 'Darkness', an extraordinarily modern work that pictures the world as a frozen wasteland where 'the icy earth / Swung blind and blackening in the moonless air'. Now, for Haushofer, it appears that a new season is coming, a long-awaited thaw that will finally bring an end to the freeze that has held Europe in its icy grip for seven years. But that thaw has not yet arrived and, all too aware of the fate that he and his fellow conspirators had suffered for misjudging the pace of history, Haushofer warns the bees – the harbingers of that coming summer, who transform its flowers, not just into honey but also into hope – not to leave the hive until it is safe:

It's winter, still, across the open fields,
You bees, be careful not to swarm too soon
Let the sun have time to warm your fur!

You will not find the hope that honey yields
until the plums are decked in red and white,
and cowslips sparkle in the morning light.

Es ist noch Winter in der weiten Flur:
Ihr Bienen, hütet euch vor frühem Schwärmen
Laßt euch die Sonne noch die Pelze wärmen!

Ihr sammelt süßes Heil im Honig nur,
Wenn rötlich-weiß die Pflaumenäste blühn,
und goldne Primeln leuchten auf im Grün.

The most moving of the poems collected in the *Moabit Sonnets*, however, is 'Heimat' (XXIII in the series), which begins by addressing the obvious question of why Haushofer did not immediately flee Germany after the failed coup, escaping, perhaps to Switzerland, when he had the chance. His stark answer is:

I did not wish to leave my homeland.

Ich wollte nicht aus meiner Heimat gehn.

The poem then goes on to illumine the deep emotional and spiritual power of *Heimat* that we touched on earlier. As has been noted, the subject is historically complex and, because of Nazism, has become for many a compromised ideal, but it was surely a key factor in the response of many German citizens to the Nazi regime who, like Haushofer, remained at home in order to resist, or at the very least, try to reduce the impact of the dangerous and highly destructive regime that had stolen their country. After all, does it matter if the tyrant is an outsider, come from abroad, or one of your own? Do such questions make a difference when it comes to resistance? Those who had left Germany by then did so because, as Jews or known communists, or as 'decadent' artists or scientists for whom the writing was already on the wall, they would have been insane to stay. For many, however, the position was not so clear. After expressing his devotion to his home, Haushofer relates, in the most matter-of-fact manner, how he went from relative protection ('Schutz') to being hunted down in earnest. There is regret here, of course. What comes through, however, is a sense that, given the options, the outcome was probably inevitable.

In retrospect, it should come as no surprise that Haushofer would feel that it had been a dangerous thing to be permitted hope. His mother was of Jewish origin, which meant that he and his brother, Heinz, were classed as *Mischlinge* ('people of mixed race'), and thus potentially subject to deportation. They had believed they could trust Hess, effectively second-in-command to Hitler until his disastrous mission to Britain in 1941. Even as war approached, Haushofer wrote to his mother at home on the family estate that he refused to leave 'this limping ship which is already on fire at several points and is largely run and steered by criminals and fools'. What kept him in Germany, first as a measured voice of reasoned opposition to Hitler's wilder policies and, later, as a conspirator with other leading intellectuals and military men implicated in a series of failed attempts to oust or kill the Führer, was what would have seemed to him a sacred duty, the duty to *Heimat*.

Yet this is not the real achievement of Sonnet XXIII. What lifts this poem into the higher level of a great European tradition is its sestet, where, after stating, simply and without self-pity, that he is unlikely ever to see his home again ('ich werde lebend kaum sie wiedersehn'), Haushofer closes the piece with a hymn to the continuing life of his *Land*, a life from which he himself will be excluded:

> Yet it remains a consolation, to know
> that the mountains above the farms and the high pasture
> remain,

even though I will no longer see them.

That those silver-grey walls will still be there,
whether humankind climbs the peaks or flees them,
until some new ice age circles the high cliffs.

Doch bleibt es tröstlich, ihrer Berge Mauern
im Hintergrund von Alm und Hof zu wissen,
muß ich auch selbst den Gipfelhauch vermissen.

Die silbergrauen Wände werden dauern,
ob sie der Mensch durchklettert oder flieht,
bis neues Eis die Felsen rings umzieht.

I am reminded, here, of a poem by Juan Ramón Jiménez, 'El viaje definitivo' ('The Definitive Journey'), where, under very different circumstances, a poet sits in his garden, reflecting on the fact that, one day, he will no longer be there:

And I will go. And the birds will go on
singing.
And my garden will remain, with its green tree
and its white well.

Y yo me iré. Y se quedarán los pájaros
cantando.
Y se quedará mi huerto con su verde árbol,
y con su pozo blanco.[3]

The speaker will be gone from this everyday idyll – dead and gone, in fact – but the simple, almost Arcadian, garden will continue, the afternoons will remain calm and blue, the bells will ring in the nearby campanile. Everyone the speaker loves will die, and the village will renew itself far into the future with new people, whom the speaker does not know, living new lives that are, in essence, the same as the life he had. And through it all, persisting, the 'secret corner' of his garden will flower and his whitewashed well will reflect the sunlight.

And I will be gone, and I will be another, without a place,
  without
a green tree, or a while well,
without a sky, calm and blue.
And the birds will go on singing.

Y yo me iré, y seré otro, sin hogar, sin árbol
verde, sin pozo blanco,
sin cielo azul y plácido…
Y se quedarán los pájaros cantando.

There is regret here, without doubt, for what will be lost, just
as there is regret in the Haushofer sonnet. Yet there is also a sense
of stoical celebration, a hymn to the continuity of life that, even
as it persists, does not include the celebrant. It is a theme found
often in European poetry, especially in the Spanish tradition, and
it marks, for me, one of the great virtues of the educated heart.
It cannot be summed up, quite – the most we can say about it is
that it accepts and celebrates not its own mortality so much as
the continuity of life in others. Or, to say it differently, Jean-Paul
Sartre notwithstanding, it is the generosity of spirit that sees in *les
autres* not Hell but something akin to eternal life.

As a historical document, the *Moabit Sonnets* still holds considerable value, comparable with the writings of Dietrich Bonhoeffer
or, in another historical context, the prison letters of Rosa Lux-
emburg. Perhaps what is most rewarding about the collection,
however, is the way in which its author moves, first, from a local,
regional sense of home (that is, of *Heimat*, in its old sense) to something larger, as that original gift of belonging is taken from him.
Just as the speakers of 'El viaje definitivo' and of 'Sonnet XXIII'
find solace in the fact of mortality by imagining a temporal continuum that they may not altogether share but from which they
are not wholly excluded, so the prisoner deprived of his homeland
must reach beyond his immediate surroundings to recover a sense

of belonging. So it is that, in one sonnet in particular (no. LXIX, 'Kosmos') Haushofer imagines that greater home in the cosmos itself. Deprived of his liberty, with the traditional values of his homeland rendered toxic by Nazi propaganda,* Haushofer had no other recourse but to look up, and out, to whatever place he could find in deep space. If nowhere else, he would make a home of the earth itself. To begin with, he roots this vision in the history of astronomical speculation, moving from hints of 'the music of the spheres' to early modern science:

> Whether in sounds that appear to arise freely,
> the nature of this world is revealed in Kepler's laws,
> it is inevitable that this world is suffused
> by the mysterious harmony of number.

> Ob sich in Klängen wie zu freier Wahl,
> im Keplerschen Gesetz ihr Sinn enthüllt,
> es muß wohl sein, daß diese Welt erfüllt
> geheimnisvolle Harmonie der Zahl.

The rough translation does not fully convey the elegance of the idea, in which order not only appears as an inevitability but is also universal; as Kepler showed, in his *De Harmonice mundi* of 1619, the natural system of order that governs the relationships and movement of heavenly bodies is founded on the same mathematical principles as the order that makes music pleasing to the ear (hence 'the music of the spheres'). This common order is everywhere, if only we can find it (a quest embodied in the more recent concept of the Unified Field). It can be observed not only in the vastness of space but also in the fine detail, the small print, so to speak, of physical matter:

---

* By now Haushofer is painfully aware of how easy it is to confound an innocent concept like *Heimat* with such ugly nonsense as *Blut und Boden*: i.e., 'Blood and Soil', the old nationalist ideal of racial purity that informed Nazi *Neues Volk* Aryanism.

In the calculable play of every beam and vibration
all matter is incorporated, then released once more,
and all forms come into being as essential links
in a [single] World-Law, with a single purpose.

In Strahl und Schwingung zu gemessnem Spiel
umwebt sich aller Stoff und löst sich wieder,
und alle Formen sind gewollte Glieder
in einem Weltgesetz, von einem Ziel.

So ends the octet, with an affirmation of unity and order in the given world, a vision of 'world law' (*Weltgesetz*) with which to counter the temptation to see the cosmos as a theatre of futility and random noise – a temptation that would have come easily to one for whom everything he had ever loved and trusted was foundering. We see that, so far, this vision of order is based on accepted scientific principles, from Kepler to recent discoveries in the nature of matter itself. From here on, however, Haushofer alters the angle of perspective, to create, if only for himself, a significant paradigm shift. Here what we normally think of – and keep separate – as 'science' on the one hand and 'poetry' on the other merges into the making of a new vision of what Haushofer calls *Weltenton*, a term that, while not identical with it, is not very far from the notion of the music of what happens, or the song of the earth.

Such shifts of perspective, whether individual or public, are not always given their full due. For example, it is easy to underestimate the impact of the famous photograph of the earth taken by the crew of *Apollo 17* on 7 December 1972, an image that allowed human beings to see their planet in its entirety, floating in space like 'a blue marble'. Suddenly, our sense of cosmic dimensions was altered, as the entire earth, and by extension all that lay beyond, become more intimate, somehow, more like home. It had not always seemed thus. Wallace Stevens, for example, felt keenly the separation between the human mind and our home planet, and the resultant sense of alienation, even dread, that such a separation can bring:

I thought on the train how utterly we have forsaken the Earth, in the sense of excluding it from our thoughts. There are but few who consider its physical hugeness, its rough enormity. It is still a disparate monstrosity, full of solitudes & barrens & wilds. It still dwarfs & terrifies & crushes. The rivers still roar, the mountains still crash, the winds still shatter. Man is an affair of cities. His gardens & orchards & fields are mere scrapings. Somehow, however, he has managed to shut out the face of the giant from his windows. But the giant is there, nevertheless.

In extremis, however, using such imaginative material as is to hand, but never sacrificing or glossing over the immensity and mystery of what surrounds him, Haushofer invokes a music that is both beyond our understanding and autonomous in its perfection:

We hardly know the smallest part of it:
Order is wonder, number is the world's music.

Wir kennen kaum den kleinsten Teil davon:
Gesetz ist Wunder, Zahl ist Weltenton.

Weltenton. The 'world tone'. To say it so plainly is to risk missing this poet's hard-won sense of celebration, a view of unfolding time and space offered up by a condemned man, in which noise is trumped by an inaudible harmony. At this stage of his life Haushofer invokes not 'the cuckoo calling from the tree that is highest in the hedge' or 'the ring of a spear on a shield', 'the belling of a stag across water', 'the song of a lark' or 'the laugh of a gleeful girl', but something that runs beneath them all, as the very source of their harmony. *Weltenton.* The hum of origin. *Das Lied von der Erde.* The music of what happens.

For the sake of poems like Sonnet LXIX, and many others, the preservation of the *Moabit Sonnets* is a piece of extraordinary good luck – but it almost did not happen. Indeed, it took a series of apparently random and far from fortunate events to bring the manuscript, first, to the light of day and, second, to publication. The first of these 'lucky' accidents was the arrest of Albrecht's brother, Heinz, who was also brought to Moabit after the failed 20 July 1944 plot to end Hitler's rule. Considered a smaller fish, he was held for eight months, then released. Meanwhile, with the Russians closing on Berlin, many of the more serious political offenders were being 'terminated' (without trial, or even stated charges) in a number of prisons across Germany, including Plötzensee. However, as we know, the facilities for executing inmates at Moabit had been damaged and, in what could have been seen as cause for hope, a group of around sixteen inmates, including Albrecht Haushofer, were officially released on 22 April 1945 – only to be handed over to a gang of SS men, who marched them unceremoniously to a patch of waste land near by and shot each of them twice in the back of the neck. That pointless act of cruelty might have signalled the end for Haushofer's clandestine poetry collection, but, having survived the Russian bombardment and the collapse of the prison system, Heinz made his way to the former exhibition grounds near the prison, where, on 12 May 1945, he found his brother among a pile of bodies, face down on the cold earth, his right hand clutching the pencilled manuscript to his heart.

I remember being told, as a child, that if you shine a torch beam up into the night sky, the light travels on for ever, to the very edge of the universe. And so it was, I guessed, with sound. Everything – all the music of what happens – travels out from the surface of the earth into farthest space. I have never been entirely sure that this is true (wouldn't the sound waves decay, eventually?) but I would like to think it is. I would like to think that everything, every murmur, every cry, every dawn chorus, becomes part of the cosmic soundtrack. I have no idea why, but I find solace in this idea, not because it suggests an afterlife, which I have never found very appealing, but because it speaks of continuum. Today the site where Haushofer's body was abandoned is a city park, designed by Berlin-based architects Glaßer und Dagenbach, who describe the project on their website as:

> a combination of people's park and a memorial developed with elements of Land Art and Minimal Art. A 5m high prison wall, which remained intact, encloses the park on three sides. A passage from the 'Moabit Sonnets' is inscribed in large letters on one of the walls. Variously designed entrances are sculpted with sandblasted concrete walls. Inside the park the star-shaped layout of the prison building is recreated by sunken or elevated lawn levels and hedgerows. In a reconstructed cell in its original dimensions a recording of Albrecht Haushofer 'Moabit Sonnets', written during his incarceration in 1944–45, is played.

It seems fitting that Haushofer's memorial should take the form of a sound installation, his words broadcast into the air around the prison where he waited so long to die, and from there out and away into the cosmos, one of the many murmurs that make up the Weltenton.

LA RAZÓN POÉTICA

Mans soul consisteth of a mind, reason and imagination; the mind illuminates reason, reason floweth into the imagination: All is one soul. Reason, unless it be illuminated by the mind, is not free from errour.

Heinrich Cornelius Agrippa

MY FIRST YEAR OF COLLEGE was a miserable time. I had no money, I didn't like the people in my classes (my fault, not theirs) and I didn't like lectures, which I dodged whenever I could. A lonely teenager whose only refuge was books, I had devoured – and formed sometimes highly idiosyncratic views about – many of the set texts already; completely lacking in any of the social graces and disdainful of the various clubs and societies on offer, I spent most of my time wandering the backstreets of Cambridge with my old Voigtländer camera, taking pictures of graveyards and bridges. I was bored, broke and randomly defiant for no good reason – and I was seriously thinking about giving up and getting a job in the wrecking business. (After a few too many beers, a demolition contractor I'd met in a pub off East Road had offered me a job and, naïvely, I had thought he was serious.)

Then, one day, while wandering the streets around Mill Road, I found an old-fashioned barber's shop, like the one my mother used to take me to when I was a boy. I had enough money for a haircut, so I went inside. The shop was unremarkable, very neat and clean, with all the usual fittings; the barber, who looked to be around sixty, was softly spoken and well groomed with short, grey hair and, as he put down the book he had been reading and stood up to greet me, I was struck by how genuinely self-contained he was, self-contained and assured, a man at peace with himself, with the confidence to be visibly *gentle* that most men lack. It was a strange sort of gentleness, however, a kind of willed restraint – or so it seemed to me – and, as I sat in front of the mirror and looked at myself for the first time in days (I didn't have a mirror in the caravan I was renting), I began to feel oddly removed from my usual day-to-day existence, as if, on entering this quiet, old-fashioned barber's shop, I had stepped back in time, or perhaps out of time, and into another space altogether.

Not that the barber said or did anything out of the ordinary. He asked me how I would like my hair cut, nodded a couple of times while I explained that I had let it grow longer than usual and that I generally kept it much shorter. Then he went to work. He didn't ask the usual barbershop questions about whether I had seen the game on Saturday, or where I was going for my summer holidays; he mostly just cut my hair. Once, he enquired about my studies, and when I told him that I was doing literature and that I was mostly reading poetry, he fell silent again. When he was finished, I looked in the mirror – and it seemed to me that he had somehow transformed me, taking me back in time to the old, short-back-and-sides days, when men wore hats and coats and called each other by their surnames. I nodded to show that I was happy, then asked how much I owed him. He told me the price and stepped away, presumably for privacy's sake; I fished out the right amount, then added 10 per cent for the tip, as I had been told to do by my father. I would have given more, if I could have afforded it, for, whatever he had done to me, this strange barber really had worked some kind of transformation – and, once again, I felt as if I had entered another world, just by crossing the threshold of his small domain. I glanced one last time at my face in the mirror, then handed him the money. 'Thank you,' I said. 'This feels great.'

He nodded, then looked at the money. 'You've given me too much,' he said.

'Oh, no,' I said. 'That's fine.'

I felt embarrassed and wondered if I'd committed some mysterious *faux pas*. I'd become uncertain of so many things, socially, living among people who were so different from me. Confident, middle-class people, full of arcane knowledge about which spoon to use and what to say when being introduced to strangers. People who were made to feel entitled, rather than menaced, by the social sphere.

He counted out the right money and handed back the rest. 'It's kind of you,' he said. 'But I told you my price when you came in, and it's still the same now.'

I didn't know how to respond to this. Some part of me wanted to be offended, but I couldn't quite manage it. 'Sorry,' I said. 'I thought …'

He shook his head. 'Don't be sorry,' he said. He glanced up at the clock above the till. 'I'll tell you what. If you have a minute or two, I'd like to show you something.'

I had nowhere to be – nowhere I wanted to be, anyhow – but I glanced at the clock too before answering. 'I've got a few minutes,' I said magnanimously.

He nodded gravely; then he led me through to the back of the shop, which turned out to be a small dining room, with a table by one wall and an old sideboard by the window. I guessed that this was where he ate his lunch, or took tea when the shop wasn't busy. Just beyond this room I could see a tiny kitchen, with a kettle on a hob and a plate rack. He walked over to the low sideboard, which was covered with photographs, all of them black and white, in cheap wooden or gilt frames. The pictures were old; they showed men and women in what looked like work clothes; in some, they were smiling, looking out at the camera and squinting against the bright sun; in others, they were drinking from thick tumblers or enamel cups, talking and laughing, engaged in something larger than themselves. To be honest, I don't remember much of the detail. They were mostly young, and they were defiantly cheerful – and the moment I looked at them, I knew that at least some of them were dead. I don't know how I knew this, but I did. The barber pointed to a man in one of the photographs. He was shorter than his companions, with very dark eyes and a full, sensuous mouth.

'*He* was a poet,' the barber said.

'Really?' I was intrigued now. 'What was his name?'

The barber laughed softly.

'Federico,' he said. 'Like Lorca. But he wasn't famous.' He looked away. 'He never published anything.'

'Ah.'

I nodded gravely and studied the failed poet's face. He had what my mother would have called a devilish smile, the smile of a man who knew who he was and had decided, in spite of his faults, not to find himself wanting. Beside him, a taller, fair-complexioned man was looking away and off to the right, presumably distracted by something he had seen in the distance, or perhaps he was just demonstrating his refusal to pose for the camera. In the background the landscape seemed uniformly bright, and slightly faded, as in a holiday snap. I remembered my cousin Donna, who had worked on a kibbutz; these snapshots reminded me of hers.

'He died in Bilbao, in 1937,' he said.

I was taken aback. 'I'm sorry?'

The barber looked at me.

'In Spain,' he said. He pointed to another of the men in the photograph. 'That was me,' he said.

I studied the face. His use of the past tense hadn't gone unnoticed and, because there was no resemblance between the man in the picture and the man standing beside me, I waited, expecting some elaboration as to what had changed him so dramatically. None came, though, and after a long pause, I nodded, as if in agreement with some abstruse lie.

The barber laughed. 'It's all right,' he said. 'I've changed a lot since then.'

I looked at him – and it was true, in every describable feature, he had changed, but I saw something in his eyes, now, that I hadn't seen before – and, looking back to the photograph, I saw the same quality in the young man gazing out at me. It wasn't something I could have described then, but I remembered that face years later when, reading Rafael Alberti's poem 'Balada de lo que el viento dijo' ('The Ballad of What the Wind Said'), I came to these lines in the second stanza:

As for the man who distances
Himself from men, the wind comes
Telling him other things now
Opening his ears
And eyes to other things.

Today, I distanced myself from men,
And alone, in this gully,
I began to gaze at the river,
And saw a horse all alone,
And listened all lonely
To the cooing
Of a lost dove.

And the wind came close,
Like someone passing by,
And told me:
Eternity may well
Be only a river
Be a forgotten horse
And the cooing
Of a lost dove.

En cuanto el hombre se aleja
de los hombres, viene el viento
que ya le dice otras cosas,
abriéndole los oídos
y los ojos a otras cosas.

Hoy me alejé de los hombres,

y solo, en esta barranca,
me puse a mirar el río
y vi tan sólo un caballo
y escuché tan solamente
el zureo
de una paloma perdida.

Y el viento se acercó entonces,
como quien va de pasada,
y me dijo:
La eternidad bien pudiera
ser un río solamente,
ser un caballo olvidado
y el zureo
de una paloma perdida.[1]

I don't want to suggest here that this encounter was some kind of epiphany. True, I did go to the library that same afternoon, where I found a handful of books on the history and the literature of the Spanish Civil War, and from that I found my way into the poetry of Alberti, and to an observation made by Stephen Spender which stayed with me for years:

> Poets and poetry have played a considerable part in the Spanish War, because to many people the struggle of the Republicans has seemed a struggle for the conditions without which the writing and reading of poetry are almost impossible in modern society.

This seemed to me to be as good a working definition of what poetry means in a social context as it was possible to formulate: a just society would be one in which the conditions for writing and reading poetry are favourable – and it didn't take long to spot that the Republic had all the best writers. But then, didn't the fascists also have their poets? Presumably, there were some who found the conditions under Franco conducive to the writing and reading of poetry. History isn't short on 'great' writers and artists whose political affinities or social prejudices were quite frankly deplorable, and many of the more liberal-minded had been sadly irresolute in the face of evil actions. I had rehearsed all these arguments before, either alone or with others, like myself, whose love for their chosen art form was matched only by a burning desire for obvious – that is, visible and verifiable – justice, but those conversations had always gone badly. Few people have Spender's insight, or it may just be that most lack his confidence, but it is an intriguing idea nonetheless to suggest that, if the Civil War was a struggle to retain the conditions that best supported the writing and reading of poetry, then the presence of poetry is a clear sign of a just society, a kind of indicator species, if you will, for a healthy communal ecology.

Still, on that particular day, in that small room behind the barber's shop, my instinctive feeling that there was, or might be, a 'good' and a 'bad' to all this was extenuated by something the barber said to me when we were parting. We had talked for a while, awkwardly at first and then quite naturally, as I relaxed into listening and he into remembering stories about his time in Spain – the friends he had made, the people he had lost, the sense of betrayal and disgust that he had felt when the Republic was betrayed, not just by its enemies but by those who had claimed to be defending it. Finally, the door of the shop opened and somebody came in.

The barber frowned and laid his hand on my arm. 'Back to work,' he said.

I nodded.

'Thank you,' he said.

I wanted to thank him, even though at that moment I didn't really know what he had given me. A sense of history? Some personal anecdotes about war and friendship? Yes, but it was more than that. I felt that I had been armed in some way, made ready for something. He waited a moment, giving me space to say whatever I wanted to say, then he smiled and patted my arm again. 'El analfabetismo ciega el espíritu,' he said. 'Soldado instrúyete.'

I shook my head. I had some knowledge of Spanish, but he'd

spoken suddenly and out of context, and before I could say anything more he led me through the shop and opened the outer door. Behind him, a man in a flat cap was sitting in the barber's chair, where I had sat before. The barber nodded to him and said something in a language that I didn't understand. The man shook his head and waved vaguely. He was easily eighty years old, or he looked it anyway. As I stepped out into the fresh spring air, the barber turned back to me. 'Instrúyete!' he said again, and it took me a moment, but I finally understood what he had been saying, just as he closed the door. *Illiteracy blinds the spirit*, he had said. *Educate yourself, soldier.** He hadn't been talking literally about the inability to read, however; he was referring to my political illiteracy and to that of the wider world – but it took me decades to appreciate, in full, how important the Spanish Republic was, as fact and idea, or how grievous had been its loss.

The Spanish Civil War lasted from 1936 to 1939, and though we remain aware of atrocities such as Guernica, and individual tragedies such as the murder of Federico García Lorca by Falangists at the very beginning of the conflict, we have been too ready to forget that Franco's army of career fascists and hired mercenaries, acting with the sometimes tangible support of most of Europe, demolished what was arguably the richest – and most democratic – artistic culture to emerge anywhere in Europe in many years. Too often we see only part of the overall history: my barber friend, for example, could have offered a heartfelt elegy for the anarchists who were killed and imprisoned, and in *Homage to Catalonia* George Orwell catalogues the slow undermining of a legitimately elected government not only by home-grown fascists but by the entire European political community. (The Vatican played a particularly shameful role, both in Spain and in the spread of fascism across Europe that followed.) Anyone who reads poetry

---

* Later I traced the quotation to an old propaganda poster by the artist Vicente Vila Gimeno, aka Wila.

will have been moved by the prison poems of Miguel Hernández, the 'peasant poet' who, lacking the resources to escape the debacle of the fascist victory, died of tuberculosis in 1942, having written some of the bleakest prison poems in modern history:

> There is no space. Laughter has capsized.
> It is no longer possible to reach for the heights.
> The heart wants to beat faster
> to force open the strict blackness.

> Falta el espacio. Se ha hundido la risa.
> Ya no es posible lanzarse a la altura.
> El corazón quiere ser más de prisa
> fuerza que ensancha la estrecha negrura.[2]

It could be argued that no one expressed more fully the pain of captivity at the hands of a brutal and unworthy enemy; certainly, there have been few who were so valiant in transcending that captivity, to write lines of pure defiance and affirmation:

> If I die, let me die
> with my head held high.
> Dead and twenty times dead,
> [...]
> Singing I await my death,
> for there are nightingales that sing
> in the midst of the artillery
> and in the heat of battle.

> Si me muero, que me muera
> con la cabeza muy alta.
> Muerto y veinte veces muerto,
> [...]
> Cantando espero a la muerte,
> que hay ruiseñores que cantan
> encima de los fusiles
> y en medio de las batallas.[3]

The 1920s and early '30s in Spain saw a flowering not only of the country's first truly democratic government but also of all the arts, both 'high' and 'popular' (and, as is frequent in a truly open society, it experienced a salutary blurring of such terms). Though it would be wrong to place that culture on a pedestal, it is hard not to regard the period from around 1920 to 1936 (the era of the so-called 'Generation of '27') without recalling Wordsworth's assessment of the first years of the French Revolution:

> Bliss was it in that dawn to be alive,
> But to be young was very heaven! – Oh! times,
> In which the meagre, stale, forbidding ways
> Of custom, law, and statute, took at once
> The attraction of a country in Romance!
> When Reason seemed the most to assert her rights,
> When most intent on making of herself
> A prime Enchantress – to assist the work
> Which then was going forward in her name!

It was Jorge Guillén who first identified that sixteen-year period as the flowering of a vital Republican poetry, naming Federico García Lorca, Dámaso Alonso, Vicente Aleixandre, Pedro Salinas, Gerardo Diego, Emilio Prados, Luis Cernuda, Rafael Alberti, Manuel Altolaguirre and himself as the principal actors, before appending a list of only slightly less venerated literary figures, including one woman (Ernestina de Champourcín, of whom more below). However, this 'Generation' was not so much a movement as a loosely knit group of individuals with shared artistic interests and a mutual preoccupation with what Guillén calls 'love, nature, life, death' (though he notes that they rarely addressed 'religion' in their output). Working 'without any dogmatic restrictions set by a school', these poets were to pursue 'a poetry that would be both art with all the severity of art and creation with all of its genuine élan. An art of poetry and therefore no mere effusion, neither in the manner of the last century nor as a violent, formless surge from the subconscious.' The group was as suspicious of 'empty formalism' as it was of the Surrealists, who had come to dominate French poetry. ('There is no babble quite so empty as that of the subconscious left to its triviality', Guillén remarked.) What they wanted was an art that engaged with *this* world – that is, with a sometimes dark celebration of the dailiness of life that required of them only that they should 'never dispense with the springs from which lyric poetry flows by eliminating the heart'.

This last remark was made as response to the charge, strange as it will seem to anyone reading the Generation of '27 poets today, that Guillén and his colleagues were too abstract, too difficult and too 'intellectual' (not the only time such a charge has been laid at the door of great poetry by careless or lazy readers). In fact, nothing could have been further from the truth. Nevertheless, even as he writes, some twenty-five years after the Spanish Civil War ended, Guillén still feels the need to clarify what his generation meant by 'poetry as an art of poetry [...] this marriage of idea and music':

> 'Idea' here means reality in a state of feeling. Reality is depicted in the poem, but not described in its external likeness. Reality, not realism. And feeling, without which there is no poetry, has no need of gesticulation. Sentiment, not sentimentalism, which was as damned by that group as the lowest of obscenities. This restraint in the displaying of emotions retains their vehemence, and indeed doubles their intensity. But for ears that hear not, harmonies such as these are almost confused with silence. That is why some of these poets were tried and found wanting for their coldness, even though they were dedicated to declaring their enthusiasm for the world, their fervor for life, their love for love.[4]

The truth is that the poets of the Generation of '27 were as far from eliminating the heart as it was possible to be, but they were so vigilant in their avoidance of *efectismo* ('sensationalism, theatricality') and so committed to the part played by *maestría*, or 'artistic mastery', in containing a deeply felt art that some mistook their restraint for coolness. This may well seem strange to us now, for it is difficult to imagine any reader missing the contained emotion and the palpable urgency of a poem such as Lorca's 'Despedida' ('Farewell'), a work of exemplary economy that draws not on that variety of epiphanic theatricality we find in Ungaretti's 'Mattina' but upon the everyday world that continues, and is affirmed, beyond the speaker's death:

If I die
Leave the balcony open

The boy is eating oranges
(From my balcony I see him)

The reaper is cutting the wheat
(From my balcony I hear him)

If I die
Leave the balcony open

Si muero
Dejad el balcón abierto

El niño come naranjas
(Desde mi balcón lo veo)

El segador siega el trigo
(Desde mi balcón lo siento)

Si muero
Dejad el balcón abierto.[5]

Sadly, Lorca would not be allowed to die in his own bed, with the balcony giving on to a simple scene of everyday life; instead he was murdered by a band of Falangists in the summer of 1936, his body abandoned, according to recent evidence, on a patch of farmland between the villages of Viznar and Alfacar.* Three

---

* It has been suggested by Miguel Caballero Pérez and others that Lorca was targeted as part of a local power play between his clan and the closely related

years later the Generation of '27, and with them the coherence of Republican culture, had been dispersed. Remembering his colleagues, Guillén would close his Charles Eliot Norton Lectures in 1958 with a moving elegy for all that had been lost:

> We shall never know how long that community of friends might have remained intact, had not a catastrophe given it the sudden ending of a drama or a tragedy. Tragedy beyond question was the assassination of Federico García Lorca, a child of genius beyond question. It was a tragedy with its traitors, its blood guilt, and its chorus: all of Spain, the whole world [...] The gatherings in Madrid ended in that fatal year of the Civil War, ominous prelude to the Second World War. But this could not be called a 'lost generation'; in spite of so many vicissitudes, these poets have gone on with their work [...] Some day it will be possible to evaluate correctly the influence of exile on these men of *la España peregrine* – wandering, and so pilgrim, Spain. Meanwhile Spain, greater than all these crises, remains standing, and will continue to do so.

Professor Fritz Schalk recalls that *Cántico*★ affirms this faith against wind and tide:

> Let the dead bury their dead,
> Never their hope.

> Que los muertos entierren a sus muertos,
> Jamás a la esperanza.

That last Norton lecture tells us a great deal in a very short time about the loss of a Republican culture; however, apart from the

---

Roldán family, who were both business and political rivals.

★Jorge Guillén's own 'lifelong' poem, which was published in several books while he was alive and brought together in a single volume of over three hundred poems in 1950.

passing reference to Ernestina de Champourcín, it leaves a huge gap in the history of the Generation of '27. In fact, Champourcín was just one of many women who contributed significantly to the development of a new Spanish Republican aesthetic, a fact that has just recently begun to receive wider recognition. Still, very little has been written, outside Spain and the academe, about the part played by women from all walks of life in establishing and defending the Republic, both on the front line and in the culture – and it is not difficult to understand why, when we consider the institutional and brutally systematic ideology of sexism imposed in every walk of life after 1939. Typical of that ideology is this remark by Pilar Primo de Rivera, leader of the Falangist *Sección Femenina*:

> Women never discover anything; of course, they lack creative talent, reserved by God for masculine intelligences; we can only interpret, for better or worse, the things that men give us.

> Las mujeres nunca descubren nada; les falta, desde luego, el talento creador, reservado por Dios para inteligencias varoniles; nosotras no podemos hacer más que interpretar, mejor o peor, lo que los hombres nos dan hecho.

At the same time, while several of the male poets of the Generation '27 welcomed and reviewed the work of their female colleagues (and Juan Ramón Jiménez was instrumental in helping Ernestina de Champourcín to get her work published), later critics and literary historians tended to ignore women poets as a matter of course, not just in Franco's Spain but also in South America and elsewhere. Translators focused on the men, and it certainly did not help Ernestina de Champourcín and Rosa Méndez that they were married to leading male poets of the day (Juan José Domenchina and Manuel Altolaguirre respectively).*

---

*This problem was not confined to Franco's Spain, of course; many women artists and poets have been routinely consigned to the shadows as soon as they marry another worker in their particular vineyard. The Abstract Expressionist painter Lee Krasner is perhaps the best-known of such cases, having dwelt in

Ernestina de Champourcín was born in the northern city of Vitoria in 1905 and produced three significant poetry collections during the high period of the Generation of '27: *En silencio* ('In silence'), published in Madrid in 1926; *Ahora* ('Now'), published in 1928, and what is arguably her finest early work, *La voz en el viento* ('The voice in the wind'), in 1931. Her writing during this period was clearly influenced by Juan Ramón Jiménez (though she was hardly alone in that) and, as we have noted, he was to champion her work in the literary press. Nevertheless, she soon established her own voice in poems that speak variously of earthly love, the natural world and, later, a mystical sense of union with the divine. Forced into exile after the Civil War, she eventually returned to Madrid in 1972. Her later work is characterised by meditations on time and death that are sometimes overtly religious and at times more ambiguous:

> But dying is not that terrible thing
> from which one always flees with eyes closed.
> Death smells sweet, like the honeycomb in the hive.
> Where is there another island that burns like a living candle
> comparable with this Janitzio of all our Novembers?

> Pero morir no es esa cosa terrible
> de la que se huye siempre con los ojos cerrados.
> La muerte huele a dulce, a panal de colmena.
> ¿Dónde hay otra isla que sea un cirio vivo
> como este Janitzio de todos los noviembres?*

One of her finest poems brings together all of her main pre-occupations: asceticism, absence, the constant play between the here and now and the eternal, and a refashioning of the language

---

the shadow of her husband, Jackson Pollock, for years both before and after his death, but there have been many others.

*Janitzio is an island in Lake Pátzcuaro, Mexico, famed for its annual celebration of the Day of the Dead, during which hosts of candle-lit boats travel across the water to the island's church cemetery, where an overnight vigil is held.

of romantic love as a means of expressing the longing for, and the absence of, the divine Beloved:

> The love of each and every moment …
> hard love, with no compensations: chain, cross, sackcloth,
> absent glory, long awaited,
> joy and torment in one breath;
> reality of the centuries, thankfulness for being,
> for being in the now and in the always.

> Amor de cada instante …
> duro amor sin delicias: cadena, cruz, cilicio,
> gloria ausente, esperada,
> gozo y tortura a un tiempo;
> realidad de los siglos, gracias por ser y estar
> en el nunca y el siempre.

It is impossible – literally – to translate these lines accurately into English, if only because of the way Champourcín plays *ser* and *estar* against each other in the fifth line. Both translate as 'to be', but there are serious grammatical distinctions between the two, the most important of which, in this context, is that *estar* suggests a temporary condition, while *ser* denotes a permanent one.* Here the thanks offered for *ser* and *estar* transcends the more conventional mode of religious poetry (which has its eyes set, as it were, on eternity) by valuing the now alongside the always, on equal terms – for, as we shall see, the Thou of God, or the Beloved, is both present and absent in both:

> My task, then, is to love you in this absence,
> to cling to this nothing because it also yours,

---

*A simple example is the distinction between saying '*Juan es feliz*', meaning John has a happy, outgoing personality, and '*Juan está feliz*', meaning John is happy at the moment – as in, he is in a good mood. As with all grammar, however, it's never that simple. For example, Spanish people do not say of a dead person '*Juan es muerto*.' They always use *estar*. Perhaps they know something other language groups do not.

to drink the dust of solitude and emptiness
that is Your gift for now and Your surest promise.

Pues mi ejercicio, ahora, es amarte en la ausencia
y aferrarme a esta nada porque también es tuya
y beber ese polvo de soledad y vacío
que es Tu don del momento y Tu clara promesa.

Everything that is, the transient and the eternal, solitude and emptiness, is both a gift, in the here and now, and a promise of what is to come – and the task of the speaker is not to endure the absence of the Beloved, but to *live* it, to relish every moment, as befits the acceptance of a gift. To live, and to welcome, not just the unknown but that which no mortal being (*nadie*) can know. It is, perhaps, tempting to see in such work the language of exile, where the love of home-place, and of those who remain there, is tainted with bitterness and longing for what is forever lost (and, as exiles soon learn, once the home-place has been corrupted, the only remaining option is to carry on, as a very different writer puts it, 'boats against the current, borne back ceaselessly into the past'. That past, however, can never be regained.

for You also, I welcome the unknown,

and I carry on walking, in all this confusion,
through darkness and light, for the sake of this bitter love,
dappled with glory …

por Ti también me acojo a lo que nadie sabe.

Y así voy caminando por este desconcierto
oscuro y luminoso, por este amor amargo,
veteado de gloria …

Yet if this ascetic path can be, not so much endured as celebrated, even in its bitter essence, the speaker will be able to continue on her spiritual journey, guided by a love that is both bitter and 'veteado de gloria' – and is there not an insinuation, here, that no obvious end is in sight? What is interesting, in this final line, is the use of the word *veteado*, which translates as 'veined', 'streaked' or 'lined', but can also suggest 'marbled' or 'grained', as when a craftsman applies a veneer to a surface, to give it a more vivid or variegated appearance. So even at the end the speaker acknowledges that any glory she may possess is borrowed from, or possibly bestowed by, the beloved Thou, whose absence (and the acceptance of whose absence) transforms the devotee in the here and now, in readiness for the eternity – not a point in linear time but a parallel state – in which the glory is complete.

While, as we have noted, a considerable number of Spanish women artists were seriously overlooked for many years after the fall of the Republic, it is Maria Zambrano who, to my mind, has been the most unjustly neglected of all. She was a writer of many gifts, a fine poet and essayist, but for now I want to confine my reading of her work to a (much too) brief review of her vision of *la razón poética*, in which she proposes a system of enquiry into the totality of human experience that not only allows for but demands the use of *all* our available faculties, and not just discursive reasoning. That philosophy is complex, and connects with the work of several other thinkers of the time in interesting ways; however, it is fair to say that the system Zambrano advocates, in which poetic reasoning does not displace or oppose scientific method but sits alongside it, as its equal and complement, adds significantly to the overall method we have for investigating our environment. With its new respect for intuition as a proven faculty, Zambrano's approach to the basic human act of perception (of, first, registering sense-data from their environment, and then ordering that data into information, and so knowledge) would bring all of our faculties into play in order to create a complete and satisfactory way of being. The vital point to remember is that this is a vision of life that neither the rational enquirer (the scientific thinker) nor the poet can achieve alone. Making a distinction between philosophy (that is, any system that uses a *method*) and the intuitive apprehension of poetry (which depends not on a predefined method but on *grace*), she says:

> We do not find the complete human being in philosophy; we do not find the totality of the human experience in poetry. In poetry, we directly encounter the specific human instance, the individual. In philosophy we see 'man' in his historical context, in his will to be. Poetry is serendipitous encounter, a gift, a matter of grace. Philosophy searches, but it must follow a method.

> No se encuentra el hombre entero en la filosofía; no se encuentra la totalidad de lo humano en la poesía. En la poesía encontramos directamente al hombre concreto, individual. En la filosofía al hombre en su historia universal, en su querer ser. La poesía es encuentro, don, hallazgo por gracia. La filosofía busca, requerimiento guiado por un método.

It is possible to detect, in these remarks, echoes of other thinkers such as Heidegger, going back as far as early Greek philosophy. A particularly illuminating example might be drawn from the work of Carl Gustav Jung, who noted in 1921: 'We should not pretend to understand the world only by the intellect; we apprehend it just as much by feeling. Therefore, the judgement of the intellect is, at best, only the half of truth, and must, if it be honest, also come to an understanding of its inadequacy.' This is an idea that we accept more readily now, perhaps, than we did in the 1920s, but then so many of the most important scientific ideas of the twentieth century arose from a searching exploration of the limits of established logical methods and assumptions. For instance, Gödel's incompleteness theorems shook the foundations of mathematical logic, while Heisenberg's uncertainty principle had the same liberating if disruptive impact on physics. As we saw earlier, Wittgenstein's closing argument in the *Tractatus Logico-Philosophicus* painstakingly revealed how logical endeavour could carry us only so far in our knowledge of the world, and that we needed to employ other, less rigid methods to apprehend the whole (and Wittgenstein had no doubt that poetry – that is, what Zambrano calls *la razón poética* – was the foremost such method).

Yet, where some philosophers proposed poetry as a *replacement* for hard scientific method as it approached the limits of what logic could say and do, Zambrano insisted that we need to work with both forms of enquiry – that is, using logic and *la razón poética* in tandem – to build a holistic vision of the cosmos. No philosopher born in Goya's Spain could forget that the sleep of reason produces monsters, and Zambrano recognises that, but by the same token she knows that the sleep of our more lyrical faculties – dream, insight, intuition, inspiration – leads first to dullness and then to something more sinister (of which the rise of fascism in Europe might reasonably be considered a symptom). In her writing she pairs the two faculties, saying, 'Philosophy asks questions, while the poetic discovers' ('Filosófico es el preguntar y poético el hallazgo'). To rephrase: we need philosophy to frame the questions, while poetry creates the possibilities of grace in which serendipitous discovery (*hallazgo*) can occur. Taken together, the two disciplines form a complete system for living a full life.

This vision had been coming for some time. With Kant, philosophers and poets had begun to accept just how significant a part the imagination plays in our experience of the world – and that individual, and even communal, ideas of 'reality' were more than the sum of what the mind constructs using sense-data gathered from its environment and duly organised according to the various rules and protocols (conventions to do with time and space, for example) that each individual learns (depending on his or her cultural milieu). Without the balancing weight of poetic reason we can be led to believe that the 'real' – as opposed to the 'imaginary', i.e., unreal – world is made up of sense-data, interpreted according to the rules of logic and nothing else. But such a worldview leads inevitably to a reductive view of how things are. It allows us to perceive all the noise of time, but little of the music of what happens.

For a number of reasons, however, some of them political, a new hard-science hegemony, allied to the forces of industrialisation, began to insist on an untenable ethos of objectivity. Discursive thinking was recognised, everything else was to be filed under superstition, fanciful thinking and, if women were involved, hysteria. And of course, hard science was genuinely useful in some situations, where rigour was more important than inspiration, scepticism essential for the avoidance of damaging mistakes. Just as it helps to know which of the berries in the woods are poisonous and which are not, so it is worth knowing how to weigh and measure things accurately – and these skills depend on rigour and close observation. On the other hand, when it comes to discriminating between love as a gift and love as currency, or what constitutes real courtesy as opposed to self-serving politesse, we may find intuition more useful. Does grace exist? We find evidence of it everywhere, but we cannot dissect or scan it. Such observations ought to be self-evident, but the history of science, as it shifted into reductionism in the service of industrial capitalism, meant that some of our native faculties were over-privileged while others were allowed to atrophy. Zambrano's concept of poetic reason can be seen as an elegant and lyrical attempt to redress the balance, and it should be more widely read than it is at present.

That there are areas of experience unknown to hard science – grace, self-sacrifice, perversity, or what it is we mean when we talk about the soul – ought to be obvious. And it is to some. In a poem composed in Rome in 1950, 'Delirio del incrédulo' ('Delirium of the Unbeliever'), Zambrano begins by invoking the nothingness we have encountered in Stevens and Montale:

> Beneath the flower, the branch
> above the branch, the star
> under the star, the wind;
> and beyond that?
> Beyond that – don't you remember? – nothing.
> nothing – listen well, my soul
> sleep, go to sleep in that nothingness.

Bajo la flor, la rama
sobre la flor, la estrella
bajo la estrella, el viento;
¿Y más allá?
Más allá, ¿no recuerdas? sólo la nada.
la nada, óyelo bien, mi alma
duérmete, aduérmete en la nada.[6]

As it opens, this poem could be an Imagist piece in the style of
Pound's famous two-liner 'In a Station of the Metro' –

The apparition of these faces in the crowd:
Petals on a wet, black bough

– but it immediately moves on into the philosophical realm, as
the speaker summons up the idea of nothingness while at the
same time singing the soul to sleep, with the traditional opening
of a Spanish lullaby.* There is an odd conflict here, however: the
gentle command, 'go to sleep' is preceded by another that contra-
dicts it: 'listen well' – but we do not know what the soul is listening *to*, since we have just been told that nothing is there. Can we
hear nothing? Can we listen to nothing? This opening recalls the
famous poem of Juan Ramón Jiménez 'No era nadie':

– It was nobody. Water. – Water?
How is water nobody? It was
nobody. The flower. – Nobody?
But, is the flower nobody?

– It was nobody. It was the wind. – Nobody?
Is the wind nobody? – It
was nobody. Illusion. – It was nobody?
And is illusion nobody?

---

*Compare Lorca's *Blood Wedding,* where the lullaby runs:

Duérmete, clavel,
que el caballo no quiere beber.

201

– No era nadie. El agua. – Nadie?
Que no es nadie el agua? – No
hay nadie. Es la flor. – No hay nadie?
Pero, no es nadie la flor?

– No hay nadie. Era el viento. – Nadie?
No es el viento nadie? – No
hay nadie. Ilusión. – No hay nadie?
Y no es nadie la ilusión?[7]

We are in familiar territory here, but where the looming non-presence in Montale and Stevens was a *nothing*, Jiménez offers instead a voice – almost childlike, as we listen to its attempts to reassure itself – insisting that what hovers on the borderline between absence and presence is a *no-body*. That voice is countered, however, by a second voice that steadily questions the apparently wishful assumptions of the first (though, when we listen closely, it is clear that who or what this *nobody* might be is not clear: it could be the bogeyman, but it could be another presence altogether, possibly even the divine).

Zambrano picks up on this uncertainty, adding a dimension of her own to the metaphysical puzzle:

Truly, is there really nothing?
There is nothing.
Nothing, listen well, my soul.
sleep, go to sleep in the nothing.
And that you do not remember it. That was your glory.

De verdad ¿es que no hay nada?
Hay la nada.
La nada, óyelo bien, mi alma.
duérmete, aduérmete en la nada.
Y que no lo recuerdes. Era tu gloria.

Here the play on 'nada' becomes a little more complicated. The childlike voice seeking reassurance (is there really nothing?) is answered by what sounds like that very assurance, there is nothing – only for everything to shift, as 'nothing' becomes something or enough of something, at least, for the soul to go to sleep in. Whatever that something and nothing is, however, it will not be remembered, which is not a loss, but is, instead, 'your glory'.

Any confusion on the listener's part here is altogether forgivable – and yet intuitively we cannot help feeling that, as much as it makes no sense according to conventional reasoning, this dialogue about nothing is profoundly meaningful. Zambrano continues:

Beyond memory, in oblivion,
listen to the sound of your breathing.
Look into the pupil within you
in the fire that will scorch you, light and water.

Más allá del recuerdo, en el olvido,
escucha en el soplo de tu aliento.
Mira en tu pupila misma dentro
en ese fuego que te abrasa, luz y agua.

It seems odd to suggest that, in the beyond (which we usually take to mean some kind of post-mortem state), in 'oblivion', a person might be able to listen to the sound of his or her own breathing – the very sign of life itself. What, then, is this afterlife where the subject still breathes and is capable of listening to itself breathe, however lightly? Whatever it may be, it is a condition that can be experienced. Meanwhile, the command to look into this inner pupil is reminiscent of the discussion of the soul in Plato's *Alcibiades I*:

SOCRATES: Consider; if some one were to say to the eye, 'See thyself' as you might say to a man, 'Know thyself' what is the nature and meaning of this precept? Would not his meaning be: That the eye should look at that in which it would see itself?
ALCIBIADES: Clearly.
SOCRATES: And what are the objects in looking at which we see ourselves?
ALCIBIADES: Clearly, Socrates, in looking at mirrors and the like.

SOCRATES: Very true; and is there not something of the nature of a mirror in our own eyes?[8]

With this deliberate echo, then, the poem implies that the imperative 'know thyself' requires the experience of oblivion, of nothing, in order to succeed. To know the self, as a soul, one must confront nothingness – for it is this nothing that defines the something the self is, just as the nothing of Montale's 'Forse un mattino' or the legendary Hidebehind of Borges's Wisconsin tale defines the one who witnesses it. Of course, the hard scientist who works only with logic might ask if any of this is *real*, but the experience of confronting the inexplicable is far from rare, and is not only recorded throughout the world, at different times, by very different cultures, but is seen as a spiritually rewarding experience – a miracle, in Montale's terms, and also a vital secret – by many. That being said, Zambrano acknowledges that it gives her speaker pause:

> But I cannot, I cannot.
> The eyes and the ears are windows.
> Lost between/inside myself
> I cannot search for anything/nothing
> I do not arrive at Nothing.

> Mas no puedo, no puedo.
> Ojos y oídos son ventanas.
> Perdido entre mí mismo
> no puedo buscar nada
> no llego hasta la Nada.

The language here is difficult and deeply paradoxical. To say that one is 'lost between myself' implies an *and*: that is, between myself and – what? Another side of myself? The nothingness that both defines and excludes me? The ambiguity that follows, with its play on 'buscar nada' only adds to the sense of paradox:* of

---

*Here, we are in a realm of wordplay familiar to readers of the English

course, we cannot search for nothing, as nothing, by definition, cannot be found; thus, the speaker of this poem does not arrive at Nothing (note the capitalisation in the last line). Is this closing stanza an admission of defeat, or is it the declaration of an existential impossibility? Hamlet's argument that that there are more things in heaven and earth than are dreamt of in our philosophy has by now become a truism. What Zambrano is attempting is to find a new mode of enquiry into those unscientific 'things' that might provide us with a different kind of knowledge, a knowledge that, apprehended, or intuited through paradox, cannot be verified by conventional means, but which might nevertheless lead to a wisdom that sits beyond the limits of discursive thinking.

---

metaphysical poets; see, for example, John Donne's 'Negative Love' for a similar play on 'nothing':

> If that be simply perfectest,
> Which can by no way be express'd
>> But Negatives, my love is so.
>> To All, which all love, I say no.
> If any who deciphers best,
>> What we know not, our selves, can know,
> Let him teach mee that nothing.

WHY LOOK AT ANIMALS?

What we habitually see confirms us.

John Berger

WHEN WE DRIVE HOME from the west of an evening, my eyes fixed on the twilit road, my sons in the back of the car, quietened by fatigue or boredom, we have to pass through a strip of dense woodland, just a couple of miles before we emerge into the open farmland where we live. Even as a grown-up, I can see that this is one of those magical woods: the trees arching over the road on either side to form a long, half-lit tunnel that could bring us out anywhere, glints and winks of silver in the darkening under-growth and, not a rare event at this time of day though always a small miracle when it happens, a hint of other lives, swimming or leaping through the greenery, sometimes to shy away at the last second and sometimes to stream across the road, two or three or five of them together, panicky, but not too quick to make out – and always, no matter how suddenly it happens, we are all aware of the eyes, of the fleeting, gorgeous exchange of a look, while we shift from the humdrum routine of a homeward journey into vivid life again, just for a moment, and the boys call out, or whisper, wonderingly: *Deer!*

It seems such a small event, yet this animal encounter is an occa-sion of quiet if short-lived pleasure every time it happens because, like the grown-up I am now, as opposed to the half-wild boy I was in a different, more populous-seeming world, my children very rarely see animals in the wild. Even when they do, it's usually through a car window, on occasions like this when, half-asleep, they get home wondering if they dreamed it all – or maybe wondering what else they are missing. It takes a true encounter, in fact, to realise that real animals, *wild* animals, have all but passed from our lives. I remember stopping my car one morning in early May and getting out to stretch my legs somewhere in north Norway: the thaw had begun a few days earlier, but then it had snowed again and the land was frozen for miles, which is probably why I saw the fox, its white winter coat just starting to turn brown. Why it didn't see or sense me sooner I don't know, but we came close enough to exchange a look, and for a long moment I felt that same rightness about the world that my sons feel when they catch sight of something in the woods: a strange immediacy that cannot be communicated but is real nevertheless. After a few long seconds the fox turned and wandered away, seemingly unconcerned but, as my excitement and wonder faded, I began to experience something else. Something like grief; or maybe the sense that I was, in the full sense of the word, *bereft*. The ecologist Paul Shepard has said:

> we hear much these days about the loss of species and bio-logical diversity, usually in terms of diminished ecosystems, destabilized environments, and the loss of unknown physical resources. I suspect that the greater loss is of another kind – the way a local fauna links the concept of the self and the unique-ness of place in different cultures. The loss of nonhuman diver-sity erases nuances in identity. We are coarsened by the loss of the animals.

We are coarsened by the loss of the animals. True, we are intel-lectually aware that species loss is a catastrophe, and some of us still feel that it is the most urgent environmental problem we face, but we have yet to understand that it is not only the presence of an acceptable number of specific creatures that matters. What is essential – the one thing that could stop us becoming further coarsened – is that we *feel* a great, living wave of animal life all around us, literally covering the earth. I may know that there are still a few pandas out there somewhere, but that sense of being bereft comes from living day to day with the near-absence of wild things. (The few exceptions, in my case, are: flocks of pink-footed geese in the winter, a few buzzards and hares, the odd frantic deer skittering across a road, a passing fox or badger, a glimpse of weasel or stoat on the road.) None of these creatures is rare, or particularly prized; in fact, there are official bodies and quangos empowered to decide how many may be killed, per annum, in order to furnish us townsfolk with more or less clear roads, automatic garage doors and patio heaters. So what hope is there, in such a world, for someone whose heart lifts at the sight of a family of rabbits, grazing on a verge, after a long day at the theme park?

With this sometimes unrecognised and generally unacknow-ledged sense of a coarsened life hanging over us, the animal presence in our culture has become more urgent than ever before. In fact, the obliteration of vast numbers of species during the last hundred years or so has been paralleled by a steady growth in animal encounter poetry. When Robert Frost wrote 'Two Look at Two' in the early 1920s, he could make it seem the most natural thing in the world that, as night approached, two humans could stand by a broken wall, gazing in wonder – and at close quarters – as a doe, and then a buck, came to greet them, and it was even possible for them to feel

> A great wave from it going over them,
> As if the earth in one unlooked-for favour
> Had made them certain earth returned their love.

Yet a few minutes earlier, when the buck first appears, he challenges the humans with a look that seems to say

> Why don't you make some motion?
> Or give some sign of life? Because you can't.
> I doubt if you're as living as you look.[1]

– and the reader, both a hundred years ago and now, feels the discomfort of being caught out, for we really aren't as living as we look; we are tamed, and we have almost lost the common stamp of creatureliness that other animals, arguably even the most domesticated, have retained. What Frost would have us understand here, even as he invokes the possibility that earth returns our love, is that there is so little of the wild in us, so little sign of life that, as dusk falls, we could easily be mistaken for inanimate objects.

Then, as the century wore on, we not only became less animate ourselves but, as we felled old woodlands and cleared the way for new super-highways, we also embarked upon the systematic destruction of life itself. There is no question now that many of us knew what we were doing, but we did it for the good of our species: good seeming to consist in floodlit golf ranges, single-use disposable razors and the clear-felling of tropical rainforests to create palm-oil plantations. More than anything else, good consisted in speeding across the land in semis and juggernauts and 4×4s that got bigger by the year, occasionally glimpsing some living creature out in the grey of it all, very frequently leaving said creature behind as that new natural phenomenon, roadkill. In 1956 William Stafford wrote the laconic and unsettling 'Traveling Through the Dark', about finding a dead doe on his drive home: a not infrequent event. Though the road is narrow, he stops, because

> It is usually best to roll them into the canyon:
> that road is narrow; to swerve might make more dead

and he is only doing his duty when he gets out to push the deer off the edge of the road and into the river. When he touches the animal, however, he realises that she is pregnant, and that the fawn is, for the moment, still alive inside her. It should be said that there is no sentimentality here: aware that he can do nothing for the unborn fawn, the speaker of the poem only wavers for a moment before carrying on with his unwanted task. Nevertheless, he hesitates and, in one of the most beautifully dramatised moments in modern poetry, he creates a scene in which the only animate, warm thing seems to be the car engine, while the man, who is in every rational sense guiltless, becomes complicit with some greater, existential sin, a sin against life to which, as he slowly realises, wild nature itself is always a witness:

> The car aimed ahead its lowered parking lights;
> under the hood purred the steady engine.
> I stood in the glare of the warm exhaust turning red;
> around our group I could hear the wilderness listen.[2]

No sense, here, that earth returns our love: the wilderness watches, listens, and the man, after having 'thought hard for us all', does what he must do, before driving on.

The animal encounter poem is now so distinct a genre that it would be possible to create a full-length anthology from deer encounter poems alone, and many varieties of experience would emerge from such an exercise, such as Mary Oliver's 'Picking Blueberries, Austerlitz, New York, 1957', in which the speaker recounts a childhood memory of having fallen asleep while out gathering fruit and then, when she woke, of frightening a concerned deer that had stopped to nuzzle her. Here there is a sense of elegy not just for the deer but for a former self, lost when she somehow lost contact with the creaturely ('Beautiful girl, / where are you?'). One of the most troubling items in such an anthology would surely be Brigit Pegeen Kelly's astonishing 'Dead Doe', from the collection *Song* (1995): here a woman and her child find a roadkill deer on the way to the school bus stop, but they do not – cannot – approach her, as Stafford's driver, or Frost's couple, so easily do:

> The doe lay dead on her back in a field of asters: no.
>
> The doe lay dead on her back beside the school bus stop: yes.
>
> Where we waited.
> Her belly white as a cut pear. Where we waited: no: off

from where we waited: yes

at a distance: making a distance
we kept.[3]

To begin with, in fact, they cannot even approach her imaginatively: the speaker struggles to describe the scene, constantly tempted by, and refusing, familiar scenarios. Indeed, this opening passage sets the scene for all that is to come: throughout, Kelly refuses the easy appeal of traditional pastoral, or the clear moral predicament that Stafford evokes; when she is tempted into images like that 'cut pear', she draws back and insists on the unbridgeable distance between the dead animal and the human family group. What sets that distance between them is not distaste for a dead, perhaps decaying corpse – or even squeamishness about death itself – nor is it the desire to avoid forced explanations of mortality, but the fear of witnessing some kind of resurrection:

as we kept her dead run in sight, that we might see if she
    chose to go skyward;
that we might run, too, turn tail
if she came near
and troubled our fear with presence: with ghostly blossoming.

From this point onwards the poem embarks on a method that Kelly has made her own, a bringing forth of the process of working through a spiritual problem, a kind of extended meditation that is also a thought experiment, aimed at a more or less provisional – one might even say 'fuzzy' – conclusion. Several attempts are made to fix the image, to say something definitive about what the woman and her child see at the bus stop –

The doe lay dead: she lent
    her deadness to the morning, that the morning might have
    weight, that
our waiting might matter: be upheld by significance: by, light
    on the rhododendron, by the ribbons the sucked mint
    loosed on the air

– but each is quickly balanced by an antithesis, an open-ended concern for the living, both the deer and the child waiting at the bus stop, who cannot be protected, cannot be kept eternally safe 'in mild unceasing rain', and our final view of the deer sets up a whole new set of possibilities: lying dead, at a distance, 'her legs up and frozen', she comes to look like two swans fighting, or coupling, or 'stabbing the ground for some prize / worth nothing, but fought over, so worth that'.

Now, in an instant, in what Emily Dickinson calls 'a certain slant of light', the feared resurrection, the 'ghostly blossoming', has come to pass, but in a wholly, unanticipated form –

> And this is the soul: like it or not. Yes: the soul comes down:
> yes: comes into the deer: yes: who dies: yes: and in her death
> twins herself into swans: fools us with mist and accident into
> believing her newfound finery

– and though this vision is not as frightening as the anticipated 'blossoming', the speaker remarks that it should be: a different fear, perhaps, like the fear we owe beauty, or the divine, a kind of sublime panic, as

> we watch her soul fly on: paired
> as the soul always is: with itself:
> with others.
> Two swans …

> Child. We are done for
> in the most remarkable ways.

All the while, language has struggled to make sense of the scene; now we close with a soft, heart-breaking wordplay, a beautiful ambiguity. Yet the poem has created in its reader an odd breathlessness, a giddy onrush similar to the rush of a panic attack, not in the usual sense but in the old, true sense of a meeting with the cloven-footed god.

Panic. If ever there was a term that needed redefinition – or rather, clarification – it is this. Panic: 'a sudden and excessive feeling of alarm or fear, usually affecting a body of persons, and leading to extravagant or injudicious efforts to secure safety.' So the *Shorter Oxford* tells us, explaining that originally this emotion was occasioned by an encounter with Pan, whose 'appearance or unseen presence caused terror and to whom woodland noises were attributed'. Yet this is much less than half the story, and it presents the Ancient Greeks in a rather patronising light, as mere superstitious pagans, fearful of the wind in the trees or some looming, possibly spectral predator in the undergrowth. It is a definition that forgets the story of Pheidippides, the Athenian youth who meets Pan in the woods as he is running to seek help from the Spartans against an invading Persian army: true, this meeting strikes terror into the young athlete's heart, but it also inspires him to continue and gives him the strength not only to finish the round trip to Sparta (where his request for help is denied) but also to go on to Marathon and take part in a great victory before running back to the waiting Athenians with news of their salvation. Here, in its Greek original, panic is more than fear, more than terror: it is a glimpse into the fabric of the world, a glimpse, after all, of the divine, and it fills its recipient with an inspired awe, a more than human vitality, as well as a terror that, while understandable, is recognisably a by-product of the encounter with the goat-god, rather than the main event.

But what causes this panic? Panic is the fear not of the unknown but of the unknowable. At the same time it is the inspiration, the dark joy, that comes of the encounter with what cannot be known: the sense that something orders the world, even if we can never comprehend that order (or, as the physicist Arthur Stanley Eddington remarked, 'Something unknown is doing we don't know what') and even if we, as individuals, are only fuel to its eternal flame. Panic is the moment when we apprehend the divine in the fabric of the everyday, and see that it moves independently of our hopes and fears, carrying us forward a little way, then letting us fall, easily, naturally, as leaves fall from a tree in the autumn. It is a glimpse of the void itself: that regenerative, all-consuming nothingness from which we all emerge, and into which we are all destined to return.

On several occasions during the 2016 presidential race Donald Trump made reference (and on one occasion, recited the full lyric) to a 'poem' that he said was written by Al Wilson 'a long time ago'. (The 'poem' was, in fact, a song written and recorded by the poet, playwright and civil rights activist Oscar Brown Jr, in 1963, though Wilson's version won it a new following, especially among British Northern Soul fans, in the late 1960s.) It's a fun piece, with a talking-point sting in the tail about a 'tender woman' who finds a half-dead snake 'all frosted with the dew' and decides to take it in and care for it. This she does, wrapping the creature in silk, warming it by the fire and feeding it on milk and honey. Soon the animal is restored to its original, seductive beauty – so much so that the woman clutches him to her, stroking his 'pretty skin' and holding him tight (the sexual innuendos are in no way subtle), but the snake responds by biting her. Naturally, the woman protests: how could he have betrayed her so, when he knows his bite is fatal? To this, the snake replies that the woman should stop complaining: after all, she knew he was a snake when she took him in.

There is a great deal of wit in the song, not so much in the sexual innuendo as in the way the refrain 'Take me in, tender woman' modulates from an innocent appeal for mercy and shelter through erotic play to the bitter fact that, whether she chooses it or not, the woman's body is bound to absorb the snake's venom. All the while, of course, she herself is being 'taken in', in the sense of being deceived, led down the garden path, seduced and then betrayed, as Eve was by the Serpent in the garden – and this, predictably, is the aspect of the poem/song that Trump picked up on. (He even interrupted his recitation with asides such as 'the Border' and references to Homeland Security.) The tender woman is the United States, a nation apparently too kind for its own good; the snake represents a catalogue of refugees, asylum seekers and migrants, 'poor' people who cry out for shelter, much like the tired and huddled masses immortalised by Emma Lazarus's poem 'The New Colossus' at the Statue of Liberty (and listening to Trump say the word 'poor' is instructive: he can barely conceal his contempt). Yet, while this performance was genuinely repulsive, it was also somewhat, if rather bitterly, amusing. To watch the candidate responsible for this revealing *faux pas* eventually rise to the position of president was disturbing, to say the least; but it is profoundly ironic, in that context, to think, not only that the original song was composed as a comic cautionary tale about the unreliability of sexual predators but also that the lyricist was a known civil rights activist and communist, whose musical *Big Time Buck White*, based on the Black Power-inspired play by Joseph Dolan Tuotti, briefly featured Muhammad Ali in the title role – complete with outsize Afro wig – during its Broadway run.

To a man whose knowledge of history could probably be inscribed in large font on the back of the 1863 Bolivar 10c green postage stamp,* 1963, or even 1968, probably is 'a long time ago', but the original source of the ungrateful snake story goes back much further than that. The earliest known version seems to be Aesop's, in which the human character is not a woman but a man (this English account is from an edition of the *Fables* published in 1867, edited by Edward Garrett):

> One Winter a Farmer found a Snake stiff and frozen with cold. He had compassion on it, and taking it up, placed it in his bosom. The Snake was quickly revived by the warmth, and resuming its natural instincts, bit its benefactor, inflicting on him a mortal wound. 'Oh,' cried the Farmer with his last breath, 'I am rightly served for pitying a scoundrel.'

> Moral: The greatest kindness will not bind the ungrateful.

---

* At 8 × 9.55 mm, this is the smallest stamp ever issued.

There is no mention, in the original Greek, or in this English version, of a 'tender woman'; what we get is simply a cautionary tale about misplaced trust and ingratitude. Not surprisingly, however, several translators have adapted the tale to their own ends. (Few Classical authors have suffered so badly from this kind of misappropriation as Aesop.) For example, Odo of Cheriton, the thirteenth-century Norman-English preacher and moral fabulist, manages to weave into his translation of the tale a warning against the perversity of the Muslim enemy of the day, the Saracens. It may be, of course, that this use of fable to demonise real and supposed enemies is a peculiarly Christian-culture phenomenon; there may be other reasons for the custom. Still, it seems fair to assume that the folklore of the generous-spirited Wampanoag people lacked a 'deceitful snake' story, or they might have taken more care over Homeland Security when Europeans first landed on their shores back in the 1620s.*

Many cultures, however, use the animal Other to stand for both the best and the worst in the human character. In many cases a moment's reflection reveals how odd this is: animals live according to their nature, responding to the circumstances in which they find themselves, and there is nothing specifically noble about a lion, or industrious about a swarm of bees. When Bernard de Mandeville writes, in his instructive work *The Fable of the Bees* (1714),

---

*History wants us to believe that the Indian was a savage, illiterate, uncivilized animal. A history that was written by an organized, disciplined people, to expose us as an unorganized and undisciplined entity. Two distinctly different cultures met. One thought they must control life; the other believed life was to be enjoyed, because nature decreed it. Let us remember, the Indian is and was just as human as the white man. The Indian feels pain, gets hurt, and becomes defensive, has dreams, bears tragedy and failure, suffers from loneliness, needs to cry as well as laugh. He, too, is often misunderstood.

From the suppressed speech of Wamsutta (Frank B.) James that was to be delivered at Plymouth, Massachusetts, on Thanksgiving 1970, to mark the 350th anniversary of the Pilgrims' arrival.

A Spacious Hive well stockt with Bees,
That liv'd in Luxury and Ease;
And yet as fam'd for Laws and Arms,
As yielding large and early Swarms;
Was counted the great Nursery
Of Sciences and Industry

he was more concerned with preaching the values of the emergent capitalist system than with natural history – and this is typical of how animals are portrayed in the arts generally. Anthropomorphism came naturally to our ancestors – and why would it not? In general, humans are primarily interested in what is human; as Flavius Philostratus remarked of Aesop himself: 'he puts animals in a pleasing light and makes them interesting to mankind. For after being brought up from childhood with these stories, and after being as it were nursed by them from babyhood, we acquire certain opinions of the several animals and think of some of them as royal animals, of others as silly, of others as witty, and others as innocent.' Those opinions are, of course, completely arbitrary. Animals in poetry, and the other arts, have appeared as symbols, emblems, allegorical figures and metaphors, but the attribution of human values and characteristics is as groundless as it is misleading, a practice in many ways as superstitious as experiencing a lightning storm as the wrath of a god, or an outbreak of plague as a punishment for sin. In the last century, however, poets began to see the animal as an Other, a locus of mystery in which assumptions about the ascendancy of humans could be interrogated and subverted.

One of the great poems in which a human subject confronts the animal as Other is D. H. Lawrence's 'Snake', perhaps the most anthologised of his works. This might seem odd, as the poem does not conform to a good many of the common expectations of verse (obvious metrical rhythms, rhyme etc.), but it is accessible, intensely visual and seems to a pose a moral question that, depending on the reader, can be seen in terms of a single question or proposition, or viewed as a multi-layered philosophical puzzle. Set in Sicily, where Lawrence was living at the time of composition in the early 1920s, the poem begins:

> A snake came to my water-trough
> On a hot, hot day, and I in pyjamas for the heat,
> To drink there.
>
> In the deep, strange-scented shade of the great dark carob-tree
> I came down the steps with my pitcher
> And must wait, must stand and wait, for there he was at the
>   trough before me.

There is no actual reason, other than a kind of creaturely etiquette, to say that the speaker 'must wait', but wait he does, as a courtesy, for the snake was there first. Does the snake know the man is there? This might well be the first question to pass through the mind of somebody finding himself in close proximity to a potentially venomous animal, but the speaker is for the moment unconcerned, caught up as he is in observing the elaborate process by which the snake comes to the trough:

> He reached down from a fissure in the earth-wall in the gloom
> And trailed his yellow-brown slackness soft-bellied down, over
>   the edge of the stone trough
> And rested his throat upon the stone bottom,
> And where the water had dripped from the tap, in a small
>   clearness,
> He sipped with his straight mouth,
> Softly drank through his straight gums, into his slack long
>   body,
> Silently.[4]

As he observes it, the man notes that the animal has emerged from the earth-wall, out of the gloom – it has come, that is, from darkness into the light of the day; he also notices that everything about the snake's behaviour and movement is smooth, soft, languid, rather sensual. A moment later, however, the snake lifts his head 'as cattle do' and looks 'vaguely' towards the speaker, 'as drinking cattle do' and it seems the repetition of the cattle comparison is reassuring: cattle are large and could be dangerous, but even though they see us, they continue to function in their own, parallel world, where, as long as we do not interfere with their drinking, they may be consigned to the vast panorama of the irrelevant. So with the snake: unless he is threatened or interfered with, he will remain harmless.

> He lifted his head from his drinking, as cattle do,
> And looked at me vaguely, as drinking cattle do,
> And flickered his two-forked tongue from his lips, and mused
>   a moment,
> And stooped and drank a little more,
> Being earth-brown, earth-golden from the burning bowels of
>   the earth
> On the day of Sicilian July, with Etna smoking.

It is not the looking that matters, of course, and the speaker knows that: it is the flicker of the scent-seeking tongue and the moment's musing that shows the snake knows the man is there. A more important detail, however, is the colour: this snake is earth-golden, which prompts the man to remember the one thing he knows about Sicilian snakes (most of which are non-venomous), which is that 'the black, black snakes are innocent, the gold are venomous'.

Meanwhile, at the very moment the man takes note of the snake's colour (this golden-brown hue suggests the asp viper, which is responsible for around 90 per cent of all snakebites in Italy, and whose bite can, albeit rarely, be fatal*), something else

---

* It must be said here that asp vipers really are beautiful creatures – and the best place to encounter them is in proximity to fresh, cool water. Admiration for their beauty, however, can be tempered by whether or not the viewer knows the snake is there. I will never forget a walk I took with a friend in

threatens – and in a single moment the snake, which has come from 'the burning bowels of the earth', is united, in the speaker's mind, with the volcano. This moment does not invoke any particular myth or legend, but one thinks of Jörmungandr, the Midgard Serpent, who must be killed by Thor at the final battle of Ragnarok – and perhaps the man thinks of some similar, residual myth of combat, in which the fiery snake/serpent/dragon is overcome by an aspiring hero:

> And voices in me said, If you were a man
> You would take a stick and break him now, and finish him off.

This impulse is not only an ugly one; it is also ignoble – and deeply impractical. If he leaves the animal alone, it will not harm him, and his killing one snake will do no great good for public safety. Besides, the speaker likes the snake, he admires its beauty and, from this point onwards, the dominant allusions come from sources that demand compassion, rather than a callow heroism from its actors. First, we hear that the snake has

> come like a guest in quiet, to drink at my water-trough
> And depart peaceful, pacified, and thankless,
> Into the burning bowels of this earth

– a clear reference to Luke 19, where Jesus comes 'as a guest' to the house of Zaccheus:

> And when Jesus came to the place, he looked up, and saw him,
>   and said unto him, Zaccheus, make haste, and come down;
>   for to day I must abide at thy house.

---

the Pfyn-Finges area of Switzerland in high summer. As was my habit, I was about to stop and scoop water from one of the conduits, or *bisses*, that guide the cold glacier melt down from the mountains and into the valley below, when my friend advised me, very quietly, but in a tone that got my immediate attention, to stay very, very still. This I did, while an asp viper, who had just that moment been drinking from the spot at which I had intended to take my refreshment, slithered between my feet and away into the dusty undergrowth.

And he made haste, and came down, and received him
    joyfully.
And when they saw it, they all murmured, saying, That he was
    gone to be guest with a man that is a sinner.

This allusion, of course, makes Lawrence's speaker the 'sinner';
but is it not already clear that, with his thoughts of killing and his
mock-heroism, he is exactly that? We should note that this reference to the life of Jesus (Jesus, that is, not 'Christ') is the first of
several, in which the impulse to murder the snake and the wise
teacher run parallel. Luke 19, in fact, ends with the lines:

But the chief priests and the scribes and the chief of the
    people sought to destroy him,
And could not find what they might do: for all the people were
    very attentive to hear him.

And indeed, the voice of civilisation, of supposed reason, of resentment of the golden other starts up again in that very moment,
confused now, by admiration and a natural curiosity:

Was it cowardice, that I dared not kill him?
Was it perversity, that I longed to talk to him?
Was it humility, to feel so honoured?
I felt so honoured.

And yet those voices:
If you were not afraid, you would kill him!

The snake, unaware of the battle being waged in the mind of his
host, has now drunk his fill, but he does not hurry away – and
there is something sensual, again, in his languor, so much at odds
with the pace of human life:

He drank enough
And lifted his head, dreamily, as one who has drunken,
And flickered his tongue like a forked night on the air, so
    black,

Seeing to lick his lips,
And looked around like a god, unseeing, into the air,
And slowly turned his head,
And slowly, very slowly, as if thrice adream,
Proceeded to draw his slow length curving round
And climb again the broken bank of my wall-face.

Reading these lines, with their reference to the lifting of the head and a slaked thirst, I cannot help but remember Psalm 110, with its magisterial opening, 'The Lord said unto my Lord, Sit thou at my right hand', and which continues with this promise to the Psalm poet's 'Lord' –

Thy people shall be willing in the day of thy power, in the beauties of holiness from the womb of the morning: thou hast the dew of thy youth.

– through to the mysterious final line, both beautiful and terrible, a line that must be read with a sense of the Lord's Lord, the He of this verse, as some glorious animal creature, combined in one body – or rather, in one breath – with the ultimate warrior hero, stooping to drink, then lifting up his beautiful, terrible face to the light: 'He shall drink of the brook in the way: therefore shall he lift up the head.' Like this divine creature, the snake lives by its own clock, or rather, by no clock at all: it is regal in its slow progress through this kingdom, of which it is in full command. Here the snake is 'like a god', another allusion to Jesus, who is not God but is the Son of God; later he will be a 'king', and eventually a 'king in exile'. First, however, something truly horrible happens, as the man gives way to his baser instincts:

And as he put his head into that dreadful hole,
And as he slowly drew up, snake-easing his shoulders, and
    entered farther,
A sort of horror, a sort of protest against his withdrawing into
    that horrid black
hole,

Deliberately going into the blackness, and slowly drawing
    himself after,
Overcame me now his back was turned.

We all know the courage that goes on behind turned backs. It is a kind of playground bravery that shows here, histrionic and stupid, as Lawrence's brief account of the childish and clumsy attack shows:

I looked round, I put down my pitcher,
I picked up a clumsy log
And threw it at the water-trough with a clatter.

This is not the courage of Thor facing Jörmungandr, this is not George facing the Dragon; this is the petty mob casting stones at the woman taken in adultery, in order more thoroughly to conceal their own lust. The log flies wide, of course, but it prompts a sudden change in the snake's movements, causing it to vanish quickly into 'the black hole, the earth-lipped fissure in the wall-front' – a black underworld to which, of course, the snake, and the poem, were always bound to return. In the meantime, however, we stay with the man, standing in his pyjamas, in the morning sunlight:

And immediately I regretted it.
I thought how paltry, how vulgar, what a mean act!
I despised myself and the voices of my accursed human
    education
And I thought of the albatross
And I wished he would come back, my snake.

The man thinks of 'the albatross', slain by Coleridge's Ancient Mariner, who is then accursed. Perhaps he also thinks of the long voyage that must be undertaken before the sin can be expiated, a voyage that brings the Mariner and his companions to the desolate and terrifying kingdom of the water snakes:

Beyond the shadow of the ship
I watched the water-snakes:
They moved in tracks of shining white,
And when they reared, the elfish light
Fell off in hoary flakes.

Within the shadow of the ship
I watched their rich attire:
Blue, glossy green, and velvet black,
They coiled and swam; and every track
Was a flash of golden fire.

O happy living things! no tongue
Their beauty might declare:
A spring of love gushed from my heart,
And I blessed them unaware:
Sure my kind saint took pity on me,
And I blessed them unaware.

The selfsame moment I could pray;
And from my neck so free
The Albatross fell off, and sank
Like lead into the sea.

Here is the moment when the petty, arrogant human finally sees beauty not just in the things that please him but in everything that lives, a beauty that resides in all subjects, if they are regarded with sufficient reverence (or, as Coleridge has it, love), and this is the moment, as the asp viper slithers back to his unknowable underworld beyond the earth wall, when the man in Lawrence's poem encounters defeat, as he realises he has missed his chance 'with one of the lords/ Of life'. It is a defeat, without doubt, one that is entirely self-inflicted – and yet, in the larger scheme of things, it is also a beginning, the start of a process of expiation that, even if such an encounter never comes again, will rid the man of that most craven of human sins: pettiness.

Pettiness, in this situation, comes of shame. Yet shame is not something to be avoided – unless it leads us, like Miss Havisham, to construct a needless and self-limiting illusion of stasis, or reversal. Lawrence's poem tells us that shame brings a desire for expiation, and that expiation is a beginning or, perhaps we should say, the beginning of a beginning – and in so doing, it reminds us that new beginnings can arise in the least promising of circumstances.

This is not surprising, however, if we consider that, whereas being lost is a simple, and wholly passive condition, being found demands, first, that we recognise that we are, in fact, lost, and, second, that we take the necessary steps to relocate ourselves and, in so doing, propose a home of some kind (however tentative, however impermanent). Lawrence's protagonist in 'Snake' can only find his way when he learns, first, to acknowledge his own pettiness and cowardice and, second, to understand that, in the reptile world, the snake is its own creature, unconnected in any way to whatever 'meaning' or symbolism we humans pin on it. We are the ones who left Eden, we are the ones who live on the near side of language. Or, as Grace Slick of Jefferson Airplane put it, rather less delicately:

> You call it rain, but the human name
> Doesn't mean shit to a tree.[5]

In the summer of 2014 a woman was taken to hospital after being attacked by a lion at a Michigan zoo. Part of her right middle finger had been bitten off after she entered the animal's enclosure. The woman claimed that she had permission from an attendant to 'pet' the lion; however, the attendant and the zoo denied this, saying that she and her daughter had been told to 'get back' and that there were 'warning signs and bite signs everywhere', which the victim had ignored. In an attempt to put the attack in context, the zoo issued a statement claiming that, when the woman went into the security area and was told by the guide to get back, she 'stated that she wanted to touch the lion and continued, against the guide's warning, to put her finger inside the fence'. Clearly, this animal lover was lucky to lose no more than a finger; events could have taken a significantly more dramatic turn. Yet such incidents are not as rare as one might think. Every year new stories emerge of individuals who deliberately enter zoo enclosures housing big cats, especially lions and tigers, and lose their lives as a consequence. These people have a variety of motives: one man thought that, like Daniel, he would be preserved by angels sent down from heaven (as described in the Old Testament book of Daniel, 6:22, 'My God hath sent his angel, and hath shut the lions' mouths, that they have not hurt me: forasmuch as before him innocence was found in me; and also before thee, O King'). A surprising number seem to have been motivated by some variety of psycho-sexual impulse; others appear to be driven by a sudden sense of privilege, or emotional kinship: a feeling that he or she understands, or has a secret connection with, a large and immensely dangerous animal.

Almost inevitably, when someone is injured or killed by an animal, even if he or she entered the enclosure deliberately, that creature is immediately 'put down' (having tasted human blood, it is seen as a permanent danger to its keepers). Sometimes they are simply shot by police or security officers on the scene. This happened, for example, when three boys broke into the polar bear enclosure at Brooklyn's Prospect Park Zoo in 1987, leading to the death of one of the boys and the subsequent shooting of both polar bears. According to the Parks Commissioner, Henry J. Stern:

> 'They were not executed. There seems to be no question but the police did the right thing in the circumstances.' When asked what might provoke such an attack, Mr Stern said, 'The mere presence of people in their cage.' He said polar bears are territorial and vicious by nature ...

Reading these comments, it is highly tempting to take issue with his language: true, bears are territorial, but this does not make them vicious; or at least, not according to the definition of that word in the Merriam-Webster dictionary: 'dangerously aggressive, savage; marked by violence or ferocity, fierce; malicious, spiteful; having the nature or quality of vice or immorality, depraved'. However, the Commissioner's abuse of the word is far from uncommon. For example, weasels and stoats are considered 'vicious' because, according to folklore, they 'kill for pleasure', a belief that grows a little in stature every time a weasel gets into the hen house, but anyone able to observe at close hand the behaviour of weasels knows that they do not kill a hen house full of birds for the love of killing: they simply see an opportunity to stock up on food, the way a human stocks up on food on market days.

This understanding based on proximity to the other animals was once common among human communities, as John Berger notes in an essay from 1980, 'Why Look at Animals?'

> The nineteenth century, in western Europe and North America, saw the beginning of a process, today being completed by twentieth-century corporate capitalism, by which every tradition which has previously mediated between man and nature was broken. Before this rupture, animals constituted the first circle of what surrounded man. Perhaps that already suggests too great a distance. They were with man at the centre of his world. Such centrality was of course economic and productive. Whatever the changes in productive means and social organization, men depended upon animals for food, work, transport, clothing.

To read this when it first appeared was poignant. Today, however, it bears all the weight of a tragedy in full flow, as we lose sight not just of our former companions at the centre of the given world but also of our own place there. We seem to be standing alone, now, without companions, only occasionally catching glimpses, in the half-light, of what Berger calls 'another visible order which intersects with ours and has nothing to do with it'. He continues:

> Our customary visible order is not the only one: it co-exists with other orders. Stories of fairies, sprites, ogres were a human attempt to come to terms with this co-existence. Hunters are continually aware of it and so can read signs we do not see.

Children feel it intuitively, because they have the habit of hiding behind things. There they discover the interstices between different sets of the visible.

When we grow up, however, we lose sight of other animals, both in the quasi-wild terrain we criss-cross in cars and trains and aeroplanes but barely inhabit and in our familiar immediate surroundings. As W. S. Merwin notes, in his short poem 'Witness':

I want to tell what the forests
were like

I will have to speak
in a forgotten language.[6]

And it should come as no surprise that, as we lose sight of the land, and the other creatures, we also lose sight of the wild in ourselves. The extinctions and species depletions we see in the world around us are, in short, mirrored in a loss of *élan vital* in our day-to-day lives, a loss of the connectedness that was once provided by clan and totem animals, or even by the simple fact of wild presences in our immediate habitat.

This being so, might it not also be the case that, for some, this loss of the wild becomes unbearable, and any contact, anything at all that brings them closer to the creaturely world, is preferable to the absolutely denatured terrain in which they have come to dwell? That grief may live on the surface of the mind and of the skin, or it may be buried deep in the well of the (un)conscious, but it is real nonetheless. Somehow, we feel the lack – and at times that lack becomes urgent and dangerously irrational. If what we habitually see confirms us, as John Berger claims, it is also true that what we never see, or see only in some denatured (domesticated, imprisoned or cartoon) form, fades from our lives – and, with it, a necessary emotional and psychological kinship with other living things dissipates. In one of his finest poems Sherman Alexie conjures up the spirit of the salmon, a sacred animal of the Spokane River people (for whom the river itself is sacred), an indigenous group who were effectively deprived of their cultural basis when the Grand Coulee Dam and the Chief Joseph Dam were built in the 1940s:*

> I am told
> by many of you that I must forgive and so I shall
> after we Indians have gathered around the fire with that
>> salmon
> who has three stories it must tell before sunrise: one story will
>> teach us
> how to pray; another story will make us laugh for hours;
> the third story will give us reason to dance.[7]

That gathering around the fire would have taken place at Spokane Falls (now part of the central business district of Spokane, it is, itself, dammed in two places), and the ceremony, centred around the totem-spirit of the Great Salmon and its three stories, renewed the three basic values of the people: reverence for the given world, laughter and kinship, and the natural connection to the earth that comes of dancing. But what happens to a people when those values are lost? And what happens to a certain kind of individual when not only the totem spirits but any and all meaningful sense of our fellow animals has dissipated?

People visit zoos for any number of reasons. However, if you are looking for some kind of communion with another animal, there is no place worse to go – indeed, for the damaged individual seeking to find some reconnection with the wild, zoos offer a terrible confirmation of his or her deepest fears. 'The zoo cannot but disappoint', says John Berger. 'The public purpose of zoos is to offer visitors the opportunity of looking at animals. Yet nowhere in a zoo can a stranger encounter the look of an animal. At the most, the animal's gaze flickers and passes on. They look sideways. They

---

* 'Irony, a hallmark of the contemporary indigenous American' (Sherman Alexie). Chief Joseph (1840–1904) spent much of his life resisting the oppression, and decrying the lies and hypocrisy, of the US government.

look blindly beyond.' So – what then? To the average visitor this aspect of the zoo is, as Berger says, a matter of disappointment. However, to the homeless woman who climbs into the lion's cage in Lucie Brock-Broido's poem 'Self-Deliverance by Lion', it is a matter of life and death.

Published in Brock-Broido's third collection, *Trouble in Mind*, in 2004, 'Self-Deliverance by Lion' was 'adapted' from Kay Redfield Jamison's study of suicide, *Night Falls Fast* (1999). A note attached to the poem tells how

> In 1995, the body of a thirty-six-year-old transient woman from Little Rock was discovered by a worker at the National Zoo in Washington. She had scaled a barrier, ascended a rough high wall, and crossed a twenty-six-foot moat in order to make her way into the lions' den. Her death by mauling was ruled a suicide.

What we note here – more important than the court ruling and the obstacles placed by the zookeepers to the intruder's intent to trespass – is that this woman is 'transient'. In the poem she has no name, she is of no fixed abode, she has no societal function and she is a thousand miles from home.* Because she has no known history, we have no way of knowing why she might have chosen to die or, more specifically, to die in a lions' den, but then, as Jamison points out, all suicides are mysterious. 'Each way to suicide is its own', she says, 'intensely private, unknowable, and terrible. Suicide will have seemed to its perpetrator the last and best of bad possibilities, and any attempt by the living to chart this final terrain of life can be only a sketch, maddeningly incomplete.' She also notes that in many cases suicides 'want both to live and to die; ambivalence saturates the suicidal act'. Paraphrasing this, we might say that, while we usually understand suicide as an attempt to escape a painful life through death, it might also be an attempt to escape from a kind of death-in-life into what might be

---

* She was to be identified as Margaret Davis King, of Little Rock, Arkansas, a woman who had a long history of 'schizophrenia' and 'religious delusions'.

a moment's intense life, the moment of mauling, which in Brock-Broido's poem not only makes 'a massive loss/ Of the history of a body's history' in which what is taken is 'the custody/ Of soft tissue, and astonishment', but also 'deliverance':

> I had hoped for, all that Serengeti
> Year, a hopelessness of less despair
>
> Than hope itself. I knew the excellent repair
> Of night fell cruel and quickly where
>
> The lions had the mastery of me – aware
> Their mastery was by my will, and fair.[8]

Brock-Broido's work is often characterised by cruel and lovely ambiguities: none more so, perhaps, than the play on the word 'aware' here. Who is aware that the mastery of the lions happens by the transient woman's will? Just the woman? It is more interesting than not to resist that conclusion – and we are then obliged to ask who the master is, here, if the lions are also 'aware', not only of who was devising this small drama but also of its intrinsic fairness. (We could, of course, go into the ambiguities of the word 'fair' here, but I think Brock-Broido has made her point.) Brock-Broido points out in her note that she has adapted Daniel 6:24 here: 'And the king commanded, and they brought those men which had accused Daniel, and they cast them into the den of lions, them, their children, and their wives; and the lions had the mastery of them, and brake all their bones in pieces or ever they came at the bottom of the den' – an example of Old Testament justice, or punishment at least (one feels sorry for the wives and children, anyway). However, there is nothing in the Bible verse to justify the use of the word 'fair', nor is there any suggestion of awareness of the lions' mastery, whether on their part or on the part of their victims – and it is this contrast that is most telling. What *is* fair – in the most appalling and genuinely tragic way – is the choice this woman makes to deliver herself, by lion, from a selfhood that is no longer bearable. This brings us back to the original definition of 'to maul', with which the poem opens –

> To maul is to make a massive loss
> Of the history of a body's history

– lines that, to me, immediately suggest another Bible passage, this time from the New Testament. It is a passage that comes in John 12, almost immediately after Jesus' last visit to Lazarus, whom he had earlier raised from the dead, and it is a fine example of John the Evangelist's own gift, not only for cruel and lovely ambiguities, but for the revelatory paradox:

> Verily, verily, I say unto you, Except a corn of wheat fall into the ground and die, it abideth alone: but if it die, it bringeth forth much fruit. He that loveth his life shall lose it; and he that hateth his life in this world shall keep it unto life eternal.

What the woman from Little Rock surrenders is her body's history, an act she commits out of a need to be released from the worst kind of despair, on the one hand, and a desire, on the other, to regain, for one astonishing moment, the mastery she has lost. What the poem grants her in return is 'the excellent repair/ Of night' in which her abandoned body is transformed into nature itself:

> Her hair was a long damp chestnut
> River-pelt spilled after an enormous
>
> And important rain. Her body was still sticky
> With the lilac repetitions in her cotton dress. [...]
>
> [...] crewelled with frost marks, cursive
> As the dewclaws on a lion's forepaw, massive
>
> And significant.

If we follow the logic of this poem, we are obliged to appreciate that deliverance from human loneliness – from an almost unbearable homesickness for our own wild selves and for the other animals – takes many forms. Sometimes, it comes from without, kindly, forgiving, just. Sometimes it shames us into changing, so that we are able to accommodate the wild in our day-to-day lives. Sometimes it must be found in ruin, but even then it is still a deliverance – and what we ask for deliverance from is always an evil. That evil can take many forms, from the *anomie* of a human subject disconnected from any sense of connection with other lives (the loss of creatureliness, as it were, that comes of living apart from the natural, both within and outside our own bodies) to the wishful fascination with a taboo that we most desire and, at the same time, fear. We can hunt them from jeeps on expensive safaris, we can turn them into symbols and metaphors for human values, we can reduce them to cartoons and company logos, but for most of us they remain too distant, too remote. Try as we may to be content with our mobile phones and gaming consoles, we are homesick for the other animals.

A STONY INVITATION TO REFLECT

I believe that banking institutions are more dangerous to our liberties than standing armies.

Thomas Jefferson

ROME, 20 JANUARY 1927. Addressing Benito Mussolini, a foreign visitor makes the following statement:

If I had been an Italian, I am sure that I should have been whole-heartedly with you from the start to finish in your triumphant struggle against the bestial appetites and passions of Leninism.

Ten years later, in remarks addressed to the Palestine Royal Commission, the same individual cheerfully proclaims:

I do not admit for instance, that a great wrong has been done to the Red Indians of America or the black people of Australia. I do not admit that a wrong has been done to these people by the fact that a stronger race, a higher-grade race, a more worldly-wise race to put it that way, has come in and taken their place.

Neither of these sincere and lasting opinions – or the history of political actions they inspired – seemed to count in 2002, however, when, as a BBC news release reported: 'Winston Churchill [has been] voted the greatest Briton ever in the much-awaited result of the BBC poll which [...] has generated more than one and a half million votes.' With 456,498 votes the wartime prime minister was a clear winner, with Isambard Kingdom Brunel (398,526 votes) an honourable second, followed by Princess Diana (225,584), Charles Darwin (112,496) and an early proponent of music hall named William Shakespeare (109,919). Yet, though this choice may seem ill judged, it should not surprise anyone. Churchill – anti-labour, pro-eugenics, racist, the architect of the Greek dictatorship and a man who openly advocated the use of chemical weapons on people he considered 'barbaric' – somehow steers past all criticism and retains the aura of wartime hero. It is difficult to understand why – maybe he is so loved for his occasional flashes of rather brutish wit? After all, this was the man who, routinely castigating the working classes of Britain – 'as for tramps and wastrels, there ought to be proper Labour Colonies where they could be sent for considerable periods and made to realise their duty to the State' – could add, in a letter to George V, no less, that 'it must not, however, be forgotten that there are idlers and wastrels at both ends of the social scale.'

Rome, 15 March 1942. Ezra Pound delivers one of his many radio broadcasts in support of Mussolini. It is a loathsome catalogue of anti-Semitic rambling and jumbled historical disinformation, deliberately contrived to be as vile as possible. Pound will continue to make such broadcasts until 1943, when the US government indicts him *in absentia* for treason. The poet's passionate support for Mussolini continues unabated, however, and he continues to broadcast under various pseudonyms. Then, on 28 April 1945, *Il Duce* is murdered and, after a brief encounter with some bemused Italian partisans, a confused and mentally unstable Pound surrenders to a group of Americans at Lavagna. From there he is transferred, first to Genoa for interrogation, then on to Pisa, where he is held in a specially fortified, open-air cell, nicknamed the 'gorilla cage'. Here he has vivid hallucinations and composes some of his finest work, before being repatriated to the United States, where he is due to stand trial for treason. After psychiatric reports find him unfit to plead, however, he is sent to a mental hospital in Washington, where he will remain, his doctors and lawyer playing a rambling cat-and-mouse game – Is he still mad? Was he ever? – until his release in 1958. During this time he receives a stream of highly respected visitors, including many of the finest American poets of the day, and, in spite of his history as a traitor and current status as a lunatic, wins the Bollingen Prize for Poetry. To this day he is the subject of fierce debate: is he a great poet or a tawdry anti-Semite? Can he be both? And, given how odious he had become by the end of the Second World War, given the fact that he continued to write and speak racist nonsense off and on for the rest of his life, is it possible to rescue *anything* from his work?

Many readers and academics think it is. Some point out that Pound's anti-Semitism, even if it was more than usually vehement and unashamed, was very much of its time and, possibly, a symptom of his mental derangement; others advance the argument that Pound was not at all as racist as he seemed, citing remarks such as 'The worst mistake I made was that stupid, suburban prejudice of anti-Semitism.'* Yet, even when we set aside the question of his bigotry, it is not at all clear what Pound's political or artistic vision really entailed. A poet who constantly spoke of making things new, his own verse regularly drew on very old Chinese, Italian and Provençal models – and the better side of his politics was a hodgepodge of half-understood Chinese philosophy, medieval morality and European courtly traditions. His hatred of 'usura'† – and so, by extension, the runaway capitalism

---

*Though an analysis of the language here rather suggests that he is more ashamed of the 'suburban' element than of the race hatred.

† *Usura*, or usury, in basic terms, meant the lending of money at an exorbitant interest; though it was usually not outlawed altogether, successive governments tried to control its excesses. In England, for example, the Usury Act of 1660, while it allowed speculative lending to be carried out, tried to limit the interest rate to 6 per cent. Gradually, the practice became more sophisticated and many-faceted, so the term 'usury', as employed by Pound, really refers to a variety of bad financial practices. He preferred to use the term *usura* because of its roots in medieval culture, especially in Dante, but

that had caused the crash of 1929 – might have provoked more serious debate had it not been riddled with obscurity and elitism:

WITH USURA
wool comes not to market
sheep bringeth no gain with usura
Usura is a murrain, usura
blunteth the needle in the maid's hand
and stoppeth the spinner's cunning. Pietro Lombardo
came not by usura
Duccio came not by usura
nor Pier della Francesca.

And yet … And yet, in spite of all this, Pound could be deadly accurate, and persuasively eloquent, as in the passage on *usura* in Canto 45, where he says:

Usura rusteth the chisel
It rusteth the craft and the craftsman
It gnaweth the thread in the loom
[…]
Usura slayeth the child in the womb
It stayeth the young man's courting
It hath brought palsey to bed, lyeth
between the young bride and her bridegroom.[1]

And few other poets have defined so well, or so poignantly, the task of maintaining a vital culture in a society crumbling under the sheer weight of modernity as Pound does at the end of Canto 81, arguably his finest poem:

What thou lovest well is thy true heritage
What thou lov'st well shall not be reft from thee

---

with that use came some ugly baggage, most notably the association with anti-Semitism.

he declares, defiantly. And he continues with a surprising invocation of 'the green world' where the poet most closely associated with European artifice celebrates the 'scaled invention and true artistry' to be found in nature, in a passage that Albertus Magnus or Spinoza might have heartily approved:

> Pull down thy vanity, it is not man
> Made courage, or made order, or made grace,
>   Pull down thy vanity, I say pull down.
> Learn of the green world what can be thy place.

A few lines later he is castigating someone – himself, no doubt, and at the same time some species of modern Everyman – in a passage of around thirty lines, reminiscent of Ecclesiastes, in which the word 'vanity' appears nine times.* Here he mercilessly strips away the 'mean hates' and 'falsity' of a character damned as 'Rathe to destroy, niggard in charity' until, all pride and arrogance spent, he testifies to the purpose of the poet, a purpose that, no matter how gravely he failed in it as a man, he had tried to fulfil as an artist and as a friend to other artists:

> But to have done instead of not doing
>   this is not vanity
> To have, with decency, knocked
> That a Blunt should open
>   To have gathered from the air a live tradition
> or from a fine old eye the unconquered flame
> This is not vanity.
>   Here error is all in the not done,
> all in the diffidence that faltered …

It is worth pointing out that Pound was not alone in viewing usury as ruinous in its social and economic effects; nor was Samuel

---

* See Ecclesiastes 1:2.

Johnson, when he said that 'the synonym of usury is ruin'.* On the contrary, writers and commentators throughout history have castigated the practice of usury as unjust, socially and economically destructive and a sign of low moral character. However, for historical reasons, this hostility towards usury has become confused with a separate and utterly irrational anti-Semitism – a huge irony when we recall that the interdict against usury has its origin in Jewish religious teachings. (See Exodus 22, 'If thou lend money to any of My people, even to the poor with thee, thou shalt not be to him as a creditor; neither shall ye lay upon him interest', or Deuteronomy 23:19, 'Thou shalt not lend upon usury to thy brother; usury of money, usury of victuals, usury of any thing that is lent upon usury', as well as Leviticus 25:37, 'Thou shalt not give him thy money upon usury, nor lend him thy victuals for increase', among many other references in the Bible.) Throughout history the damage done by usury was clearly recognised and frequently condemned. As Marx points out, it has always been a problem, a sore in any community that eats away at freedom and creativity:

> Usury centralises money wealth, where the means of production are disjointed. It does not alter the mode of production, but attaches itself to it as a parasite and makes it miserable.

---

*Johnson, in fact, had much to say about usury. For example, he once remarked to James Boswell that 'The law against usury is for the protection of creditors as well as debtors; for if there were no such check, people would be apt, *from the temptation of great interest, to lend to desperate persons,* by whom they would lose their money. Accordingly, there are instances of ladies being ruined, by having injudiciously sunk their fortunes for high annuities, which, after a few years, ceased to be paid, in consequence of the ruined circumstances of the borrower' (my italics). Anyone who lived through the 2008 market crash, caused in part by unscrupulous lending of 'sub-prime' mortgages to 'desperate people', will appreciate the chilling foresight of Johnson's observation. Even he, however, would perhaps not have envisioned anything so cynical and callous as the behaviour of some of the institutions involved in that circus of runaway capitalism. See Michael Lewis's 2010 account of that circus, *The Big Short: Inside the Doomsday Machine.*

It sucks its blood, kills its nerve, and compels reproduction to proceed under even more disheartening conditions. Hence the popular hatred against usurers, which was most pronounced in the ancient world, where the ownership of the means of production by the producer himself was at the same time the basis of the political conditions, of the independence of the citizen. To the extent that slavery prevails, or to the extent that the surplus product is consumed by the feudal lord and his retinue, while either the slave owner or the feudal lord falls into the clutches of the usurer, the mode of production remains the same. Only, it becomes harder on the labourer. The indebted slave holder or feudal lord becomes more oppressive, because he is himself more oppressed. Or he makes finally room for the usurer, who becomes a landed proprietor or a slave holder himself, like the knights in ancient Rome. Into the place of the old exploiters, whose exploitation was more or less patriarchal, because it was largely a means of political power, steps a hard, money-mad parvenu.[2]

It was not until this century, when the citizenry of Western Europe and the Americas – and finally the world – saw banks and the financial institutions take control of the public sphere as never before, that usury was, very grudgingly, accepted as a temporarily necessary evil. 'For at least another hundred years,' says John Maynard Keynes, 'we must pretend to ourselves and to every one that fair is foul and foul is fair; for foul is useful and fair is not. Avarice and usury and precaution must be our gods for a little longer still.' Such a position, even if Keynes was being facetious, is untenable, even in a bad joke. Yet how do we go about loosening the grip of financial institutions over every aspect of our lives? We may recognise ourselves in the protagonist of Ursula Le Guin's *The Dispossessed*:

He tried to read an elementary economics text; it bored him past endurance, it was like listening to somebody interminably recounting a long and stupid dream. He could not force himself to understand how banks functioned and so forth, because all the operations of capitalism were as meaningless to him as the rites of a primitive religion, as barbaric, as elaborate, and as unnecessary. In a human sacrifice to a deity there might be at least a mistaken and terrible beauty; in the rites of the moneychangers, where greed, laziness, and envy were assumed to move all men's acts, even the terrible became banal.

Now 'the moneychangers' have a new face, and the ways in which they do business have become ever more recondite. Instead of talking about usury, we use terms like 'runaway capitalism', or the 'One Percent', but the outcomes are much the same as they were in earlier epochs, when greed not only reigned but was normalised, even admired. As the French economist Frédéric Bastiat pointed out almost two centuries ago: 'When plunder becomes a way of life for a group of men living together in society, they create for themselves, in the course of time, a legal system that authorizes it and a moral code that glorifies it.' Whatever his flaws, Ezra Pound saw the dangers of runaway capitalism, and in Canto 45 he offered a clear diagnosis of the damage done by usury to the human spirit, to the land and to communities everywhere. Indeed, Pound biographer and critic Michael Alexander calls it 'perhaps the clearest and most cogent statement of principle in the poem. Its Old Testament litany of the effects of usury on natural life is full of torrential moral indignation, a passion which remains, in spite of reservations, deeply impressive.'

So did that poem make any difference? Who can say? As Chairman Mao is said to have remarked, when asked about the impact of the French Revolution, it's too soon to tell. Yet, even if we take the long view on the political poem, as exemplified by Pound and others I shall discuss below, it seems naïve to expect a literary work – or any single action by a lone individual – to change the world. As we know, poetry makes nothing happen. But what if this assumption should prove to be a mistake? In recent years the old models of historical cause and effect, in which powerful nations, armies or dictators decide all outcomes in a fairly linear if-then-else manner are gradually being replaced by a more chaos-based, 'butterfly effect' system of thought, in which the emergent, the granular and the fuzzy can play a significant part. For example, Carne Ross, whose book *The Leaderless Revolution* has helped to change the paradigms for observing change since its first publication in 2011, has remarked that:

> [the] battle will not be won by marches on Washington, but by myriad small but substantive changes wrought by individuals and groups acting upon, as well as declaring, their convictions (for not only systemic change is needed, but also cultural). This revolution does not need a manifesto, or leaders. It can be, and perhaps needs to be, a leaderless revolution: a million acts of change, driven by individual conviction [...]
>
> But these multiple acts of change must also inhabit the simple choices of the everyday: what we buy and where we bank, and how we treat others – celebrating the compassionate, shaming the greedy. And though simple, the decision to enact our beliefs in every circumstance is profound and liberating, not least because this is harder than it sounds. Dull, it is not.
>
> The many steps towards a just and sustainable economy, and a truly inclusive democracy will be taken not by those we vote for, or petition. They will not emerge from the inevitable dialectic of history either. These steps require action and choices by us, individually, and then together.

Following this argument, in which an accumulation of seemingly diverse but interconnected events combine to effect tipping points and chain reactions in the social sphere, it seems as reasonable to treat a poem (or any other work of art) as a potential catalyst. If we recall Auden's words – that poetry 'makes nothing happen' but that it offers a context, a 'way of happening' – we begin to see that the social function of the poem, if it has one at all, is both to provoke us to reflection and, at the same time, to cast a new light on the matter at hand, a light that is not necessarily available when we rely solely on conventional reasoning.

Certainly such a position offers more, and is more courageous, than that taken by some post-war poets who, following Theodor Adorno, suggested that, after Auschwitz, poetry should be seen as a dead or, at the very least, a merely decorative art. In fact, this sense that poets are morally obliged to go beyond the hollowness of the dominant culture was not new: writing immediately after the First World War, Pound denounced the materialism and cynicism of 'a botched civilization' that, by then, amounted to little more than 'two gross of broken statues' and 'a few thousand battered books', while his poetic collaborator Eliot cited Hermann Hesse's *Blick ins Chaos*, as an influence on *The Waste Land*:

> Already half of Europe [...] on the way to Chaos, drives drunk in sacred infatuation along the edge of the precipice, sings drunkenly, as though hymn singing, as Dmitri Karamazov sang. The offended bourgeois laughs at the songs; the saint and the seer hear them with tears.

Adorno's challenge to a corrupted society was, however, the starkest: he asked not simply whether it is possible to write poetry after Auschwitz, but whether it is possible to *live*. Meanwhile, Anne Sexton's poem 'After Auschwitz' seems to go several steps further:

> Man is evil,
> I say aloud.
> Man is a flower
> that should be burnt,
> I say aloud.
>
> [...]
>
> Man with his small pink toes,
> with his miraculous fingers
> is not a temple
> but an outhouse,
> I say aloud.

Let man never again raise his teacup.
Let man never again write a book.
Let man never again put on his shoe.
Let man never again raise his eyes,
on a soft July night.
Never. Never. Never. Never. Never.[3]

Again and again the poem's speaker says these things aloud –
but in the last line of the poem she says, 'I beg the Lord not to
hear.' Why this prayer? Is it because the speaker recognises that
her loathing for the evil 'other' is a mirror image of the Nazi's
loathing and contempt for his victims, and that, as the opening of
the poem suggests, she is humanly diminished by the anger that
'as black as a hook/ overtakes' her? She then goes on to repeat an
atrocity story that, with its regularity, universality and fixed time,
strikes us as highly unlikely:

Each day,
each Nazi
took, at 8:00 A.M., a baby
and sauteed him for breakfast
in his frying pan.

Each day? Each Nazi? At exactly 8:00 a.m.? With the entire catalogue of horrors, from the gas chambers to Mengele's horrifying
'experiments', why does the poet offer us a story that is so far-
fetched? That is, in fact, absurd? It is a story intended to make its
audience feel, not a justifiable anger that might lead to resistance
to political evil but a black rage that overtakes us – so much so
that, caught on its hook, we become as irrational and unforgiving
as the perpetrator of the original crime. 'Man' is not a temple, it
is true, but that does not make him a cesspit. Such judgements are
too black and white, too final, leading the average reader to retort
that our awareness of suffering, our awareness of evil, should not
drive us to reject the human condition altogether but to search
harder, and dig deeper, to find the compassion that 'the Lord'
would approve.

Considered in this light, it becomes apparent that what was required in the twentieth century's confrontation with the Angel of History was not the kind of rearguard action advocated by Wyndham Lewis, in which superior people launched a rescue mission to save the European cultural silver, but it wasn't Sexton's defeatist, baby-with-the-bathwater, 'Man is Evil' approach either. What was needed was a radical re-envisioning of those shared values and manners – and, more broadly, of life itself. That being the case, it seems profitable to consider the position taken by certain other twentieth-century philosophers with regard to poetry and, in particular, that taken by Heidegger and Wittgenstein, two thinkers who, having examined and questioned philosophy's ability to apprehend reality in a holistic way, both turned to poetry as an alternative method to envision the world and our dwelling in it. Both expressed their belief in the importance of poetry on numerous occasions. 'To be a poet in a destitute time means: to attend, singing, to the trace of the fugitive gods,' Heidegger said. 'This is why the poet in the time of the world's night utters the holy.' As we have already seen, Wittgenstein, who once remarked that 'Man has to awaken to wonder […] science is a way of sending him to sleep again', was quite categorical. 'Philosophy,' he said, 'ought really to be written only as a form of poetry.' When we consider these statements alongside Maria Zambrano's writings on philosophy and poetry, we begin to discover a new and very different sense of what poetry's potential role in a society might be.

At the same time, we can perhaps learn a useful lesson on what can reasonably be expected from the political poem – and from political art in general – from another discipline or, rather, from a critic in another discipline. When the eminent music critic Richard Taruskin proposed that, in his Holocaust memorial piece *Different Trains*, Steve Reich had composed 'the only adequate musical response – one of the few adequate artistic responses in any medium – to the Holocaust', he took a gleeful, and not entirely fair side-swipe at the After Auschwitz hypothesis:

With famous and flatulent self-importance, Adorno announced that after Auschwitz, poetry had become impossible. The kind of art Adorno upheld – pretentiously abstract, ostentatiously alienated and self-involved – surely did ring hollow after the art-loving Nazis, co-opting the masterpieces of the past, had unmasked the moral contingency of high 'humanistic' aesthetics. What was desperately needed, though, was a poetry that gave significant form to that contingency and disillusion. Most of what was put forth, from the heavy tomes of existentialist philosophy to the bloated cantatas of the Socialist Realists, ludicrously contradicted by its bombast the sensibility it sought to embody. Or else it sought with mendacious sentimentality to retrieve a message of uplift from the abyss.

He then went on to discuss art that falls into such traps:

> Arnold Schoenberg's 'Survivor from Warsaw' (1947), the most famous musical memorial to the Holocaust, falls easy prey to these pitfalls. Were the name of its composer not surrounded by a historiographical aureole, were its musical idiom not safeguarded by its inscrutability, its B-movie clichés – the Erich von Stroheim Nazi barking 'Achtung,' the kitsch-triumphalism of the climactic, suddenly tonal singing of the Jewish credo – would be painfully obvious, and no one would ever think to program such banality alongside Beethoven's Ninth as has become fashionable. That kind of post-Auschwitz poetry is indeed a confession of art's impotence.

Finally, after a brief analysis of Reich's method in *Different Trains* (an astonishing work for string quartet and voices), Taruskin distils the political valence of the art work to its true essence: a bearing witness, a refusal of false solutions and, at the most basic level, a starting-point for thought, and for the possibility of dialogue:

> There are no villains and no heroes. There is no role for a Ralph Fiennes or a Werner Klemperer to flatter your sense of moral superiority. And there is no bathetic glory to comfort you with

a trumped-up Triumph of the Human Spirit. There is just the perception that while this happened here, that happened there, and a stony invitation to reflect.

It seems ironic, now, that arguably the best repudiation of the last century's runaway capitalist ethic should have been written not by a Marxist, or even a poet from the left of the political spectrum, but by a man whose every expressed idea would be seen as tainted by his association with Italian fascism and his virulent anti-Semitism. Sadly, for reasons that are hard for his poetic admirers to understand, when Pound reached the conclusion that 'USURY is the cancer of the world', he also decided that 'only the surgeon's knife of Fascism can cut it out of the life of the nations'. This was a terrible error of judgement, and literary critics and biographers will no doubt continue to argue as to whether his convictions arose out of deliberate thought or as the result of his madness. Yet Pound was not the only modern American poet to reject usury; he was just the easiest to dismiss. William Carlos Williams, for example, was perfectly sane, and his views are remarkably similar to those Pound laid out in Canto 45. Here he is in Book IV of *Paterson*, composed in the mid-1940s:*

> Money sequestered enriches avarice, makes
> poverty: the direct cause of
> disaster   •

---

*Earlier in the same poem (Book II), he had attacked the Federal Reserve Banks as constituting:

> a Legalized National Usury System, whose Customer No. 1 is our Government, the richest country in the world. Every one of us is paying tribute to the money racketeers on every dollar we earn

adding that:

> The people must pay anyway; why should they be compelled to pay twice? THE WHOLE NATIONAL DEBT IS MADE UP ON INTEREST CHARGES. If the people ever get to thinking of bonds and bills at the same time, the game is up.

           while the leak drips.
Let out the fire, let the wind go!
Release the Gamma-rays that cure the cancer
  • the cancer, usury. Let credit
out • out from between the bars
before· the bank windows

    • credit, stalled
in money, conceals the generative
that thwarts art or buys it (without
understanding), out of poverty of wit, to
win, vicariously, the blue ribbon

   •••

          to win
the Congressional Medal
for bravery beyond the call of duty but
not to end as a bridge-tender
on government dole •

         Defeat may steel us
in knowledge : money : joke
to be wiped out sooner or later at stroke
of pen •[4]

The analyses are almost identical; the only difference is in the quality of each man's anger. Where Williams clearly speaks of a system, Pound identifies that system with a specific community. Why he should have so persistently done so remains something of a mystery – but then, prejudice on anyone's part is hard to understand. As it turned out, Pound threw away his political insights by allowing them to become sullied with the vilest of prejudices, at a time when that prejudice was fuelling genocide. Had he never come to his bizarre anti-Semitic conclusions, would we take those insights more seriously today? This is a hypothetical question – but it is a pity that, as he said late in life: 'If the individual, or heretic, gets hold of some essential truth, or sees some error in the system being practised, he commits so many marginal errors himself that he is worn out before he can establish his point.'[5] As the century continued, poets across the world began to develop more sophisticated political arguments, especially in their application to social justice, feminist and environmental issues. As we shall see in the next chapter, Robert Frost even dreamed of a kind of alliance between poets and politicians that, if carefully managed, might yield real fruits in the public sphere. That he was to be disappointed almost goes without saying, but those who came after him, from the 1960s onwards, developed a new, and more radical, poetics that, adhering neither to left nor right, in many cases, attempted, with the tools at their disposal, to speak truth to power.*

---

* See the American Friends Service Committee's document of that name, from 1955:

> Our title, *Speak Truth to Power*, taken from a charge given to Eighteenth Century Friends, suggests the effort that is made to speak from the deepest insight of the Quaker faith, as this faith is understood by those who prepared this study. We speak to power in three senses:
>
> To those who hold high places in our national life and bear the terrible responsibility of making decisions for war or peace.
>
> To the American people who are the final reservoir of power in this country and whose values and expectations set the limits for those who exercise authority.
>
> To the idea of Power itself, and its impact on Twentieth Century life.

A GOLDEN AGE OF POETRY AND POWER

If more politicians knew poetry, and more poets knew politics,
I am convinced the world would be a little better place in
which to live.

John F. Kennedy

ON 20 JANUARY 1961 a poet read for the first time during a presidential inauguration. The idea to invite Robert Frost to 'say' a poem during the ceremony originated not with John F. Kennedy himself but with Stewart L. Udall, an environmentalist, activist, former Arizona congressman and Secretary of the Interior designate, who had got to know Frost during his residency at the Library of Congress. It was a great notion and, though Kennedy joked that it could turn out to be a mistake because 'you know that Robert Frost always steals any show he is part of', he immediately saw the advantages in having the US's most distinguished poet by his side as he was sworn in. He must have seen, as the poet William Meredith later remarked, that Frost's presence would focus attention on the incoming president as 'a man of culture' and, on a purely analytical level, this was a sufficient PR coup in itself. Yet there were other reasons for including Frost in the celebrations, not least the fact that the notoriously oppositional old 'Puritan' had backed the Kennedy campaign from the beginning. In fact, he had shown his support even before Kennedy announced his candidacy. 'The next President of the United States will be from Boston,'

Frost declared during a gala dinner for his eighty-fifth birthday on 26 March 1959. 'He's a Puritan named Kennedy. The only Puritans left these days are the Roman Catholics. There. I guess I wear my politics on my sleeve.' Frost would reiterate his admiration for the junior senator from Massachusetts on numerous occasions, and just as Eleanor Roosevelt's eventual endorsement appeared to align Kennedy's political vision with the spirit and values of the New Deal, so Frost's backing linked the youthful candidate to the latter-day Puritan ethic that Frost had come to embody, both in his writing and in his person. What Frost brought, in short, was *resonance*.

Having made his decision, Kennedy telegraphed Frost early in December 1960. The old poet replied by telegram the next day, his acceptance of the honour tinged with a sly dig at Kennedy's supposed inexperience (to which Richard Nixon had made repeated reference during the presidential campaign):

IF YOU CAN BEAR AT YOUR AGE THE HONOR OF BEING MADE PRESIDENT OF THE UNITED STATES, I OUGHT TO BE ABLE AT MY AGE TO BEAR THE HONOR OF TAKING SOME PART IN YOUR INAUGURATION. I MAY NOT BE EQUAL TO IT BUT I CAN ACCEPT IT FOR MY CAUSE – THE ARTS, POETRY, NOW FOR THE FIRST TIME TAKEN INTO THE AFFAIRS OF STATESMEN.

This latter remark, as naïve as it sounds today, is crucially important in our understanding of the relationship between Frost and Kennedy. We could dismiss his talk of a cause as rhetorical, the high-sounding language of public discourse, but that would be unfair for, like his friend Udall, Frost was prepared to pursue a careful but committed working relationship with those in power in order to pursue higher goals than mere fame or reflected glory. Frost cared about the arts, and about poetry especially, both in the US and elsewhere (when he visited Russia in 1962, he would be sufficiently impressed by Khrushchev's encouragement of poets such as Yevgeni Yevtushenko and Andrei Voznesensky – and by the rehabilitation of Anna Akhmatova – to call the Soviet leader 'a great man'), and he felt artists should be ready to work with the state to serve a higher cause. Years later, Stewart Udall recalled the following exchange with André Malraux during a Washington luncheon, in which Frost's seeming naïveté about art and politics seems all too obvious in the face of a more sophisticated and politically experienced writer:

> Frost: The Government can use a poet to serve its purpose – *but when he is no longer useful, the Government has a right to cast him off.*

> Malraux: Yes, but that is not the ultimate truth. Think of Caesar Augustus. The poet Virgil was used by him, was part of his circle of advisers. But today Virgil is the one we remember.

> Frost: But that was a long time coming.

> Malraux: But isn't that what we're for?

But was Frost really being naïve here? Considering his commitment to democratic politics, on the one hand, and his chosen art, on the other, he would have felt that it was his duty to work with government, whenever he could, to further both causes, rather than to oppose power purely as a matter of course. He fancied himself a political animal, among other things. When he discovered that he was not (as he did later, on his return from Moscow), it hurt him badly, and even though he would still maintain that, when he was no longer useful, his government had every right to cast him off, he was dismayed by his failure.

The initial telegram exchange gave way to a telephone conversation, during which Kennedy suggested the old poet might write something new for the ceremony. Then, when Frost rejected that idea as too demanding, they agreed he might read 'The Gift Outright' – though, in a move that could have jeopardised the entire enterprise, Kennedy asked that the poem's final line be changed to sound a more optimistic note than the original, which had been written during the Depression. That original poem ends:

Such as we were we gave ourselves outright
(The deed of gift was many deeds of war)
To the land vaguely realizing westward,
But still unstoried, artless, unenhanced,
Such as she was, such as she would become.[1]

Kennedy suggested that 'such as she would become' be altered to read 'such as she will become' and, surprisingly, Frost agreed, if rather grudgingly. However, in spite of his refusal to contemplate such a task, he soon began working on a new poem especially for the occasion, a sixty-seven-line variation on the heroic couplet form that both celebrates the arts in public life and provides a revealing elaboration of a historical perspective that 'The Gift Outright' only partly addresses. Frost called this new poem simply 'Dedication' – and it was his plan, until the very last minute, to read this, and not the altered version of 'The Gift Outright', at the inauguration.

That new work, conceived and executed in a remarkably short space, is in many ways a revelation of Frost's mature political vision, an affirmation of a certain type of power that both echoes and interrogates Kennedy's own vision of 'what together we can do for the freedom of man', especially in its final lines:

There is a call to life a little sterner,
And braver for the earner, learner, yearner.
Less criticism of the field and court
And more preoccupation with the sport.
It makes the prophet in us all presage
The glory of a next Augustan age
Of a power leading from its strength and pride,
Of young ambition eager to be tried,
Firm in our free beliefs without dismay,
In any game the nations want to play.
A *golden age of poetry and power*
Of which this noonday's the beginning hour.[2]

However, a close reading of 'Dedication' reveals a darker side to its politics. It could be argued, for example, that the kind of imperialist thinking that led to Vietnam, just a few years later, is implied in the lines

> We see how seriously the races swarm
> In their attempts at sovereignty and form.
> They are our wards we think to some extent
> For the time being and with their consent,
> To teach them how Democracy is meant.

And, while no direct mention is made of the wholesale eradication of native peoples and the invasion of Mexican land, the following lines would come to seem, at the very least unfortunate, as the 1960s began:

> The new world Christopher Columbus found.
> The French, the Spanish, and the Dutch were downed
> And counted out. Heroic deeds were done.
> Elizabeth the First and England won.
> Now came on a new order of the ages
> That in the Latin of our founding sages
> (Is it not written on the dollar bill
> We carry in our purse and pocket still?)
> God nodded his approval of as good.

Reading that last line, it is hard not to think of Bob Dylan's satirical song 'With God On Our Side', in which God's approval is affirmed at the end of every verse, a scornful expression of disdain for America's wars, from the killing of the Indians through the Spanish-American and Civil conflicts to the Cold War, about which Dylan's young Midwestern protagonist knows nothing, except that he is supposed to hate and fear all Russians. In the final analysis, 'Dedication' comes across as a rather thin piece of Augustan pastiche, in which Frost's hopes for the arts blend with an outmoded triumphalist vision with an all too evident whiff of Manifest Destiny taken for granted. Luckily the glare off the snow on Inauguration Day, combined with his weak eyesight, forced him to abandon this new and complex work; instead, he said 'The

Gift Outright', its last line altered as agreed, and Kennedy became the thirty-fifth president of the United States.*

Clearly, many in 1960s America were still very much in tune with the sentiments that Frost expresses in 'Dedication', but, as we shall see in the following chapter, numerous critiques of post-war American society were already in the air. Social commentators such as Vance Packard and David Riesman had begun to dismantle the illusions that concealed the US's wasteful consumerism, the insidious power of Madison Avenue and the 'sexual wilderness' to which the average suburbanite was consigned by a moral system predicated on the denial of human tenderness and sensuality. The Beat poets were forging a new poetics to attack a society prepared to destroy 'the best minds' of a generation in pursuit of conformity, and the civil rights movement was beginning to organise itself more effectively in the face of brutal police tactics. Meanwhile, as he left office just days before Kennedy's inauguration, President Eisenhower delivered this ominous warning:

> In the councils of government, we must guard against the acquisition of unwarranted influence, whether sought or unsought, by the military-industrial complex. The potential for the disastrous rise of misplaced power exists and will persist. We must never let the weight of this combination endanger our liberties or democratic processes.

It was clear, then, that the crisis of American identity did not begin with the Kennedy assassination, or with Vietnam or Watergate; it had already begun long before Kennedy took office. In 1961, however, the American Dream still felt real, or at least salvageable for many – and to understand fully the resonance that

---

*Not that the original choice was entirely innocent of such problems. It is highly unlikely, for example, that Native American/Indian readers would have appreciated the idea of 'the land vaguely realizing westward' in 'The Gift Outright'.

Frost brought to the Kennedy camp, it is worth looking again at Eleanor Roosevelt's 'Citizens for Kennedy' campaign advertisement. Mrs Roosevelt had initially opposed Kennedy's nomination, coming out in her *My Day* column for Adlai Stevenson: 'Of course, I know I am prejudiced,' she wrote, as late as June 1960, 'but it seemed to me that the man who made the most sense, who analyzed the situation before us most clearly and told us what should and could be done about it, was this undeclared candidate, Mr. Stevenson.' Winning her over, therefore, had been a significant victory, though, reading the advertisement today, it is clear that the doyenne of the Democratic Party is more comfortable talking about general principles than the photogenic young senator from Massachusetts:

> Our country is the oldest democracy in the world, but it is less than two-hundred years old. It is a country with ample room for growth. It is a land which needs today just as much as ever before to live by the prayer written about the Statue of Liberty […] If we are to be the spokesmen for the free world we must begin at home by assuring all our peoples regardless of religion, race, or national origin, equal opportunity under law and under God. When you cast your vote for the president of the United States, be sure you have studied the record. I have. I urge you to vote for John F. Kennedy for I have come to believe that as president he will have the strength and the moral courage to provide the leadership for human rights we need in this time of crisis.

The 'prayer' to which Roosevelt refers here is a rather conventional Petrarchan sonnet written in 1883 by one Emma Lazarus; the full text was eventually engraved on a bronze plaque and placed inside the Statue of Liberty. In its entirety, it reads:

> Not like the brazen giant of Greek fame,
> With conquering limbs astride from land to land;
> Here at our sea-washed, sunset gates shall stand
> A mighty woman with a torch, whose flame
> Is the imprisoned lightning, and her name

Mother of Exiles. From her beacon-hand
Glows world-wide welcome; her mild eyes command
The air-bridged harbor that twin cities frame.

'Keep, ancient lands, your storied pomp!' cries she
With silent lips. 'Give me your tired, your poor,
Your huddled masses yearning to breathe free,
The wretched refuse of your teeming shore.
Send these, the homeless, tempest-tost to me,
I lift my lamp beside the golden door!'[3]

Though not a major work, 'The New Colossus' resonates with the high rhetoric of a new democratic ideal, an inclusive politics based not on conquest but on 'world-wide welcome'. American Liberty, this 'Mother of Exiles', has snatched the very lightning from the sky and imprisoned it to illumine the way for everyone, no matter how lowly, to the free world. Politically it may be a work of supreme naïveté – but it is also, given its context, irresistible, and it became an inspiration for countless refugees fleeing the conflagrations, pogroms and death camps of the Old World.

While it is infinitely more sophisticated, Robert Frost's 'The Death of the Hired Man', first published in his 1914 collection *North of Boston*, raises similar questions about shelter and the morality of giving and accepting refuge. In this dramatic dialogue a farmer named Warren and his wife, Mary, are discussing their unreliable, even rather feckless, hireling who after a period of unexplained absence has turned up at their farm again, looking for work. Warren is inclined to send the man away, complaining:

'When was I ever anything but kind to him?
But I'll not have the fellow back,' he said.
'I told him so last haying, didn't I?
If he left then, I said, that ended it.
What good is he? Who else will harbor him
At his age for the little he can do?'

Mary, however, feels sorry for the prodigal and argues that he should be allowed to stay, at least for a time: the man has come home to die, she believes, which leads to the following exchange, one of the best-known in twentieth-century poetry:

'Home,' he mocked gently.

        'Yes, what else but home?
It all depends on what you mean by home.
Of course he's nothing to us, any more
Than was the hound that came a stranger to us
Out of the woods, worn out upon the trail.'

'Home is the place where, when you have to go there,
They have to take you in.'

          'I should have called it
Something you somehow haven't to deserve.'[4]

Two definitions of home are offered here: the first suggests obligation, duty, and has about it something of a grudging quality; the second, a generosity of spirit that goes beyond ordinary morality. The first is predicated, essentially, on pity (which implies superiority), the second on egalitarian compassion. Neither is very heartening when treated as a comprehensive definition of home – and neither actually prevails, as Frost avoids an easy resolution of the conflict by having the hired man die at the end of the poem – but as a baseline, as it were, both have their virtues. It is the second of these that most resonates with the sentiments of the Lazarus 'prayer', however; and it is a resonance that runs throughout Frost's *oeuvre*. In Frost, all traces of the high-flown, of the idealistic, of the merely rhetorical are stripped away, leaving what passes for homespun, 'Puritan' wisdom, though it is far more complex than appearances suggest. At its best, Frost's moral vision comes not from human-scale values (from, as it were, a 'father's saying'), and not from some divine or otherworldly source, but from the land itself.

That this is so is illustrated by a poem from the same collection, the psychologically complex 'Mending Wall', with its famous opening:

> Something there is that doesn't love a wall,
> That sends the frozen-ground-swell under it
> And spills the upper boulders in the sun,
> And makes gaps even two can pass abreast.

The tone here – as that 'doesn't' suggests – is informal, conversational. At the same time, it raises a deeply philosophical question. What is the 'something' that doesn't love a wall? Where does it originate? What causes the gaps? 'No one has seen them made, or heard them made', the speaker notes, but they appear at 'spring mending-time' and, the neighbour beyond the hill duly informed of the need to go to work, the men come together to rebuild a wall that neither of them needs:

> My apple trees will never get across
> And eat the cones under his pines, I tell him.
> He only says, 'Good fences make good neighbours.'

Yet the speaker cannot help thinking that a wall, and the mending of it, go against some natural principle that he cannot quite identify, though he knows what it is not:

> 'Why do they make good neighbours? Isn't it
> Where there are cows? But here there are no cows.
> Before I built a wall I'd ask to know
> What I was walling in or walling out,
> And to whom I was like to give offense.
> Something there is that doesn't love a wall,
> That wants it down.' I could say 'Elves,' to him,
> But it's not elves exactly, and I'd rather
> He said it for himself.

Now the speaker says aloud what had been, at the poem's opening, a private thought, and he does so because 'Spring is the mischief' in him. Clearly, the unseen 'mischief' that rises from the earth to topple the wall is the mischief that enters into the speaker's mind, provoking him to question the other man's inherited – and unconsidered – principles:

He moves in darkness as it seems to me,
Not of woods only and the shade of trees.
He will not go behind his father's saying,
And he likes having thought of it so well
He says again, 'Good fences make good neighbours.'[5]

For his part, the neighbour is too benighted by ignorance and a stale tradition to recognise the natural force, the 'something' that wants the wall down. He lives by a received code – the thought he comes up with, and repeats, is not an original one, but an *idée reçue* – and so the mischief of spring cannot work in him. Yet, while it works in the speaker, it does not lead him to some easy, and essentially superstitious, conclusion and he cannot name the 'something' he recognises as originating in the land itself, a force greater than any human order but not supernatural as such. Nor does his questioning of the wall's purpose – or of whom, or what it might 'like to give offense' – lead him to abandon the work: what he is witnessing may be the effect of a more fundamental but entirely organic order, one that brings mischief to human boundaries and conventions, but he is still bound by societal obligations and *politesse*. This says something significant about Frost as a thinker: in stark contrast, say, to Henry Miller, or the better Beat writers, his enlightened protagonist does not rail at conformity, even when he understands how futile it is, because he recognises that his neighbour needs this ritual in order to give his life meaning. He has broken out of the illusion, but he does not rebel against the societal obligation (from the Latin *obligationem*, 'an engaging or pledging') that, artificial as it may be, still allows for some sense of community.

The Kennedy inauguration was a historic moment, and a real success – a good note to rest on, perhaps. However, Robert Frost was not yet done with political life. In the summer of 1962, as the inner circle of Washington braced itself for the Cuban Missile Crisis, Stewart Udall proposed a kind of cultural exchange programme that would take Frost to the Soviet Union for meetings with poets and other writers in Moscow and Leningrad, along with some public readings and press events. The Soviet Ambassador, Anatoly Dobrynin, who had met Frost in Washington, warmly supported the scheme and issued a formal invitation – though it seems possible, in retrospect, that he had an ulterior motive for this. At first, Frost hesitated: the state of his health was unpredictable, the journey to Russia would be long and he had suffered heart strain during a trip to Israel the previous spring. At the same time he wanted very much to meet Nikita Khrushchev, to talk to him 'man to man' and lay out his own ideas for a 'noble rivalry' between the United States and the Soviet Union. As Udall recalls it, this was never a firm part of the plan: he was travelling to the USSR as Secretary of the Interior at the head of a delegation to view hydro-electric plants and had, initially, no expectation of meeting the premier himself. Nevertheless, he continued to encourage Frost to make the journey, and the old poet agreed that he would, if President Kennedy invited him to do so. To the last, Frost was never quite sure of his role or the real purpose of the visit, and he wondered about 'going all the way over there just to show off', but he felt in his heart that he could make a difference, and on 29 August 1962 he arrived in Moscow, to be greeted by a delegation from the Russian writers' union, led by Yevgeni Yevtushenko.

Almost everyone, other than Frost, saw this 'adventure' (as the old poet had described it to F. D. Reeve, a young poet and translator who travelled with him) as mainly cultural. For both sides it was convenient window-dressing while the diplomats worked to avert the coming crisis, as well as a chance for Khrushchev to showcase the cultural and political benefits of his de-Stalinisation programme, a project that, from its inception in the 1950s, had been regarded by many in the Politburo as deeply suspicious. (It would last until 1964, when Khrushchev was removed from power.) That programme had made a cherished figure of Yevtushenko and, more importantly, it had rehabilitated Anna Akhmatova, who, in spite of the years of persecution and enforced poverty had remained a powerful critic of Stalin's regime. A year later Reeve published a useful account of the trip, including the meeting between Frost and Akhmatova at the dacha of the literary critic Mikhail Alexeyev, near Leningrad:

> Akhmatova arrived. She came in a dark dress, a pale lilac shawl over her shoulders, august and dignified with her white hair and deep eyes. She and Frost greeted each other with polite deference. At table Alexeyev toasted Frost and then toasted both Akhmatova and Frost, referring to their meeting as one of the great literary events of our time. The rumor was then pervasive that the two great poets were in competition for the Nobel Prize. They themselves were conscious of the stakes, the rumors, and the pressures, but neither one let on.[6]

However, even competition for the Nobel Prize was not at the forefront of Frost's mind, and both Reeve and Udall recall his 'increased desire' to meet Khrushchev, who was staying at his summer house in Georgia. At the same time Frost had once again begun to experience a variety of health problems. Nevertheless, he received an invitation to fly to the Crimea for a meeting, and on 7 September, 'fatigued and running a 101-degree fever', he finally achieved his goal. Stewart Udall describes the meeting in some detail:

> The talk began and rapport came easily to these two men, both masters of the art of banter. Khrushchev chided Frost for not taking care of himself and suggested he follow doctor's orders if he was going to live to be 100. Robert said he was 'half as old as his country' and didn't trust physicians, but would be around for his nation's 200th anniversary anyway.

The two men then had a brief discussion about poetry and the poet's role in society, and Frost gave a warm account of his travels in Russia and his meetings with other writers. He praised Khrushchev for his support of writers, though he said nothing about Boris Pasternak, who had been prevented from accepting a

Nobel Prize in 1959 for *Doctor Zhivago*. (Frost was very sensitive to the fact that the West's politicking over the affair might well 'get him killed'.) Then, 'having tested each other', Khrushchev asked Frost if he 'had anything special in mind', at which point, Frost

> went right to the issue he had come to discuss – a modus vivendi for the long haul that would allow both countries to survive, contend and prosper [...] He conceded that the Soviet system was destined to be a vigorous force in the world, and he outlined his belief that constructive rivalry would lead to a gradual convergence of the two systems [...] He underscored his point with one of his own aphorisms: 'A great nation makes great poetry, and great poetry makes a great nation.' Khrushchev studied Frost's face as Frost expounded his argument. He intervened only once to say that the fundamental contest would be in the area of 'peaceful economic competition.' Otherwise, the Soviet leader took no issue with Frost and at one point he exclaimed, 'You have the soul of a poet!'[7]

So far so good. Frost proceeded to raise the question of a code of conduct between the two superpowers, leaving room for noble rivalry and creating 'a climate hospitable to wide-ranging contact and competition'. Now the old poet was in full rhetorical flow and clearly enjoying himself, in spite of his illness – and Khrushchev appeared to be enjoying the exchange too. True, he was evasive on the two or three occasions when the old man tried to steer the conversation around to the Berlin Wall, but it would have been over-optimistic on Frost's part to expect any great movement there. Finally, after ninety minutes, the conversation came to an end and Khrushchev departed with a volume of Frost's poetry inscribed 'To Premier Khrushchev, from his rival in friendship, Robert Frost'.

Frost returned to the United States almost immediately, triumphant and feeling he had done some good – and indeed, viewed as a whole, the visit had been a success. Frost had connected with some of the leading Russian poets of the day, and he had carried himself well through the meeting with Khrushchev, in spite of his ill-health. When the conversation ended, Frost is reported by one of his travelling companions as saying, 'Well, we did it, didn't we?' as he lay back on his sick-bed to rest for the journey home. He knew what he had achieved, and he was proud of it. However, as Udall recalls, that success turned to ashes in a moment, after the exhausted old man made an unguarded – and quite inaccurate – remark about his conversation with the Soviet premier during an unexpected press conference at the airport in New York:

> Though Frost was in a mellow mood, he had been awake 18 hours by the time we finally deplaned and was bone-tired. I should have stopped any further press interviews, but the reporters were out in force and anxious to persuade him to expand on his impressions of Khrushchev. As he was beginning to repeat himself near the end [...] Frost astonished me by suddenly blurting out, 'Khrushchev said he feared for us because of our lot of liberals. He thought that we're too liberal to fight – he thinks we will sit on one hand and then the other.' This was the fresh news the reporters were waiting for, and the next day *The Washington Post* carried a banner headline: 'Frost Says Khrushchev Sees U.S. as "Too Liberal" to Defend Itself.'

Within hours other papers were repeating the supposed quote in various wordings. *The St Louis Post Dispatch* was saying that Khrushchev believed 'American liberals were too soft to fight', while Philip Benjamin, in *The New York Times*, wrote: '"Khrushchev said he feared for us modern liberals," the 88-year-old poet said. "He said we were too liberal to fight"' – but however Frost's supposed quote was reported, the old poet would have known immediately that his late-blossoming political career was over. It was a disastrous moment, a defeat plucked from the jaws of real success. But the strangest thing is that, having made so many other remarks about US–Soviet relations, Khrushchev had *never* said that America was too liberal, or too soft, to fight. He had declared that he was not afraid of NATO, and he had reminded Frost that Kennedy had been inclined to draw up a pact between the two superpowers but had been prevented from doing so by political pressure at home – though this would hardly have come from 'liberals'. (In fact, the real pressure was coming from hard-liners who wanted Kennedy to invade Cuba immediately.)

Frost's 'liberal' remark was, then, a mysterious gaffe by any account. He had, at the very least, misquoted Khrushchev – and certainly he had misrepresented his overall position – and there was absolutely no reason for him to have said such a thing. However, conservative 'Puritan' that he was, Frost himself very much mis-trusted 'liberals' as being indecisive and weak (he once remarked, 'A liberal is a man too broadminded to take his own side in a quarrel') and, in his exhausted, sleep-deprived state, coming off a seventeen-hour flight, he may have allowed his own prejudices to emerge during a press conference that Stewart Udall says he himself 'should have stopped'. Was this the classic Freudian slip of the tongue that reveals a deeper truth, an underlying attitude that waits for the right moment of fatigue, stress or weakness to surface? Freud himself said that 'these phenomena are not accidental, that they require more than physiological explanations, that they have a meaning and can be interpreted, and [...] one is justified in inferring from them the presence of restrained or repressed intentions'.[8] If so, it was a tragedy, not for US politics – in which the real game was being played elsewhere – but for an old patriot who, having sacrificed his health for the sake of peace and understanding between the US and the Soviet Union, was left with nothing but the taste of ashes. After this gaffe Kennedy snubbed him, but Frost remained stoical and, though he made what Udall calls 'negative references' to 'those guys around the President', he said nothing ill against Kennedy himself. Frost had, of course, known what he was doing, and he was aware, as he had remarked to Malraux, that once a poet had served his purpose he might well be cast off, but it is hard not to believe that he was played, by both Khrushchev and Kennedy, as an expendable piece in a highly complex and dangerous game.

Certainly, Stewart Udall saw it in that light, reflecting on events ten years later:

At the time, I wondered why Khrushchev was so solicitous about Frost, and why he spent so much time with me. We realize later that [...] he was obsessed with President Kennedy's forthcoming response to his nuclear lunge. Would Kennedy order an invasion of Cuba? Would nuclear weapons be used by the United States? The condition of Kennedy's nerve, and his initial interpretation of Khrushchev's intentions would be decisive. The Soviet Premier saw us, then, because he needed us. In a few days, the real purpose of the Cuban installations would be discovered. Khrushchev needed to send tidings of his sanity, to prove that he was still in charge. Our visits would give Kennedy a window into his mind. When I look back now with the benefit of hindsight, Khrushchev's conduct was both conservative and cunning. He was trying, with deceptive twists and turns, to keep Washington guessing, to present a peaceful face one day and a tough stance the next.

Robert Frost died of a pulmonary embolism on 30 January 1963, just a few weeks before his eighty-ninth birthday. His passing was recognised as a massive loss to American poetry (though it had been John Steinbeck and not Frost who took the Nobel Prize a few months earlier). That the president felt the loss keenly is clear from the eulogy he delivered later that year at Amherst, just a month before his own death, a deeply moving speech in which he began by praising a poet who had once said, 'Were an epitaph to be my story I'd have a short one ready for my own. I would have written of me on my stone: I had a lover's quarrel with the world.' His quarrel had always included the powers-that-be, as Kennedy noted:

Strength takes many forms, and the most obvious forms are not always the most significant. The men who create power make an indispensable contribution to the Nation's greatness, but the men who question power make a contribution just as indispensable, especially when that questioning is disinterested,

for they determine whether we use power or power uses us
[…] The artist, however faithful to his personal vision of reality,
becomes the last champion of the individual mind and sensibility against an intrusive society and an officious state.

And he continued:

In a free society art is not a weapon and it does not belong
to the spheres of polemic and ideology. Artists are not engi-
neers of the soul. It may be different elsewhere. But democratic
society – in it, the highest duty of the writer, the composer, the
artist is to remain true to himself and to let the chips fall where
they may. In serving his vision of the truth, the artist best serves
his nation. And the nation which disdains the mission of art
invites the fate of Robert Frost's hired man, the fate of having
'nothing to look backward to with pride, and nothing to look
forward to with hope'.

It seems likely that Kennedy had not been entirely straight with
Frost regarding the Russian trip – it may even be that he 'played'
the old man for reasons of state – but he still liked and admired
Frost, and this speech is not only one of the most moving eulo-
gies ever delivered for an artist but arguably unique in the often
troubled relationship between politics and poetry. Perhaps it is the
particular quality of a politician that he or she can like, admire,
respect and even love someone and still use that person for their
own ends. Kennedy did what he had to do. Nevertheless, it seemed
clear to Stewart Udall, during that autumn memorial service, that
the president deeply regretted the loss of his former friend:

Reserved men are often thoughtless men, and John Kennedy
was essentially a very private person. This trait made him a
person who usually chose to ignore his critics, and was slow
to either praise or blame his associates. Kennedy and I never
discussed the final phase of his relationship with Frost. To my
knowledge, he only mentioned the subject once. Nine months
after Frost's death, at the Robert Frost Library dedication at

Amherst, in a quiet corner he said apologetically to Kay Morrison, Frost's secretary, 'We didn't know he was so ill.'

John F. Kennedy was murdered in Dallas in November 1963. That Robert Frost did not live to witness his former friend's death meant that the US lacked the one man who might have offered an adequate response to the assassination. Yet, while we can only speculate as to what he might have written, we do know that his poetry was everywhere in the air as the nation came to terms with what had happened. As former WBC correspondent Sid Davis told NPR on the fiftieth anniversary of the killing:

> The body came back to the White House about 4:15. And when I saw that gray Navy ambulance come up the driveway, and Mrs. Kennedy sitting with the casket – I had to close the broadcast. And I was signing off, and I decided unwisely to quote from a poem that Robert Frost had written. And Kennedy was very close friends with Robert Frost and at the end of his speeches on a long campaign night, Kennedy would say: The woods are lovely, dark and deep. But I have promises to keep, and miles to go before I sleep. And I tried to say that on the air, and I couldn't get through it. And that's where I broke up on the air. This is sixteen or seventeen hours after the shooting but up until that point, it hadn't hit me that – the finality of his now being dead, and it's all over for the great adventure that he brought to us.

It is hard not to think that this story best sums up the demands of the days following Kennedy's death – days when the only possible response, poetic or otherwise, was a measured silence.

It was not long, however, before poets began to respond to the loss of a man who, whatever his personal faults, had seemed to usher in a new era. Perhaps the most affecting was Wendell Berry's 'November Twenty-Six 1963', published in *The Nation*'s issue for 2 December. In spite of its long lines and almost documentary attention to everyday detail, this fairly conventional poem is set firmly in the tradition of pastoral elegy: it opens with an image of 'the winter earth upon the body of the young President, and the early dark falling', and continues through a series of cinematic, or rather televisual, images of the funeral ('the mourners standing in the rain, and the leaves falling', 'his death's horses and drums; the roses, bells, candles, crosses; the faces hidden in veils') to invoke 'the time he is not alive, filling with our footsteps and voices [...] and the light of all his lost days' and concludes with a stately and unashamedly beatific image of 'the long approach of summers towards the healed ground where he will be waiting, no longer the keeper of what he was'. It is odd, then, that this final observation, separating the mortal man from the burdens and privileges of office (and so from the system his presidency continued to represent around the world, especially in those places where American foreign policy had been less than kind), chimes rather eerily with remarks attributed to Fidel Castro by *The New York Times*, just three days after the shooting:

> We have to make an objective analysis of the facts, consequences and repercussions that the assassination of President Kennedy might have. We should comprehend it very well. This kind of act affects the sensibility of every man. Before an act of this nature I react in this way and I believe this is the reaction of most human beings, who repudiate assassination [...] As Marxist–Leninists we recognize that the role of a man is small and relative in society. We should be glad about the death of a system. The disappearance of a system would always cause us joy. But the death of a man, although this man is an enemy, does not have to cause us joy. We always bow with respect in front of death. The death of President Kennedy can have very negative repercussions for the interests of our country, but in this case it is not the question of our interest, but of the interests of the whole world.

It seems that friends and enemies alike were unable to do anything but reach for traditional forms of expression – pastoral, in the main – to mark the assassination. Meanwhile, in response to a request from Igor Stravinsky, W. H. Auden produced a short 'Elegy for J.F.K.', whose brief, almost haiku-length stanzas bring together a mix of simple declaration and Biblical rhetoric ideally suited to the composer's intentions but strangely at odds with the details of what had happened. In this poem Kennedy could have been anyone:

> When a just man dies,
> Lamentation and praise,
> Sorrow and joy, are one.
>
> Why then, why there,
> Why thus, we cry, did he die?
> The heavens are silent.
>
> What he was, he was:
> What he is fated to become
> Depends on us
>
> Remembering his death,
> How we choose to live
> Will decide its meaning.[9]

This is writing that does nothing, says nothing, moves only the susceptible. It lacks all specificity, as if the poet were simply completing a literary exercise, an assortment of truisms strung together more or less at random. Other poets followed in similar vein, and through the years a few have returned to that defining moment of their generation, when a beautiful illusion melted away in a matter of televised minutes, the first time (though, as the coming decades would prove, not the last) that massive, incomprehensible public events were beamed into suburban living rooms like soda commercials or episodes of the latest sitcom. (It should not be forgotten that Kennedy's death was the first murder ever shown live on TV.) Not surprisingly, such images are both indelibly printed on the mind for ever and, at the same time, qualitatively interchangeable with other, purely narrative images, scenes from old B-movies like Lewis Allen's disturbingly prescient *noir* flick *Suddenly* (1954), in which Frank Sinatra plays a ruthless assassin who takes over the home of an everyday suburban family with the intention of killing the US president as he passes through their peaceful Californian town. This conflation of entertainment and the brutally real informs Floyd Salas's response to the events in Dallas, 'Kaleidoscope of an Assassination in Black and White':

Memory is like a motion picture
He is waving
The President is waving
from the back seat of a car.[10]

By now, televised, the assassination has no meaning: it is a frame in a movie, an image. At the same time, what most unites those poems that treat the assassination as a televised event is the sense that what happened in Dallas is public property, a shared drama, an item in the collective memory that, in spite of its appalling nature, unites the nation in the same way that a televised sporting event (the Olympics, say) or a much-loved comedy show like *The Beverly Hillbillies* might do. That unity offered a sense of community, a system of belonging – but it was as artificial and remote as the rhetoric of politics itself or the various conspiracy theories that both framed the assassination and left it for ever open, unresolved, beyond closure.

This sense of belonging that community provides (in exchange for a degree of social conformism and a tacit acceptance of mediocrity) would seem, for most individuals, a desideratum – but it would appear that the inevitable by-product of such belonging is that individual spontaneity and critical thinking must be carefully managed or suppressed. *In extremis*, a sense of community can be preserved only when history is stripped down to an acceptable myth, an agreed version of *what really happened* that is at once reductive, colourless and lacking in the manifold detail of creaturely experience. Perhaps this is why so many poems about the assassination fail as poems, even when they seem to succeed as public utterances. To maintain the myth, and so perpetuate a workable sense of community, events that we have lived through together will sometimes be so transformed that we doubt our own experiences and begin to adopt the cinematic and televisual 'memories' that are established as society's authorised version. Possibly it is to this condition that Henry Ford was referring when he said that 'history is bunk', but it need not necessarily be the case that history mires us in a dry, colourless past. Real history is made using memory and individual imagining, and with vigilance – and time – a society can win back not only the shared narrative of past events that genuinely communal life permits but also a fabric shot through and vivified by a private, sensual and variable set of personal and familial strands that controvert that authorised version of events.

Such an opposition of fine-grained specifics and the official account is nowhere more elegantly revealed than in Lucie Brock-Broido's remarkable 'Self Portrait on the Grassy Knoll', from her collection *Trouble in Mind* (2004). The poem begins with an insistence on the colour red:

> The only real place to gather consolation
> Is from the back-talk of the dead, and they
> Do not speak to me.
> Miss Jean Hill, the lady in red who named the hummock
> 'Grassy Knoll' in Abraham Zapruder's grainy film is
> Dead tonight at sixty-nine.
>
> In her red rain-coat, she had been hoping
> To loom small and pleasing on the glassy hill
> Like a poppy anemone in bloom.

On one level this is a playful opening, with those repetitions of 'dead' and 'red' invoking the Cold War adage 'better dead than red', or with the play on looming *small* or the way 'grassy knoll' shifts arbitrarily to 'glassy hill' (the original term, which became so significant in the aftermath of the Kennedy assassination as to have entered the language, being just as arbitrarily chosen, in the heat of the moment). Yet it remains a poignant reminder of

a historical event that, for many, signalled the loss of a compendium of values and hopes that were jettisoned for ever during the
administrations that followed. Equally poignant is the reference to
Jean Hill herself (whose testimony about the number of gunmen
present in Dallas that day was first disputed then summarily dismissed by the authorities), a reference that introduces a powerful
emblem of the difficult relationship between individual experience and an authorised communal version of history designed
not to seek out the truth but to maintain a *status quo ante*. Meanwhile, the colour red is itself a reminder of a highly significant
element of the assassination scene that the authorities censored:
in Zapruder's film, the other instance of a deep 'poppy anemone'
red, besides Miss Hill's coat, is the blood spray of the impact shot
that was excised from Abraham Zapruder's home movie after he
handed it over to *Time* magazine. Those frames then became a
matter of controversy, until Geraldo Rivera showed the entire film
on *Good Night America* in March 1975. Rivera justified this action by
citing the public's right to review all the evidence. (One conspiracy theory held that the excised frames would prove the existence
of the second gunman Jean Hill claimed to have seen fleeing the
scene.) But it is also the case that, in a wider sense, the omission of
the head shot created a sanitised version of the assassination, one
which, while officially intended to avoid creating undue distress,
also reveals a manipulative (and patronising) stance among those
who made the decision. The most vivid image, the blood image,
is excluded from history, and with it the living colour is drained
away. At the same time, remaining true to the most ancient of
Classical traditions, in which poetry has its origins in the underworld via such personages as the oracle at Delphi or Orpheus,
the poem reminds us that consolation is only obtained from 'the
back-talk of the dead' and, because we are separated from those
Classical roots by the loss of a pagan accord with the land and
several hundred years of rationalism, those oracular dead do not
talk to Brock-Broido's speaker, or to us.

As we enter the second stanza, the poem modulates from red to
yellow, as its speaker shifts from public to personal history. Like all

the other ordinary people who remember what they were doing when Kennedy was killed, the speaker of Brock-Broido's poem recalls the 'schoolguard in her yellow slicker/ Crossing us toward home/ Too early in that afternoon, in rain' and some 'honeybee / In a field of mustardseed/ Flickering like radium or memory', but this personal past is a confused, golden haze, fuzzed with rain, the light flickering and the early departure from school unexplained. (Note also how that reference to 'mustardseed', invokes Matthew 13:31 – 'the kingdom of heaven is like to a grain of mustard seed which a man took and sowed in his field' – thus reminding us of the significance of all that which 'looms small' in our lives.) Actual history, with its accompanying sense of the vivid and manifold kingdom of heaven, consists of all these small loomings, some confused (as in Jean Hill's testimony, or in a child's memory), some too intense to contain ('radium'), and is therefore beyond the scope of an official version of events – and so, having moved from blood red to mustardseed yellow, the poem slides, in the final stanza, towards the world 'of fact and time and black and white', clutching, first, at the shadows thrown by an 'anemic slippery light', then at 'the hem/ Of the sorcerer's tattered cloak'. And while the identity of the sorcerer (about whom we know only that 'he has given up/ The ghost') is left unspecified, the sense of loss and the speaker's urgent desire to hold on to the vivid colour and fuzziness of the lived experience are powerfully conveyed. Overall, the poem suggests a descent into the underworld (in both the Classical and the Christian senses), but there is no resurrection and no return, only the substitution of 'fact' for lived experience, and the 'black and white' of newsprint and binary logic for life's colour and fuzziness – and it might be this admission of failure, this rejection of easy closure or pastoral resolution, that marks 'Self Portrait on the Grassy Knoll' as the only truly successful poem about the Kennedy assassination and one that, had he been able to read it, Frost might have recognised as a worthy memorial to all we have lost, real and imaginary, since Dallas.

WHERE TURTLES WIN

Goodbye I'm walking out on the whole scene.
Close down the joint.
The system is all loused up.
Rome was never like this.
I'm tired of waiting for Godot.
I am going where turtles win.[1]

Lawrence Ferlinghetti

ROBERT FROST might have been prepared, if not entirely happy, to play Virgil to John F. Kennedy's Caesar Augustus, but a number of the younger poets, not just of the 1960s but also among those who matured during the 1940s and '50s, were less forgiving, both of government and of socio-political conditions in general. That said, anyone looking to American writers for the kind of political engagement found among Europeans in the 1950s and '60s was in for a disappointment. It is hard to imagine an American Sartre, for example. This may have had something to do with McCarthyism, but there were surely other factors in play, certainly up until the mid-1960s. In fact, American dissidence immediately after the war seems rather naïve (at least in retrospect). Was this because everybody knew, on paper, what their guiding principles were? Uniquely, US citizens had the Constitution, a Bill of Rights, the rhetoric of the Declaration of Independence and the apparent moral example of the Founders to look to when injustice presented itself. They had Tom Paine and Thoreau. Emerson had long ago established the idea that 'every actual state is corrupt', and that it was every good citizen's duty to work with other like-minded republicans to prevent tyranny from taking hold. Just as American political heroes were usually portrayed as Capra-esque individuals of extraordinary integrity and not as organised, conscious revolutionaries, so McCarthyism had to be seen as the aberration of one man and his near associates, rather than as a systemic disease infecting the entire body politic. Similarly, it was considered eccentric, or unpatriotic, to portray the US's increasingly imperialist interventions abroad as anything more or less than defending the world from the spectre of totalitarianism. In fact, many decent and far from stupid people were proud to echo Harry S. Truman's claim, in the State of the Union address of 1946, that the US, having seen off 'the Nazi-Fascist terror in Europe, and also the end of the malignant power of Japan', was now dedicated to leading the world in 'the substantial beginning of [a] world organization for peace', rather than simply safeguarding the interests of any number of American coffee, oil and banana companies. With some significant exceptions, it took American political thinkers until the 1960s to see the direct link between racial oppression on the streets of Chicago and Alabama and Watts to the country's various interventions in Central and South America and Asia.*

Americans were troubled at home, however. By the middle of the twentieth century widely accepted notions of success were being painstakingly interrogated in the US by writers who had begun to see through the American Dream and the characters who inhabited its country clubs and cocktail bars. Men like Neddy, from John Cheever's elegant short story 'The Swimmer', an initially glamorous figure described as 'determinedly original [with] a vague and modest idea of himself as a legendary figure', or Tennessee Williams's Brick, a 'thirty-year-old kid' living in the

---

* To the best of my knowledge, the term 'US Imperialism' first appeared in a Students for a Democratic Society paper written in 1967 by the Columbia University activist David Gilbert.

wreckage of a heroic sporting past, nursed by alcohol and a wife whose desperation is matched only by her tenacity. The route to this new critique of social success had been paved (in varying ways) by realist writers and social commentators such as Theodore Dreiser and Sherwood Anderson, by Henry Miller's excoriating examination of American life during the Second World War, *The Air-Conditioned Nightmare*, and by Beat writers such as the former college football star Jack Kerouac, the anarchist poet and publisher Lawrence Ferlinghetti and the renegade scion of a famed business equipment empire, William Burroughs. Now, as the Cold War deepened and the US waged a disastrous war in Vietnam, a younger generation of writers was wielding newly honed scalpels, dissecting the underlying, even existential, fear on which the Dream was founded. At the same time, it is hard not to acknowledge that they were working in a kind of vacuum, with little to no theoretical underpinning and no unified and lasting political vision. They thought that in the abstract beauty of the Constitution they already had a worthy model for social good; all they had to do now was fix it.

In 'The Great Society', a quietly damning poem from his collection *The Light Around the Body* (1966), Robert Bly shows Americans from various walks of life engaged in the everyday activities that occupy their days. Dentists routinely tend their gardens, making sure the lawns are kept well watered, even when it rains; a janitor worries about his boiler; a band of dark children play on the further shore at Coney Island. It sounds like an ordinary day, until we hear what is happening alongside these banal events:

> Hands developed with terrible labor by apes
> Hang from the sleeves of evangelists;
> There are murdered kings in the light-bulbs outside movie
> theaters:
> The coffins of the poor are hibernating in piles of new tires.

Meanwhile, up in the White House and in the properties of the rich

The President dreams of invading Cuba.
Bushes are growing over the outdoor grills,
Vines over the yachts and the leather seats

while the beach where the children are playing is described as 'chilling'. Soon, after barely getting started, the poem ends on the one image that an earlier American poet might recognise, but it is dry, brittle, the detritus of a day at the seaside after it has ended:

a sprig of black seaweed,
Shells.[2]

In the last line we see the mayor alone in his office, his head in his hands, seemingly at his wits' end. This, Bly seems to be saying, is the Great Society, Lyndon B. Johnson's model for a more just America,* a place where everyone, from the janitor to the

---

*During his exposition of the Great Society in a speech made at University of Michigan in 1964, Johnson said:

Many of you will live to see the day, perhaps 50 years from now, when there will be 400 million Americans – four-fifths of them in urban areas. In the remainder of this century urban population will double, city land will double, and we will have to build homes, highways and facilities equal to all those built since this country was first settled. So in the next 40 years we must rebuild the entire urban United States.

Aristotle said: 'Men come together in cities in order to live, but they remain together in order to live the good life.' It is harder and harder to live the good life in American cities today.

The catalog of ills is long: There is the decay of the centers and the despoiling of the suburbs. There is not enough housing for our people or transportation for our traffic. Open land is vanishing and old landmarks are violated.

Worst of all expansion is eroding the precious and time-honored values of community with neighbors and communion with nature. The loss of these values breeds loneliness and boredom and indifference.

Our society will never be great until our cities are great. Today the frontier of imagination and innovation is inside those cities and not beyond their borders.

president himself, sits uselessly burdened by minor responsibili-
ties and vague fears that they seem either unable, or unwilling to
deal with, while the children play on the *farther* shore, in a city
that resembles nothing so much as one of George Bellows's lurid
urban landscapes of 'ash cans and darkening mortar'.

The poem is hard to like and difficult to understand – but that
is Bly's intention. He means to unsettle his reader, and in so doing
provoke questions about the status quo. Technically, his approach
is deceptively simple: influenced by Asian and Imagist poetry,*
in which a single, unqualified image is presented to the reader,
followed by another and (depending on the form) yet another,
each demanding a two-level response – one based on the visceral, in-the-moment reaction, the other drawing on allusions
and cross-currents from other works of art – he shows us images
of absurdity, neglect, futility and decay that prompt a variety of
responses, from dismay to humour. That hands 'developed with
terrible labor by apes/ Hang from the sleeves of evangelists' is a
fairly easy joke at the expense of those whose religious biases are
disputed even by their own physical make-up (in the notorious
Scopes Monkey Trial of 1925 a young schoolteacher from Tennessee lost his job and was threatened with prison for talking about
evolutionary theory in his science class), while Bly borrows from
the imagery of Surrealist painting to create a dark and fairly dismal
atmosphere in which death waits, patiently, to reap its harvest:

> There are murdered kings in the light-bulbs outside movie
>   theaters:
> The coffins of the poor are hibernating in piles of new tires.

On the other hand, we cannot help seeing the next two lines
as a vision of hope, of nature re-asserting itself as it rises and

---

* The twin influences that nourished the economical style of the poets of the
1960s were the Japanese haiku and the work of Imagist poets such as Ezra
Pound, H. D. and others. The aim of both approaches was not just brevity
('use absolutely no word that does not contribute to the presentation') but a
kind of distillation process in which the image presents 'an intellectual and
emotional complex in an instant of time'.

overwhelms the luxury possessions of the idle rich –

> Bushes are growing over the outdoor grills,
> Vines over the yachts and the leather seats.

– and Bly works in a wonderfully sly image for decay and the passing of time in the reference to the 'darkening mortar' in the last stanza, a deft touch that we possibly do not notice at first, until we consider how many other, more obvious images he could have substituted here. What he wants is a long, slow, inevitable and mostly (because it happens so slowly) invisible process, not a conventional emblem of *tempus fugit*. There is no explanation as to why the mayor has his head in his hands, yet we see it as a powerful image, a stock photo almost, of the failure of American cities and the increasingly obvious indifference of Federal authorities to the real conditions of inner-city residents, who, unable to join the exodus to the suburbs, are left to make do amid the ruins. The poem does not preach its politics; it is not a diatribe on inner-city decay or public policy, though the title, with its direct reference to the policy that LBJ most treasured, is enough to point the reader in that direction. At the same time, while it could be argued that race is not overtly mentioned, those last four lines do inform us that the children are 'dark':

> On the far shore, at Coney Island, dark children
> Playing on the chilling beach: a sprig of black seaweed,
> Shells, a skyful of birds,
> While the mayor sits with his head in his hands.

As the poem ends, we are no better informed, factually, as to why these scenes have come about. We might assume that the city is now bankrupt for the usual historical reasons: the mass of white taxpayers have moved out to self-sufficient communities in the suburbs; the corporation that once employed half the population has migrated its entire operation to a place where labour is cheaper and regulation almost non-existent; discriminatory lending practices are preventing African-American citizens from investing in property, leaving the housing market in the hands of unscrupu-lous landlords. A few years before Bly's poem was written, Jane Jacobs had published *The Life and Death of Great American Cities*, in which she critiqued the many reasons why American cities were failing, while at the same time introducing terms (such as 'social capital' and 'self government') that at least attempted to human-ise the process. What Bly is presenting in 'The Great Society' is the aftermath of a great squandering of social capital. That he titles it with the name of Lyndon Johnson's flagship social policy is bitterly ironic.

Lawrence Ferlinghetti was in his eighties when he wrote one of his best-known poems, an angry cry against George W. Bush and his advisers entitled 'Pity the Nation', in 2007. It begins

> Pity the nation whose people are sheep,
> and whose shepherds mislead them.
> Pity the nation whose leaders are liars, whose sages are
> silenced,
> and whose bigots haunt the airwaves

and the poem continues, using the now established refrain, to 'pity the nation whose breath is money' that acclaims 'the bully as hero' and 'aims to rule the world with force and by torture' while remaining ignorant of any other culture but its own. Finally, partly as a sideswipe at the erosion of civil rights under Bush's Homeland Security Act (2002), he concludes:

> Pity the nation – oh, pity the people who allow their rights to
> erode
> and their freedoms to be washed away.
> My country, tears of thee, sweet land of liberty.[3]

Throughout, the poem drips irony, especially in that last, bitter reference to the American patriot's Ur-song;* yet the most telling stroke of all, considering the political climate of the time of composition (and since), is that Ferlinghetti used – and fully acknowledged – as his model a poem written in the 1930s by the Lebanese-American painter-poet Gibran Kahlil Gibran (someone who, though actually Christian in upbringing, would almost certainly have become a target of Bush's 'security' measures).

'Pity the Nation' was not Ferlinghetti's first foray into political commentary, however. A native of Yonkers, NY, he served in the navy during the Second World War before moving to San Francisco, where he founded the City Lights Bookstore in 1953. He had been writing poems throughout his life; now he began work on the collections that would establish him as one of the leading American poets of the day (*Pictures of the Gone World* in 1955; *A Coney Island of the Mind* in 1958). Meanwhile, as a publisher, he disseminated contentious work by others, including the first edition of Allen Ginsberg's *Howl*, in 1956 (for which he was arrested on obscenity charges, subsequently winning the ensuing court case and so setting a landmark for free speech publication in the United States). Rejecting the label 'Beat' (he preferred to be seen as an 'insurgent'), he moved seamlessly from the 1950s into the more politically engaged '60s, taking an active part in the anti-Vietnam and civil rights movements. A pacifist and anarchist, he expresses his fundamental hopes and beliefs in poems that, in spite of their sometimes bitter ironies, look to the possibility of a new world, one that has achieved social and environmental justice. One of the

---

* 'America', aka 'My Country 'Tis of Thee', was composed in 1831 by Samuel F. Smith, while he was still a student. It contains the lines: 'Author of liberty,/ To Thee we sing./ Long may our land be bright,/ With freedom's holy light', sentiments much abused by presidents and presidential candidates throughout the last few decades. (See Mitt Romney's 'Faith in America' speech of December 2007, which, after attacking the 'theocratic tyranny' of Islam, on the one hand, and secularism, on the other, concludes with the lines: 'let us give thanks to the divine author of liberty. And together, let us pray that this land may always be blessed with freedom's holy light.')

finest of these is 'I am Waiting' (from *A Coney Island of the Mind*), with its refrain of 'perpetually awaiting/ a rebirth of wonder':

I am waiting
for the meek to be blessed
and inherit the earth
without taxes
and I am waiting
for forests and animals
to reclaim the earth as theirs
and I am waiting
for a way to be devised
to destroy all nationalisms
without killing anybody.[4]

In 'Baseball Canto', a poem written in 1973 about the San Francisco Giants team of the 1960s, he sets not just two baseball teams but two cultures against one another. On one side, the great 'Anglo-Saxon tradition' of white baseball, dominant in the American imagination for many decades for the simple reason that, until Jackie Robinson signed to Branch Rickey's Brooklyn Dodgers in 1947, non-white players were not allowed to play at the highest levels, but were forced to content themselves with less pay and recognition in the 'Negro Leagues'. With Robinson's success – hard-won, as he faced down racist colleagues and fans alike – the floodgates began to open, and soon the game was transformed, with new levels of artistry and athleticism (and new records in hitting, fielding and pitching). For a hundred years, baseball had been the quintessential blue-collar American pastime,* and Ferlinghetti has a little fun with this in the opening line:

Watching baseball, sitting in the sun, eating popcorn,
    reading Ezra Pound.

---

* It is interesting that in the US, with its myth of classlessness, people are referred to not as working- or middle-class but as blue- or white-collar.

It is a nice opening play: by breaking the usual fan stereotype with the introduction of Pound (and as we shall see later, the anti-*usura* Pound at that), Ferlinghetti reminds his audience of something that should go without saying – that the usual stereotype of the passive, uneducated working man is absurd. At the same time, he introduces another informing strand from Pound's *Cantos* – the tradition of the *Anglo-Saxon Chronicle*, with which Pound engages near the start of the poem, thus setting up another stereotype/expectation about 'the culture'. Yet what follows is even more slyly subversive of conservative America, represented by

> the National Anthem,
> with some Irish tenor's voice piped over the loudspeakers,
> with all the players struck dead in their places
> and the white umpires like Irish cops in their black suits and
> > little
> black caps pressed over their hearts,
> Standing straight and still like at some funeral of a blarney
> > bartender,
> and all facing east,
> as if expecting some Great White Hope or the Founding
> > Fathers to
> appear on the horizon like 1066 or 1776.

It should come as no surprise here that an anarchist like Ferlinghetti should choose to link 1066, when Norman invaders set up a viciously feudal state in England, and 1776, when a small band of white, slave-owning men established an idea of America that any anarchist thinker would be bound to question.* Now, however, there is a new player in town – and he is a black man:

---

*The term 'Great White Hope' originated in another sport, when white fans started calling for a white boxer capable of defeating the black heavyweight legend Jack Johnson. From 1908 to 1915 Johnson reigned as champion, triumphing over all-comers, including the former champion Jim Jeffries, whom he defeated on 4 July 1910. Jeffries had returned to the ring after a long campaign that included an openly racist appeal from Jack London: 'Jim Jeffries must emerge from his alfalfa farm and remove the golden smile from

But Willie Mays appears instead,
in the bottom of the first,
and a roar goes up as he clouts the first one into the sun and
    takes
off, like a footrunner from Thebes.

Willie Mays. One of the best ever all-around players, a formidable athlete and a true gentleman, an example to players everywhere and a mentor to younger black players coming into the Big Leagues, where they still faced a diet of daily racism. Willie Mays is a legend, a man of myth, the living legacy of a Golden Age, a foot-runner from Thebes indeed. For an astonishing two decades, from 1951 to 1973, his name was synonymous with baseball, partly because he was so good and partly because he played with integrity and an exemplary respect for the game. Now, back in the poem, Mays gets on base and everyone waits to see what will happen next. What happens next is Tito Fuentes, who comes in

looking like a bullfighter
  in his tight pants and small pointy shoes

– a sly jibe at the fashion sense of many white players, who wore their uniforms with all the grace a convict brings to prison clothes. Tito, on the other hand, is *stylish*, individual – though he matches his swagger with skill by 'smack[ing] one that don't come back at all' before fleeing 'around the bases like he's escaping from the United Fruit Company' (a rather dark joke, aimed at those American corporations who knowingly supported oppressive and often murderous regimes in Central and South America in pursuit of higher profits and minimal regulation). Now

---

Johnson's face. Jeff, it's up to you.' After the fight, Jeffries graciously remarked: 'I could never have whipped Johnson at my best. I couldn't have hit him. No, I couldn't have reached him in 1,000 years.' Others were less generous, however, and Johnson, who had married a white woman and become successful in the entertainment business, suffered constant government persecution and even served gaol time on trumped-up sex crime charges.

sweet Tito beats it out like he's beating out usury,
not to mention fascism and anti-semitism.
And Juan Marichal comes up,
and the Chicano bleechers go loco again,
as Juan belts the first ball out of sight,
and rounds first and keeps going
and rounds second and rounds third,
and keeps going and hits paydirt
to the roars of the grungy populace[5]

and the only way the keepers of the Anglo-Saxon epic can restore order is to hit 'the backstage panic button for the tape-recorded National Anthem again'; but this does nothing, not this time, as whole-scale revolution breaks out, ending the age of the 'the great Anglo-Saxon epics' and leaving the poem itself to move forward into 'the *territorio libre* of Baseball'.

Poems like 'Baseball Canto' raise many questions, of course, chief of which is, how successful it actually is as a political satire. Ferlinghetti often uses humour in his work to make serious observations about socio-political issues, but that humour is based on a close understanding of, and care for, the working population of the US. He knows how important baseball is (or was at that time) in the composition of the American Dream, and he knows that, as families and groups of neighbours gather around the radio, and later the TV set, tuning in to the ball game, they are taking part in a communal activity just as vital to the group as listening to the bard retell the epic poems of origin and purpose that informed ancient societies. Sports commentators and writers, especially in baseball, were folk poets who wove and renewed the narrative of America many times over each year, and these tellings could be as cohesive for the group as the accounts of creation myths, decisive battles or the birth of a god. The fact that black athletes and players from Central and South America could become heroes of the national game was vital proof that they were not just an integral but also a heroic part of the American story. That this should seem a threat to some is, to Ferlinghetti, reason for pity and mockery in equal measure. Rather than diminishing the American narrative, the arrival of these new heroes only enriched it further, and 'Baseball Canto', for all its sense of fun, is a powerful argument not for racial tolerance but for an all-out celebration of diversity.

Robert Bly consciously dedicated himself to finding a poetic idiom that was open and democratic: 'the language you use for your poems,' he said, 'should be the language you use with your friends.' At the same time he recognised that 'the democratic culture doesn't exist without highly informed citizens capable of thinking well.' Similarly, Ferlinghetti chooses to make poems that anyone can read, as opposed to the kind of work that, in his view, confines itself to the ivory towers of academia. He habitually uses pop culture, sports, demotic speech and the textures of street life in his work, as in the unrelenting surge of anarchist ideas that form one of his finest pieces, 'Junkman's Obbligato':

> Goodbye I'm walking out on the whole scene.
> Close down the joint.
> The system is all loused up.
> Rome was never like this.
> I'm tired of waiting for Godot.
> I am going where turtles win
> I am going
> where conmen puke and die
> Down the sad esplanades
> of the official world.
> Junk for sale!

This does not mean, however, that he is in any way anti-intellectual, or dismissive of the existing literary canon per se. Far from it. 'Junkman's Obbligato', for example, is full of references to Yeats's 'The Lake Isle of Innisfree' (to which it is, in fact, a sly response) as well as to Samuel Beckett and the classical traditions of pastoral. In fact, one of Ferlinghetti's main points of contention is the assumption that 'the culture' belongs to the rich and well educated, that, as T. S. Eliot contends, it is 'the function of the superior members and superior families to preserve the group culture' just as they 'preserve and communicate standards of manners'. His poetry discovers and fosters the plain fact (one that ought to have been self-evident) that the appreciative intellect is as democratic in its workings as taste, or a basic sense of justice. He has told interviewers that he set up the City Lights Bookstore as 'a center of intellectual activity', and his publishing list includes Julio Cortázar, Pier Paolo Pasolini and Howard Zinn, among others. Asked by a reporter during a television appearance how it felt 'being on mainstream media', he responded: 'The mainstream media is still the high culture of intellectuals: writers, readers, editors, librarians, professors, artists, art critics, poets, novelists, and people who think. They are the mainstream culture, even though you may be the dominant culture.' This distinction is crucial to an understanding not only of Ferlinghetti but also of many of his contemporaries: to be a democratic writer does not mean to talk down to the reader (an attitude that would only serve to reinforce the idea that the culture, like everything else, belongs to the rich and powerful); it demands a clarity of language and vision that allows the poem to open itself gradually to any reader, no matter what their background. Reading Ferlinghetti, we are reminded that it is as foolish to confuse a 'good education' with intelligence as it is to confuse wealth with success or, *pace* Eliot, the mere politesse of 'manners' with the radical responsibility that fosters mutual respect.

While their methods may differ in some respects, what Bly and Ferlinghetti share is: first, a commitment to democratic speech that, while it by no means simplifies language or reduces ideas to some kind of cartoon accessibility, nevertheless communicates directly, using all the tools the poem has to offer, with a non-academic readership; and, second, a quest for something larger and more inclusive to set in place of the nation-state and the conventional institutions, something truly humane in which the poem can place its trust. Their poetry of dissidence does not consist solely of rejection; they may express an abhorrence of a 'loused up' system, but they also seek to discover an alternative to that system, a set of possibilities, at the very least, that we can believe in. This search was not new. Even in the 1930s the Catholic poet, novelist and film critic James Agee was summoning an internationalist vision of social justice to set in place of the US, which, having foundered as a republic, was now stumbling into Empire:

> From now on kill America out of your mind.
> America is dead these hundred years.
> You've better work to do, and things to find.
> Waste neither time nor tears.
>
> See, rather, all the millions and all the land
> Mutually shapen as a child of love.
> As individual as a hand.
> And to be thought highly of.[6]

There are many forms of dissidence, and many forms of political poetry, but in the second half of the twentieth century this approach, in which the poem moves on from an initial critique – even a denunciation – of the corrupt state to pledge allegiance to something larger than that state: not to the flag but to the land, not to the leaders but to the people, and not to the tribe but to the race as a whole. A black poet in the US such as Haki R. Madhubuti has more in common with a North Vietnamese resistance fighter than he has with the powerful elite in the US:

> Viet brothers come give us a hand
> We fight for freedom
> We fight for land.

Give me my forty acres
Give me my mule –
Broken promises and hypocrisies.*

Yet, while such appeals to 'kill America out of your mind' or to form fraternal bonds with a fellow victim of imperialism on the other side of the world might have been seen by some as treason, they were not usually acknowledged as such by their authors. However, in 'Alta Traición' ('High Treason') a poem written in the 1970s, the Mexican poet José Emilio Pacheco appears to indict himself of exactly that crime, opening with the outright declaration that:

I do not love my country,
its abstract brilliance
is beyond my grasp.

No amo mi patria.
Su fulgor abstracto
es inasible.

As a journalist, Pacheco had witnessed the brutal attacks on students during the Tlatelolco massacre of October 1968, when students using the public events surrounding the Mexico City Olympic Games to protest against social inequality, injustice and environmental degradation were fired on by government troops. Official sources put the number of dead at four, but most observers estimate that somewhere between two hundred and three hundred people were killed, with thousands arrested in the aftermath. Not surprisingly, this brutal act, and the cover-up that followed, led many Mexicans to abandon what little trust they still

---

*A reference to a pledge made out of political expediency by Union General William Tecumseh Sherman to the black residents of Savannah, Georgia, that, under specific conditions, they would be provided with forty acres of land to work of their own account after the war. This promise was quickly reversed by the incoming president, Andrew Johnson, the moment hostilities ceased, and the land was returned to its former owners, many of them slave-owners loyal to the Confederacy.

had in the government, and Pacheco was giving voice to a widely held sense of disillusionment and disgust. These opening lines, in which he rejects *'patria'*, do not mean, however, that he also rejects his home-place, or the community with which he shares it (we might, perhaps, oppose the term *'patria'* here with the word *'país'*, thus setting apart the political homeland from the geographical and communal place). And he continues:

> [but] I would give my life
> for ten of its places,
> certain people,
> ports, pinewoods,
> strongholds,
> a washed-up city,
> gray, monstrous,
> a few characters from its history,
> mountains
> – and three or four rivers.

> daría la vida
> por diez lugares suyos,
> cierta gente,
> puertos, bosques de pinos,
> fortalezas,
> una ciudad deshecha,
> gris, monstruosa,
> varias figuras de su historia,
> montañas
> – y tres o cuatro ríos.[7]

It is here that this brief, clearly articulated and profoundly elegant poem ends, a perfectly economical utterance that is both conversational and deeply moving. Overall, the effect is utterly to contradict the opening claim, that this speaker does not love his homeland – he loves it deeply, and it grieves him to witness its shame, under the control of a corrupt governing elite. Indeed, it would be high treason for him to support that government,

considering how utterly it disdains the values inherent in the land
and in the people – and ironically, this is why he does not abandon
hope. He knows that the real *'patria'*, the *'patria'* that he deserves
and is prepared to die for, along with the 'certain people' of whom
the poem speaks, has nothing to do with the 'abstract brilliance'
of self-proclaimed patriots and self-appointed leaders. It lies in the
land itself, in the woods, in the rivers and in the people, for whom
justice is a shared aspiration, and that space in which the music of
what happens can be heard is a matter of continuing hope.

SÓLO TÚ, ALMA MÍA

Greatly ought we to rejoice that God dwells in our soul;
and more greatly ought we to rejoice that our soul dwells
in God. Our soul is created to be God's dwelling place, and
the dwelling of our souls is God, who is uncreated. It is a
great understanding to see and know inwardly that God,
who is our Creator, dwells in our soul, and it is a far greater
understanding to see and know inwardly that our soul, which
is created, dwells in God in substance, of which substance,
through God, we are what we are.

The Cloud of Unknowing

IN APRIL 2003, towards the end of a balmy Argentine summer, I
set out on a more or less impromptu field trip to Entre Rios with
Mary and Diana, two friends from Buenos Aires. It was already
late in the day when we left the city, heading out across the
pampas into a wide, eerie twilight that, even in the small hours,
never quite became night. On the map the journey had seemed
pretty straightforward, but I had already begun to learn that in
Argentina nothing on the map corresponds very closely to the
terrain, and after three hours or so we stopped at a nondescript
lean-to by the side of the road, a narrow box of light and familiar
scents into which the two women disappeared for a coffee and a
smoke, leaving me to explore the immediate vicinity alone. By
now they had become accustomed to my poking around in the

dust, looking for plants and insects, or even small animals, and they were content to leave me to it; the trip itself was an indulgence on their part. City folk by choice, they had generously agreed to take me to see the great Yatay palms at El Palmar national park, and they had quickly realised that only a steady regime of creature comforts, however modest, would prevent them from allowing their regret to become apparent. Meanwhile, I was trying to be sensible; but there, by the road, in the near-dark, I caught a hint of a scent and then, almost immediately, a pungent drift of what I knew could only be skunk and, immediately, stupidly, I was off. Out into the darkness I went, away from the box of light and the aroma of coffee, hoping for a glimpse of something wild.

Inevitably, I wandered too far. But it didn't matter. Suddenly I was out in the open, the land flat and vast around me, the ghostly plumes of pampas grasses – nothing like the ornamentals I knew from the parks and gardens of my childhood – catching the star-light like feathers turning in the wind. And once out into the open, those were the first things I was aware of: the wind and the stars. The sky was massive, cloudless and, away from the artificial lights, a vast, detailed map of constellations that I mostly didn't know. Immediately, I began to search for the Southern Cross – but then I heard a rustle off to my left and I looked down, thinking the skunk had re-emerged from a nearby clump of spear grass. Another rustle came off to my right, and then a new set of impres-sions – this time, the warm, ropy smell and the looming bulk of horse – and two gauchos appeared, presumably as surprised to see me as I was to see them, though nothing was visible in their faces. Silently, indifferently, they continued on their way, barely pausing to take me in, and after a long moment they were gone. Maybe that was when the full immensity of the pampas struck me, or maybe it was later, as we drove on into the night and I gazed out at the vastness, not quite finding the words for what that land-scape was doing, somewhere at the back of my head. At the time I might have said it was a dreamlike landscape, and perhaps – aware of the fact that (in Argentinian miles) we weren't that far from the place where Olga Orozco grew up, back in the 1920s and '30s –

I might have said *surreal*. But that wasn't quite right. What I was seeing, as we headed north, was an insomniac kingdom, a landscape for the sleepless and, like those other places that are flat and wide and open to the sky for thousands of miles, it was both beautiful and unsettling. At the same time it was not altogether real, or not in everyday terms; it stood immersed in its own separate reality, where magic could happen at any time, because, in this place, magic was natural, even inevitable, like weather. It was, if not exactly here, then in similar terrain that Olga Orozco began to conceive a new kind of mystical poetry, her imagery and language haunted by a God who preceded Christianity, a God who 'in some way' is diffused or dissolved in all of us but will eventually return to reunite us as a single entity.

Olga Orozco was born Olga Noemi Gugliotta on 17 March 1920 in Toay, La Pampa province. She moved away as a child, first to Bahia Blanca, and then to Buenos Aires; reading the poems, however, it is the sleepless, dreamlike landscape of the open plain that clearly sits at the heart of the work. 'I was born in the Pampas,' she told interviewers. 'There the flatness seems at a zero level. That place is filled with mystery. It has such an intense flatness that it is dizzying to look at from wherever you may stand. Any detail on that flatness becomes prominent. Just as in a picture by Magritte.' In an autobiographical sketch she wrote many years later, she would point to Basque and Irish roots on her mother's side and Sicilian blood on her father's, but it was her maternal grandmother who nurtured the poet in her: 'Every day she told me a new, fantastical story, full of fairies, goblins and demons; each story had its own terrors and salvations, all miraculous, of course.' She seems to have had a happy childhood, the one shadow falling in her seventh year, when her brother Emilio died of polio; in her first collection, *Desde lejos* ('From Afar'), published in Buenos Aires in 1946, she would write movingly of that loss in the poem 'For Emilio in His Heaven' ('Para Emilio en su cielo'):

Wait, wait, my heart:

it is not the cold countenance of the dreaded snow, nor that of
    the recent dream.

Once more, once more, my heart:

the unmistakable sound of the sand brushing the gate,

the grandmother's cry,

the same solitude, immune to all lies,

and the long destiny of gazing at our hands as they grow old.

Espera, espera, corazón mío:

no es el semblante frío de la temida nieve ni el del sueño
    reciente.

Otra vez, otra vez, corazón mío:

el roce inconfundible de la arena en la verja,

el grito de la abuela,

la misma soledad, la no mentida,

y este largo destino de mirarse las manos hasta envejecer.[1]

Settling in the capital on the completion of her studies at the
Facultad de Filosofía y Letras, Orozco worked as a journalist and
editor, pursuing what seems to have been, on the surface at least,
a not atypical literary career for the time and place in which she
worked.* In the course of that career she published eighteen collections of verse and several prose works, becoming a member,
in name and allegiance, of the Generación del '40 group, which
included such poets as Alberto Girri, Roberto Juarroz and Enrique
Molina, now seen by most critics as the leading Argentinian Surrealists of the period. Yet, while she enjoyed the camaraderie of the
group, Orozco never felt herself to be a Surrealist, declaring that
she mistrusted their inclination to believe 'that everything begins
from zero' – and this is not surprising. Like other artists, poets
come together to protect and nurture a shared sensibility, but if

---

*Not an easy time, it should be said, for a journalist and poet, as the period
known as the 'Infamous Decade' (beginning with the deposition of Hipólito
Yrigoyen in 1930) merged into a series of military dictatorships through the
1940s and '50s and beyond.

they are to last any time at all (and most do not), such schools have to be extremely fluid. Movements that impose rules and methods on their membership, such as André Breton's Paris Surrealist group, soon lose the best of those participants, if only because the making of art, and certainly of poetry, tends to be individual, heuristic and ungovernable. Perhaps the photographer Edward Weston expressed it best: 'To consult the rules of composition before making a picture is a little like consulting the law of gravitation before going for a walk. Such rules and laws are deduced from the accomplished fact; they are the products of reflection.' As Orozco later remarked about that period:

> Our generation was driven to get together and keep in touch to write something that did not exist, and to learn what was going on because we could not read about poetry in the newspapers. In fact, we were probably very much like all other groups of poets in the immediate post-war and early Fifties: we had to start afresh because everything had been done and then dramatically destroyed. We were probably no more than small animals locked up together all of a sudden in a cage and we had to share what we had.

And in a poem from those early years entitled 'Olga Orozco' she speaks of herself as one might speak of the dead in an obituary, the better to draw, with the kind of finality only an obituary can provide, a definitive portrait of an artist who, her poetic affiliations notwithstanding, remained independent, a distinct voice dedicated to her own vision:

> I loved solitude, the heroic endurance of all faith,
> the idleness where strange animals and fabulous plants grow,
> the shadow of a great era that passed between mysteries and
>   hallucinations,
> also the faint tremor of candle flames when night falls.

> Amé la soledad, la heroica perduración de toda fe,
> el ocio donde crecen animales extraños y plantas fabulosas,

la sombra de un gran tiempo que pasó entre misterios y entre
    alucinaciones,
y también el pequeño temblor de las bujías en el anochecer.[2]

This solitary and independent persona was one that Orozco
would elaborate on throughout her later life, seeing herself as a
witness to 'a deeper and darker law' ('una ley más honda y más
oscura') than those that govern other lives. For her, poetry comes
from that deeper and darker order, where the named self has no
jurisdiction:

When I look, there is always someone in me who says that I
    am not me,
someone who slips away step by step as I advance
leaving me blind, clutching only at a name, at ignorance.
For there are incomprehensible extensions that reach into the
    beyond,
unnavigable regions where the footsteps of God may appear,
transparent substrates that sometimes penetrate the gardens
    of another world
and when they return they release a perfume like the perfume
    of dawn.

Siempre hay alguien en mí que dice que no estoy cuando me
    asomo,
alguien que se desliza paso a paso a medida que avanzo
hasta dejarme a ciegas, asida solamente a un nombre, a la
    ignorancia.
Porque hay prolongaciones inasibles que llegan más allá,
zonas inalcanzables donde tal vez se impriman las pisadas de
    Dios,
subsuelos transparentes que se internan a veces en los jardines
    de otro mundo
y al regresar expanden un perfume semejante al del alba.

Yet, though Orozco allies herself as a poet with 'a deeper and darker law' than that of the social realm, this does not mean that she rejects the world she inhabits for some otherworldly realm. On the contrary, like Rilke confronting the angels, like Stevens and Montale coming face to face with the nothing that surrounds them, the encounter with the unnameable only serves to heighten the sense of poignancy – and of inherent beauty – she feels, living in the contingent world where, even when home is in question, it is still possible to find *refuge*. Indeed, the idea of refuge becomes vitally important in her work, but she finds it – tentatively, at least to begin with – in places where others might not look, places that are overlooked and neglected or even, in one of her finest works ('Balada de los lugares olvidados') not only in the places but in *everything* that others fail to recall:

> My loveliest refuges,
> the places that best adapt to the ultimate colours of my soul,
> are composed of all that others have forgotten.

> Mis refugios más bellos,
> los lugares que se adaptan mejor a los colores últimos de mi
>   alma,
> están hechos de todo lo que los otros olvidaron.[3]

We should note here that these refuges are not given, the speaker of the poem does not find them to hand in the immediate environment; they must be made (*hechos*). They are built from the wild grasses of the pampas, from the shadows cast by birds in flight, from the music of what happens:

> They are solitary places excavated in the caress of grass,
> in a shadow of passing wings; in a song that happens.

> Son sitios solitarios excavados en la caricia de la hierba,
> en una sombra de alas; en una canción que pasa.

The poem goes on to offer a catalogue of moments and images from a particular life, with its own particular memories and phantasms, providing a history of images, both fantastical and quotidian, in which the speaker imagines a private realm, through the use of magical invention and ritual. Having opened a kind of clearing, a debatable yet enchanted land in the midst of the world of others, it closes with a confident invocation of a claimed space, where the spirit cannot be deprived of its magical powers:

> My loveliest refuges are solitary places where no one else goes
> and where there are only those shadows that come to life
> > when I am their sorceress.

> Mis refugios más bellos son sitios solitarios a los que nadie va
> y en los que sólo hay sombras que se animan cuando soy la
> > hechicera.

The reference to sorcery in 'Balada de los lugares olvidados' marks a distinct strand in Olga Orozco's work; she makes frequent reference to magic, talismans, cartomancy, horoscopes and other occult arts. It is inviting, however, to see those interests as sources of imagery and an arcane iconography, while the philosophical edifice of the poetry is founded on medieval theology. This comes through most forcefully in her idea, noted above, of a god who is at present dispersed through all creation, but who will eventually return, together with everything that has ever been.* However, like T. S. Eliot, she is also deeply influenced by the ideas of the medieval mystics. For example, asked to speak about a recurrent theme in her work, at a conference in Córdoba in 1991, Orozco chose 'time and memory', which she described as two constant and fundamental 'presences' in her writing. Reminding her audience of Augustine's famous dictum ('If no one asks me, I know

---

* This idea can be traced to the medieval theologian and suspected heretic Johannes Scotus Eriugena: 'God is the beginning, middle, and end of the created universe. God is that from which all things originate, that in which all things participate, and that to which all things eventually return' (*Periphyseon III*).

what it is. If I wish to explain it to him who asks, I do not know') and declaring her intention to avoid discussions of the 'fugitive and perverse' behaviour of linear time, she chooses:

> to protect myself in eternity, the one favourable place to con-
> template the hours and the centuries, since eternity is lethal
> to time, as garlic is to vampires, laughter to monsters and
> morning to ghosts […] from that beatific refuge, I can say that I
> have no interest in knowing whether time is a form of thought,
> or an aspect of reality experienced as duration, or a measurable
> entity like space.

> ampararme en la eternidad, único lugar venturoso para con-
> templar las horas y los siglos, porque la eternidad es mortal
> para el tiempo, como el ajo para los vampiros, la risa para los
> monstruos y la mañana para los fantasmas […] desde ese bien-
> aventurado refugio, puedo decir que no me interesa saber si
> el tiempo es una forma del pensamiento, o un aspecto de la
> realidad hecha duración, o una entidad mensurable junto con
> el espacio.

She is aware of linear time, and she is aware of Kierkegaard's concept of the present as 'that which has no past or future', but what interests her now is the fact that 'time flows in all directions, that it happens, that it accumulates in reverse and that it returns transformed and dynamic' ('el tiempo fluya en todas direcciones, que pase, que se acumule hacia atrás y que vuelva transformado y dinámico').

This is the beginning of a vision of time that is architectural, rather than merely linear. Time as an edifice, a structure. It is difficult to describe this concept of time, but one way of thinking about it might be to compare the music to which we are most accustomed, essentially a linear, melodic flow, with the musical structures created by Minimalist composers such as Steve Reich or La Monte Young. Here, especially in longer pieces like Reich's *Music for 18 Musicians*, say, the nature of listening is gradually altered, which in turn alters the overall nature of the listener's attention, creating an entirely different experience of how time operates. Absorbed in the music's multi-storeyed, multi-current organic structure, the listener's experience of time is not linear, on the one hand, or suspended in the 'eternal moment', on the other. Instead, Orozco says:

> I am the active scenario where time circulates in both directions, without limitations, without borders, as in dreams.

> soy el escenario activo por donde el tiempo circula hacia ambas direcciones, sin limitaciones, sin fronteras, como en los sueños.

With a nod to T. S. Eliot, Lewis Carroll, Borges and Stephen Hawking, she goes on to add:

> In the same way that the present influences the future, so the future influences the present and corrects the past [...] This incessant, circular action transforms memory itself into an active instrument against time, disrupting its tyranny, so that each repetition turns what would seem an act of clairvoyance into a reading of the past, reversing the relationship between cause and effect.

> De modo que así como el presente influye en el porvenir, el porvenir influye en el presente y corrige el pasado [...] Esta acción incesante, circular, hace de la memoria misma un instrumento activo contra el tiempo, desbaratando su tiranía, haciendo que la repetición convierta lo que parecería una clarividencia en una lectura del pasado, invirtiendo la relación entre causa y efecto.

This sounds mystical – and Orozco is fully aware of this, which is why she now moves into a more anecdotal exposition based on folk beliefs about the nature of time that occur in several cultures –

> It may be that this is no more than a superstition, but I have heard it said that the exact repetition of a certain atmosphere, that is, of special conditions that occurred once, can cause the

reappearance of an image or of a fact that was particularly intense, particularly significant. In this way, the *Marie Celeste* could be seen on certain days, just as she was before her shipwreck; The Flying Dutchman wanders the oceans waiting to renew his pact with the Devil to cross the Cape of Good Hope, and at Marathon, the Athenians rise up from their graves and resume the battle amongst the neighing of their horses.

Se dice, tal vez sea una creencia supersticiosa, que la repetición exacta de la atmósfera, de unas condiciones especiales que se dieron una vez, pueden provocar la reaparición de una imagen o de un hecho que fueron particularmente intensos, particularmente significativos. Así la María Celeste podría verse intacta ciertos días, como antes de su naufragio; el Holandés Errante deambula por los mares dispuesto a reanudar su pacto con Satán para cruzar el Cabo de Buena Esperanza, y en Maratón los atenienses se levantan de sus tumbas y prosiguen su lucha entre el relincho de los caballos.

– and she recognises in this old belief a parallel with her own practice as a poet. She combines the central idea of these stories with the memory of her home landscape on the pampas:

> Maybe this open and mysterious vision I have of time has something to do with the fact that I was born in La Pampa […] The pampa is a space where nothing is lost, where everything stands out […] From this space I received, long ago, my first lessons in the abyss and the absolute.

> Tal vez tenga que ver con esta visión abierta y misteriosa de todos los tiempos el hecho de que nací en La Pampa […] La pampa es un espacio donde nada se pierde, donde todo se destaca […] De ese espacio recibí, hace ya muchos años, mis primeras lecciones de abismo y de absoluto.

Rarely has a poet set out so thoroughly the relationship between home-place, philosophical preoccupations and the poetic process – and this lecture calls for close attention, if we are to come to terms with Olga Orozco's work. A child of the pampas, she seems to have lived a full life as a journalist and writer in Buenos Aires without attracting undue attention from the powers-that-be. What she brought with her from the pampas, however, was a magical sensibility, a vital apprehension of something that she chose to shroud in the language of cartomancy and witchcraft. A few commentators have argued that the image she projected, of an eccentric obsessed with the occult and the otherworldly, was, partly at least, a mask, a persona that deflected the potentially unwelcome attention of the authorities. Her sense of home, intertwined as it is with her vision of time and of an audacious variety of negative theology, is fundamental, however. Some readers have been tempted to see her work as pessimistic, because she locates the absolute so firmly in an ever elusive elsewhere, but this seems to me a serious mistake. For while it is true that she cannot enter those 'unnavigable regions where the footsteps of God may appear', she at least knows that they exist, just as she knows that, above and beyond the noise of Benjamin's 'progress', above and beyond all the distractions the social realm imposes on us, the music of time continues, unbroken.

When Olga Orozco died, on 15 August 1999, she was highly regarded among Spanish-language readers, a recipient of such prestigious awards as the Juan Rulfo Prize (but barely known outside academic circles elsewhere). Since then, her work has begun to be translated into English and other languages and appreciated by a wider audience and, without doubt, will continue to find new readers. Reading her work, and gleaning from articles and interviews what she felt about her chosen art, it becomes clear that, for her, poetry was a matter of process, a spiritual, even shamanic practice in which the idea of a posterity was secondary to the immediacy of that practice. To be a poet, she said, was to feel 'incomplete, limited and imprisoned in this self and in this tangible reality, face to face with an unknown universe

that exceeds us'; however, the recognition of this plight leads to
'a continuous quest [...] to find, through symbolic operations, the
recovery of a lost unity, of the essential freedom in which it is possible to experience all metamorphoses, all times, all associations'.*
Towards the end of her life, when she was being garlanded with
prizes throughout the Spanish-speaking world, she remarked that
she had never felt herself to be a poet, but that she 'still aspired to
that title'.†

---

* 'Es sentirse incompleto, limitado y prisionero en este yo y en esta realidad
tangible, frente a un universo desconocido que nos excede ... Ser poeta es
también una incesante, una continua búsqueda. Es buscar, por medio de
operaciones simbólicas, la recuperación de una unidad perdida, de la libertad
esencial en la que es posible vivir todas las metamorfosis, todos los tiempos,
todas las asociaciones.'

† 'Sentir que soy una poeta, no lo sentí nunca, todavía estoy aspirando al
título.'

LIKE A STRIPÈD PAIR OF PANTS

And what I know best
                has nothing to do with Point Conception
And Avalon and the long erasure of ocean
Out there where the landscape ends.
What I know best is a little thing.
It sits on the far side of the simile,
                the like that's like the like.[1]

Charles Wright

IN 1969, WHEN I WAS FOURTEEN, my mother would turn up the radio whenever they played a song called 'MacArthur Park', and I would have to listen, torn between conflicting emotions but, essentially, trying not to laugh or, worse, snigger while she hummed or, worse, sang along. It was a strange choice for her, a woman who usually liked Andy Williams and Perry Como, and it was an even stranger situation. This song (schmaltzy, sentimental and yet annoyingly affecting for reasons I did not understand) was one that she had deliberately *chosen* to like, because it was officially of my era rather than hers, and she was pleased to enjoy something out of her usual taste that might offer us common ground on which to meet. (Around that same time, as I recall, we had disagreed rather forcefully about the Rolling Stones' double-A side of 'Ruby Tuesday'/'Let's Spend the Night Together'). That fact, along with the tragic sense of lost love and thwarted ambition that I was getting from the music, might have moved me to genuine tears, but almost every time I stopped politely to listen, any upsurge of emotion was undermined by the sheer *stupidity* of the lyrics. What in the hell was going on here? Why was MacArthur Park melting? How had it turned into a cake with sweet green icing? And how, by any stretch of the imagination, could the doomed lovers who seemed to float through this tortured landscape be compared, in any meaningful way, to 'a stripèd pair of pants' caught in 'love's hot, fevered iron'? It was all very confusing, not to mention altogether silly – and on a couple of occasions I had to rush away and perform some inessential chore. And once, out of context, as it were, I wept silently, my head bowed for a different reason now, the tears running down my cheeks as I rehearsed a heartache that was not mine, though I sensed, without knowing why, that it was my mother's.

I remember this scenario as the first, or perhaps the most glaring, example of the discord that arose when the lyrics of a song and its music struck me as being desperately, even wilfully, at odds. Never the hard-bitten type, I could melt silently (like sweet green icing in the rain, presumably) when Ella Fitzgerald came on the radio with 'Every Time We Say Goodbye'. I could even admit to a certain guilty melancholy when Simon and Garfunkel launched into 'The Only Living Boy in New York', but then, in both cases, the words worked together with the music and so played an equal, or nearly equal, part in drawing out emotions that at fourteen I could not readily identify by name. By now, there is no need for further analysis of Cole Porter's lyric (its sad, playful rhymes, its wit, its smoky but genuine stoicism), and in 1970 it would have been well-nigh impossible to find a fifteen-year-old who did not respond wistfully to Paul Simon's lyric – 'Half of the time we're gone, but we don't know where' – especially considering the fact that these words are sung over Joe Osborn's elegant, restrained bass lines. (Osborn, one of the great session musicians who *made* pop music in that era, also played on 'MacArthur Park'.)

Nevertheless, I learned what I still think was a valuable lesson, sitting by the radio in my mother's kitchen – a lesson that, while it is hard to put into words, installed in me a caution about comparing poetry and pop songs. For while so many moving songs fall apart when the music is taken away and the lyric is left exposed on the page, the truth is that this is neither here nor there, for in a good song the music and the words are intricately interdependent. To strip the lyric of its melody would be like surgically removing the bones from a horse and then complaining when it could not stand up or run. (This is easily illustrated by taking any national anthem, pretty much at random – 'O Canada!', say – and trying to glean anything more than empty rhetoric from the words, while Peter Sellers's versions of hit Beatles songs like 'Help!' and 'Hard Day's Night', when stripped of their musical backing and performed in the voice of Laurence Olivier's *Richard III*, or a pompous rural vicar, even had fans of the Fab Four rolling in the aisles back in the early '60s).

None of this is surprising. Music brings essential underpinning to a song lyric, drawing on folk and 'high art' traditions alike, or weaving blue notes, waltz rhythms and skipping rhymes with hymn-like cadences that, even for the non-believer, evoke childhood walks to chapel or midnight Mass, usually in new snow, along long-lost roads with long-ago loved ones. The best songwriters use these musical allusions the way poets echo the Bible, or Shakespeare (or, for that matter, Child's *English and Scottish Popular Ballads*). What *is* surprising is the not uncommon impulse to 'elevate' the best songwriters to some supposedly higher level: to suggest that, because they make such great songs, a Bob Dylan or a Joni Mitchell or a Neil Young deserves to be called a poet, rather than a 'mere' songwriter. As if this was an honour. As if all the nonsense handed down to us by a class-based system about 'high' and 'low' culture was ever anything more than a way of maintaining a cultural hierarchy commensurate with a class-based social order. Why didn't we always know, as a matter of common sense, that there is no such thing as 'high' or 'low', only good and bad? I didn't need to go to this or that school to respond immediately to Handel or Benjamin Britten, and nobody had to tell me that most of the commercial 'pop' peddled on radio and

TV was manufactured, a 'hit parade' of watered down R&B, deep soul and blues music made anodyne by white people with excellent teeth: some A&R guy's idea of edgy new material that, in the end, turned out to be more or less polite rehashes of Bob Dylan by pretty young men who wouldn't scare my mother, or covers of Screamin' Jay Hawkins by art school dropouts who looked good in pageboy haircuts and ruffs. I didn't have to believe that a song lyric was somehow a disguised poem in order to be moved by it. Songs were songs, poems were poems. Both were made, in part, of words, and both were musical in some way; but, other than that, they were distinct entities, and I enjoyed them in quite different ways.

Nevertheless, during the 1960s, in particular, ardent fans of singer-songwriters like Dylan or Joni Mitchell would frequently deploy the 'poet' epithet.* The press and the publicity people didn't help, and Dylan, in particular, had fun muddying the waters, most famously in the 'I Shall Be Free No. 10' lines

Yippee! I'm a poet, and I know it
Hope I don't blow it.

Nevertheless, and in spite of the mock-naïve tone, it is hard not to agree with his public contention – oft quoted by an adoring press – that, if he could sing something, he called it a song, and if he couldn't, he called it a poem. Dylan may have been deliberately stripping a complicated argument down to its barest bones when he made such remarks (perhaps because, like so many others, he found the whole controversy tiresome), but the essence of truth

---

* I still recall the snooty older brother of a friend remarking, when he came across me listening to *Songs of Love and Hate*, that I would never 'get' Leonard Cohen because, unlike my more usual musical heroes, Cohen was a poet, not just some sell-out from Tamla Motown or Stax (he had recently discovered that I was a fan of Otis Redding and, stupidly, despised me for it). I can only imagine this hipster's confusion when, asked during a press conference, 'What poets do you dig?', Bob Dylan replied: 'Rimbaud, I guess; W. C. Fields; The family, you know, the trapeze family in the circus; Smokey Robinson; Allen Ginsberg; Charlie Rich – he's a good poet.'

is there. No matter how beautiful, or incisive, or surreal its lyric might be, a song, even when performed without accompaniment, must have a strong musical underpinning. Read cold, on the page, it is diminished, not because it is of any less worth than a poem but because it has been taken out of its true element. For example, when we simply *read* the lyric of a highly affecting hymn like 'All is Well', from the renowned hymnal *Revival Melodies, or Songs of Zion*, published in 1842 by John Putnam –

> What's this that steals, that steals upon my frame,
> Is it death, is it death?
> That soon will quench, will quench this mortal flame,
> Is it death, is it death?
> If this be death, I soon shall be
> From ev'ry pain and sorrow free,
> I shall the King of glory see,
> All is well, all is well.

– we are drawn in by the immediacy of the first lines, and stirred by the stoicism and deep faith of those that follow, just as, later in the hymn, we respond to the imaginative leap, wrought by the dying man, in which the mourners who surround him are transformed into

> Bright angels [...] from glory come,
> They're round my bed, they're in my room.
> They wait to waft my spirit home.

It has to be said, however, that the hymn relies for its fullest effect on the melody, which slows the piece down and gives the words a halting, tentative rhythm that does not come over on the page. It is the rhythm of a dying man whose breath has begun to waver, and whose sight is clouding over in this world, even as he prepares to enter the next. Taken together, the music and words have what some would call a spiritual power that the lyric alone does not possess. To see how this is so, we need only compare the not unrelated, but more open-ended, Emily Dickinson poem, 'I heard a Fly buzz – when I died' to see how differently the poet works the same territory:

I heard a Fly buzz – when I died –
The Stillness in the Room
Was like the Stillness in the Air –
Between the Heaves of Storm –

The Eyes around – had wrung them dry –
And Breaths were gathering firm
For that last Onset –- when the King
Be witnessed – in the Room –

I willed my Keepsakes – Signed away
What portion of me be
Assignable – and then it was
There interposed a Fly –

With Blue – uncertain – stumbling Buzz –
Between the light – and me –
And then the Windows failed – and then
I could not see to see – [2]

It would be possible to set this poem to music, but that music would not add anything essential to a work whose musicality is already fully formed and perfectly appropriate to the subject at hand. Which is not to say that Dickinson's poem is better than Putnam's hymn – they are simply different in form, and thus in effect.

Any further comparison is complicated by the fact that the Dickinson poem is mediated by its appearance *on the page* in a way that a hymn lyric is not – and while there can be real traffic between a song (or, for that matter, a 'spoken word' piece) and a page poem, the differences between them are more important than the similarities. Put simply, song is probably the oldest art form practised by humans, while the page poem, as we understand it now, is a much more recent phenomenon. With the invention of printing, the page poem started to evolve in new directions, encompassing philosophical speculation, on the one hand, and linguistic and visual play that could only happen within the white space of the page, on the other. The page poem could draw on traditions of theatre and philosophical or scriptural commentary in ways that would not have worked in song; it could play elaborate games with time and with semantic expectations that, in a song lyric, would have seemed cumbersome. Finally, because of its association with literacy, page poetry began to be seen as a 'high' art, while popular song was consigned to some lower level – but that had everything to do with societal values, and nothing at all with the intrinsic value of the respective forms.

In short, when song lyrics and page poetry parted company, they did so for a number of reasons,* but it wasn't because page poetry was in any way superior to popular song. In fact, by the time Bob Dylan was awarded the Nobel Prize for Literature, in October 2016, many readers and listeners had come to see such hierarchical distinctions as entirely historical, the product of a

---

*Walter Pater's famous claim that 'all art aspires to the condition of music' has often been misunderstood. In the same essay he would go on to contend that:

> Poetry, again, works with words addressed in the first instance to
> the pure intelligence; and it deals, most often, with a definite subject
> or situation. Sometimes it may find a noble and quite legitimate
> function in the conveyance of moral or political aspiration, as often
> in the poetry of Victor Hugo. In such instances it is easy enough for
> the understanding to distinguish between the matter and the form,
> however much the matter, the subject, the element which is addressed
> to the mere intelligence, has been penetrated by the informing, artistic
> spirit. But the ideal types of poetry are those in which this distinction is
> reduced to its minimum; so that lyrical poetry, precisely because in it we
> are least able to detach the matter from the form, without a deduction
> of something from that matter itself, is, at least artistically, the highest
> and most complete form of poetry. And the very perfection of such
> poetry often appears to depend, in part, on a certain suppression or
> vagueness of mere subject, so that the meaning reaches us through
> ways not distinctly traceable by the understanding.

It is this radical new way of conveying its meaning that distinguishes what I am calling the page poem from more traditionally oral-based works.

system that had always assumed a direct link between social rank and real merit, an asumption previously noted in T. S. Eliot's conception of the social elite as a 'repository' of 'higher values'. This is nonsense, of course. It was nonsense in Eliot's day, and it is nonsense now, but that doesn't prevent people from continuing to make the association. This error can lead, on the one hand, to bad songs with pretentious lyrics from people who might otherwise have made something perfectly decent in their chosen form and, on the other, to facile and frequently condescending poetry that, the more it tries to acquire the common touch or some kind of 'street' relevance, the more it reveals its inherent cultural and socio-political prejudices.

It may be a symptom of some natural perversity, but when I listen to those singers whose lyrics are most likened to 'poems', I am struck by how often they succeed when they eschew the more obvious literary techniques. As a page poet, for example, I find Leonard Cohen – how to say it? too poetic? – but his songs are often breathtaking. Even Dylan, with his compendious knowledge of every kind of popular music, could fall foul of the overliterary mode in his earlier work. (For me, the turning point comes with 'Brownsville Girl', from *Knocked Out Loaded*; after that he never strayed from the purity of song again. It took him a while, though.) When, having been asked during an interview if he thought of himself 'primarily as a singer or a poet', he responded: 'Oh, I think of myself more as a song-and-dance man', he wasn't just being flippant. The poet label was mostly imposed from without, by those who arrived at his work with the old hierarchical, high-culture vs. low-culture baggage. It would have been well-nigh impossible not to slip into the odd bout of poeticising, even for a song-and-dance man of his calibre.

Similarly, Jim Morrison's work with The Doors is full of howlers, but only when he is *trying* to be a poet.* When he honours the

---

* All that snake nonsense.

song tradition, drawing on the work of his greatest predecessors, like the Delta Bluesmen, or turning a standard '60s love song on its head, he can do astonishing, if deceptively simple, things. For instance, in the song 'Break on Through' (1967) he sings

> I found an island in your arms
> Country in your eyes

– lines that embody the clichés of every 60s love song while throwing in an off-the-cuff reference to John Donne's elegy 'To His Mistress Going to Bed':

> O, my America, my new-found-land,
> My kingdom, safest when with one man mann'd,
> My mine of precious stones, my empery;
> How am I blest in thus discovering thee!
> To enter in these bonds, is to be free;
> Then, where my hand is set, my seal shall be.

But then, in a ferocious and brilliant rejection of these received ideas, Morrison snaps:

> Arms that chain us
> Eyes that lie
> Break on through to the other side.

As anyone who was a child in the radio days can attest, it was songwriters, more than anybody else back in that golden era, who shaped our experiences at every stage, from the life of the mind to the greasy squalor of the heart. If asked out of context the name of the first girl I ever really (seriously) danced with, or even what she looked like, I wouldn't be able to answer; play me 'Standing in the Shadows of Love', by the Four Tops, however, and I see it all as if it had happened yesterday. Songs are our life, the warp and weft in the fabric of our dailiness. They are also, or can be, the means to our betrayal. Without Jim Morrison's fierce riposte to the conventions of co-dependency romance, I might have wandered placidly from the disco floor to the altar with someone I barely knew. What gave us all a chance of snapping out of those romantic conventions was that snarl, and the words: 'Your ballroom days are over, baby [...] Night is drawing near [...] Shadows of the evening [...] Crawl across the year.'*

If poetic aspirations sometimes get in the way of good songwriting, however, almost any song can inform the shaping of a great poem. Sometimes, like a jazzman picking up a 'pop' standard or show tune (Miles Davis, say, reinventing 'Some Day My Prince Will Come', from the Disney feature cartoon of 1937, *Snow White and the Seven Dwarfs*, or the same artist's extraordinarily moving version of Cyndi Lauper's 1984 chart-topper 'Time After Time'), the poet will respond to some formal aspect of the original, rather than to the semantic content. (Robert Burns, for example, drew his inspiration for many works from popular songs, while, as we have noted, Lorca was quick to acknowledge his debt to flamenco *music.*†) At other times, however, it is what the song says in (or in opposition to) an established tradition that piques the poet's interest.

A very good example of this is Charles Wright's response to 'California Dreamin', a three-minute pop classic originally composed in the winter of 1963 by John and Michelle Phillips,‡ and released first as a single by Barry McGuire and then by the Mamas and the Papas themselves (with Joe Osborn, naturally, on bass) on their album *If You Can Believe Your Eyes and Ears* (1966). Wright's poem shares the song's title but, unlike the song, which captures a single moment when John Phillips took refuge from the New York winter in a church (where he pretends to pray while

---

*By way of contrast, see Bobby Vinton's 'Please Love Me Forever', from the same year (1967).

† Intriguingly, it is rumoured that Michael Jackson was inspired to write 'Thriller' by Burns's poem 'Tam o' Shanter'.

‡ With Mama Cass and Denny Doherty they would become the Mamas and the Papas in 1965.

fantasising about being 'safe and warm' in Los Angeles), the poem is composed of nine diary-like sections, each capturing a fleeting vignette of a mood or a scene that the poem's speaker experiences in the period between October and Christmas. (This approach was to become a central element of Wright's poetic practice, leading to works that spanned whole seasons or years, such as the fifty-page 'A Journal of the Year of the Ox' in the 1988 collection *Zone Journals*.) This strategy allows Wright to develop a persona who stands at times as a kind of Everyman figure and at times as the poet's alter ego (a character modulated through echoes of Tang Dynasty poets such as Du Fu and Li Bo). This allows Wright to draw on the fine detail of quotidian experience, while placing his speaker at one remove from the burdens of the obviously auto-biographical. The result is often highly individual, but it is so in such a way that the author, if he does not altogether yield, at least offers the lyrical space that the poem creates for the reader's own reflections.

At the time 'California Dreamin' was composed, almost anyone would have considered the West Coast an earthly haven: prosper-ous, comfortable, hedonistic, 'safe and warm' and, most of all, *easy*. What Wright's lyrical but sometimes scathing retort to that myth of California does is to show that such easiness is not only not enough but is also a trap. The prosperity and safety are real, no doubt, but *easy* quickly becomes facile, and the maintenance of a dream may eventually demand a willingness to numb the usual experiences of day-to-day existence – unease, anxiety, dread – with pharmaceutical supplements, or worse. It is on these points that Wright takes issue not only with his initial source material (the song 'California Dreamin'') but also with the entire myth of California-as-earthly-paradise.

To see what Wright does with his source material, we have to examine the song itself – a task that is rarely very satisfying. At best, it can feel like stating the obvious to point out how a lyric achieves a certain effect; at worst, it can spoil the thing for ever. In the case of 'California Dreaming', we might note that the rhyme scheme is limited throughout to just six sounds: gray, day, way, pray, stay and the rogue two-syllable L. A; or we can note the use of phrases like 'pretend to pray', and 'if I didn't tell her' to reveal the speaker's indecisiveness and bad faith; but none of this adds up to very much. It is a persuasive, accomplished pop song, and it helped to shape a myth about California that, for a while, made that state seem like the happiest place on earth. A place of peace and love and an easy, if somewhat vague, 'spirituality'. A place where it was sunny all the time and everybody had some kind of vegetation, if not in their hair, then about their person. What Wright takes from the song, however, is a prompt: just as John Phillips's persona is homesick for LA sunshine in a drab New York winter, the leaves brown, the sky grey, so the speaker in Wright's poem is homesick – but what he is desperate to escape is the very place Phillips would most like to be. What California represents for Phillips is safety and warmth; for Wright's protagonist it is a place without history, a region whose people are 'not born yet':

> another nation,
> 　　　　living by voices that you will never hear,
> 　Caught in the net of splendor
> 　　　　of time-to-come on the earth.
> 　We shine in our distant chambers, we are golden.[3]

Here, from the start, is a vision of the perfect location to live out Emily Dickinson's famous poem 'I Dwell in Possibility':

> I dwell in Possibility –
> A fairer House than Prose –
> More numerous of Windows –
> Superior – for Doors –
>
> Of Chambers as the Cedars –
> Impregnable of eye –
> And for an everlasting Roof
> The Gambrels of the Sky –

> Of Visitors – the fairest –
> For Occupation – This –
> The spreading wide my narrow Hands
> To gather Paradise – [4]

And, while we are considering possible allusions, it may be instructive to note that sly use of a fleeting quote from another Southern Californian singer-songwriter: 'we are golden', from Joni Mitchell's hymn to the Woodstock Nation:

> We are stardust.
> We are golden.
> And we've got to get ourselves back to the garden.

Already Wright is weaving in a host of what we now think of as classic '60s allusions, from the Mamas and the Papas through Mitchell to 'Age of Aquarius' ('everything's crystal under our feet' echoing the 'mystic crystal revelations' of The Fifth Dimension's 1969 hit). This new dawning, however, is seen through a 'Darvon dustfall off the Pacific' (Darvon was a trade name for the opioid Dextropropoxyphene), suggesting that this New Age vision of a West Coast Paradise might have been gained, or is at least sustained, with the aid of mind-altering substances. It is a *dream*, after all – and to dream we have to be, if not asleep, then at least in a state of suspended disbelief.

Having established this sense of unease, Wright (a native of Pickwick Dam, Tennessee, and a former counter-intelligence officer who taught at Irvine, in Orange County, California, from the mid-1960s to the early '80s) makes clear how he feels about his life in what was frequently cited at the time as the safest place in the US:

> I've looked at this ridge of lights for six years now
>   and still don't like it
> Strung out like Good Friday along a cliff
> That Easters down to the ocean.

A few lines earlier the poem has identified its current season as October (it will move between this non-autumnal fall to a very unseasonal-seeming Christmas), which ought to be a time of brown leaves and the first autumn frosts, but this place is stuck in what feels like a perennial Good Friday, a constant Easter that, nevertheless, is now subject to the 'hot breath' of the Santa Ana wind (also known as the 'devil wind') that troubles Southern California late in the year.* In this unrelenting weather all living things are fretful:

> High in the palm tree the orioles twitter and grieve.
> We twitter and grieve, the spider twirls the honey bee,
> Who twitters and grieves, around in her net,
> > then draws it by one leg
> Up to the fishbone fern leaves inside the pepper tree
> > swaddled in silk
> And turns it again and again until it is shining.

Here even the deadly game of a predator and its victim is transformed into something that shines, catching the uniform, monotonous light, while the mocking repetition of 'twitter and grieve' implies that, in a place like this, even mortality is a trivial matter, to be dismissed as mere histrionics. (The poem does not even say why *we* twitter and grieve, suggesting that our woes are scarcely worth mentioning.) The poem's fifth section is a night scene, a favourite time for Wright, who has been influenced, throughout his career, by the moon-viewing tradition of Chinese poetry.† Yet where that tradition emphasises the serenity and continuity of

---

* The Santa Ana wind is a feature of California-based songs by artists as various as Tim Buckley through the Beach Boys to Steely Dan and, more recently, Sons of Bill. It features in the works of many writers, from Philip K. Dick to Joan Didion. Raymond Chandler, in his short story 'Red Wind', describes Santa Ana season as a time when 'Meek little wives feel the edge of the carving knife and study their husbands' necks.'

† A pose he will occasionally ironise, while still retaining the poignancy of his model; see 'After Reading Wang Wei, I Go Outside to the Full Moon', from the 1995 collection, *Chickamauga*.

the natural world, here the poem's speaker is disturbed, first by a rock-and-roll band rehearsing in the next house, then by a last helicopter 'thwonking' back to the nearby Marine base, while the moon is nothing more than a gold lamé prop and the country that sleeps around him, weightless and inconsequential, is 'like flung confetti', leaving the speaker to wonder

>   just what in the hell I'm doing out here
> So many thousands of miles away from what I know best.
> And what I know best
>   has nothing to do with Point Conception
> And Avalon and the long erasure of ocean
> Out there where the landscape ends.
> What I know best is a little thing.
> It sits on the far side of the simile,
>   the like that's like the like.

It is this recognition – of displacement, of spiritual exile – that becomes the pivot point of the poem. From here on, the speaker observes his surroundings with a kind of bemused detachment touched with curiosity about the game he is playing and why he continues to play it –

> Who are these people we pretend to be,
>   untouched by the setting sun?
> They stand less stiffly than we do, and handsomer,
> First on the left foot, and then the right.
> Just for a moment we see ourselves inside them,
>   peering out,
> And then they go their own way and we go ours

– and this *is* a game, though it is a solemn one: a pose, a gesture towards a lifestyle that probably does not exist outside glossy advertisements and the cinema, an attempt on the part of these California dreamers to live the life, even as

>   everything we have known,
> And everyone we have known,

Is taken away by the wind to forgetfulness,
Somebody always humming,
                    California dreaming …

So they go on, in their wetsuits, riding 'wave after wave …
glossed slick as seals', their surfboards rising and falling 'like the
sun', each day merging imperceptibly with the next. It is hard not
to find, here, an echo of what might be the tragically short-lived
Weldon Kees's most powerfully elegiac work, an untitled eight-
line poem that opens with the celebrated line 'The smiles of the
bathers fade as they leave the water', and continues:

> These perfect and private things, walling us in, have imperfect
>   and public endings –
> Water and wind and flight, remembered words and the act of
>   love
> Are but interruptions.[5]

At the same time the Eliot of 'Burnt Norton' hovers in the
background:

> Distracted from distraction by distraction
> Filled with fancies and empty of meaning
> Tumid apathy with no concentration.

Meanwhile, Wright's dreamers carry on, humming the soundtrack to their illusory West Coast lifestyle absently, while the
Santa Ana blows through their somnambulist heaven, incongru-
ous Christmas lights draped in the pepper trees, and the known
world falling away 'like spores / From a milkweed pod'.

It could be said, with some fairness, that Wright's work in 'California Dreaming' is, on one level at least, not unlike that of the
jazz musicians he much admires,* as it takes a pop tune and

---

* And pays tribute to, as in 'Body and Soul II', from the 2002 collection *A Short
History of the Shadow*, a poem Wright dedicates to jazz saxophonist

makes something new from it. In this instance, however, he goes further, to engage in a profoundly moving interrogation of the assumptions that lie at the heart not only of his 'standard' but of the mythology that was created around California as a locus of earthly perfection. The mythological California is a place that not only contrasts favourably in every way with the rest of the world (a world that Joni Mitchell describes as 'old and cold and settled') but is also, in the words of 'California Calling' (the Beach Boys' best song about the state), a land of 'permanent vacation' where 'the good sun shines every day'. Just as, musically, Miles Davis might draw from a Top Ten single the tragic recognition that, even if we do find one another 'time after time', we are nevertheless mortal creatures, subject to temporal limits and thus bound to be lost sooner or later in the flow of unrecorded history, so Wright poetically exposes the artificial paradise of the dreamed California that may well 'Dwell in Possibility' but remains, nevertheless, a figment of a wishful imagining. Indeed, that dwelling place outside the limits of 'Prose' can only be maintained by the persistence of a dreamlike, possibly pharmaceutically induced, slumber. Yet even as the exposure of this flaw in the mythology has its own worth (as a useful diagnostic act, perhaps), the poem also reveals something important about the nature of home, and of belonging. It is a revelation that recalls one of the essential narratives of the tribe, narratives about place and community and the nature of reality that are essential to our knowledge of ourselves and our world – in this case, a story that pretends to be for children but is not, a necessary story about what we wish for and what we eventually come to see as needful.

This story, which has several variants, usually tells of a brother

---

Coleman Hawkins:

> The structure of landscape is infinitesimal,
> Like the structure of music,
>> seamless, invisible.
> Even the rain has larger sutures.
> What holds the landscape together, and what holds music together,
> Is faith, it appears – faith of the eye, faith of the ear.

and sister who, having strayed too far from their parents' house, meet the Fairy King at the edge of an enchanted meadow in the first grey of dusk. The King is very beautiful, and the children see that he is kind; so when he tells them that, if they will follow him, he will take them to a place where everything is perfect, a place free of sickness and work, where anyone can have anything he or she desires, simply by wishing for it, they willingly go with him into the gathering twilight, only to emerge, on the far side of the meadow, in a land of eternal sunshine and safety and warmth, where nobody sickens or grows old. Here they are happy and have all they desire – and the Fairy King is genuinely happy to welcome them into his magical realm.

After a time, however, the children begin to think again of their parents' house, and of the family and friends they left behind. They have everything they could possibly want – and yet they feel a strange melancholy, a sadness shot through with the sense that nothing they know, in this place, is altogether real. They reminisce about their old life; they miss their playmates and pets. Finally, they go to the Fairy King and explain that, as kind as he has been and as beautiful his kingdom seems to them even now, they must go back to the life they left behind. They love their parents and, as imperfect as it might be, they miss their true home.

Naturally, the King is saddened by this news, and he explains to them that, if they go back, their lives will no longer be charmed. They will not only have to watch helplessly as their loved ones waste away and die, but they too will sicken and grow old. They will no longer have anything they want just by wishing for it; instead, they will work long and hard to no avail and be subject to the miseries of unrequited love and frustrated ambition. Worst of all, having returned to the realm of linear time, they will be obliged to live with the fact that, in times of trouble, the days will be long and wearisome, while the handful of happy occasions will go flashing by, never to be repeated. The children nod sadly; they appreciate everything the King is telling them. They know that his kingdom is perfect, but they also know that, for them, that perfection is not quite real. It's an existential trick, a lived illusion – and as imperfect and fleeting as it may be, the world they left behind is the only place that they can think of as home. This is why they are returning to that world; this is why they are leaving the King's apparent paradise; they are going back to the place where they belong. It is a sad moment, but it is also a salutary one; for just as Wright's poetic response to 'California Dreamin' reveals the necessity to search beyond some fantasy of 'easy living', so the story tells us that it is better to find our true home, even a home that is flawed and temporary, than to dwell with bad faith in a place that is not our own.

TANTALUS IN LOVE

And yet, within this deception,
true happiness occurred.[1]

Louise Glück

ACCORDING TO PHILIP LARKIN, sexual intercourse began in the *annus mirabilis* of 1963, between the lifting of the ban on *Lady Chatterley's Lover* two years earlier and the appearance of The Beatles' *Please Please Me*, which featured songs such as 'Love Me Do', 'I Saw Her Standing There' and the disarmingly direct title track, in which pleasure is very much a negotiation between the lovers.* Before that year of wonders, Larkin says,

> there'd only been
> A sort of bargaining,
> A wrangle for the ring,
> A shame that started at sixteen
> And spread to everything.[2]

Now the bargaining was more specifically directed, as songs like 'Please Please Me' sought to dispel adolescent shame altogether and initiate an honest, if somewhat crude, quid pro quo approach to sexual relations. Nevertheless, the 'wrangle for the ring'

---

*The ban on *Lady Chatterley's Lover* was lifted in November 1960. During the year that followed, 2 million copies would be sold, temporarily knocking the Bible off the Number 1 spot. *Please Please Me* was released on 22 March 1963.

continued and, even as the new era was ushered in with refreshing frankness by such no-nonsense offerings as The Rolling Stones' 'Let's Spend the Night Together' (in 1967) and Bob Dylan's 'Lay Lady Lay' (1969), Solomon King could still top the charts during the self-proclaimed 'Summer of Love' with the mawkish and highly suspect Boudleaux and Felice Bryant number 'She Wears My Ring' ('to show the world', naturally, 'that she belongs to me').

In theory, at least, none of this was new. The challenge to staid society over the assumed link between love and marriage had been posed back in 1940 by the Swiss cultural historian Denis de Rougemont, whose study of romantic attachment *Love in the Western World* had contended that: 'Passion and marriage are essentially irreconcilable. Their origins and their ends make them mutually exclusive.' In fact, European literature abounded with cautionary tales and quips about the pitfalls of marriage as an institution – almost all of them from men.* One frequent critic was Robert

---

*It may be that women, having been schooled so long in the courtesies and anticipated joys of wifehood, were too dismayed for casual repartee when they came up against the state of affairs that George Eliot noted in *Middlemarch*:

> How was it that in the weeks since their marriage Dorothea had not distinctly observed, but felt, with a stifling depression, that the large vistas and wide fresh air which she had dreamed of finding in her husband's mind were replaced by anterooms and winding passages which seemed to lead no whither? I suppose it was because in courtship everything is regarded as provisional and preliminary, and the smallest sample of virtue or accomplishment is taken to guarantee delightful stores which the broad leisure of marriage will reveal. But, the door-sill of marriage once crossed, expectation is concentrated on the present. Having once embarked on your marital voyage, you may become aware that you make no way, and that the sea is not within sight – that in fact you are exploring an inclosed basin.

Mae West notwithstanding, not much had changed by the 1950s. Fast-forward to Betty Friedan:

> The problem lay buried, unspoken, for many years [...] it was a strange stirring, a sense of dissatisfaction, a yearning that women suffered [...] Each suburban wife struggles with it alone. As she made the beds, shopped for groceries, matched slipcover material, ate peanut butter

Louis Stevenson, who, in spite of severe ill-health, travelled half-way around the world to marry Fanny Van de Grift Osbourne. Stevenson gleefully explained that 'In marriage, a man becomes slack and selfish, and undergoes a fatty degeneration of his moral being',* while Leonardo da Vinci, who remained a bachelor, presumably did so because he was wise enough to heed his own observation that 'Marriage is like putting your hand into a bag of snakes in the hope of pulling out an eel.' Love, it seems, is one thing, marriage another – but does this mean that we are bound to agree with Lord Illingworth, in Oscar Wilde's *A Woman of No Importance*, when he says: 'One should always be in love. That is the reason one should never marry.' Or should we perhaps consider with all due seriousness the opposite argument, in which passion is eschewed for the sake of a common good that marriage is thought to embody? 'It is not the first love that matters,' according to the French essayist Jacques Chardonne, 'nor the second, nor the last. It is the one that folds two destinies into the life of the community.'

To a contemporary reader, no doubt, this is an old-fashioned idea. We think of marriage as a private matter, a continuation of the romance with which a couple's love began, a stab at Happy Ever After whose apparent failure, even if it comes decades after that honeymoon spell, somehow negates, or at least devalues, the initial bond. Denis de Rougemont would claim, however, that this approach to love is a recipe for disaster: 'Passion is by no means the fuller life which it seems to be in the dreams of adolescence, but is on the contrary a kind of naked and denuding intensity, verily, a bitter destitution, the impoverishment of a mind being emptied of all diversity, an obsession of the imagination by a single image.' In short, romantic love, passion, *amour fou*, not only cannot last

sandwiches with her children, chauffeured Cub Scouts and Brownies, lay beside her husband at night – she was afraid to ask even of herself the silent question – 'Is this all?'

* Though this is less severe than this remark, from his *Virginibus puerisque* (1881): 'Once you are married, there is nothing left for you, not even suicide.'

but actually *depends* upon not lasting. According to the model of domestic order proposed by Rougemont and Chardonne, the only way to succeed in marriage is to abandon, or perhaps transcend, that initial passion, while the only way to remain 'in love' is to stay single and move on when the spectre of matrimony rears its problematic, if not necessarily ugly, head. Love is a narrative, possibly a fiction; marriage is an institution (defined as 'an established law or practice' – which is to say, a convention), and during the twentieth century this polarity of romantic engagement versus institutional obligation found expression in the works of poet after poet, as unrealistic matrimonial expectations were more openly discussed and divorce rates soared, giving a new and sometimes disturbing dimension to those famous lines from Shelley's 'Epithalamium',

> O joy! O fear! what may be done
> In the absence of the sun?

However, before considering the marriage poem – by which, I mean, not just the traditional epithalamium but the poem that gets out its dissecting kit and digs deep into what makes modern marriage so difficult, on the one hand, and so rewarding when it is sustained, on the other – it is worth thinking about the modern love poem *as* love poem. I have to confess, I have always found this difficult as a theme; for example, when I first read e. e. cummings as a lovesick teenager, I was charmed to begin with –

> i carry your heart with me (i carry it in
> my heart) i am never without it (anywhere
> i go you go, my dear; and whatever is done
> by only me is your doing, my darling)
>   i fear
> no fate (for you are my fate, my sweet)[3]

– especially when he delved into his bag of Platonic sleight of hand, as in:

one's not half two. It's two are halves of one:
which halves reintegrating, shall occur
no death and any quantity.[4]

But all this philosophical flummery soon became tiresome for
the very obvious reason that there *was* death, and there *was* fate
and, if I was being frank, the thought of another person going
everywhere I went, even figuratively, gave me the heebie-jeebies.
Better, perhaps, to look to Robert Graves, the man who once
defined love as a 'universal migraine'. Perhaps with that perspective he would be the one to sift out the rhetorical excess and offer
a love poetry that was both passionate and realistic – or even, as in
'At First Sight', a measured intimacy informed by a more seasoned
and less possessive ardour:

'Love at first sight', some say, misnaming
Discovery of twinned helplessness
Against the huge tug of procreation.

But friendship at first sight? This also
Catches fiercely at the surprised heart
So the cheek blanches and then blushes.[5]

From his earliest, sometimes knockabout, poems about sexual
and romantic love to the measured work of his maturity, Graves
was cautious about the irrational impulses that lust fostered
('Down, wanton, down') and the various ways in which one lover
or the other might use the romantic occasion to satisfy more
primal psychological needs (and in the age of Freud such suspi-
cions could never be far from any lover's mind*). The early love

---

* Graves had little time for Freud, as he makes clear in *The Meaning of Dreams*:

Freud's position is briefly this [...] that every dream is expressing some
sort of desire which the dreamer in his waking life has not been able
to attain and, more than that, has not even dared to consider, because
somehow horrible, or unnatural or very strongly disapproved of
[...] These wishes are centred in the passions and in order to account
for children dreaming, Freud has been forced to say that even very
small children are subject to the same inclinations and passions as

poems are haunted by the dread of being absorbed into the life of the beloved, on the one hand, and of becoming the object of a cloying dependency, on the other – so much so that the only respite seems to be in letting go and moving on, as in 'A Former Attachment':

> And glad to find, on again looking at it,
> It meant even less to me than I had thought –
> You know the ship is moving when you see
> The boxes on the quayside slide away
> And become smaller – and feel a calm delight
> When the port's cleared and the coast is out of sight,
> And ships are few, each on its proper course,
> With no occasion for approach or discourse.[6]

Such freedom is an illusion, however, and Graves knows it. In poem after poem he expresses the recognition that love, even attachment, is part of a full life; he just wants to find a way to reconcile that with what was clearly a deeply felt need for personal integrity. In fact, what has always seemed most admirable in Graves's mature love poetry is his honest determination to love without compromising himself *or* the beloved, to balance passion with respect, to claim but also to give space. He steadily refuses to use the occasions of love dishonourably, a crime for which he indicts no less a figure than Dante, whose supposed beloved, Beatrice, was really a philosophical pretext for the poet's perfectionist fantasies:

> He, a grave poet, fell in love with her.
> She, a mere child, fell deep in love with love
> And, being a child, illumined his whole heart.
>
> From her clear conspect rose a whispering

---

grown persons; it is this theory that has given Freud most ill-fame and frightened away the common-sense man more than ever from the subject, particularly as the Freudian theory soon attracted to Vienna a number of students who liked nastiness for its own sake.

With no hard words in innocency held back –
Until the day that she became woman,

Frowning to find her love imposed upon:
A new world beaten out in her own image –
For his own deathless glory.

'Deathless glory' was never an object for Graves; instead, he recognised that, at the very least, the temporary, sometimes provisional, but genuinely shared attention of lovers-as-friends might
well be the only means by which we are able to make sense of an
impossible world:

When the immense drugged universe explodes
In a cascade of unendurable colour
And leaves us gasping naked,
This is no more than the ecstasy of chaos:
Hold fast, with both hands, to that royal love
Which alone, as we both know certainly, restores
Fragmentation into true being.

Of course, it could reasonably be argued that what Graves is
making here is not love poetry but poetry *about* love. It speaks
of dilemmas specific to a given individual at a given time – and
Graves was nothing if not frank about his younger self's dread
of being absorbed in some way by a needy other. To the true
romantic such concerns might seem unworthy, even ugly, but they
have strong roots, and Graves's researches into the neurotic and
possessive side of love are as honest as they are uncompromising.
So much so that it feels like a victory of sorts when the mature
poet emerges with an honourable vision of a considered, non-
possessive and egalitarian love-friendship – and the greatest
achievement of Graves's writings about love is that, at the end,
he discovers what he had hoped for from the first: that, far from
losing themselves in one another, true lovers turn outward to the
world and learn how to live there more skilfully than they would
otherwise have done.

But, as has been noted, this is poetry about love, in which, for the most part, the beloved appears only as a hypothesis. What, then, of the love poem itself, a poetic artefact that, even as we recognise it as a crafted and therefore self-conscious utterance, nevertheless comes across as a sincere address to the beloved? Did the twentieth century even do such things any more? Or rather, did it do such things unselfconsciously, as Byron or Leopardi might have done.* Where better to seek a continuation of the genre than in the works of the Chilean Nobel Laureate Pablo Neruda, who wrote literally hundreds of poems about love – and, indeed, there are magical things in his *oeuvre*, where he manages to side-step the usual hyperbole. Not surprisingly, considering he was such a prolific artist, there are occasions when he comes across as too histrionic for some tastes:

> In this story I am the only one who dies
> and I will die of love because I love you.

> En esta historia sólo yo me muero
> y moriré de amor porque te quiero.

At his best, however, he speaks in a way that allows the reader to slip quietly into what, in less skilled hands, might feel uncomfortably like a private drama – one that I, for one, might easily have been tempted to avoid.

Here, for example, in the seventeenth of *One Hundred Love Sonnets*, he is working at his highest powers. The poem begins with an echo of the 'negative love' tradition, in which the speaker attempts to say what something is by telling what it is not:

> I don't love you as if you were a rose of salt, topaz,

---

*Perhaps what is most disarming about 'She Walks in Beauty' is that it was written by the author of *Don Juan*:

> She walks in beauty, like the night
> Of cloudless climes and starry skies;
> And all that's best of dark and bright
> Meet in her aspect and her eyes.

or arrow of carnations that propagate fire:
I love you as one loves certain obscure things,
secretly, between the shadow and the soul.

No te amo como si fueras rosa de sal, topacio
o flecha de claveles que propagan el fuego:
te amo como se aman ciertas cosas oscuras,
secretamente, entre la sombra y el alma.[7]

This idea – to love the other as one loves the interior landscape of the self, that shadowy region where the soul becomes a possibility – sets the stage for a drama in which both lovers are presented with the possibility of mutual discovery; this is followed by a beautifully organic image in which, through his love of the other, the speaker's entire being is connected intimately with the earth itself, like a plant

   that doesn't bloom but carries
the light of those flowers, hidden, within itself,
and thanks to your love the tight aroma that arose
from the earth lives dimly in my body.

   que no florece y lleva
dentro de sí, escondida, la luz de aquellas flores,
y gracias a tu amor vive oscuro en mi cuerpo
el apretado aroma que ascendió de la tierra.

Finally, in a series of direct, declarative statements that are among the most cited in this poet's work, the speaker expresses his sense of wonder at having achieved this condition and, at the same time, speaks of the humility of one who not only loves without pride but is also capable of merging with the beloved without the fear of self-abnegation that so troubled Graves:

I love you without knowing how, or when, or from where,
I love you directly without problems or pride:
I love you like this because I don't know any other way to love,

except in this form in which I am not nor are you,
so close that your hand upon my chest is mine,
so close that your eyes close with my dreams.

Te amo sin saber cómo, ni cuándo, ni de dónde,
te amo directamente sin problemas ni orgullo:
así te amo porque no sé amar de otra manera,

sino así de este modo en que no soy ni eres,
tan cerca que tu mano sobre mi pecho es mía,
tan cerca que se cierran tus ojos con mi sueño.

This sonnet – songlike in its steady, measured rhythms – does not seek to persuade or to control; rather, it is a genuine love poem that, in its surrender to a force that is incomprehensible to both protagonists, permits them a moment of unity in which, together, they are magnified. Yet it seems to me that such works are rare in the twentieth century; and when they do succeed, they often emerge from a specific tradition and from established aesthetic and even linguistic conventions. What can be said in Spanish or Italian is often more difficult to utter with a straight face in, say, English – and for poets with, say, Anglo-Saxon attitudes, romantic love might well be regarded, on one level at least, as a kind of existential curiosity, to be treated lightly, and preferably with a touch of humour. W. H. Auden puts it nicely, in 'Tell Me the Truth about Love':

Will it come like a change in the weather?
Will its greeting be courteous or rough?
Will it alter my life altogether?
O tell me the truth about love.

Yet, humour notwithstanding, there is something genuinely poignant about this enquiry; and Auden could break a reader's heart with just as light a touch, when he chose to:

He was my North, my South, my East and West,
My working week and my Sunday rest,

My noon, my midnight, my talk, my song;
I thought that love would last forever: I was wrong.

The stars are not wanted now; put out every one,
Pack up the moon and dismantle the sun,
Pour away the ocean and sweep up the wood;
For nothing now can ever come to any good.[8]

Nevertheless, his now famous command to 'stop all the clocks' notwithstanding, even Auden could not ignore the looming impetus of time – and this comes clear in what seems to me his best poem *about* love, 'As I Walked Out One Evening', a seemingly straightforward ballad that is haunted throughout by an atmosphere of near-tragic mutability, the lover's voice raised to affirm his undying passion a futile protest against inexorable loss, in a city whose population is as perishable as 'fields of harvest wheat':

And down by the brimming river
      I heard a lover sing
Under an arch of the railway:
      'Love has no ending.

'I'll love you, dear, I'll love you
      Till China and Africa meet,
And the river jumps over the mountain
      And the salmon sing in the street.'

These are the clichés of every Valentine's card verse and teenage *confessio amantis* in which love endures 'till the ocean/ Is folded and hung up to dry' (the echo of Burns here seems almost mandatory). Yet the truth is that love is a fleeting event, while the passage of time is relentless and never-ending –

But all the clocks in the city
      Began to whirr and chime:
'O let not Time deceive you,
      You cannot conquer Time'

– and the poem continues with one of the bleakest invocations of mutability in the history of English literature:

> The glacier knocks in the cupboard,
>   The desert sighs in the bed,
> And the crack in the tea-cup opens
>   A lane to the land of the dead.

It concludes with the image of the 'deep river' – already characterised, in Auden's elegy to Yeats, as an elemental 'peasant' phenomenon that flows on 'untempted' by human concerns. This same river was there at the start of the lover's speech – when it was described as 'brimming' – and it has been present throughout, flowing on relentlessly to become the one thing that is still moving at the poem's end, after the crowds have melted away and the clocks have 'ceased their chiming':

> It was late, late in the evening,
> The lovers they were gone;
> The clocks had ceased their chiming,
> And the deep river ran on.[9]

Yet, while there are moments of real bleakness and the observations on the nature of passing time are painfully on the mark, this is not as pessimistic a poem, about love or about the human dilemma, as a first reading might suggest. True, the crowds of people and the lovers are ephemeral – but their drama happens, in their span of time, and the river runs on, when all is played out, out of, and into, another day. Like so many of the old ballads, 'As I Walked Out' takes note of its characters' fate but regards them tenderly, even in their moments of folly, and looks on mortality stoically, taking the something that happened as better than the nothing that might otherwise have been. This sense of stoicism would come into play, in a different guise, in poems about the bonds of matrimony, and the inexorability of time and tide, as the lovers become husband and wife and find the change unsettling, at best.

With so many twentieth-century poets intent on proclaiming the difficulty, even the impossibility, of sustaining love over time, the modern epithalamium showed signs of foundering alongside the blither conventions of love poetry, at least in English. 'Till a' the seas gang dry, my dear,/ And the rocks melt wi' the sun' simply did not stand up to scrutiny in an era when divorce became as commonplace a life-event as marriage, birth and death, and women were finally able to express their reservations about what the institution meant for them. In fact, the poetic celebration of marriage was even more vulnerable to such scrutiny for, as painful as its effects might sometimes be, romantic love can still be regarded as a kind of play, or a fleeting joy that is all the more precious for being transitory. 'I'm a romantic,' says F. Scott Fitzgerald. 'A sentimental person thinks things will last, a romantic person hopes against hope that they won't.' What better foundation for an aesthetic than this ironised acceptance of transience?

Marriage, on the other hand, came increasingly to be portrayed as a business of steady and sometimes tedious negotiation. Stevenson may have travelled all the way to California to win his bride, but when he actually found himself trapped in wedlock, the glamour would soon dissipate. Oscar Wilde, ever ready with a crushing epigram when it came to matters of the heart, would claim that 'Marriage is the triumph of imagination over intelligence' – though in this, I think, he is mistaken. To *fall in love* is the real triumph of the imagination, and it calls on all our gifts to maintain that condition. Always and everywhere, falling in love is, at least in part, a work of art, but marriage is a contract. That contract is an agreement to carry love forward in time, to achieve, if not Happy Ever After, then at least a willed continuity in which, while accepting, as William Carlos Williams does in his 1954 poem 'The Ivy Crown', that we 'cannot live/ and keep free of/ briars', we may come to a point where we have:

> no matter how,
>> by our wills survived
>> to keep
> the jeweled prize
>> always at our finger tips.
> We will it so
>> and so it is
>> past all accident.[10]

Here the most important word is not 'briars' or 'prize'; it is 'we'.
Where the love poem is almost always a solitary utterance, the
poem of marriage must find a way to speak for both parties, and
even for the community into which their two destinies have been
folded. This is no easy feat, and most attempts fail; but the failure
is honourable when the speaker – a solitary Ego in the midst of
what ought to have been a shared narrative – can bear adequate
witness to what went wrong, or salvage some kind of instruction
from the wreckage.

'Mock Orange', Louise Glück's rather painful account of matrimonial impasse – though not, as yet, failure –unflinchingly describes
the female speaker's visceral disillusionment with the married
state. That the poem is about marriage is revealed at first glance
by the title: mock orange is a flowering shrub closely associated
with weddings: bouquets and table settings are often composed
entirely, or at least partly, from these highly scented white flowers.
The plant itself (not a citrus variety, in fact, but an ornamental
shrub of the genus *Philadelphus*) flowers plentifully in June, and
is best known for its heady scent and snow-white flowers, so it
comes as no surprise that, as the poem opens:

> It is not the moon, I tell you.
> It is these flowers
> lighting the yard.[11]

What does come as a surprise, immediately after these opening lines, is the vehemence of the speaker, who immediately associates the flowers with an unwanted sexual intimacy:

I hate them.
I hate them as I hate sex,
the man's mouth
sealing my mouth, the man's
paralyzing body –

and the cry that always escapes,
the low, humiliating
premise of union –

Where the cry originates (with the woman? the man? both?) is not specified, but the cry itself is not what matters. What matters is the humiliation of the *premise* of union – the word 'premise' here (Oxford Dictionaries definition: 'A previous statement or proposition from which another is inferred or follows as a conclusion') bestowing on that union a logical inevitability that everything else in the poem denies. Like the wedding flower that is not an orange but an imitation of the orange in colour and scent, this is a *mockery* of true union – and we see now, remembering the title, that this union was predicated from the first on a deception. The speaker continues:

In my mind tonight
I hear the question and pursuing answer
fused in one sound

and again the lines are loaded with unsettling ambiguities. What is the question and the pursuing answer? The formulaic promises of the wedding ceremony? Or some later, more unseemly query? Here, as with the cry in the previous lines, there is a sense of something involuntary happening in the 'fused' sound:

that mounts and mounts and then
is split into the old selves,
the tired antagonisms. Do you see?

With this new question – a question that goes unanswered and is, in fact, unanswerable – the reader enters new and even more uncertain territory. Until now, the poem could have been a soliloquy, an unhappy wife's personal meditation on the disappointments of marital sex and the assumptions of power and provenance that it brings. Now, however, a question is asked that cannot be taken as rhetorical. Yet what 'Do you see?' is really asking is, 'Can you not understand that all of this, the heady scent, the false moonlight of the flowers, the formality of the wedding vows and, most of all, the blind appropriation of the woman's body in the sex act adds up to a parody, and a diminishment, of love, in which all this urgency and inherent force contravene the basic premises of liberty and mutual respect?' In short, the speaker wants to know if, whoever her interlocutor is, he or she is able to understand that, at some point,

We were made fools of.

Notice that it is this line, and this line alone, that enters the past tense – and, significantly, it contains the only instance of the word 'we' in the entire poem. The scent continues into the now, as does the man's paralysing weight, but the trick, the deception, happened once, in the past, and at the same time, as it would seem from this wording, once and for all, not just to the speaker but also to her spouse. This is a vital turning point: the speaker may complain of the scent, the weight, the feeling of having been deceived, but she also acknowledges that the deceit was mutual, that it was not perpetrated by the other, but originated elsewhere. At this point, to emphasise this sense that the decisive moment is consigned to the past, we return to the present and the persistence of the mock orange's perfume –

And the scent of mock orange
drifts through the window

– and so to the speaker's continuing disgust, and her sense, or perhaps her fear of *self*-betrayal, during that moment of consummation and in the subsequent instances of 'union':

How can I rest?
How can I be content
when there is still
that odor in the world?

There is no arguing here that 'Mock Orange' expresses a disgust with sexual intercourse (or at least, with intercourse of a specific kind), but it is hard not to see that disgust as directed not towards the body, or bodies themselves, but towards the way sex is incorporated into an institutionalised act in which, as soon becomes apparent to the new bride, the male 'mounts and mounts' while the female is suffocated – only for the whole exercise to end with the supposedly united couple splitting into their usual selves, nursing their 'tired antagonisms'. (And the tone of the poem obliges us to feel that these tired antagonisms are never adequately voiced.) In short, this poem is not about sex, as such, but about married sex as it is enacted in a patriarchal society. That the poem does not allocate blame to 'the man' as such but situates the error elsewhere entails a bearing witness to the suffocating power of convention that is both diagnostic and salutary. Reading it, we might recall the words of the political activist Emma Goldman, who summarised the difference between natural love and institutionalised marriage thus:

> Love, the strongest and deepest element in all life, the harbinger of hope, of joy, of ecstasy; love, the defier of all laws, of all conventions; love, the freest, the most powerful moulder of human destiny; how can such an all-compelling force be synonymous with that poor little State and Church-begotten weed, marriage?[12]

The other deception implicit in marriage as institution is Chardonne's idea – desirable in itself, perhaps, but scarcely achievable for most couples in a highly fractured and rootless society – of marriage as a kind of sacramental binding of the lovers to their community. This idea poses a social model in which the married couple and the wider group share common cause, and where the health and prosperity of the one is bound up with that of the other. In the twentieth century, however, this condition would come to seem rare (if it ever actually existed at all). In Robert Lowell's 'Skunk Hour', for example, the speaker reels off a humorous but altogether jaundiced account of his local community – the dotard heiress in her 'Spartan cottage' whose thirst for 'hierarchic privacy' drives her to buy up her neighbours properties just so she can let them fall; the 'fairy decorator' who

> brightens his shop for fall;
> his fishnet's filled with orange cork,
> orange, his cobbler's bench and awl[13]

– before moving on to castigate himself ('My mind's not right') as a pathetic, lonely voyeur, gone out into the night to watch for 'love-cars' on a dark patch of land 'where the graveyard shelves on the town'. As is now known, Lowell suffered terribly from spells of debilitating depression.[14] Here, he notes, as the car radio 'bleats' the old Blues song 'Love, O careless Love',* that:

> I myself am hell

– and surely that 'myself' is intended to qualify those infamous lines from Sartre's best-known and most frequently performed play, *Huis Clos (No Exit)*:

---

*The song is of unknown origin: W. C. Handy copyrighted it in 1926, but the best-known version is surely Bessie Smith's, in which some of the added verses seem signally appropriate to Lowell's poem:

> Love, oh love, oh careless love,
> All my happiness bereft.
> Cause you've filled my heart with weary old blues
> Now I'm walkin' talkin' to myself.

On the other hand, considering the year of composition, the radio could have been playing a version by any one of the following: Fats Domino, Emile Barnes and the Louisiana Joymakers, The Pilgrims, Big Bill Broonzy or the Christie Brothers Stompers.

So this is hell. I'd never have believed it. You remember all we
were told about the torture-chambers, the fire and brimstone,
the 'burning marl'. Old wives' tales! There's no need for red-hot
pokers. Hell is – other people!*

In Lowell's case, however, hell is not imposed by others but is
born of his own *original* shame, his own self-objectification – and
now, as the poem ends, it is in this degraded condition that the
speaker has his celebrated encounter with

a mother skunk with her column of kittens swills the garbage
   pail
She jabs her wedge-head in a cup
of sour cream, drops her ostrich tail,
and will not scare.

The scene is rendered deliberately grotesque: compared with the
skunks, who 'march on their soles up Main Street', the speaker
is helpless, clumsy, ineffectual; the vision of himself that he presents, flapping his arms and jumping up and down trying to scare
the animals (who clearly own this night) is altogether ridiculous.
At the same time, his maudlin response to the radio songs, his
hyperbolic self-pity and, adding a sinister touch, his presumed
voyeurism strip him of whatever dignity to which he might still
have clung.† It could be argued, justifiably, that part of the problem
arises from Lowell's mental state – and by all accounts, he was a
difficult person to live with when his mania was at its height. On
the other hand, it is hard to imagine even a less vulnerable person

---

*Jacqueline Audry's film of the play, with Arletty as Inès, premiered just two
years before 'Skunk Hour' was written.

† We are reminded here of the ageing Honda, from Yukio Mishima's *Sea of
Fertility* tetralogy, a man who had once been witness to great love and great
historical events, now reduced to one of the infamous voyeurs who haunt
Japanese parks and other public places, spying on young lovers. This was a
common practice in the 1970s; see *Dokyumento: Kōen*, by the photographer
Kohei Yoshiyuki (Tokyo: Sebun-sha, 1980).

drawing enough sustenance to sustain a happy marriage from the fractured and essentially facile society that Lowell describes here. When nobody thinks of anyone but themselves, when a crazed man is left to wander the streets in a hell of his own making, when all our institutions are veiled in suspicion, we are obliged to abandon any and all pretence of the vital community that, in Chardonne's vision, both sustains and is itself enriched by the sum of its happy marriages. At the same time, we can allow ourselves the cold comfort of knowing that it is not love that fails us when a marriage founders; instead, the fault lies, more often than we think, with the supposed infrastructure that was supposed to uphold and strengthen the institution to which the newlyweds so trustingly consigned their union on the day they made their vows.

Perhaps the most painful aspect of the failing marriage, however, is the private loss of dignity, the sense of complicity in dishonour that comes of being obliged to continue living with a spouse or lover who has turned against us. We do this for several reasons – for the sake of the children being the one most frequently cited, though hope of a return to former happiness, financial constraints or even routine apathy can enliven this particular passion play. In his brave and difficult book *Tantalus in Love*, Alan Shapiro explores a marriage that is quietly disintegrating, in an atmosphere of suspicion, regret and, especially, anger (in both its more understandable and its most petty forms). The poem that best reveals the complexities of this wrath – not in a wildly enraged but in a thinking, self-aware man living a more or less examined life – is simply titled 'Anger', though it could just as easily have been called 'Shame'.

The poem runs to five and a half pages and is part narrative, part reflection. Its narrative is straightforward, but far from simple. A man wakes one morning, after twenty years of marriage, and watches his wife sleep:

> her back to him,
> the covers pulled up tight and clutched in both hands,
> her eyes tense, everything about her stiffened
> even in dream against him, sealed away.[15]

Immediately alarm bells are ringing in the reader's mind: is this defensive posture real or constructed by the husband's imagination, possibly to spite himself? Is the woman so opposed to the man that even sleep cannot offer relief from that tension? If this is how *she* sleeps, how does *he* look when he is unconscious? We learn that the woman is usually the first to wake – that, most days, she would already be doing yoga 'in pajama bottoms and a skimpy tank top', a situation that the man finds both upsetting (they have not made love, or even touched now, for several months) and sexually arousing.

In the next stanza the man continues to observe the sleeping woman, running through the possible reasons for their estrangement, what he 'might have done' –

> he has his reasons for his anger, he is never
> at a loss for reasons for his anger:
> his sister's death, and then his brother's, and he
> the youngest child, the baby, the last one you'd
> expect to carry out the task, as in the old tale

– the task being to take care of the dying, to shoulder the burden of care, to become invisible, really, even to the extent of knowing that, since 'the kind of thing you do less well the more / you do it', he will not come out of it all looking skilful, or admirable. Indeed, his actions will barely be visible to others, since that is the nature of caring. The focus is on those who are experiencing the dramatic life change and so can be judged as brave, or thoughtful, or skilled in some way in preparing for the end. Yet, even as he runs through his failings, the man emerges as partly admirable after all, at least in the self-awareness he shows, as he wonders:

> How could she stand it, really? What did she feel,
> seeing him make his airtight case

against the world, proving again all through
his brother's dying what he had proved in
no uncertain terms throughout his sister's,
that there was never enough that anyone
could do for him, especially his wife?

Here the man shows an undeniable self-awareness, but there is no humility. In the next stanza he recalls an argument in which he smashed a chair, frightening the woman, forcing him to apologise and then searching for a way to get past the conflict and so find some kind of peace:

wanted to make love, it had been so long,
and she said, How can I touch you when you're like this?
And he snapped back, Well, maybe if you did
touch me I wouldn't be like this.

This memory is the first turning point of the poem as we move from narrative towards reflection, the man running through a series of questions that he has clearly asked himself many times. Has he 'willed these losses'? Are they somehow answered prayers? Is he not someone with an insatiable appetite to be 'betrayed, neglected, shunted aside'? Does he not like playing the part of righteously aggrieved husband? So far, so typical: in the post-Freud age we are obliged to suspect ourselves of all manner of 'subconscious' desires; in the pit of the self there have to be so many demons that we can barely list them all; and, most importantly, whatever the reason for what is happening, the only shame greater than that of the guilty party, is that of the hapless non-combatant. The passive victim. The mocked. The cuckold. The final question in all this is, of course, *who*? Who is she seeing? The yoga teacher? The chiropractor? As he runs through this multiple-choice test of his own petty devising, the man is fully aware of how low he has come, suspecting his wife of only doing yoga – which she clearly does well from the foregoing description – as a cover for some tawdry affair. At this point, however, he reaches the crux of his problem, a jealousy that, initially surprising, explains much of what has gone before.

The following stanza details an occasion 'a few weeks back' when, exhausted by one of their many fights, they had sunk into

> an almost elegiac closeness, as if
> they were remembering themselves like this,
> being a couple, lovers, talking in bed

– a beautiful and hugely poignant observation – and while they talked, almost man and wife, almost together, she had, quite innocently, ruined everything by playing what she did not even know was her trump card:

> telling him about this vision
> she'd had while doing yoga, of this white light,
> this warm miraculous white light that filled her
> with inexplicable well-being. The vision
> was all her own, it seemed, and no one's. Deep
> within the self and yet completely separate.
> A vision, she said, of being beyond the self,
> even beyond life. Imperturbable,
> Immovable. Eternal. Perfect and whole.

Now, all at once, the yoga teacher and the chiropractor fade into insignificance. For they can only offer romance, or sex, while this is self-realisation as a transcendent condition, a condition even beyond selfhood, in which the husband has no place. While he has been floundering about, trying to cope with grief and inadequacy and guilt, she has been following some mystical path to a kind of nirvana. That the memory is painful we know from the way his own hands are now 'twisted in the sheets'; adding insult to injury, however, the sleeping woman relaxes the moment her husband slips from the bed, falling into 'untroubled sleep'.

At this point the poem introduces its second turning point, but before we move into the new space that is about to open, we must remember that, throughout, the woman herself has not been present (other than in the man's memory). We have seen into the man's sometimes ugly, mundanely selfish, petty yet self-aware spirit; we have seen him exposed, laid bare, humiliated by his own self-recognition, as well as by the memories of his clumsy attempts to regain his wife's sexual favour, if nothing else. Yet we have seen nothing of the wife. We cannot know how she feels, whether she shares her husband's sense of inadequacy and shameful rage or is genuinely untouched by them. Her apparent serenity is seen through the eyes of the husband, who has already admitted that he feels neglected and distanced by her yoga practice. The story of spiritual liberation she recounted at the very moment the husband betrayed a desire to regain their former closeness was exactly the narrative most likely to alienate him, deepening his sense of isolation in the face of her serene, detached, other-worldly life. It might even have been a construct – if not an outright lie, then an exaggeration, at least – to drive him away at a difficult moment. We simply do not know. This poem is about the man, not the woman. If there is to be a release, or a transformation, or just the summoning up of enough courage to leave this destructive marriage – after *twenty years* – it must happen to him, not to her.

On the surface, what happens next is minimal. The man recalls his wife's yoga routine and how, when she moves into the Cobra posture, she seems formed 'by some higher power' and he wonders what it is like

> to be held
> that way, to hold yourself, so poised, so still?
> As if you could be all one thing, complete,
> enclosed.

The significance of what happens next, if any, is left undefined. Where, a generation earlier (as in, say, one of Robert Frost's narratives), there would have to be a conclusion, as such, Shapiro is able to work by suggestion, setting up an ambiguous moment in which the man, adopting a pose that his wife might adopt, stands on her yoga mat and

                    as if
he too were being moved by something, he
turns sideways, toward the window, his gaze fixed
on a single star whose faint light makes the black
sky all around it even blacker.

Neither the reader nor the man himself is concerned with what the 'something' might be here: he has entered the realm of 'as if', the point at which conventions, names, comparison, denotation are no longer of interest; or, as Wallace Stevens says in the 'It Must Be Abstract' section of 'Notes towards a Supreme Fiction':

> Phoebus is dead, ephebe. But Phoebus was
> A name for something that never could be named.
> There was a project for the sun and is.
>
> There is a project for the sun. The sun
> Must bear no name, gold flourisher, but be
> In the difficulty of what it is to be.[16]

What matters to the man is not the name or nature of the 'power' he is trying to find (a power that would originate, at least, in a conscious surrender of his anger) so much as the turning of his attention *outward*, away from himself – and so from the tawdry theatre of his dying marriage – towards a star whose 'faint light' nevertheless makes the blackness around it seem even blacker. Everything that happens now belongs to the *as if*: the bow he holds in his hand is imaginary; the arrow he will loose into the night is metaphysical; the power or force to which he surrenders cannot be named or explained rationally. Seen from the outside, as

                    he raises
his arms until his right's extended straight
out toward the star, his left bent at the elbow,
two fingers pulling the string back farther and farther,
aiming into the darkness till he lets go

his action might well appear clumsy. (In fact, the description Shapiro offers begins clumsily, deliberately so, in that 'until his right's extended straight' and only eases into more flowing and musical language as the man himself eases into the release of his invisible arrow.) This does not matter, however. In fact, the very point is that this man, so taken up with how he looks to others – his failure to be a perfect carer, his shame at his lapses into self-righteous anger, how his wife might perceive his ill-timed attempt to force a reconciliation by making love – is able to forget himself in what the reader hopes is not a mere gesture but the beginning of a movement, or even just an aspiration, to enter what Stevens calls 'the life that is lived in the scene that it composes [...] not that external scene but the life that is lived in it'. And it is in the midst of this gesture that Shapiro leaves the man. He is at the end of one stage in his life, perhaps, but now that he has turned from self-absorption, he finally seems capable of moving on into the next.

That 'Anger' ends with a suggestion, at least, of a transition from helpless and mostly undirected rage to an acceptance in which healing may begin is the main key to the poem's success. The significant moments of our lives begin and end better if we mark them well; there are times, however, when we fail even to recognise them as transitional. This is what the old, pagan calendars did so well: they marked life stages not with some orthodox ceremony based on a piece of doctrine or a set of rules but in celebration of individual beings, or communities, in their place and season. We have almost no contact with those old calendars now; they were taken over first by Christianity (the first wave of globalisation) and then by consumerism. Where we sometimes find makeshift but satisfying rites of our own is in the poetry of those who, like us, need to find some way to mark those life events that would otherwise go unremarked – not just the births, marriages and deaths but the days and hours that precede and follow them. All our changes demand observance and the necessary rituals, even if they are only enacted in the privacy of a dim room, in half-formed gestures that an objective witness might find redundant or clumsy.

After the caustic diagnosis of a toxic marriage offered by 'Mock Orange', it may seem surprising to return here to Louise Glück for a last word rooted in hope, if not optimism. Yet it is in another of her poems about love and marriage, 1999's 'Earthly Love', that we find a possible if qualified rejoinder to the earlier work's outright disgust with the system of power relations to which women are all too often subjected in traditional marriages. Here the first couple we encounter have been married for a 'very long' period, and have learned to live within the 'conventions of the time' that held them together:

> in which
> the heart once given freely
> was required, as a formal gesture,
> to forfeit liberty: a consecration
> at once moving and hopelessly doomed.

The reader is not told, but is left to guess, who these people are: whether parents or older friends of the speaker, certainly they are citizens of an era where the choices were limited and the need to adapt was strong. The speaker of the poem, however, is of a more recent generation:

> As to ourselves:
> fortunately we diverged
> from these requirements,
> as I reminded myself
> when my life shattered.

Unlike the previous generation, the speaker's life shatters when the marriage ends; leaving her the sole consolation that what she had, for as long as it lasted, was

> more or less,
> voluntary, alive.[17]

Of course, this sense of relationship is not just consoling; if it can be made to work, it is also logical. Under societal rules and expectations a marriage that does not last 'till death us do part' is a failure, which seems both logically unfounded and a bitter pill to swallow. Is a relationship that is nurturing and loving for five or ten years a failure if it does not continue through an entire lifetime? For that matter, is a stolen night of love, or a holiday romance, still fresh in the memory from thirty years ago, nothing more than a sham? How realistic is it to expect a pair of love-struck twenty-two-year-olds to love, honour and whatever each other, through all manner of personal and social changes, until they are in their dotage? Can we not take nourishment and a tempered sense of continuing respect from the five-, or ten-year burn-out? The speaker seems able to regard that period of the marriage that was voluntary and alive as worthwhile, until 'long afterward', when she begins 'to think otherwise'. What has changed? The speaker offers no concrete explanation, only an aside that cycles around a vague idea of self-preservation –

> We are all human–
> we protect ourselves
> as well as we can
> even to the point of denying
> clarity

– which might be expanded as a defence of pride and the persistence of folly: as alive and voluntary as the marriage may have been for as long as it lasted, it is not the ideal, the marriage that lasts, the 'one love' against which all others must fade in comparison, if the dream of matrimony is to continue to hold sway. Few of us have escaped the awkward vaudeville of watching a former couple meet at some family event, each now with a new significant other in tow, both pretending that what had once seemed as vivid as today's affair had actually been little more than a youthful flight of fancy, not so much a mistake as a simple twist of fate.

The speaker of 'Earthly Love' refuses to accept this compromise, however – and it is here that the title comes into full play. The love we are capable of, as humans, living in this world, is 'earthly' – not divine, not a matter for eternity.* The lovers, like all humans, are creatures of earthly time, earthly limitations, personal and shifting moral and imaginative qualities. All things considered, a marriage is no different from any of the other acts of imaginative play that make our existence on earth liveable. Like home, like community, like the self even, a marriage is an *inventio*, the imaginative construction of something meaningful from what we have been given – and seen in that spirit, every game that we play with sincere love and respect for the other is as valid as every other:

> And yet, within this deception,
> true happiness occurred.
> So that I believe I would
> repeat these errors exactly.
> Nor does it seem to me
> crucial to know
> whether or not such happiness
> is built on illusion:
> it has its own reality.
> And in either case, it will end.

It is this earthly reality that we must accept, then, if marriage is to work. We may recognise the deception, but we should not despise the possibilities of matrimony – and when it can no longer be sustained, it is only the foolish or the most arrogant who disdain all hope of salvage in a new beginning. Meanwhile, if we begin to see marriage as an exception rather than the rule – a condition to which a couple might naturally progress rather than a starting-point – perhaps we can create more interesting and rewarding models of wedlock for both parties. Certainly, marriage has been

---

* 'For in the resurrection they neither marry, nor are given in marriage, but are as the angels of God in heaven' (Matthew 22:30).

historically problematical in a patriarchal society, and it seems
certain that the institution will not change unless the overall infrastructure that sustains it changes. It has been said before – rather
loudly since that *annus mirabilis* when sexual intercourse began –
and it will be said again, but it is still worth seeing marriage as one
within a whole framework of other options. One of those options
may be solitude, but then, as Charles Bukowski says:

> there are worse things than
> being alone
> but it often takes decades
> to realize this
> and most often
> when you do
> it's too late
> and there's nothing worse
> than
> too late.[18]

Meanwhile, if we can accept being alone, it may be that we
become more inventive in proposing new ways to live together.
Surely it is a mistake to see marriage as a once-and-for-all matter,
a project that, if it does not last an entire lifetime, is by definition
a failure. Not long before the end of his too short and emotionally
cluttered life, William Matthews would conclude that

> Love needs to be set alight
> again and again, and in thanks
> for tending it, will do its very
> best not to consume us[19]

– the implication being that even 'its very best' might not be
enough. We are all at risk from the 'hole' in ourselves, 'unnoticed
before', that Anne Carson identifies, a hole that desire reveals
and marriage can all too often compound. That hole takes many
forms, from mistrust of self through the fear of being absorbed
or possessed by the other to the subtler flaw that Robert Graves

identifies in the poem 'Perfectionists':

> Interalienation of their hearts
> It was not, though both played resentful parts
> In proud unwillingness to share
> One house, one pillow, the same fare.
> It was perfectionism, they confess,
> To know the truth and ask for nothing less.
>
> Their fire-eyed guardians watched from overhead:
> 'These two alone have learned to love,' they said,
> 'But neither can forget
> They are not worthy of each other yet.'[20]

It might be easier if we were all worthy of each other; then again, it might be fairly inhuman, not to mention rather dull. What persists in all our musings about modern love and not so modern marriage, however, is an underlying sense that, as much as one would wish it otherwise, the only humane alternative to conventional wedlock is imaginative invention, not refusal. Never to have loved does not bring freedom. To fulfil its institutional obligations, marriage has always demanded that the participants forfeit at least some of their liberty, if only as 'a formal gesture' (and it would be wrong to underestimate the significance of such formalities). To be entirely free, one must be alone. For some, that may be the best recipe for a worthwhile life, even a lucky escape. The rest of us, however, are doomed to find a way of making good on Benedick's pledge, in *Much Ado about Nothing*:

> I did never think to
> marry. I must not seem proud. Happy are they that hear
> their detractions and can put them to mending [...]
> The world must be peopled. When I said I would die a
> bachelor, I did not think I should live till I were married.

A GIFT TO THE FUTURE

Sans la culture, et la liberté relative qu'elle implique,
la société, même parfaite, n'est qu'une jungle. C'est
pourquoi toute création authentique est un cadeau
pour l'avenir.

Albert Camus

IT WAS ROBERT FROST who said that poetry is 'what gets lost in
translation' – and, like much of what Robert Frost said, this
adage achieves the ring of wisdom by being a half-truth. Few
would argue that any translation entirely 'carries over' both the
music and the associative power of the original, never mind the
'meaning', but the real value of translating poetry becomes clear
only after we have accepted this limitation. To call translation 'the
art of failure', as Umberto Eco does, is not a condemnation but
a realistic assessment: to translate is, inevitably, to fail; nevertheless, it is still an art – and a useful one at that. The failure here has
little to do with those highly dubious notions of success (approxi-
mation to the original, verisimilitude) imposed on all art by the
soi-disant 'real world'. Like poetry itself, like all art, translation
occupies the delectable hinterland of Samuel Beckett's famous
maxim: 'All of old. Nothing else ever. Ever tried. Ever failed. No
matter. Try again. Fail again. Fail better.' All art fails, but some of
it fails so beautifully as to be breathtaking – more so, in fact, than
if it had 'succeeded' in worldly terms.

The reason we sometimes insist that translation as a practice is particularly and inevitably doomed, however, has to do with a failure to understand its intent. For while it is true that the *act* of translating will usually (but not always) result in a product of some kind in the target language, the *art* happens in the process itself, and what is forged there. In that respect, we could see translation as a form of particularly rigorous or attentive reading. John Berger has said that 'true translation is not a binary affair between two languages but a triangular affair. The third point of the triangle being what lay behind the words of the original text before it was written. True translation demands a return to the pre-verbal.' This remark is key to understanding the importance of translation (in all its forms) to the making of culture – and to the proposal of a 'world culture' that Osip Mandelstam saw as the principal aim of Acmeism. To begin with the pre-verbal in one's own tongue is the first step in making an original poem; to do so in another is a tentative and heuristic venture in the discovery of common interests – as well as of rich hoards of difference. A good translator will go to great lengths to preserve the difficulties and discomforts of the original, even as he or she tries to assist the reader in finding the doorway to the labyrinth. This involves either a good knowledge of the original text's language and culture or, in rare but genuine cases, the kind of arrogance that only comes with genius. In either case, what matters is not just the original text but the original moment of its finding. That moment has to be repeated somehow in the translation: the vision has to be repeated, but repeated in what might be an entirely new atmosphere, a new weather. When this happens, the result is not only extraordinary but also mysterious: even the translator does not know how she plucked that bird out of the air without once interrupting its flight.

There have been high and low points in the history of translation. Yet, while it may seem fanciful to say so, the highest points have always happened for worldly reasons – because translation is a form of trade, it is an art that seeks to discover the world of the other and, in doing so, creates common ground when common ground is most urgent. At the most basic level, my *Heimat* is connected to your *Heimat* in a very obvious way: if I invade your space for place-making, you are obliged to fight for a place to stand, and vice versa. But if instead I trade your vision of place for my own, and make echoes and mirror images and variations of your art in my culture, then it becomes harder for me to demonise or dismiss you. This, of course, is a simplification, and there are myriad qualifying factors, but it seems to me that peace- and place-making lie at the heart of translation and, even when errors arise, as long as the initial impulse is to respect the other, to honour the text and to honour the experience that gave birth to the text, then we can echo that delicious idea of the *I Ching*, usually translated into English as 'No Blame'.

No Blame – truly, because while it is the case that we lose musical and semantic nuance in the carrying over of poetry from one language to another, what we gain outweighs that loss, as long as we approach the task with a humility worthy of Beckett. By translating, we venture on a dialogue with an *otherness* – another human mind, another way of experiencing Berger's 'pre-verbal', another era – that both challenges and enriches our own host culture. Every literary culture is a unique, mysteriously self-organising (and, not to state the obvious too vehemently, it must also be said: constantly changing and so never fixed) storehouse of ideas, observations, natural history and wisdom that have been set down in the most memorable form, as in that old adage of Pope's:

> True Wit is Nature to advantage dress'd
> What oft was thought, but ne'er so well express'd;
> Something whose truth convinced at sight we find,
> That gives us back the image of our mind.

However, the 'our mind' to which Pope refers is not necessarily or immediately available to others. Translation demands a faith in the other that has to be capable of surmounting not insignificant barriers – of which, often enough, the least is linguistic differences. At the same time, no recognition, no intuition, no path to understanding or wonder endures other than in the ether of what Ezra Pound called 'a live tradition' – and as part of that tradition each of us is already plugged into our own vast and variably familiar hoard of imagery and narrative and metaphorical nuance. To read in another tradition, however, is to be obliged to start again – with a new way of seeing, sometimes initially in a cloud of unknowing, a willingness to work slowly and tentatively, learning how to ask questions where no questions even existed in the original culture, and to take other things on trust. This is a demanding discipline, but it licenses anyone who reads a poem, by any poet, living or dead, to venture on an intimate encounter with the subjectivity of another witness to this world. That is, poetry – in the original and in translation – is a way of conversing with the previously exotic other,★ or with the dead, on an intimate, one-to-one basis, the way one listens and responds to a family member or a close friend. Or, as Mark Doty remarked in a 2012 interview in the *Kenyon Review*:

> I think what poems do is preserve something of the flavor or texture of subjectivity; that's why they give us the uncanny sense of presence we get when we read, say, Whitman. There is the voice of a man long gone, and that voice has not vanished from the earth. But the visual has a different quality, in that instead of giving us language and inviting us to see how one perceiver saw, let's imagine, dewdrops on rose leaves, that perception is rendered in a far more precise, physically evidencing way.

★ See the Online Etymology Dictionary: exotic: 'belonging to another country', from Middle French *exotique* (sixteenth century) and directly from Latin *exoticus*, from Greek *exotikos*, 'foreign', literally 'from the outside' from *exo* 'outside'. The sense of 'unusual, strange' in English is first recorded in the 1620s, from the notion of 'alien, outlandish'.

Now, the commonality of experience we enjoy with our own dead is extended by translation into conversations with complete strangers, dead and living – conversations that not only open up cultural trade routes and pathways between us but also mutually enrich the home culture to which the translator belongs. This last point is, perhaps, the least dramatic, or perhaps the least visible, but it is central. The vitality of a culture, the maintenance of a live tradition, depends on commerce as much as it does on home-grown inventiveness;* like any other communal activity, from the making of a city state to the establishment of safe trade routes, the life of every society, however grand, depends on the just and free exchange of all manner of 'goods'.

In the middle of the twentieth century, in response to the ruin brought about by a global war of unprecedented horror and as a response to the appearance of The Bomb, poets around the world began to translate each other with a rare commitment to hon-ouring differences and to seeking mutual understanding – and, even if many of the supposed products of that enterprise were 'failures', the process, the conversation itself, was sometimes close to miraculous. The gross displacement of populations led to productive if not happy accidents that saw poets of the highest calibre working in close proximity† – conditions that allowed for

---

* As compelling and enjoyable as etymology mostly is, it also has its tragic moments. For example, one need only look up 'commerce' in a good etymological dictionary to get a sense of how far, and how clumsily, societies fall from best practice.

† The Spanish diaspora brought poets from the Iberian peninsula not only to South America but also to the United States, where two generations of poets from Robert Bly to Forrest Gander and others became active; Charles Wright's own work was vitally informed by his time in Italy as an American serviceman, and by his translations of Montale, Foscolo and others; the appointment of Czesław Miłosz to the Department of Slavic Languages and Literatures at Berkeley led to a rich exchange of work and ideas with Robert Hass; Joseph Brodsky in exile not only worked fruitfully on translations of

discussion, exegesis, outright refusal and a determination to move beyond acceptable compromise into a realm of discovery that could startle both the original poet and his or her collaborating translator. One of the more interesting phenomena was the emergence of self-translation, or even a switch from first language to that of one's place of refuge. After he was released into exile from a Soviet labour camp in 1972, the Russian-language poet Joseph Brodsky was forced by circumstances to accept that he would never again swim in the pool of his native language and (unwilling, as he put it, to be absorbed into some expat community whose language he saw as a museum of pre-Revolutionary speech, frozen at the moment of diaspora) began to write in English.

Yet, while it would be fascinating here to speculate on how certain poets who matured in the second half of the twentieth century grew as poets in their own language from their adventures and misadventures in translation (Charles Simic, say, or the inimitable Mark Strand, whose versions of Carlos Drummond de Andrade are unparalleled in their wit and sensitivity), what is perhaps more interesting is how the mere act of translating contributes, by small yet incremental degrees, to the creation of the world culture for which Mandelstam so fervently longed. When Frost observed that poetry is what is lost in translation, he was not only speaking for a specific time and place; he was also mistaken, at least in part. True, no translation will ever catch, in its entirety, the music and sense of the original, but it offers at the very least a glimpse, an echo, of something that would otherwise have gone unseen and unheard. Today translation resembles trade more than the direct conveyancing of some kind of inviolable artefact. Now it has less to do with finding the words and grammar to 'carry across' an idea in one language to another than with finding the basis of cultural exchange.* It calls for a fine line

---

his own work with Stanley Kunitz but also engaged in a vital and provocative controversy with Kunitz on the question of translating Anna Akhmatova. The list continues.

* 'translate' (v.) early fourteenth century: 'to remove from one place to

that demands, paradoxically, a deep respect for the original text, combined with a risky but altogether necessary assumption of the imaginative freedom to render in the target language a new work that is, nevertheless, true to the original in its essentials.* Every translation, even the making of a literal 'crib', is a gamble. This is what makes translation dangerous – and this is what makes it interesting. At the same time, we should resist the idea that a 'bad translation' is altogether a 'bad thing'; the truth is, we can learn a great deal, even from those renderings that go astray, not only about how language works but also about how complex the interface between cultures can be. Every translation is a hypothesis; at the same time, no translation is ever final.

In the synoptic gospels (for example, Matthew 19:24) Jesus says: 'And again I say unto you, It is easier for a camel to go through the eye of a needle, than for a rich man to enter into the kingdom of God.' As a child, I remember being perplexed by this. Why a camel? And what, exactly, was the 'eye of a needle' in Jesus' time? At that age I did not consider the problem as translation-based; it was just odd, considering the pains Jesus usually took to ground his teachings in the practical realities of his audience, using imagery

---

another', also 'to turn from one language to another', from Old French *translater* and directly from Latin *translatus* 'carried over', serving as past participle of *transferre* 'to bring over, carry over' (see 'transfer'), from *trans* 'across, beyond' (see 'trans-') + *lātus* 'borne, carried' (see 'oblate' (n.)). Related: translated; translating. A similar notion is behind the Old English word it replaced, *awendan*, from *wendan* 'to turn, direct' (see 'wend').

* See the Online Etymology Dictionary: 'render' (v.) late fourteenth century, 'repeat, say again', from Old French *rendre* 'give back, present, yield' (tenth century), from Vulgar Latin *rendere* (formed by dissimilation or on analogy of its antonym, *prendre* 'to take'), from Latin *reddere* 'give back, return, restore', from *red-* 'back' (see re-) + combining form of *dare* 'to give'. Meaning 'hand over, deliver' is recorded from the late fourteenth century; 'to return' (thanks, a verdict, etc.) is attested from the late fifteenth century; the meaning 'represent, depict' is first attested in the 1590s.

related to vineyards, seed-sowing and the daily lives of fishermen. Now here he was talking about threading a camel through the eye of a needle. It was as if, with a stroke of the pen, King James' committee of scholars had turned an earthy, grounded teacher into a proto-surrealist. So I was rather pleased when I began to find new and maverick theories about this verse, theories that proposed, as Anthony Burgess puts it: 'When Christ says it's as easy for a camel to pass through the eye of a needle as for a rich man to get into the kingdom, he uses the Greek word *kamelon*, which means camel. But another Greek word very close to *kamelon* is *kamilon*, which means a rope. The rope to many sounds more plausible than the camel.'

I could not argue with that. The rope and sewing-needle hypothesis seemed far more plausible, especially when I remembered, once more, that the people Jesus is addressing in this passage are fishermen, nimble-fingered artisans who would have made and mended their nets with the typical wooden needles available at the time, and so would easily have grasped the conundrum of threading such a needle with a thick rope. In short, the king's translators had made an understandable error, confusing two words that looked and sounded very similar – though this begged the question as to how much attention they had been paying to Jesus' typically practical, even homespun, style. The substitution of the surreal camel image seemed oddly egregious. And yet there was more to this controversy, still, than the question of what a single word meant in a specific context: for, if accuracy (in the sense of avoiding errors) is the *yin* of translation, its *yang* is a search for the correct degree of flexibility, the leeway, that is, that can fairly be taken in 'carrying across' an image, or an idea, not only from one language but also from one culture to another. For example: what if the King James scholars had known about the camel–rope controversy and decided on camel anyhow, as more effective *in this instance*? Would it matter; or rather, if it *did* matter, would such a choice make sense? The camel saying is more memorable, however phrased; the new target audience is not composed mostly of fishermen (and their needles would look very different from those used by James and John in their net-making); and, overall, the import of the saying is conveyed at least as well, if not more accurately, by the camel image. This same argument might be extended to plants and animals, who may have either a different significance from one culture to another or no equivalent between geographical locations, weather events or the emotional registers of colour terms, to name just a few possible discrepancies at random. All this considered, then, what is a mistranslation? Is it possible, or even common, for the most accurate translation to be the least effective? Finally, when we have left the question of sense behind, what of the music? Is the Duchess right when she says 'Take care of the sense, and the sounds will take care of themselves' – or is the exact opposite true, that the sense can only be fully realised in a poem when the sounds – the music – have been realised to an equivalent level in the target language? Might this be what Frost meant when he talked about what gets lost in translation: this loss of the music on which the sound so much depends? And is it even possible to create a new music, appropriate to the target language, that sufficiently echoes the music of the original? Or is that to make an entirely different poem altogether?

Translation, at its inception, is, to my mind, the most intimate of crafts, especially when we attempt to translate the work of someone 'long gone' (as Mark Doty notes above). As a reader, I am drawn back again and again to certain key works; when they are in another language, I not only want to read them over, I want to try to render them into my own tongue one more time. And, in a case like the poem below, published by Jorge Guillén in the 1950 edition of his lifelong work *Cántico*, there is no end to the possibilities of failure, and so to what can be learned from the attempt. To begin with, I shall quote the poem in full, in the original Spanish, with an epigraph in French from a poem by Paul Valéry:

Muerte a lo lejos

Je soutenais l'éclat de la mort toute pure.
Paul Valéry

Alguna vez me angustia una certeza,
Y ante mí se estremece mi futuro.
Acechándolo está de pronto un muro
Del arrabal final en que tropieza

La luz del campo. ¿Mas habrá tristeza
Si la desnuda el sol? No, no hay apuro
Todavía. Lo urgente es el maduro
Fruto. La mano ya lo descorteza.

… Y un día entre los días el más triste
Será. Tenderse deberá la mano
Sin afán. Y acatando el inminente

Poder diré sin lágrimas: embiste,
Justa fatalidad. El muro cano
Va a imponerme su ley, no su accidente.[1]

When encountering a new poem, it is useful to read it, or hear it read, aloud; when translating, this should be done several times, at the very least. It is, quite simply, a mistake to believe that the sense of a poem is only in the words, phrases and sentences on the page; the fact is that it depends equally, or more so, on the sound. A poem is a form of music; it works through nuance, resonance, echoes and, importantly, as much through what is withheld as through what is enunciated (just as music depends for its effect as much on the rests and the harmonics in the score as it does on the notes played). At this point, it is important to move slowly: hear the poem before proceeding to address the technical matter of how it is made and how it might be 'carried over'. Then, when the time is right, begin the search for the first stage of its meaning.

To begin with, we have a title: 'Death in the Distance'. This is a key – but it need not be brought fully into play just yet. Another key is the epigraph, which is from a poem Guillén very much admired, but also felt the need to work against as an influence. The line, from Paul Valéry's long poem of 1917, *La Jeune Parque*, can be rendered as (something like) 'I withstood the splendour of pure death'. The work from which it comes is a five-hundred-line meditation on life and death, from the point of view of Clotho, the youngest of the Three Fates, who is debating whether to continue her semi-divine existence as an immortal or to enter into the fullness of human life, with all its joys, sorrows and perishability. *La Jeune Parque* is a long and difficult work (it took Valéry five years to complete), grounded in Classical myth but full of the sensuality of French Symbolism; in response, Guillén creates a short, somewhat enigmatic but self-contained work of fourteen lines whose argument is brilliantly held within the traditional Petrarchan sonnet form (the rhyme scheme is *abba abba cde cde*). All of this may seem like background detail, but it actually is important: the epigraph is there not for ornament but for a logical reason. Like the title, it is a key to a full reading of the poem – which begins (in a first-stage, rough translation):

> Sometimes I am worried by a certainty
> And before me my future shudders
> [and] waiting in ambush suddenly a wall
> Of the last suburb upon which falls
>
> The light of the field.

There is much to unpack here. First, the speaker is worried (troubled, made anxious) not by the unknown but by a certainty. This anxiety is transferred to his field of vision, where the future shudders – and it is carried forward, with a sense of dread, to a wall (for now, just a wall, though later it will become a 'grey wall', 'un muro cano', with overtones of hoariness, even of age). This wall, we discover, is that of the last suburb – i.e., the cemetery – where the light of the 'campo' (the open fields, the countryside outside the city) falls.

The poem continues:

> But will there be sadness
> If the sun strips / denudes it? No, there is no hurry
> Yet. What is urgent is the ripe
> Fruit. The hand already peels it.

There is a question here, to begin with: what is the 'it' that the sun is denuding / stripping? Logically, because the question asks

> ¿Mas habrá tristeza
> Si la desnuda el sol?

we are obliged to conclude, from the 'la', that the bright sun is denuding the usual light that falls on the field – and, after a moment's thought, this comes across as an extraordinary image, first of a natural event in which the intense light of a southern sun cancels out everything, abandoning the gazing eye to a kind of unearthly whiteness (a phenomenon that not only reminds us of the light of which Seferis speaks in, say, *The Thrush*, a searing light that cancels out 'the light of the day', but one that also hints at the white light experienced by those who, brains flooded with dopamine and noradrenaline, entertain near-death experiences every day on hospital gurneys and operating tables). However, the time to die has not come – or not *yet*. Instead, the now continues, the ripe fruit of the given moment, which the hand is already reaching to peel and to savour. Nevertheless:

> … one day, amongst [all] the days the saddest
> Will come. The hand should offer itself
> Without eagerness. And obedient to the imminent
>
> I shall be able to say, strike
> Just fatality. The grey wall
> Will impose on me its law, not its accident.

Again, there is much to come to terms with here. We may see, behind the lines of this closing sestet, something that at first resembles the religious stoicism of earlier Spanish poets confronting death, but there is no invocation of divine providence or of

God's will; on the contrary, we remain in the realm of the abstract, the vital distinction being that which separates 'law' and 'accident' – which is to say, natural order and mere contingency. To have lived, attentive to the mature fruit of experience, and then come, without fear or eagerness, to the moment when death strikes is not a random event, or a matter of blind chance, but an expression of the universal law, of which death is a central element. If the hand reaches to offer itself up to that 'just fatality' without fear, but also without eagerness or hurry, then the man who is destined to die is simply obeying the laws of the cosmos in real time. (The word 'acatando' is key here: more than mere acceptance, it implies a deliberate choice to comply with a system whose justice is respected.) On this note the poem ends, not as a lament for the self who will die, and not as a devout man's acceptance of God's plan, but as an assertion of a power that is both larger than the individual will and generous in its allocation of the moment in which the 'mature fruit' of experience can be enjoyed.

And here, finally, we have reached the point at which the real work of translation begins. That work will end in a failure of one sort or another – to capture the semantic meaning of the words on the page is barely a first step – but each time the exercise is attempted, something new will come to light, not just about a particular poem but about the craft of making (and of reading) in general. At the same time, the way we think about our own language – the language in which we write, the language we speak and think every day – will be a little richer than it was before we began.

THE PANIC OF THE ADVERSARY

Force does not work the way its advocates seem to think it does. It does not, for example, reveal to the victim the strength of his adversary. On the contrary, it reveals the weakness, even the panic of his adversary, and this revelation invests the victim with patience.

James Baldwin

BACK IN 1963, when Steve McQueen, in a cutaway sweatshirt and specially tailored khakis, ran rings around a Nazi pursuit team during *The Great Escape*'s renowned motorcycle chase, the young, white, working-class Scots child that I was had no doubt that the word 'cool' signified a form of anti-establishment self-reliance that was North American, almost certainly male, youthful (if not necessarily young) and most probably white, a mix of improbable charisma and elegant self-containment that only life's more fortunate sons could mimic. 'Cool' was about masculine remoteness and a fine veneer of disdain: it was the look on the face of James Coburn as the *The Magnificent Seven*'s imperturbable knifefighter, Britt; it was fast cars, Le Mans and sleek motorcycles; it was Mick Jagger and the Stones, midnight-rambling through their contemptuous, male-power 1966 classic 'Under My Thumb', with complete disdain for the so-called Summer of Love. More than anything it was about an innate aloofness from everything and everyone, especially women, and a performed reticence that, in many cases, had less to do with emotional economy than with everyday inarticulacy. On TV and at the movies, it was perfect, brittle, glamorous; in real life, it usually crumbled the moment it was put to the test. (Abandoned by his father, McQueen, 'The King of Cool', was not only insecure, terrified of failure and a self-confessed 'chauvinist pig', but also, according to co-stars, 'paranoid', 'aggressive' and 'demanding'; while Jagger, white society's favourite counter-cultural hero, was always more astute business-man than revolutionary. He even accepted a knighthood from the British establishment, ignoring Keith Richards' advice to turn it down.)

Cool. No epithet was more coveted by the boys I grew up with and, when we had the money, we enthusiastically acquired the clothing ranges, cigarette brands and records that signified this ultimate state of grace, blind to the fact that there was nothing intrinsic to those commodities that made any difference at all to how we might carry ourselves, or what we stood for, because to admit that would be to admit that 'cool' was little more than a pose.

Historically, however, there was a variety of cool that had far less to do with lifestyle than with philosophical stoicism. This idea of coolness was predicated on self-restraint and pragmatism, as in Claudius' advice to Hamlet:

> O gentle son,
> Upon the heat and flame of thy distemper
> Sprinkle cool patience.

In such a form, cool could be seen as the prerogative of a classic view of manhood, in which passion and energy are tempered by realism; it became more complicated, however, when exercised by the least privileged, or the disenfranchised. In such circumstances, cool might be the ironic unresponsiveness of a superior individual in the face of unjustifiable power (growing up, I saw it directly, working in factories and mills where the safety or well-being of my fellow-workers was routinely threatened by the incompetence or indifference of 'management'). Anyone who has done any kind of supervised work will know that such jobs demand high levels of self-restraint, at the very least, when faced with a bullying charge-hand, or a jumped-up official. (I still recall losing a good, fairly clean job when, aged nineteen, I 'hot-headedly' attacked a supervisor who was 'pushing me around'). For a working person, the cost of failing to 'sprinkle cool patience' on their distemper can be disastrous in real terms, especially for someone who has dependents and debts.

That call for restraint has to be magnified a thousand times for a person of colour in a racist society, however – which is why the term 'cool', in the sense of self-control, takes on more urgent, and subtler, meanings in the work of twentieth-century African-American writers. The reasons are painfully obvious in a society where even the most basic resistance to constant oppression on the part of the individual citizen can mean death. Take, for example, the moment in Ralph Ellison's 1952 novel *Invisible Man*, when, man-handled by a police officer, Tod Clifton pushes back for once, and is fatally shot for that momentary lack of circumspection. He has failed, in this most pressing sense of the word, to keep his cool, as the book's anonymous narrator says, during a bitter and desperate funeral oration:

> So in the name of Brother Clifton beware of the triggers; go home, keep cool, stay safe away from the sun. Forget him. When he was alive he was our hope, but why worry over a hope that's dead? So there's only one thing left to tell and I've already told it. His name was Tod Clifton, he believed in Brotherhood, he aroused our hopes and he died.

This sense of 'cool', however, is only one of several associated with a word that, as the twentieth century progressed, came to have a rich, complex, often tragic and occasionally inspiring significance for African-American writers.[1] For, while cool initially signified self-control harnessed to the desire for self-preservation in a violent society, it also came to include elements of style, elegance, generosity of spirit and dependability. It recognised that, while self-presentation was important in public affairs, it had to be combined with inner strength and honour. In short, as cool was developed into a moral nexus of specific virtues – not just restraint in the social sphere, but also keen judgement, appreciation and fine judgement in art, philosophical thought and, especially, music – there was never any question that substance was more important than outward style. It is ironic, then, that when mainstream (white) society appropriated 'cool', it took only the superficial elements, the sideshow features; in short, the *pose*. In the late 1950s and early '60s, white America had everything else it thought it needed: the cars, the money, the glamorous jobs. In the 'popular' arts, however, what mainstream white culture produced was far less vivid, and less rewarding, to younger people in particular, than the makeshift, improvised, but highly inventive African-American culture that, county by county, town by town, city district by city district ran parallel with it and, in many respects, put it to shame. Faced with prejudice and exclusion by white radio owners and publishers, black musical culture was hard-won, but all the more resplendent for that, emerging as it did from the creativity under pressure that typified the bluesmen, jazz musicians and other African-American artists whose songs and dance-steps the white mainstream could not match, and so continually appropriated and reduced to sexless, artless saccharine for its hungry 'youth market'. At a certain point, the most obvious and attractive aspects of cool became part of this appropriation. At the same time, the commercial mainstream sought to profit by selling the surface paraphernalia of African-American cool back to the people – black and white – just as it marketed the outward trappings of Eastern religion, or Native American tradition, to young whites hungry for a new spirituality that was not tainted by association with war, empire and moral hypocrisy as (in their view at least) Christianity was.

This complex state of affairs demanded of African-American poets a sophisticated and rigorous critique, not only of white appropriation of the philosophy of cool, but also of black collaboration with that project. Born Donald Luther Lee in Little Rock, Arkansas, in 1942, Haki R. Madhubuti's individual journey to reclaim and redefine his own identity had been so painful and considered that it rendered him more than usually aware of the distractions and gimmicks on offer to black men as they rejected the slave names and social stereotypes imposed upon them by the white establishment, and this gave his work in the 1960s and '70s an urgency that still shines through today. Here, in an early poem, 'But He Was Cool, or: he even stopped for green lights', he satirises a 'super-cool', 'ultrablack' cliché whose whole identity is a self-revealing performance:

&his beads were imported sea shells

    (from some blk/country i never heard of)

he was triple-hip.

his tikis were hand carved
out of ivory
&came express from the motherland.[2]

Like the pool players in Gwendolyn Brooks' 'We Real Cool: The Pool Players, Seven at the Golden Shovel',* who are identified as *wanting* 'to feel contemptuous of the establishment' rather than actually posing a threat, the object of Madhubuti's satirical swipe is a poseur, wholly lacking in both depth of awareness and political purpose:

he would greet u in swahili
&say good-by in yoruba.

---

* 'We real cool. We / Left school. We // Lurk late. We / Strike straight. We // Sing sin. We / Thin gin. We // Jazz June. We / Die soon.' Brooks, the first African American to receive a Pulitzer Prize, was born in Kansas in 1917 and raised in Chicago. She was a consummate poet of daily life, who described her poetic project as a search 'for an expression relevant to all manner of blacks, poems I could take into a tavern, into the street, into the halls of a housing project'.

woooooooooooo-jim he bes so cool &ill tel li gent

This satirical portrait is so effective perhaps because Madhubuti understands his subject all too well; indeed, in a key early work, 'the self-hatred of don l. lee', (Donald Luther Lee being Madhubuti's slave name) he had described his transition from being a writer and academic who, for a time, was content to pass through

> doors of
> tokenism
> &
> acceptance.
>   (doors called, 'the only one' & 'our negro')

until, after some years spent wrestling with the work and ideas of classic black writers like W. E. B. Dubois, Alaine Locke, Richard Wright, J. A. Rogers and others,

> my blindness
> was vanquished
> by pitchblack
> paragraphs of
> 'us, we, me, i'
> awareness[3]

However, Lee immediately recognises that this is not the end of his struggle, and the poem ends with a new contradiction, and a new phase of self-doubt:

> i
> began
> to love
> only a
> part of
> me –
> my inner
> self which
> is all

black –
&
developed a
vehement
hatred of
my light
brown
outer.

In fact, it was only when the man who had been taught to call
himself Don L. Lee adopted the Swahili name Haki Madhubuti
(*haki* meaning 'justice', and *madhubuti* meaning 'reliable'), after
making a number of trips to Africa, that he began to heal this split
between those inner and outer selves. That slow and considered
process, however, is a world away from the subject of 'But He
Was Cool', a character wedded to self-deceit who signally fails to
acknowledge any inner conflict at all, so determined is he to maintain a façade whose effectiveness can only be guaranteed by complete dedication to the unexamined life. As 'But He Was Cool'
continues, it spirals off into a riff on the word 'cool' reminiscent
in its rhythmic play of Ornette Coleman or Don Cherry:

cool-cool is so cool he was un-cooled by other niggers' cool
cool-cool ultracool was bop-cool/ice box cool so cool cold
    cool
his wine didn't have to be cooled, him was air conditioned
    cool
cool-cool/real cool made me cool—now ain't that cool
cool-cool so cool him nick-named refrigerator.

However, as the title of the poem itself suggests, this cool *pose* is,
in itself, worthless, its exponent so unthinkingly attached to his
coolness that 'he even stopped for green lights', and so politically
out of touch that he has not realised that, 'after detroit, newark,
chicago &c',

to be black

is
to be
very-hot.

We die soon. African-American writers like Gwendolyn Brooks, Amiri Baraka and Haki Madhubuti would resist white suprema-cism in various ways, not only in their writing, but in the establish-ment of specialist publishing houses (such as Madhubuti's Third World Press) and groups like Black Arts Repertory Theatre / School (founded in Harlem in 1965), whose outline ethos and aims were expressed in Baraka's 1966 poem 'Black Art':

> We want a black poem. And a
> Black World.
> Let the world be a Black Poem
> And Let All Black People Speak This Poem
> Silently
> or LOUD[4]

The beauty of that resistance notwithstanding, however, it was evident that, on a day-to-day basis, people of colour were obliged to live with the constant threat of attack, regardless of how suc-cessful they might be in mainstream or artistic terms – even more so, in fact, now that the beauty and skill with which resistance was expressed had begun to attract what James Baldwin called 'the panic of the adversary'. No one who has seen it can forget the image of Miles Davis in the lobby of the West 54th Street Station House, New York, his shirt and coat spattered with bloodstains, arms akimbo, his shocked face staring out at the camera, as if to ask, *What do I have to achieve to be treated with decency by these people?* (Later, in fact, he would write in his autobiography that the incident 'changed my whole life and my whole attitude again, made me bitter and cynical again when I was really starting'.) Most of those involved agree that the trouble started around mid-night on 25 August 1959, a hot night in New York City. Davis had come to Birdland to play work from his new album *Kind of Blue*, the much-lauded follow-up to 1957's *The Birth of the Cool* and a superlative work of art that would literally change the culture. It was, as has been said, a hot night – very hot – and after escorting 'a pretty young white girl named Judy' to her taxicab, Davis had lingered a moment outside the club to cool down. At this point, he was told to move on by a police officer, to which he replied, 'Move on, what for? I'm working downstairs. That's my name up there, Miles Davis.' And it is here that the police account and that of witnesses begin to differ. According to another policeman who just happened to be passing by, Davis attacked the arresting officer, and was then subdued using reasonable force, but it was soon to emerge from witness testimony that the musician was only preserved from a much worse beating by the intervention of a crowd of around 200 people, who gathered around the policemen, calling for them to stop. Davis himself was clear: 'I was surrounded by white folks,' he said, 'and I have learned that when this happens, if you're black, there is no justice. None.' We can suppose, using the perverse logic that applies in what, for some of its citizens at least, is a police state, that Davis was lucky. In the immediate vicinity of the attack, outside Birdland, a fair number of people would have recognised this most famous of jazzmen, and his recent success with *Kind of Blue* – with its celebrated cover portrait – would have enhanced that recognition. Who knows what might have happened if the incident had taken place elsewhere?

Others would not be so fortunate. Some years later, in 1968, when a disgruntled white official encountered the poet and short story writer Henry Dumas – whose poem 'Kef 24' contains the poignant plea of a brutalised Southern cotton worker, 'pray with me brothers that I hold my cool' – it was in a near-deserted subway station. This time the assailant was a New York City Transit policeman named Peter Bienkowski, who claimed that the poet (who was on his way home from a rehearsal with his sometime collaborator, the visionary musician Sun Ra) had pulled a knife on him. This was hard to believe, to say the least; those who knew Dumas would have agreed with his editor, Quincy Troupe, that 'Henry Dumas did not carry a gun and he wasn't a flaming revolutionary. That cop just shot and killed him, and those types of murders are still happening today. Just think about what he would've done, not just for African-American writing, but for world literature. Because of that cop, we lost a lot.' As so often happens, there is no way of checking the officer's story: no witnesses were cited and, in due course, the official records of the case disappeared. All we know now is what the *Yonkers Herald Statesman* reported:

> NEW YORK (AP) – A Transit Authority patrolman shot and killed a 33-year-old man on a Harlem IRT subway platform early today after the man had allegedly attacked the patrolman with a knife. Police said Patrolman Peter Bienkowski observed Henry Dumas, 33, threaten another man with the knife about 12:15 a.m. on the southbound platform of the 125th Street Lenox Avenue station. Bienkowski said he ordered Dumas to drop the knife but that the man turned and attacked him, slashing him on the cheek. He said he fired three times.

It is a sickeningly familiar story for us now, in this era of Black Lives Matter. Yet it was just as familiar then. In fact, the killing of African-American citizens (by lynch mob, armed police and enthusiastic civilians eager to 'defend' their neighbourhoods) is the Ur-narrative of American history – which is, for all that some stakeholders try to deny it, a history of race, from the genocide visited upon the 'Indians' through the 'strange and bitter crop' in Southern trees recorded by songwriter and poet Lewis Allan, to the recent, and long overdue, opening of the National Memorial for Peace and Justice in Montgomery, Alabama. That the level of violence applied to oppressing black people in particular is clearly indicative of Baldwin's 'panic of the adversary' is small consolation to those whose family members and spouses are cut down on a whim; nevertheless, in such circumstances, it surely is one of the roles of poetry to speak out about that violence, and the grief that it causes – and not only to speak out, but to *insist*, over years, and decades, and even centuries, that this violence be acknowledged, and properly atoned for, for the greater good of all.

Arguably the most important, and certainly the most cynical murder perpetrated by the American government on young black men during the civil rights struggle was the slaughter of Fred Hampton and Mark Clark by a combined force of FBI agents and Mayor Daley's Chicago Police Department, at an apartment on Monroe Street in the early hours of 4 December 1969. This killing is the subject of one of Madhubuti's most powerful poems, 'One Sided Shoot-Out (for brothers fred hampton & mark clark, murdered 12/4/69 by Chicago police at 4:30 AM while they slept)', which begins:

> only a few will really understand:
> it won't be yr/momma or yr/brothers & sisters or even me,
> we all think that we do but we don't.
> it's not new and
> under all the rhetoric the seriousness is still not serious.
> the national rap deliberately continues, 'wipe them nigger
>   out.'
> (no talk do it, no talk do it, no talk do it, notalknotalk do it)[5]

This opening is urgent and close to brutal. As well it should have been, for even the official version of this act of state murder is chilling, while the eye-witness accounts are heart-breaking. As with the killing of unarmed people of colour on the streets today, by police and others, it is not just the waste of life and violence that appals us; it is also the fact that, in almost every case, we see no real attempt at serious judicial enquiry, and if a case does go to court, the acquittal of the perpetrators is almost guaranteed. Each case is treated as an isolated incident; each death becomes an opportunity for the police, or some other authority, to 'learn from its mistakes' – until the same drama happens, in almost identical circumstances, a month or two later, or in the next state but one. The pattern is never acknowledged – and the pattern is everything, because patterns show how systems work.

As chairman of the Illinois chapter of the Black Panther Party, Fred Hampton was widely admired by those in the civil rights movement, both black and white, for his intellect and character. It is not surprising, then, that this event would become a landmark in the history of civil rights, after full details of the incident were publicised. Having pressured an insider to lace Hampton's and Clark's drinks with soporific drugs, the joint FBI/police task force stormed the building, killing Clark immediately and wounding several others, including Hampton. By then, as planned, the Panther chairman was unconscious and in no condition to engage in a 'shoot-out'; nevertheless, as the dust settled and one of the police officers remarked that he was still breathing, an FBI operative stepped forward, shot Hampton twice in the head and said, 'He's good and dead now.' For many, this changed the nature of the struggle for ever: because of prompt action by the Chicago Panthers, the police did not get the opportunity to cover up the details of the killing, as the Monroe Street building was opened up to local people, reporters and even to delegations from other cities, so they could see that, whatever else might have happened in the apartment, it had not been the 'violent' and 'extremely vicious' Panther attack to which the police would later claim they had been subjected. (One elderly woman, having viewed the scene, remarked that 'This was nothing but a Northern lynching.') In fact, it soon became clear that, contrary to police claims, there had been no 'shoot-out' at all.[*]

---

*Jeffrey Hass, who later acted as an attorney for the Panthers in a civil suit against Chicago police, would comment later (in an interview with Amy Goodman and Ralph Gonzalez, *Democracy Now*, 4 September 2009):

'While I was interviewing the survivors, my partners went to the apartment. And when we gathered all the evidence, it turned out that the police had fired 90 shots into the apartment with a submachine gun, shotguns, pistols and a rifle. There was only one outgoing shot, and that came from a Panther who had been fatally wounded, and it was a vertical shot, after he was hit himself. So, Hanrahan … was on the TV

So it was that, because of the Panthers' swift and determined action, which not only brought an informed local community and press into the discussion, but also pushed a few of those in the city's legal establishment to re-examine their own basic assumptions about the FBI, the police and the civil rights movement, there was a significant broadening in the number and backgrounds of people who wanted to ask, with Madhubuti,

> were the street lights out?
> did they darken their faces as in combat?
> did they remove their shoes to creep softer?
> could u not see the whi-te of their eyes,
> the whi-te of their deathfaces?
> didn't yr/look-out man see them coming, coming, coming/
> or did they turn into ghostdust and join the night's fog?

As it poses these questions (essentially to the murdered men), the poem takes on the role assigned to the chorus in classical Greek drama, both in probing the veracity of the active characters, and in speaking for the community at large. Consider, for example, the chorus in Aeschylus' *Agamemnon*, as they question the Herald:

> Is there no means to speak us fair, and yet tell the truth?
> It will not hide, when truth and good are torn asunder

or when they sing their lament for the slain ruler:

> Oh king, my king
> how shall I weep for you?

---

that morning saying the Panthers opened fire. It turned out, we proved, that, quite to the contrary, it was a shoot-in, not a shoot-out.

What we uncovered years later – we also filed a civil rights suit after the charges were dropped against the Panthers. And in addition to proving, as I said, that it was a one-sided raid, that the police came in firing, the evidence also showed that Fred Hampton was in fact killed with two bullets, parallel bullets, fired into his head at point-blank range. He wasn't killed with the bullets through the walls.'

What can I say out of this heart of pity?
Caught in the spider's web you lie,
Your life gasped out in indecent death,
struck prone to this shameful bed[6]

Similarly, the 'we' who lament in 'One Sided Shoot-Out' is an entire community, involved in, and tainted by, the murder of the Panther chairman,

> & we.
> running circleround getting caught in our own cobwebs,
> in the sense old clothes, same old words, just new adjectives
> we will order new buttons & posters with; 'remember fred' &
>   'rite-on mark.'
> & yr picture will be beautiful & manly with the deeplook/ the
>   accusing look
> to remind us
> to remind us that suicide is not black

It follows that, if those responsible for seeing justice done clearly have no intention of bringing the killers to trial, that community must insist, as Aeschylus' chorus insists, and as Madhubuti insists in the following lines, on naming the crime for what it was:

> it was murder.
> & we meet to hear the speeches/ the same, the duplicators.
> they say that which is expected of them.
> to be instructive or constructive is to be unpopular (like: the
>   leaders only
> sleep when there is a watchingeye)
>
> but they say the right things at the right time, it's like a
>   stageshow:
> only the entertainers have changed

Finally, after invoking the spirit of Bobby Hutton, (another black leader, shot to death in April 1968 while attempting to surrender after a street battle with Oakland police), Madhubuti draws a lesson for all who seek equality under the law, at the same time deriding the enemy for his cynicism and cowardice (just as the *Agamemnon* chorus derides Clytemnestra and the upstart Aegisthus), and expressing, even in this seemingly bleakest of times, at least some hope for those who adhere to the principles of justice:

the seeing eye should always see.
the night doesn't stop the stars

The men who murdered Fred Hampton and Mark Clark were never punished. In 1970, a coroner's inquest found that the police actions constituted justifiable homicide, and it was only after a long-drawn-out civil action on behalf of those who had been wounded in the police attack at Monroe Street that the full truth of the morning of 4 December and of the events leading up to it was exposed. During the mid-1970s, a committee chaired by Idaho senator Frank Church exposed the extent and illegality of COINTELPRO (or COunter INTELligence PROgram), which had been set up to undermine domestic activist groups, especially the Black Panthers, the American Indian Movement and Puerto Rican liberation groups such as the Young Lords; their tactics had included burglary, falsifying documents and a process known as 'snitch-jacketing' (whereby the FBI spread dangerous and sometimes fatally misleading disinformation about targeted individuals in political groups, with the intention of driving other members of the harassed group to violent reprisal). At last, in 1982, damages to the sum of $1.85 million were paid to the Monroe Street survivors (though even then, police and FBI spokespersons insisted that this did not constitute any acceptance of culpability on their part). In spite of witness testimony regarding the deliberate killing of Hampton, no police officer or FBI agent was ever punished for participation in the killing.

This and other verdicts only added credence to the assumption that law enforcement officers and property owners enjoy immunity, both then and now. Black men would continue to die, on the streets, in their own homes, in their cars, shot or beaten by police officers and others who, whether from fear, hatred or cynicism, were unable to see those they were attacking as altogether human. At the same time, inspired by brave individuals like Hampton, poets (and other artists) have worked to give expression to African-American values, a black culture, and a 'Black Poem / ... [that] All Black People [can] speak ... / Silently or LOUD, according to how they feel, and not to the dictates of a panicked spectator culture intent upon traducing, commercialising and ripping off their work. To date, what has emerged, in the work of Haki Madhubuti, Amiri Baraka, Gwendolyn Brooks, June Jordan and others, is a combination of a sophisticated aesthetic of cool with a 'very-hot' critique of how white supremacism works. This critique has spread into the general culture in some surprising and encouraging ways, from the work of Madhubuti's own Chicago-based Third World Publishing company, or Eugene Redmond's championing of Henry Dumas and other neglected black writers, to websites dedicated to giving black writers a wider readership. Yet, even as we consider these success stories, it remains clear that the language, methods and means of poetic resistance must ever be called forth anew. As Madhubuti says, in his 2004 poem 'For the Consideration of Poets',

> where is the poetry of resistance,
>   the poetry of honorable defiance
>   ...
> where is the poetry of doubt and suspicion
> not in the service of the state, bishops and priests,
> not in the service of beautiful people and late night promises,
> not in the service of influence, incompetence and academic
>   clown talk?[7]

This poetry is not applicable *only* to black people in America: it is a poetry of justice whose key insight is that, as Malcolm X said, 'the only way we'll get freedom for ourselves is to identify ourselves with every oppressed people in the world. We are blood brothers to the people of Brazil, Venezuela, Haiti, Cuba.' As long as we see a poet like Madhubuti as relevant only to black culture and civil rights, we are failing to read his work in good faith; for, just as we read the New Testament, or Tom Paine, or the poetry of the French and German Resistance for its relevance – not to mention its beauty, the expression of justice being intrinsically beautiful – to all human life, so should we read those like Madhubuti, whose gifts were forged in the heat of what, if it cannot finally face up to and make some reparation for its racist history, will continue to be a critically divided society.

THE BAT-POET

And, I've found, there's no children's book so bad that I
mind your having liked it: about the tastes of dead children
there is no disputing

Randall Jarrell

OUR APPROACHES TO READING (the texts chosen, the level of attention
and analysis, our sensual and intellectual responses) are formed,
in large part, during childhood and early youth. This is especially
true in the case of poetry; we have all heard someone say, with
regard to verse, that they do not read it because they do not, or
are afraid that they might not, 'understand' it – and, as Marianne
Moore says (in the longer, early version of the poem 'Poetry'), we
'do not admire what/ we cannot understand'. We might contend
that poetry does not seek admiration, or even understanding, but
over the years, mainly for educational policy reasons, we have
been led to feel that understanding and admiration are *exactly*
what poetry demands. The children of my generation might have
grown up with John Masefield or Walter de la Mare or, better still,
the nonsense of Edward Lear ringing in our heads, the sheer pleasure of playing with language, subverting conventional logic and
giving free rein to the imagination considered an indirect source
of instruction as well as delight; my children, however, are more
likely to read a poem with some kind of sociological agenda at the
back of their minds. When the children in my English class read

John Masefield's 'Cargoes', the main point was to take pleasure in the music and playfulness of the verse:

> Quinquireme of Nineveh from distant Ophir
> Rowing home to haven in sunny Palestine,
> With a cargo of ivory,
> And apes and peacocks,
> Sandalwood, cedarwood, and sweet white wine.

As we read, we might learn what a 'quinquireme' was, we might even pick up some knowledge of the ancient Assyrian city of Nineveh (now part of Mosul, Iraq), but these things were secondary to listening to the sound and gradually taking in the form of the poem. If this kind of reading taught us anything, it did so without fanfare, and it did not set homework. If to some extent it insinuated a sense of the larger geographical drama in which I was involved, as it moved from the banks of the Tigris to a

> Dirty British coaster with a salt-caked smoke stack
> Butting through the Channel in the mad March days,
> With a cargo of Tyne coal,
> Road-rail, pig-lead,
> Firewood, iron-ware, and cheap tin trays[1]

it did so unobtrusively, creating an atmosphere, rather than delivering a lesson or, worse, a message from somebody's sponsors.

In recent years, however, the teaching of poetry has shifted further towards the pursuit of extra-literary understanding. Skimming through a child's poetry sampler (from a British school curriculum), we might find a few classics with obvious themes and any number of contemporary or recent works that I have started to think of more and more as 'sociological', poems that an educational policymaker at educational policy HQ believes might be 'good for' a child's development. There is nothing wrong with the poems as such (some of them I very much admire), but I wonder why it has to be these, and why so many of them are so darn solemn. There is no nonsense, no linguistic pizzazz, and the music is fashionably subdued. The only common factor I can find is that they are all identifiably thematic (some form a section called 'Love and Relationships', in which, for example, pupils can 'discuss the purpose of marriage and […] explore marriage in the context of the poem'*), and all seem conducive to lateral thinking, nesting puzzles of metaphor and allusion that, in the end, are solvable in some way. As I say, there is nothing wrong with any of this, on one level; nevertheless, I cannot help thinking that, when they finally emerge from English class, the students will be thinking more about marriage, or war, than about poetry. To my possibly jaundiced eye, the poems are there as prompts, to provide food for sociological musings, but nothing in the curriculum suggests that they are to be seen as unique or marvellous in their own right. To demonstrate this latter point, the study session for many of the chosen poems concludes with a creative writing exercise – proof if it were needed, not only that everyone can 'understand' verse by relating it to contemporary issues, but also that pretty much anyone can write their own poem, on a 'relevant' subject like 'marriage' or 'war', in the ninety-minute gap between assembly and double physics.

Randall Jarrell, that gentlest of poets and most acerbic of critics, was exaggerating, I think, when he maintained that 'poetry is a bad medium for philosophy', but his point is certainly useful in any critical consideration of the 99 per cent of philosophical poems that fall short of the standard set by, say, 'Burnt Norton'. 'Everything in the philosophical poem has to satisfy irreconcilable requirements', Jarrell says. 'For instance, the last demand that we should make of philosophy (that it be interesting) is the first we make of a poem; the philosophical poet has an elevated and methodical, but forlorn and absurd air as he works away at his flying tank, his sewing-machine that also plays the piano.' Yet children (for whom Jarrell wrote some of his finest work) are natural

---

* Another grouping is 'Power and Conflict'.

philosophers and will engage with any and all manner of logical or metaphysical conundrum – Where do we come from? What happens when we die? Why is the sky blue? – just so long as they do not feel manipulated. They also have an instinctive suspicion of *the didactic*, which is to say, any exercise that sets out to teach them a specific set of attitudes or skills, as opposed to those meaning-ful games that create a space in which they can learn something freely and, mostly, of their own accord. It has been said that the mother of invention is not necessity but play – and, to my mind, the best children's writers are those who work at this playful level. They are no less serious in their engagements with the 'big questions' of life (questions to do with identity, say, or fair play); they just manage to avoid being solemn – and few pressures are more damaging to free learning in children (or, for that matter, in adults) than solemnity.

On the other hand, children are happy to engage with all manner of serious philosophical enquiry, if they can sneak up on it through play. I remember very little of the formal education I received as a school-age child, but I vividly recall the delight – the joyous sense of affirmative conundrum – that I experienced reading this exchange from *Winnie-the-Pooh*:

> 'Hallo, Rabbit,' [Pooh] said, 'is that you?'
> 'Let's pretend it isn't,' said Rabbit, 'and see what happens.'

Meanwhile, I cannot imagine a whole posse of academic commit-tees coming up with a better answer to that currently fashionable enquiry – 'how does creativity work?' – than this:

> 'Hallo, Pooh,' said Rabbit.
> 'Hallo, Rabbit,' said Pooh dreamily.
> 'Did you make that song up?'
> 'Well, I sort of made it up,' said Pooh. 'It isn't Brain,' he went on humbly, 'because You Know Why, Rabbit; but it comes to me sometimes.'
> 'Ah!' said Rabbit, who never let things come to him, but always went and fetched them.

It could be argued, of course, that we need certain kinds of philosophy at certain points in our life that we will have no use for later. Children face problems that adults cannot begin to imagine – and later, when they are adults, those problems, if not forgotten entirely, may well come to look like so many paper tigers. At the critical moment – aged seven, or twelve or fifteen – the oddest things can seem grievous. Certainly, my own childhood demanded, at times, the certitude and occasionally the dismissive wit of an Ogden Nash –

> The hunter crouches in his blind
> 'Neath camouflage of every kind
> And conjures up a quacking noise
> To lend allure to his decoys
> This grown-up man, with pluck and luck
> is hoping to outwit a duck.[2]

– or the sense of mystery, which is to say, the sense of a wider narrative that included me, without my knowing how, that sometimes came through in a poem by Walter de la Mare:

> And he felt in his heart their strangeness,
> Their stillness answering his cry,
> While his horse moved, cropping the dark turf,
> 'Neath the starred and leafy sky;
> For he suddenly smote on the door, even
> Louder, and lifted his head:
> 'Tell them I came, and no one answered,
> That I kept my word,' he said.[3]

Not all of the poems I stumbled across as a child were strictly 'for' children; some were what was then called 'light verse', and some were presumed appropriate because they contained small people (all too often small people preoccupied with the acquisition of moral precepts, willingly or otherwise), but what I remember most clearly, in retrospect, is how often and how utterly I took refuge in poems that were everything my usual environment was not. This is not to say that they necessarily opposed that environment; they simply ignored it. They were touchstones, talismans against the world of what my elders and betters called 'common sense', and all too often they were either 'nonsense poems' of one variety or another or they had animals in them that could talk to other animals.

One of the surprise masters of children's writing, in both verse and prose, is the poet, critic and academic Randall Jarrell. Something of an *éminence grise* in his own time, he could make a reputation with single incisive review. (His writing on such near-contemporaries as Robert Lowell and Marianne Moore did much to broaden their readership, even as his own poetry remained under-appreciated for decades.) At the same time, he was an acerbic critic when acerbity was justified; here he is, for example, reviewing a new anthology of modern poetry, edited by our friend, Oscar Williams:

> [*A Little Treasury of Modern Poetry*] has the merit of containing a considerably larger selection of Oscar Williams's poems than I have seen in any other anthology. There are nine of his poems and five of Hardy's. It takes a lot of courage to like your own poetry almost twice as well as Hardy's.*

He was often a very astute observer of those flaws in systems of thought that others failed to notice, especially as they related to literary fashions:

> We live in an age which eschews sentimentality as if it were a good deal more than the devil. (Actually, of course, a writer may be just as sentimental in laying undue emphasis on sexual crimes as on dying mothers: sentimental, like scientific, is an adjective that relates to method, not to matter.)

---

*In a later review, discussing one of Williams' own slim volumes, he said that this 'new book is pleasanter and a little quieter than his old, which gave the impression of having been written on a typewriter by a typewriter'.

There was, however, another side to this formidable and unforgiving champion of what would now be called 'elitist' values,* a side rarely apparent to his academic peers but clearly visible in his writing. For not only was Jarrell a man who loved children; he also understood something about them that made him a perfect companion on the page. This understanding took in some astute observations on the generation gap between children and their parents, as in his Afterword to Christina Stead's 1940 novel *The Man Who Loved Children*:

One of the most obvious facts about grown-ups, to a child, is that they have forgotten what it is like to be a child. The child has not yet had the chance to know what it is like to be a grown-up; he believes, even, that being a grown-up is a mistake he will never make – when *he* grows up he will keep on being a child, a big child with power. So the child and grown-up live in mutual love, misunderstanding, and distaste. Children shout and play and cry and want candy; grown-ups say *Ssh!* and work and scold and want steak. There is no disputing tastes as contradictory as these. It is not just Mowgli who was raised by a couple of wolves; any child is raised by a couple of grown-ups. Father and Mother may be nearer and dearer than anyone will ever be again – still, they are members of a different species. God is, I suppose, what our parents were; certainly the ogre of the stories is so huge, so powerful, and so stupid because that

---

*There can be no more absurd controversy than the arguments that periodically erupt about 'elitism' in the arts. When Pope Julius II called on Michelangelo to paint the Sistine Chapel, nobody said he was being elitist. Or, as art critic Robert Hughes once observed:

I am completely an elitist in the cultural but emphatically not the social sense. I prefer the good to the bad, the articulate to the mumbling, the aesthetically developed to the merely primitive, and full to partial consciousness. I love the spectacle of skill, whether it's an expert gardener at work or a good carpenter chopping dovetails. I don't think stupid or ill-read people are as good to be with as wise and fully literate ones. I would rather watch a great tennis player than a mediocre one, unless the latter is a friend or a relative.

is the way a grown-up looks to a child … Grown-ups forget or cannot believe that they seem even more unreasonable to children than children seem to them.

He also appreciated something vital about the way in which children read, if left to their own devices, that gave him a rare freedom as a poet writing for a younger audience: 'It is better,' he said, 'to have the child in the chimney corner moved by what happens in the poem, in spite of his ignorance of its real meaning, than to have the poem a puzzle to which that meaning is the only key.' In short, children intuitively understand that the poem is the thing – and if they are able to hold on to that understanding, they grow into the kind of readers most likely to engage fully with a poet's poet like Jarrell. Not surprisingly, then, he saw that the persistence of a child's sensibility into adulthood was a sign not of immaturity, or narcissism, but of good luck and the preservation of something essential. As Leo Zanderer notes in reference to Karl Shapiro's essay 'The Death of Randall Jarrell': Shapiro 'rightfully suggests that all his poetry shows an overriding concern not only with the experiences of childhood but with a general theme of childhood as a human experience continuing well into maturity'.[4]

This is a key point: historically, most 'developed' societies (even those, such as Victorian England, that romanticised childhood) have been intolerant of any continuation of 'childhood' beyond a certain age. In 1867, for example, just two years after the appearance of *Alice's Adventures in Wonderland*, Karl Marx was writing, in the first volume of *Capital*:

> In so far as machinery dispenses with muscular power, it becomes a means of employing labourers of slight muscular strength, and those whose bodily development is incomplete, but whose limbs are all the more supple. The labour of women and children was, therefore, the first thing sought for by capitalists who used machinery. That mighty substitute for labour and labourers was forthwith changed into a means for increasing the number of wage-labourers by enrolling, under

the direct sway of capital, every member of the workman's family, without distinction of age or sex. Compulsory work for the capitalist usurped the place, not only of the children's play, but also of free labour at home within moderate limits for the support of the family.

At this time children as young as three might be employed as chimneysweeps, though as Marx points out, 'there exist plenty of machines to replace them'; occasionally, they would become trapped in the chimneys, where many died of exposure, smoke inhalation or, of course, fire. It seems strange, now, to think that, in an age that not only idealised the child but is considered by many the era in which 'childhood' was invented, the sheer misery of most children was so studiously ignored. But then, like the idealisation of agricultural workers in the English landscape tradition, or of women in any society where men nevertheless retain economic and political power, the idealisation of the child in Victorian times was little more than a process of fetishisation, in which the actuality of the subject's life is systematically obscured by the myth of pastoral contentment, unapproachable beauty or eternal innocence. As the historian Paula S. Fass has pointed out:

> the 'modern' perspective on children as sexually innocent, economically dependent, and emotionally fragile whose lives are supposed to be dominated by play, school and family nurture, provides a very limited view of children's lives in the modern western past. While some children did experience this kind of childhood, for the vast majority, it is quite literally only in the twentieth century that these have been enforced as both preferred and dominant.

As a critic, Jarrell was keenly aware of the perpetuation of those Victorian myths into the literature of his own time, and he knew the burden of mythic responsibility that adults place on children when they themselves have 'forgotten what it is like to be a child'. At the same time he was alert to the potential that children are all too often obliged to conceal, while gamely playing the roles they are assigned. When in in an early poem, 'Children Selecting Books in a Library', he writes that we live

> By trading another's sorrow for our own; another's
> Impossibilities, still unbelieved in, for our own

he is showing us that children, just as much as adults, seek more than mere entertainment, or diversion, in books. He is saying that, on the contrary, all imaginative reading is a quest in which

> The world's selves cure that short disease, myself,
> And we see bending to us, dewy-eyed, the great
> CHANGE, dear to all things not to themselves endeared.

However, this writing *about* childhood – as a social construct and the way that it extends into adult life – is paralleled, in his work *for* children, by an exploration of life's wonders and an enquiry into how they may be discovered, even in a rigidly controlled world in which, as Jarrell notes in yet another poem about a young person in a library, 'the ways we miss our lives are life'.

At first glance, Jarrell's finest work for children, *The Bat-Poet*, comes over as a standard, if charming and well-made, 'once upon a time' animal story. Its protagonist is 'a little light brown bat, the color of coffee with cream in it', who, for his own reasons, becomes separated from his home colony and, having achieved what could be seen as a form of Romantic isolation in the manner of Thoreau's *Walden,* begins to stay awake in the daytime, in the process discovering a very different environment from the night world to which he is accustomed.* This daytime realm is a source of great wonder (sunlight, other animals, birds) – so much so that the bat wants to find a way to describe it to his former companions. The

---

* Though few would express it as forcefully as Thoreau himself ('I love to be alone. I never found the companion that was so companionable as solitude'), artists and writers have a long history of finding their beginnings in solitary contemplation. See Anthony Storr, *Solitude: A Return to the Self* (2005).

question is, how to convey it in all its strangeness and beauty. He quickly learns that plain description fails to impress:

> The bat told the other bats about all the things you could see in the daytime. 'You'd love them,' he said. The next time you wake up in the daytime, just keep your eyes open for a while and don't go back to sleep.
>
> The other bats were sure they wouldn't like that. 'We wish we didn't wake up at all,' they said.*

At this stage the little bat could be seen as just another Romantic outsider, one of those for whom the doors of perception have been miraculously cleansed, so that everything appears to him as it is, lit by the sun, all 'green-and-gold-and-blue'. While the other bats insist on closing themselves up, only seeing the world through the narrow chinks of their cavern (or, in this case, barn), the little bat enjoys privileged glimpses of the infinite. However, there is a cost here: first, his individual vision of the world sets him outside his community; and, second, he has no way to articulate for others, and so to validate, what he has seen. Unlike the conventional nonconformist, he cannot pretend to be altogether happy in his isolation (he is, after all, a bat), and so, in order to share his solitary visions, he turns to poetry, composing three short pieces in which he describes an owl, his new friend the chipmunk and a sceptical mockingbird. Finally, having refined his craft to a level at which he can use poetry as a means to self-exploration and discovery, he writes about his own life. In the process he comes upon a kind of vision of the essence of bat-ness, a game of pretend that nevertheless allows space for the reader to ask questions about what can and cannot be known, and, of that, what can and cannot be articulated. What does language do in relation to experience? How do we convey the wonder of what we have witnessed to

---

* See the American organisational analyst William H. Whyte, whose book *The Organization Man* was a bestseller in the 1950s: 'People very rarely think in groups; they talk together, they exchange information, they adjudicate, they make compromises. But they do not think; they do not create.'

those who live in an entirely different world from ours? And what is it, in all this wealth of sense-impressions, that comes together to make a 'self'? Describing the mother bat's flight through the air – with her baby hanging on to her body through all the 'doubling and looping, soaring, somersaulting' – Jarrell elegantly illustrates this process of seeking and finding:

> All night, in happiness, she hunts and flies.
> Her high sharp cries
> Like shining needlepoints of sound
> Go out into the night and, echoing back,
> Tell her what they have touched.

This is beautifully done. At first sight, it comes across as a charming description of echolocation in a creature that 'lives by hearing'; its real function, however, is to remind us that what we know of the world is the result of a moment-by-moment sensory and imaginative quest. At the same time, we cannot ignore the fact that this game is *shared*: the mother plays it to find her place in the world, and the child is nourished not only directly, by the 'milk she makes him/ In moonlight or starlight, in mid-air', but also by all that she sees and does.

What makes *The Bat-Poet* special as a work of children's writing is partly the way in which it reveals how (and why) art is made and partly its emphasis on the outward, a regard for the world around its subject that is larger than curiosity, and wider than a basis for self-identification. The bat's urge simply to find a language for what it has seen is one that many a child shares (we all remember coming home with stories of the big world we encountered for the brief time that we were outside the usual home ground), but it is also coloured by the impulse to praise, to see the value of the other as at least equal to that of the self – and, reading Jarrell's charming picture book (with illustrations by Maurice Sendak), I cannot help but remember Rilke's praise poems, in which the revered world brings unlooked-for blessings upon the witnessing self, in spite of conflict and existential doubt. As with the sentimental and the scientific, what is of the essence here is method, and the method a praise poet like Jarrell adopts is an attitude, a stance, in which more is achieved by looking outward, *at the world*, than by peering back into the self.

There is an old saying, attributed more often than not to some anonymous Chinese thinker, that 'he who remembers, forgets'. As a child, I used to puzzle over what it meant; now I believe that it may be a timely warning not to become too attached to the idea of memory. If the ways in which we miss our lives are life, one of those distractions may well be the irritable, obsessive, supposedly Proustian search for specific moments in the past, key images, or occasions, or triggering stimuli, that quite possibly never actually happened – or not in the way we choose to think. Is it not conceivable that the specific data (the relatable memories, the mental images and album leaves, even those 'madeleine' moments) for which we constantly, and often fruitlessly, search are not as important to growth as the marks and traces that experience lays down in the body as a whole? Becoming – unfolding in time, realising a selfhood, growing up – is not a matter of querying some kind of inner database, or picture library, where we are unlikely to find anything more than a repository of anecdotal evidence; it is a way of seeing and doing, a way of being, that we summarise, for convention's sake, under the rubric of character. We do not – cannot – live in the past. The childhood each of us has is not a matter of long ago and far away but, like history, like memory, is happening here and now. Childhood continues; perhaps it never ends. As Jarrell reminds us, in the poem that opens this book, we live, sometimes painfully, in the present, all the while longing for 'well water/ Pumped from an old well at the bottom of the world'. We feel incomplete without the sense of an origin, a source, and we locate it, wilfully, in the past, or in some ideal history. All this while, however, we have the means to drink, if only we could abandon such illusions:

The pump you pump the water from is rusty
And hard to move and absurd, a squirrel-wheel
A sick squirrel turns slowly, through the sunny
Inexorable hours. And yet sometimes
The wheel turns of its own weight, the rusty
Pump pumps over your sweating face the clear
Water, cold, so cold! you cup your hands
And gulp from them the dailiness of life.[5]

TO RECLAIM LOST SPACE

First warm
spring winds up from Ohio, I
pause at the top of the ladder
to take in the wide world reaching
downriver and beyond.[1]

Philip Levine

A DAY TRIP FROM school, some time in the early 1960s. This is our
third, that I can recall. The first was to a local pet shop to look
at a baby crocodile the owner had just acquired, the second to
the cinema for a special viewing of a film I have forgotten, but
this is the most exciting, the one with a hint of danger, dust and
darkness mingled in the lungs and on the skin, the unlooked-for
descent into a world that, under normal conditions, is reserved
for our uncles and fathers. Every day we see the pit-head from
the playground as we walk into the schoolhouse in ordered rows,
boys from one playground, girls from another, the two separated
by a spiked fence, a masterstroke on the part of our wardens that
only makes the forbidden contact sweeter to the imagination and
that much more poignant. Every year we hear of some mishap,
and twice during my time at this Catholic Primary in the old heart
of coal country the Deputy Head has come to my class to call out
children by name and send them home, for reasons that we all
know so well that Cathy Allan is already trembling with fear when

she rises from her chair and tries to walk, invisibly, and unseeing, to the door. This is Cowdenbeath, a pit town dying on its feet, surly and proud, the men silent and capable of rare violence, the women tough and tender by turns, weeping inexplicably at the kitchen table on a Saturday afternoon when the man of the house is at the football, laughing fit to cry among their own kind at Sunday tea, safe in their secrets and destined for something better when that day comes when evening shall be light.

Under normal circumstances, I would go anywhere to be away from school. Even standing in the backroom of a narrow shop, staring at something that looks like an elm log half submerged in greasy water is preferable to chanting the Times Tables or making cardboard models of Roman forts, but somewhere at the back of my mind I know why we are being taken to the pit today, and everything in me baulks at it. If somebody could sit me down and promise, absolutely, that work as a miner was most assuredly not on the cards, then the whole trip would be instantly transformed into an adventure, a Journey to the Centre of the Earth with the great James Mason as Professor Lindenbrook (though on a more modest budget). But the reason for this visit – rumours are we are even going to go down in 'the cage' – is that the mining life is more likely than not the future I am destined for, and I do not want to see, in advance, what it holds.

I had read, and would read, poems about work, mostly agricultural or sea-related, at school, and all of them were prettier, and far more meaningful than what I knew about coal mining or the construction industry. (My father, alone among our extended family, worked 'on the building', which made him a seasonal employee, laid off with the first frost and re-hired in the spring. This meant that Christmas in our house was hedged about with worry, as he would have to travel far and wide to find any kind of work and sometimes came home with nothing. Sad to say, it was a blessing to him when a foot-and-mouth outbreak occurred as, back then, casual men were needed for the slaughter and disposal of the corpses.) Most poems we read, however, were about farm work, and even they reflected a pastoral ideal, rather than hard graft.

John Masefield, for example seemed to be letting the side down, rather, in poems like 'Autumn Ploughing', where no mention is made at all of the man or men doing the work. Here the autumnal scene is quickly established in familiar, bucolic terms –

> After the ranks of stubble have laid bare,
> And field mice and finches' beaks have found
> The last spilled seed corn left upon the ground;
> And no more swallows miracle in air;

– until, out of nowhere, with nobody in attendance, the apparatus of ploughing appears:

> Then out, with the great horses, come the ploughs,
> And all day long the slow procession goes,
> Darkening the stubble fields with broadening strips.[2]

Apart from one missing feature, the scene is well observed: we see scarlet hips in the hedge, we see robins, we see grey gulls following the plough. Although this Herefordshire landscape was not exactly my own, it was close enough to the Platonic ideal to be instantly recognisable. (And in fact, even at an early age I somehow guessed that a Fife farming scene, with its windswept, straggling trees and its sparser pastures, was just that little bit inferior to the lusher, English Arcadia on which the ideal was based. This somehow made us, as residents of an inferior, harder landscape, inferior in turn: colder, more austere, less generous.)

The missing feature is, however, critical. Somebody – an agricultural worker, probably on a casual contract, if his employment was even that formal – had hitched those horses to the plough; somebody had kept the line straight, perhaps struggling to control the horses' pace a little, if the beasts were a little fresh; somebody took care of the animals when the job was done. Yet this person goes unmentioned, just as nobody seems to have made the hay in the pretty scene glimpsed from the train in Edward Thomas' 'Adlestrop':

And willows, willow-herb, and grass,
And meadowsweet, and haycocks dry,
No whit less still and lonely fair
Than the high cloudlets in the sky.[3]

Clearly, the absence of working people in these landscapes belongs to a convention of the picturesque in which rural folk are either invisible – their work done, they have retreated to some scullery or shebeen somewhere, not to spoil the view – or shown at rest, ruddy and oddly clean, perched among the haystacks, eating apples or quaffing ale from earthenware jugs. Sometimes a goose-girl goes by, as in this poem by Edna St Vincent Millay, but she is predictably clean and wholesome, and carries with her an unmistakable moral burden:

Spring rides no horses down the hill,
But comes on foot, a goose-girl still.
And all the loveliest things there be
Come simply, so, it seems to me.

That the girl is lovely – she is, after all, the personification of Spring – is to be expected, but why is this goose-girl so obviously simple, and why, in the next lines, does she become the very embodiment of honesty?

If ever I said, in grief or pride,
I tired of honest things, I lied.

We do not know why, of course, but we can guess – and the close of this poem reveals the truth that the speaker is not in the least interested in the girl, who is simply a pastoral type, but is poking a sly dig at the many vices of the non-bucolic class, who are just as vaguely drawn but are at least observed enough to possess flaws:

And should be cursed forevermore
With Love in laces, like a whore,
And neighbours cold, and friends unsteady,
And Spring on horseback, like a lady![4]

Non-agricultural workers are even less visible in much of the poetry written during the Industrial Revolution, which ought to seem troubling but for some reason is altogether to be expected. Every era has its winners and losers: those who make and write history, and those who are expunged from the cultural record.

In 'Nottingham and the Mining Country', an essay he wrote in 1929, D. H. Lawrence talks frankly about the life of the Nottinghamshire colliers, remembering how his father 'loved the pit. He was hurt badly, more than once, but he would never stay away. He loved the contact, the intimacy, as men in the war loved the intense male comradeship of the dark days.' His father, however, belonged to a mining tradition that, as described in *Sons and Lovers*, had only a little impact on the land:

> Hell Row was a block of thatched, bulging cottages that stood by the brookside on Greenhill Lane. There lived the colliers who worked in the little gin-pits two fields away. The brook ran under the alder trees, scarcely soiled by these small mines, whose coal was drawn to the surface by donkeys that plodded wearily in a circle round a gin. And all over the countryside were these same pits, some of which had been worked in the time of Charles II, the few colliers and the donkeys burrowing down like ants into the earth, making queer mounds and little black places among the corn-fields and the meadows. And the cottages of these coal-miners, in blocks and pairs here and there, together with odd farms and homes of the stockingers, straying over the parish, formed the village of Bestwood.

This was all to change, with the coming of industrialised coal-mining, when the miners' families were moved into terraces and obliged to live at close quarters with the dirt and squalor of the new methods:

> Now though perhaps nobody knew it, it was ugliness which betrayed the spirit of man, in the nineteenth century. The great crime which the moneyed classes and promoters of industry committed in the palmy Victorian days was the condemning

of the workers to ugliness, ugliness, ugliness: meanness and formless and ugly surroundings, ugly ideals, ugly religion, ugly hope, ugly love, ugly clothes, ugly furniture, ugly houses, ugly relationship between workers and employers. The human soul needs actual beauty even more than bread.

For a time the colliers had managed to preserve a sense of beauty, and they felt a proud independence from the material world outside the pit – but they could not be altogether independent, or the married men could not, and it was not long before the industrialisation of mining had a damaging effect on the miners' family life:

> Now the colliers had also an instinct of beauty. The colliers' wives had not. The colliers were deeply alive, instinctively. But they had no daytime ambition, no daytime intellect. They avoided, really, the rational aspect of life. They preferred to take life instinctively and intuitively. They didn't even care very profoundly about wages. It was the women, naturally, who nagged on this score. There was a big discrepancy, when I was a boy, between the collier who saw, at the best, only a brief few hours of daylight – often no daylight at all during the winter weeks – and the collier's wife, who had all the day to herself when the man was down the pit […] The collier went to the pub and drank in order to continue his intimacy with his mates. They talked endlessly, but it was rather of wonders and marvels, even in politics, than of facts. It was hard facts, in the shape of wife, money, and nagging home necessities, which they fled away from, out of the house to the pub, and out of the house to the pit […] The collier fled out of the house as soon as he could, away from the nagging materialism of the woman.

Lawrence, whose own mother was a collier's wife, is being deliberately provocative here, and there is no doubt that the passage reveals more than he intended about his own attitudes to the pit-town women he grew up with (as evinced, say, in *Sons* *and Lovers*).* Nevertheless, we catch a glimpse of the dilemma of those women who, wanting more for their children than hard labour, danger and grime, were perceived as disloyal to their husbands, and to their community, when they took actual measures to educate those children for a better life. Excluded from the camaraderie of the pits (excluded, for that matter, from the public bars where men gathered), the wife may have been unable to see anything but the ugliness of her industrialised surroundings, and the lonely life she lived, with 'all the day to herself' giving her time to brood on the dangers of mining and the fate she and her children would suffer if the man was to be disabled or killed. (In 1920, 1,130 men died in British pits, three-quarters of them below ground, just under half of them buried in 'falls of ground'. This figure only includes fatalities, however: many more were so badly disabled that they could no longer work below ground, and so saw their wages cut when they were obliged to take surface jobs.) It is not surprising, Lawrence says, that these women should want a cleaner, safer, healthier life for their children. Yet these conflicting perspectives between miner and wife led to unhappy, ugly marriages – and Lawrence's portrait of one such relationship, in the poem 'The Collier's Wife', published in 1928, is brutal in its combination of humour, Lawrence's astute use of Nottinghamshire dialect and unsparing honesty on the part of the woman for whom bad news has become a matter of habit. The poem begins in a time-honoured tradition, with somebody knocking at a door in the night:

> Somebody's knockin' at th' door
> Mother, come down an' see!
> – I's think it's nobbut, a beggar;

---

* Lydia Lawrence, *née* Beardsall, had been educated for a career in teaching, but after financial problems struck her family she was unable to fulfil her academic ambitions. Nevertheless, she continued to aspire to a better life after she married Arthur Lawrence and settled in Eastwood, running a small clothes shop from home and ensuring her children received a better education than the local schools could offer.

Say I'm busy.

It's not a beggar, mother; hark
How 'ard 'e knocks!
– Eh, tha'rt a mard-arsed kid,
'E'll gie thee socks!

Shout an' ax what 'e wants,
I canna come down.

As the dialogue between child and mother unfolds, we come
to understand that the 'mester's/ Got hurt i' th' pit'. The wife's
response to this news, however, is far from what might have been
expected:

　　　– Eh dear o' me,
If 'e's not a man for mischance!

Wheer's 'e hurt this time, lad?

The messenger cannot answer, he only knows that 'it wor bad', to
which the woman's reply is even more surprising:

It would be so!

Out o' my way, childt! dear o' me, wheer
'Ave I put 'is clean stockin's an' shirt?
Goodness knows if they'll be able
To take off 'is pit-dirt!

An' what a moan 'e'll make! there niver
Was such a man for a fuss
If anything ailed 'im; at any rate
I shan't 'ave 'im to nuss.

From here on, the poem is a monologue on the part of the wife,
who is not so cold-blooded that she does not show a little sympa-
thy for the man, but the main burden of her soliloquy, apart from
a sidelong grumble about the inconvenience of getting herself to
the infirmary, is money:

An' there's compensation, sin' it's accident.
An' club-money – I won't growse.
An' a fork an' a spoon 'e'll want – an' what else?
I s'll never catch that train!
What a traipse it is, if a man gets hurt!
I sh'd think 'e'll get right again.[5]

This portrait of a hard-bitten, brutalised woman is far in character from the 'mother who smiles as she sings' in Lawrence's
'Piano', but it is perhaps franker, and more truthful, to how
industrialisation systematically desensitised the colliery workers
and their dependants, denying them the basic rewards of life that
ought to have been regarded as human rights, from the sense of
a home landscape to marital love, and even to the extent of transforming the mutilation of a loved one into the crude cash value of
injury compensation money.

I knew why my teachers had planned a visit to the pit, I could even
see how the trip could be seen as educational, but I also knew the
lesson I was meant to learn, as the cage descended. That lesson
– first, that I had a future, and second, that I should think of it in
certain terms and not others – was to be a preparation for life as a
worker. The future was coming, and it would not be pretty – but
it was all there was. Boys became men, and men went to the pit,
(and, as we know, women became pit-wives). I didn't want to go
to the pit that day, not because I was afraid of the cage, or the
darkness, or the claustrophobic descent; I just didn't want to see
'the future' my elders had planned for me – just as the speaker in
Philip Levine's poem 'The Future' doesn't want to linger on his
prospects:

> One spring day
> the whole class went by bus
> to the foundry at Ford Rouge

to see earth melted and poured
like syrup into fire. 'Look up,'
someone said, maybe Dougie
or Alan, so I did, and saw

way up above the collisions
of metal and men, a family
of sparrows in the trapped light,
trapped themselves, or perhaps

out to reclaim their lost space.

Here the predicament of the sparrows echoes the predicament of the present and future workers in this foundry: not only are both 'trapped', but any space they might have laid claim to is lost, making escape impossible. Their new habitat is so alien, so denatured, that even the light is trapped, and the only thing that is sure to expand, as the future keeps rolling in, is that alien industrial apparatus.

Later the class
picnicked on egg salad
beside a wide stream that fed

our filthy river. Alan,
or maybe it was Dougie,
managed to cross the water
leaping from rock to rock

and then back again,
his balance was that good.
Alan, or maybe Dougie,
whoever had crossed, dared me

to try, but I knew enough
even then not to.

Already the speaker has been trained not to give in to childish impulses: the water is dangerous, but not in the usual way. In fact, it may be so toxic that it isn't really water any more.

As the poem moves to its end, we remember its beginning, a piece of wordplay by the class wit that, with a little tweaking, wouldn't have seemed out of place in *Four Quartets*:

> The past is no more past
> than the future, or so said
> Moradian, the unlikely seer
> of my senior shop class.

Now, for as banal a reason as it is possible to find, the school trip becomes 'endless', but even that is not enough to prevent the onward rush towards a fate that the speaker knows he does not want, but cannot imagine himself avoiding:

> The bus driver
> lost the way and had to stop
> at a filling station in Delray
>
> to get directions, so the trip
> was endless. I got back before
> nightfall, but the day kept going
> on and on into the future.[6]

It is almost redundant, here, to point to how these last lines evoke the end of *The Great Gatsby*, the great American novel about the illusory nature of both future and past:

> Gatsby believed in the green light, the orgiastic future that year
> by year recedes before us. It eluded us then, but that's no matter
> – tomorrow we will run faster, stretch out our arms farther …
> And then one fine morning –
> So we beat on, boats against the current, borne back ceaselessly
> into the past.

Levine's allusion, however, is painfully ironic. In Nick Carraway's Keatsian vision, with its exquisite alliteration ('beat … boats … borne … back') and its rich, worldly melancholia, there is a certain weary elegance in the Sisyphus-like ordeal he sets out and, most importantly, there is a 'we' that, no matter how vainly, acts on its own volition: run faster, stretch out our arms further. This 'we' aspires, and there is sad beauty to that drama. For the child in 'The Future', however, there is no volition, no aspiration: the future is something that happens to him. He is not an actor, merely an extra in a crowd scene. Even the way in which time is portrayed here is revealing: for Fitzgerald's 'ceaselessly', Levine substitutes the brutal, and matter-of-fact, 'on and on' into a future that, according to Moradian's offhand observation on the way to the school outing, is no more future than the past.

One of the quietly unsettling aspects of industrial work is the possibility of exposure to contaminants: not just the carefully labelled HAZCHEM variety but the random leak of killer gas or dust, or some viscous blue fluid that clings, burning, to the skin and will not wash off; the hand plunged into a crate from the West Indies finding a tarantula or a rusted blade smeared with tetanus; that pallet-load of boxes, empty but for the spores or the fine vapour that, as they are loaded on to the fire, emit toxic gases and bio-toxins. Warehouse workers tell those stories the way steelmen tell the story of the boy on his first shift, working alongside his father at the furnaces, who loses his footing or is pushed by a bogey into the scorching heat, the story that ends with the father taking a pole and pushing the boy's body into the flames, so his mother will never see him 'like that'. I heard that story in Corby, when I started at the steelworks there; then I heard it in Pennsylvania (twice) and again, later, from a Japanese friend. Everybody swore, of course, that it was true.

The hand follows where the eye sees. Not every contaminant is a choking powder or a spill of burning tar; sometimes it arrives as a mystery, beguiling, even beautiful, 'like a jewel', as in Levine's 'Something Has Fallen':

You pick it up, not sure

if it is stone or wood
or some new plastic made

to replace them both.[7]

The poem opens out as if it were heading for sci-fi territory: something falls (from where? overhead, presumably, which means it comes from the sky), and, overcome by curiosity, somebody picks it up, opening the door, or Pandora's Box, to all kinds of possibility. Examined more closely, however, it turns out to be nothing but a shadow:

When you raise your sunglasses

to see exactly what you have
you see it is only a shadow

that has darkened your fingers,
a black ink or oil

Notice the anticipation in 'to see exactly what you have', the moment of hope the you of the poem permits himself that this might be something of value, whether financially or otherwise. It is 'only a shadow', however, a shadow that is immediately transformed into ink, or oil, and the contamination – in the form of a troubling memory – has begun:

and your hand suddenly smells
of classrooms when the rain

pounded the windows and you
shuddered thinking of the cold

and the walk back to an empty house.

That memory spreads and grows, colonising the mind the way the alien spores from the fallen spaceship take hold and rapidly colonise the victim's brain:

You smell all of your childhood,

the damp bed you struggled from
to dress in half-light and go out

into a world that never tired.

This line, this reference to a world 'that never tired', is the pivot
point, where the burdens of the working-class child suddenly
become the burdens of the worker – no accident, of course, for
as we have seen, the child's schooling is meant to prepare him
for the tireless world of work and disadvantage that he will have
to endure as an adult – and the memory shifts seamlessly into a
hand, 'thickened and fat', sliding from its rubber glove so the now
adult 'you' can take a smoke break

while the acid tanks that were

yours to clean went on bathing
the arteries of broken sinks.

A hardened veteran now, the man remembers his first impres-
sions of this workplace, the 'great hissing jugs' and the 'stories …
of flesh shredded to lace' that once frightened him, the physical
danger amplified by moral squalor –

Women spoke of men
who trapped them in corners

– before coming to rest in the everyday, almost banal contamina-
tions of grease, oil, paint, blood – his own blood, sometimes

sliding across

your nose and running over
your lips with that bright, certain

taste that was neither earth
or air.

Worst of all, however, 'there was air':

the darkest element of all,
falling all night

into the bruised river
you slept beside, falling

into the glass of water
you filled two times for breakfast

and the eyes you turned upward
to see what time it was.

The contamination that comes through the air usually comes unseen and cannot be protected against, for it is constant; and because it cannot be avoided, and because its poison is invisible to the naked eye, air is the greatest danger of all:

Air that stained everything
with its millions of small deaths,

that turned all five fingers
to grease or black ink or ashes.

As the poem ends with this echo of its opening, there is a final shift in perspective. From that initial mild anticipation, the desire to see 'exactly what you have' (and now, on reflection, is there not a cruel ambiguity in 'what you have' here?) slides into fatalism: in the final analysis, everything is, or could be, a contaminant; however, since every breath you take is poison, you might as well give up on any hope of coming through unharmed.

This sense of contamination belongs entirely to an unjust labour 'market', however. Were they to be treated more fairly, by which I mean, were they to be able to govern themselves, workers in what are currently low-paid jobs might see their work in a different light. In fact, reading poets like Philip Levine makes us realise that the great error we make as a society is to think that there is such a thing as demeaning work per se. Work can be dirty, it can be dangerous, it can be demanding – but even where it is all of these, it cannot be called demeaning where it is properly remunerated and respected. In fact, this lack of respect or care for the worker comes across again and again in Levine's work: while it is true that manual work can be boring, what is humiliating is the understanding that, in the great scheme of things, one's own flesh and blood are of considerably less value than the product being assembled or packed on the line. In 'Making It Work', for example, Levine opens with a ghostly, silent vision of:

> 3-foot blue canisters of nitro
> along a conveyor belt, slow fish
> speaking the language of silence.

The first thing we notice is that there is no verb to indicate the kind of movement (or stillness) of the gas canisters. They are not 'moving', or 'sliding' or 'gliding' or anything else, they are simply there, as if guided by some force or logic native to the factory in which they are produced, a factory that is described later, by an unknown commentator (presumably the speaker's work companion), in organic terms:

> 'These here are
> the veins of the place, stuff
> inside's the blood.'

In fact, everything here has an organic quality: the canisters are fish, the gas is blood, the asbestos gas lines are not only veins but are also 'as big around as the thick waist/ of an oak tree'. (The reader will also note, though it is never made explicit, that everything the speaker works with, not just the gas itself but the asbestos lines that he is 'patching', is toxic.)

There is one respite from boredom, alienation and danger, however. As the poem progresses, we see that the men are on the roof, and, even though they work in 'rain, heat, snow, sleet', there are moments of quiet and solitude, moments when the speaker can lift his head, or turn, and feel the 'spring winds up from Ohio' on his face. Notice here that the 'we' at the start of the poem is now an 'I', who, grateful for the least glimpse of a beyond, pauses:

> at the top of the ladder
> to take in the wide world reaching
> downriver and beyond. Sunlight
> dumped on standing and moving
> lines of freight cars, new fields
> of bright weeds blowing, scoured
> valleys, false mountains of coke
> and slag.

There is not much to go on here – the wind, sunlight, bright weeds, clouds – but anyone who has ever done factory work will recognise this moment; a glimpse of freedom, a sense of a wider perspective; when a very little can make a great deal of difference. Levine does everything to undermine the least trace of the picturesque in the scene – the sunlight is 'dumped' on the freight cars, the 'mountains' are actually slag heaps. Even the green element in the scene comes from weeds, and, as bright as they are, their transitory nature is revealed by the word 'blowing' followed so closely by 'scoured', so the reader cannot help but think of the verses from the 103rd Psalm: 'As for man, his days are as grass: as a flower of the field, so he flourisheth. For the wind passeth over it, and it is gone; and the place thereof shall know it no more.' Yet, even as carefully qualified as it is, this scene is a flake of manna in the working day, a breath, a respite.

However, the poem does not end here, and the last three lines draw the speaker's mind back, through the momentary vision of the land, to the real force that guides his days, the money that makes him, and the factory, work:

> At the ends of sight
> a rolling mass of clouds as dark
> as money brings the weather in.

No need to linger on the ambiguity of 'ends' here, but it is worth noting that, trumping the organic machinery of the factory below, the clouds are elemental, a 'rolling mass' as unstoppable, and as dark, as capital itself. For, where the organic and the lifelike 'work' according to a logic that either is or could be within human comprehension, the elemental does not. Money, like the weather, works according to its own laws and, because it is as impersonal as any other elemental force, it cannot be governed. Or can it? It is not money but the love of money that is the root of all evil, and those black clouds are only as dark as money that is loved more than human dignity, or for that matter, humane safety and environmental regulations. Take away the greed, and we begin to take away the darkness, paving the way for a world in which no work, however dirty, dangerous or demanding, is necessarily demeaning.

A TOWERING STRANGENESS

A chaffinch flicked from an ash and next thing
I found myself driving the stranger

through my own country, adept
at dialect, reciting my pride
in all that I knew, that began to make strange
at the same recitation.[1]

Seamus Heaney

I ARRIVE AT THE Seamus Heaney HomePlace, in Bellaghy, South Derry, on a day that is, alternately, bright and sunny for half an hour at a time then suddenly fast and fierce in the downpipes and gutters, fat raindrops bouncing off the flags in the courtyard, followed by brief spells of glance and glitter in the sudden shock of quiet when it all stops, only to start again, faster and fiercer than ever, pooling in the grass and darkening the trees in the back hedge. It all feels appropriate, almost staged, the place living up to its history, earthy and lush and slightly wild, the air shot with something akin to ozone, only for the sun to emerge again, clear and pale along the road that leads up from here to the churchyard of St Mary's, where the man himself is buried under a stone that reads: 'Walk on air against your better judgement' (the line is drawn from his Nobel acceptance speech of 1995).

I have been bothered by the name – HomePlace – since I started out from the location that, despite some reservations, both personal and political, I do my best to think of as home. This is not a *birth*-place (that house is now a private dwelling), nor is it the particular locus of any of Heaney's most familiar poems; indeed, it is a new building, elegant, well designed and, in its use of local materials and architectural discretion, nicely in keeping with the immediate environment. True, it sits at the heart of Heaney country, and members of the Heaney family still farm close by; it can even be considered something of a triumph for political progress, in that it is built on the site of the old RUC headquarters, which was placed here (according to one local I spoke to) so that the police could spy on the comings and goings of Catholics residents affiliated with the church up the hill. From here it is an easy matter to explore the relics of Heaney's youth: the family home at Mossbawn, the wetlands around Lough Beg (a haven for snipe, herons, redshank, curlew and lapwing), Barney Devlin's forge on the Hillhead Road, a former schoolhouse that Heaney would transform imaginatively into a 'door into the dark', peering into the dim interior to witness the alchemy that went on there like a child at the door of a pagan temple:

> The anvil must be somewhere in the centre,
> Horned as a unicorn, at one end and square,
> Set there immoveable: an altar.[2]

A little further out lies the Toome Road, revealed in 1979's *Field Work* as the place where the poet first encountered the armoured cars of the British Army:

> In convoy, warbling along on powerful tyres,
> All camouflaged with broken alder branches.

It is an invading force that moves him, first to anger –

> How long were they approaching down my roads
> As if they owned them? The whole country was sleeping

– and then, almost involuntarily, to imagine a defence of the invaded territory, using all he can muster, by identifying the quotidian paraphernalia and the daily tasks that fall to those who rightfully inhabit such a place:

> I had rights of way, fields, cattle in my keeping,
> Tractors hitched to buckrakes in open sheds,
> Silos, chill gates, wet slates, the greens and reds
> Of outhouse roofs.*

Finally, he invokes mythology – in the figure of the Greek *omphalos* (of which more below) – as an imaginative if not practical defence against these invading 'charioteers':

> O charioteers, above your dormant guns,
> It stands here still, stands vibrant as you pass,
> The invisible, untoppled omphalos.

Here we see, in the ambiguity of the word 'pass', an assertion, on behalf of the occupied citizenry ('sowers of seed, erectors of headstones'), of the long-term power of the home-place against those who, even if their vehicles warble as they move into position, and even if they try to pass for local with their 'broken alder branches', have no place here, since they not only do not see but cannot even sense the presence of the *omphalos* that makes this location on the map more than a mere space that they can enter by force. Or rather: enter, they may, but they have no rights of way, no roles, no work to do and no memories to guide them; they are for ever strange, mere ciphers, universal soldiers who, like the charioteers of earlier invading armies, while they are only obeying orders, have no real purpose in this land.

There can be few more beautiful or moving invocations of such a home-place – a place in which the mind and body are *attuned*

---

*The image of the buckrake here is perfect: an implement used in hay harvesting, it has long, sharp tines that, at a push, might serve as a crude defensive weapon.

to the environment – than that offered by Seamus Heaney in his Nobel address:

> It was an intimate, physical, creaturely existence in which the night sounds of the horse in the stable beyond one bedroom wall mingled with the sounds of adult conversation from the kitchen beyond the other. We took in everything that was going on, of course – rain in the trees, mice on the ceiling, a steam train rumbling along the railway line one field back from the house – but we took it in as if we were in the doze of hibernation. Ahistorical, pre-sexual, in suspension between the archaic and the modern, we were as susceptible and impressionable as the drinking water that stood in a bucket in our scullery: every time a passing train made the earth shake, the surface of that water used to ripple delicately, concentrically, and in utter silence.

Here the characteristics of home are not property-related, nor are they specifically territorial; what matters is attunement, attentiveness, susceptibility. For many of us, born in the more geographically mobile decades since Heaney was a child at Mossbawn, and so deprived of a fixed abode where memory may find a legitimate and permanent shelter, such a vision of home-place is more than beguiling. Yet it is also misleading, if we take its promises purely at face value. Like any museum, the Heaney HomePlace is a source of inspiration and fond recollections of much-loved poems;* but the truth is that to go to Bellaghy in search of Seamus Heaney is to embark on a pleasant but elusive wild goose chase, in pursuit not just of the man himself but also of his final abode. This is not to say that what the HomePlace offers is an absence; on the contrary, the *poet* Heaney is everywhere – in photographs, in recordings, in the fond memories of those who knew him and in the pride this

---

* The word 'museum' is derived from the ancient Greek term, meaning 'shrine of the Muses', or more generally, a place for the study of the arts. It seems only fair to add that it is not a place where art works originate but where they are contemplated and treasured, when the heat of making is over.

community takes in having given the world a Nobel Laureate. And yet, at the same time, the man is nowhere at all. It's like walking into a house an hour after the previous occupant has moved out: you sense him still, you can almost hear him moving about in the next room, but the truth is that he is long gone. As Auden said of Yeats, he has become his admirers; it is not a man that lives here now, it is the poetry. Still, what that poetry says about this place, in particular, makes of Mossbawn and its surrounds a sacred site, in the fullest, if not in the conventionally religious, sense. By being here, and giving voice to the experience of this patch of ground, in all its nuance, as well as in all its uncertainties, Heaney created a holy ground, a sense of *omphalos*, that reveals, even to us, the 'inconstant ones', who see ourselves as rootless and shifting, not only the essence of home but also its eternal contradictions.

Omphalos: the word in Greek means 'navel', and the original *omphalos* was the stone at Delphi, considered by the Ancients to be the centre of the world, and so of the cosmos. Heaney returns to the idea of Mossbawn itself as such a central point in several works in different genres; here, for example, in a short prose memoir, he remembers how his child self would repeat the word, the way we repeat magical spells and incantations:

> I would begin with the Greek word, *omphalos*, meaning the centre of the world, and repeat it, *omphalos, omphalos, omphalos*, until its blunt and falling music became the music of somebody pumping water at the pump outside our back door.

This is a marvellous stroke, wedding high Classical mythology to the most commonplace circumstance,* and in so doing, re-sacralising, in the ubiquitous water pump, one object of quotidian experience. The idea is most fully realised, however, in the poem 'Sunlight' (dedicated to the poet's mother), in which that sense of a centre is given an extraordinary gravity:

---

*And, like Randall Jarrell's 'Well Water', to a 'dailiness of life' that depends on the extraction of water, the principal element required for the continuation of life.

There was a sunlit absence.
The helmeted pump in the yard
heated its iron,
water honeyed

in the slung bucket
and the sun stood
like a griddle cooling
against the wall

of each long afternoon.[3]

From this gravitational centre, from this given *place*, the child's imagination is free to venture out into a kind of weightless and conditional agora – *space* – where he is able to participate in a range of adventures, which might be defined, roughly, as acquisition (or appropriation, or colonisation), on the one hand, and, on the other, as exploration (appreciation, under-standing*). The difference between these two activities – the one more or less reprehensible, the other capable of leading to a state in which the poet becomes, in Heaney's words 'one of the venerators' – lies at the moral heart of poetry, certainly from the Romantics on. The energy of the child, moving out from the home-place, can manifest itself as a kind of petty imperialism, as Wordsworth knew all too well, when he describes his boy-self's fury of acquisition in 'Nutting':

> Then up I rose,
> And dragged to earth both branch and bough, with crash
> And merciless ravage: and the shady nook
> Of hazels, and the green and mossy bower,

---

* See the Online Etymology Dictionary: Old English *understandan*, 'comprehend, grasp the idea of', probably literally 'stand in the midst of', from *under* + *standan* 'to stand' (see 'stand' (v.)). If this is the meaning, the 'under' is not the usual word meaning 'beneath', but from Old English *under*, 'between, among, before, in the presence of' (the source also of Sanskrit *antar* 'among, between', Latin *inter*, 'between, among', Greek *entera* 'intestines'; see 'inter-').

Deformed and sullied, patiently gave up
Their quiet being: and, unless I now
Confound my present feelings with the past;
Ere from the mutilated bower I turned
Exulting, rich beyond the wealth of kings,
I felt a sense of pain when I beheld
The silent trees, and saw the intruding sky.

It need not be so, however. For the lucky child whose *omphalos* is, as it were, sufficient in its gravity, exploration can be a noble pleasure – and, importantly, what such a child-adventurer brings back from 'abroad' helps to strengthen the home-place. Yet what this new explorer also learns is that threat (and terror) are naturally part and parcel of the cycle of being and becoming, elements of the overall experience that, as we confront them, help to define us in finer detail, and so help us grow. Gradually the child comes to appreciate that the question of home-building, of how far one can safely venture from the *omphalos*, is for ever twofold: there is the societal issue around what constitutes an inhabitable political territory, on the one hand, and the existential, or ecological, problem of dwelling within the natural order, on the other. As a writer working out of 'The Troubles', but also keenly aware of the complexities of 'Nature', Heaney is, arguably, the arch-poet of this sense of disciplined reverence and wonder, a 'venerator' (see below) who, more than any, excavates a poetry of home from personal memory, history and native myth, even as he is engaged in an equally determined process of 'making strange'. But then, these two activities are not as contrary as they might at first appear; in fact, they might even be mutually dependent, more *yin* and *yang* complementarities than opposites.

In Heaney's work overall, the concept of 'making strange' can mean different things, depending on context. In Hiberno-English, the word 'strange' can mean 'new' (as in the expression 'Anything strange?' meaning, 'What's new?'), while the phrase 'to make strange' can be used to signify coming across as distant or unfriendly. (For example, a mother might shrug off her child's wariness about a new acquaintance by saying that he or she is 'just making strange'.) In an interview with James Campbell concerning the composition of the poem 'Making Strange' (from 1984's *Station Island*), Heaney tells how, on a visit home with the poet Louis Simpson, the two men

> stopped at a public house about 150 yards from where I grew up. We were standing on the street at the pub and my father came up – 'unshorn and bewildered/ in the tubs of his welling-tons' – and in a sense I was almost introducing him as subject matter … Or I could see that Simpson would see him as that.

From such instances it is clear that, at times, making strange can occur as the recognition of what is strange, sometimes uncomfortably so, in one's surroundings, while at others it becomes an imaginative act on the part of the poet, through the 'making new' – and so, potentially, the re-enchantment – of familiar sights and happenings.*

In the title poem from his first collection, *The Death of a Naturalist* (1966), Heaney explores all the ramifications of this strangeness. From the first, he locates the potentially disturbing, alien environmental event – the festering flax dam† – at the centre of the familiar world:

> All year the flax-dam festered in the heart
> Of the townland; green and heavy headed

---

* See Shelley's *A Defence of Poetry*: 'Poetry lifts the veil from the hidden beauty of the world, and makes familiar objects be as if they were not familiar; it reproduces all that it represents, and the impersonations clothed in its Elysian light stand thenceforward in the minds of those who have once contemplated them, as memorials of that gentle and exalted content which extends itself over all thoughts and actions with which it coexists.'

† Not so much dams as ponds, flax-dams were employed after the harvest of the flax to 'ret' the flax bundles, thus separating out the fibres that were to be used in linen manufacture.

Flax had rotted there, weighted down by huge sods.
Daily it sweltered in the punishing sun.[4]

The child knows this flax-dam 'all year', he has visited at various seasons to see 'dragonflies, spotted butterflies' and 'the warm thick slobber/ Of frogspawn that grew like clotted water/ In the shade of the banks'. In the springtime he has filled:

> jampotfuls of the jellied
> Specks to range on window sills at home,
> On shelves at school, and wait and watch until
> The fattening dots burst, into nimble
> Swimming tadpoles.

Notice the use of the word 'fattening' here, a term that cannot help but connote satisfaction in a farming community, where the growth of livestock (the fattening of lambs and beef calves, say) is a principal source of wealth. Meanwhile, the process by which these tadpoles have come into being is explained, in the kindest possible terms, by a teacher who adds a detail or two of folk wisdom to her lesson:

> Miss Walls would tell us how
> The daddy frog was called a bullfrog
> And how he croaked and how the mammy frog
> Laid hundreds of little eggs and this was
> Frogspawn. You could tell the weather by frogs too
> For they were yellow in the sun and brown
> In rain.

Up until this point the reader might be forgiven for thinking that Heaney has made an error in titling the piece: for, here, in the first half of the poem, what we are witnessing is the birth of a young naturalist, guided by a kindly schoolmistress who introduces him to the natural world in language and imagery appropriate to his age: 'daddy' and 'mammy' frogs, 'hundreds of little eggs' to make sense of and give a purpose to, all that 'warm thick slobber'. The boy brings back samples for the nature table, samples that fatten nicely and then burst individually – and in a nicely satisfying way – into nimble, discrete tadpoles. There is a sense of evolution here, from swampy mass to recognisable life forms, and the resultant order lends itself to observation and tax-onomising. Soon, however, this kindly world is disrupted by the frantic, even violent displays of the mating season, a time when the day is hot and the fields are 'rank/ With cowdung'. As the 'angry' frogs invade the flax-dam, the young naturalist has his first taste of fear – a fear born of exposure to wild appetite and the undercurrent of irrationality in the urge to life:

> I ducked through hedges
> To a coarse croaking that I had not heard
> Before. The air was thick with a bass chorus.
> Right down the dam gross bellied frogs were cocked
> On sods; their loose necks pulsed like sails. Some hopped:
> The slap and plop were obscene threats. Some sat
> Poised like mud grenades, their blunt heads farting.

Here the language is ribald and scatological ('gross bellied', 'cocked', 'farting'), the imagery suggestive of an unaccountable fleshliness ('their loose necks pulsed like sails'), but we have to remember that this language, unlike the images the child is wit-nessing, comes not from a strange, exterior reality but from his own, buried vocabulary. In the classroom he and Miss Walls may trade in terms like 'daddy' and 'mammy', but we feel at this moment of revelation that the boy has always suspected there is more to life than is accounted for in his teacher's sanitised vision, and, though he is frightened and shocked by what he witnesses, there is a relish in the language that he dredges up from his darker self to acknowledge that rude life, just as there is a dark relish to the idea of vengeance in the closing lines:

> I sickened, turned, and ran. The great slime kings
> Were gathered there for vengeance and I knew
> That if I dipped my hand the spawn would clutch it.

Those old stories about frogspawn that comes to life and clutches at the child who carelessly dabbles his hand in the ripe water, like the tales of Jenny Greenteeth or Iron Hans, those monstrous beings who form out of the duckweed on a woodland pond and drag unwary passers-by into the depths, are undoubtedly frightening to the child listening, but they are also heard, and retold, with considerable élan by the very children they are intended to caution.

At the same time, such experiences could be seen as transition points at which the child graduates from the innocence of the classroom naturalist, with his jam jars and bowdlerising language, to the experience of the one who knows nature well enough to recognise its darker side. For this child to evolve into what Heaney will later identify as a 'venerator', he has to understand his world in its full complexity – and that includes an irrationality that is bound to make him uneasy, testing his most fundamental convictions, first about the nature of things and then, gradually, as he moves further into the public space, his ideas of justice and human decency. 'Reverence toward the world can come with the belief that it is God-bearing', says Tim Lilburn.

> The wheatgrass stem bears the charge of the sacred. Here is sufficient impetus for a careful, courteous attentiveness to things that might be expected to end in an awful silence, the eye and feeling swallowed by root system, leaf shape, feather colour. But often some contemplative writers […] appear to pull away from such a gaze with troubling quickness, their inspection transmogrifying into rumination on essences or the web of being or bolting into the language of piety and praise. Their looking seems not wild and helpless enough, seems too nicely contained in understanding; it travels into the world only far enough to grasp the presence it anticipates; it appears to lack the terror of ecstasy. If you look hard enough at the world, past a region of comprehension surrounding things, you enter a vast unusualness that defeats you. You do not arrive at a name or a home. Look at a meadow long enough and your bearings

vanish. The world seen deeply eludes all names; it is not like anything; it is not the sign of something else. It is itself. It is a towering strangeness.[5]

For Heaney, this 'towering strangeness' has to be acknowledged, wherever it appears. At the same time, however, he sees that strangeness in the public sphere, a realm that by rights should be governed by reason, humanity and just compromise. This communal strangeness manifests itself principally in a tribal impulse that this poet, at least, sees on all sides of the conflict he witnesses in Northern Ireland, and, just as he is prepared to train a look that is 'wild and helpless enough' on the festering pit of the flax-dam, so he is also prepared to confront the political realm without benefit of what Lilburn reminds his reader is '*your* names for things and *your* sense of centrality'.

In September 1994 Heaney revisited Tollund in Denmark, the imaginative locus of his fourth collection of poems, *Wintering Out* (1972). With the glimmer of an end to 'The Troubles' in view after the Provisional IRA's cessation of violence over the summer and Albert Reynolds's recent meeting with Gerry Adams and John Hume in Dublin, the conclusion of the poem Heaney wrote that same month (the date is carefully noted) reflects a mood of growing hope:

>   it was user-friendly outback
> Where we stood footloose, at home beyond the tribe,
>
> More scouts than strangers, ghosts who'd walked abroad
> Unfazed by light, to make a new beginning
> And make a go of it, alive and sinning,
> Ourselves again, free-willed again, not bad.[6]

Until that point, being 'at home beyond the tribe' seemed possible only at the individual level, a matter of personal integrity that, for all its innate decency, was lonely, uncertain and nurtured mostly by friendship, books and the non-human world. What it lacked was a sense of community: integrity, at that point, meant standing outside, being one of the uncommitted.

In fact, ten years earlier, in *Station Island*, Heaney, who had become acutely aware of Yeats's dictum that 'the best lack all conviction, while the worst/ Are full of passionate intensity', had conveyed the position of the non-combatant perfectly in 'Sandstone Keepsake', where the poet finds himself under surveillance during a walk at Inishowen:

> Anyhow, there I was with the wet red stone
> in my hand, staring across at the watch-towers
> from my free state of image and allusion,
> swooped on, then dropped by trained binoculars:
>
> a silhouette not worth bothering about,
> out for the evening in scarf and waders
> and not about to set times wrong or right,
> stooping along, one of the venerators.[7]

It is interesting how Heaney portrays himself as a near-childlike figure here (A. A. Milne's Christopher Robin, that champion of 'just going along, listening to all the things you can't hear', comes to mind), and there is more than a hint of self-deprecation in the irony of 'my free state of image and allusion' (not to mention the wryness of 'not worth bothering about'). But the achievement of remaining 'one of the venerators' is significant. It was a position that many shared in the mid-1980s, not because of any single or local issue but because 'the worst' appeared to be firmly in the ascendant in every area of public life, from civil strife to the new spirit of deregulation initiated during the Reagan–Thatcher era, a loosening of government control that, while it was presented as a boon to individual entrepreneurs, actually heralded a collapse in political responsibility that would affect the majority of people around the world very badly for decades to come.

For some, faced with this unforeseen rise of a dog-eat-dog, no-such-thing-as-society mind-set, the only honourable path that

remained seemed to be what Heaney calls, later in that same collection, a 'migrant solitude'. Everywhere the times were out of
joint, and the question of what was to be done – politically, culturally, environmentally – grew ever more urgent. In such circumstances many felt that poetry was nothing more than an effete
gesture of right-mindedness, or a mere entertainment, like some
intellectual puzzle or game of literary trivia. Like many others
on 'both sides' of the divide, Heaney himself had long been troubled by the sense of standing helplessly in the midst of dishonour-
able competing factions, unable to align himself with either, as he
points out in a 1997 interview with Henri Cole in the *Paris Review*:

> SH: I see the Bog Poems [as] a kind of holding action. They
> were indeed a bit like the line drawn in the sand. Not quite an
> equivalent for what was happening, more an attempt to rhyme
> the contemporary with the archaic. 'The Tollund Man,' for
> example, is the first of the Bog Poems I wrote. Essentially, it is
> a prayer that the bodies of people killed in various actions and
> atrocities in modern Ireland, in the teens and twenties of the
> century as well as in the more recent past, a prayer that some-
> thing would come of them, some kind of new peace or resolu-
> tion. In the understanding of his Iron Age contemporaries, the
> sacrificed body of Tollund Man germinated into spring, so the
> poem wants a similar flowering to come from the violence in
> the present. Of course it recognizes that this probably won't
> happen, but the middle section of the poem is still a prayer that
> it should. The Bog Poems were defenses against the encroach-
> ment of the times, I suppose. But there was always a real per-
> sonal involvement – in a poem like 'Punishment,' for example.

> HC: In what respect?

> SH: It's a poem about standing by as the IRA tar and feather
> these young women in Ulster. But it's also about standing by as
> the British torture people in barracks and interrogation centers
> in Belfast. About standing between those two forms of affront.
> So there's that element of self-accusation, which makes the

poem personal in a fairly acute way. Its concerns are immediate and contemporary, but for some reason I couldn't bring army barracks or police barracks or Bogside street life into the language and topography of the poem. I found it more convincing to write about the bodies in the bog and the vision of Iron Age punishment. Pressure seemed to drain away from the writing if I shifted my focus from those images.

HC: So often your poems are about the disenfranchised (as in a poem like 'Servant Boy') or the victimized (as in 'Punishment') – do you feel yourself to be among them as an Irish Catholic coming from a country with tanks, posted soldiers and other degradations?

SH: I don't think consciously in that way. I would hate to think of the poems as a parade of victim entitlement. Something that irks me about a lot of contemporary writing is the swank of deprivation. One of the poets who meant most to me and whom I now believe I have always underrated as an influence is Wilfred Owen. The influence wasn't quite at the level of style, more in the understanding of what a poet ought to be doing. I think Owen's assault upon the righteousness that causes greed in people, and his general tilting of poetry's sympathies towards the underground man, I think all that had an effect upon my notion of what poetry's place in the world should be. At any rate, in the early 1970s I did surely identify with the Catholic minority. A poem like 'The Ministry of Fear' is a very deliberate treatment of the subject of minoritydom. An attempt to encompass that element of civic reality. It's written in blank verse; there's not much sport between the words of it.

'The Ministry of Fear' (from the 1975 collection, *North*) is about language: about how we identify others by their speech, by idiom, by the proper nouns they use, the names they bear, their dialect:

Those hobnailed boots from beyond the mountain
Were walking, by God, all over the fine

Lawns of elocution. Have our accents
Changed? 'Catholics, in general, don't speak
As well as students from the Protestant schools.'
Remember that stuff? Inferiority
Complexes, stuff that dreams were made on.
'What's your name, Heaney?'*

Then, later, during an encounter at a checkpoint, he describes this chilling exchange:

And heading back for home, the summer's
Freedom dwindling night by night, the air
All moonlight and a scent of hay, policemen
Swung their crimson flashlamps, crowding round
The car like black cattle, snuffing and pointing
The muzzle of a Sten gun in my eye:
'What's your name, driver?'
'Seamus ...'
Seamus?

Another poem that attempts to encompass the bounds of civic reality is 'Servant Boy', inspired by the stories told by an elderly neighbour:

He is wintering out
the back-end of a bad year,
swinging a hurricane-lamp
through some outhouse;
a jobber among shadows.[8]

This is Frost's hired man seen from the other side of the fence. Among the shadows he is little more than a shadow himself, just

---

* The poem's title refers to Graham Greene's novel of the same name, published in 1943, while Greene was working for MI6. The book concerns a Nazi spy ring who use personal information about their targets to compel their obedience.

a 'jobber' who goes from work fair to work fair hiring himself out:

> Old work-whore, slave-
> blood, who stepped fair-hills
> under each bidder's eye.

And yet he is, nevertheless, admirable in his endurance –

> and kept your patience
> and your counsel

– as he traipses back and forth from the hayrack to the stable, feeding the animals:

> Your trail
> broken from haggard to stable,
> a straggle of fodder
> stiffened on snow

– his other job being to gather eggs from the henhouse and deliver them warm to his master's house (but to the back door, of course – that is, to the servants' entrance). Note the use of 'haggard' here, in its dialect meaning of 'hay or feed rack', but suggesting, in a poem otherwise in plain English, its more usual meaning in that language, 'careworn, tired, drained'.*

That the poem ends with a single image of warmth, a warmth that the 'boy' must yield to the 'little barons' who own and control his land, is particularly poignant:

> comes first-footing
> the back doors of the little
> barons: resentful
> and impenitent,

---

* Would it be going too far to add the other known meaning, in falconry: i.e., a hawk trapped in its adult plumage that, having known flight (as opposed to a bird taken from the nest, known as a 'pasager'), could be said to resent its restrictions more keenly?

carrying the warm eggs.

Heaney discusses this poem, and his memories of how his own family 'got along' fairly well with their Protestant neighbours, in *Stepping Stones,* but he also notes how that peace was kept through a process of accommodation to the dominant group, a process of concealing one's resentment of the

> overall shape of things because you also knew that the Orange arches erected in the villages and at various crossroads were what the Romans might have recognized as a form of *jugum* or yoke, and when you went under the arches you went *sub jugum,* you were being subjugated, being taught who was boss, being reminded that the old slogan, 'a Protestant parliament for a Protestant people', now had real constitutional force.[9]

And, as history was soon to reveal, when the resentment boiled to the surface, and the minority began to show signs of resistance, the 'little barons' were quick to redraw and fortify old tribal lines.

It would be invaluable if we could work out the process by which a political impulse – for shared community, for equal rights, for justice – descends into a tribal imperative; such an analysis might begin, however, with these remarks of Che Guevara's, in *Socialism and Man in Cuba:*

> At the risk of seeming ridiculous, let me say that the true revolutionary is guided by great feelings of love. It is impossible to think of a genuine revolutionary lacking this quality.
>
> Perhaps it is one of the great dramas of the leader that he or she must combine a passionate spirit with a cold intelligence and make painful decisions without flinching. Our vanguard revolutionaries must idealize this love of the people, of the most sacred causes, and make it one and indivisible. They cannot descend, with small doses of daily affection, to the level where ordinary people put their love into practice.

This is not ridiculous at all. On the contrary, what Guevara is talking about here is, partly, what Keats means when he talks about seeing the subject *as* subject, or what Levinas means when he talks about the face of the Other as opening 'the primordial discourse whose first word is obligation'; as has been noted, it is also apparent in what Lois Shepherd has called 'radical responsibility'. In Heaney's poetic lexicon, this variety of responsible discourse arises in what he called 'through-otherness'.

Yet, 'self-accusations' aside, there are real merits in what Heaney's poetry refuses to do, not just in steering clear of 'victim entitlement' but also in what it will not aid and abet, as when the poet, returning from New York to Belfast, is confronted on the train by his old adversary, the man of violent action, in 'The Flight Path', from 1996:

> So he enters and sits down
> Opposite and goes for me head on.
> 'When, for fuck's sake, are you going to write
> Something for us?' 'If I do write something,
> Whatever it is, I'll be writing for myself.'
> And that was that. Or words to that effect.[10]

A decade or so later, in the series of conversations with O'Driscoll collected in *Stepping Stones*, Heaney said, when asked to expand on the meeting that was the basis for this poem:

> The account of what went on in the train is as it happened, yes. I make the speaker a bit more aggressive than he was at the time, but the presumption of entitlement on his part, which was the main and amazing aspect of that meeting, is rendered faithfully.
>
> It was all done pretty discreetly, actually. My interlocutor was the Sinn Féin spokesman, Danny Morrison, whom I didn't particularly know at the time. He came down from his place in the carriage and sat into the seat in front of me for maybe eight or 10 minutes … I didn't feel menaced. It was a straightforward face-to-face test of will or steadiness.
>
> I simply rebelled at being commanded. If anybody was going to pull rank, it wasn't going to be a party spokesman.

This was in pre-hunger-strike times, during the 'dirty protest' by Republican prisoners in the H-Blocks. The whole business was weighing on me greatly already and I had toyed with the idea of dedicating the Ugolino translation [his version of an episode in Dante's *Inferno*] to the prisoners. But our friend's intervention put paid to any such gesture. After that, I wouldn't give and wasn't so much free to refuse as unfree to accept.

This is a dilemma Heaney also works through carefully in 'Weighing In', where he interrogates the efficacy (through the figure of the mocked and crucified Jesus) of 'the power/ Of power not exercised, of hope inferred// By the powerless forever'. Yet although it may be easy, in moral terms at least, to reject a gunman's invitation to 'drive a van/ Carefully in to the next customs post', it is also the case that, in a world where the centre no longer holds, the temptation to 'Prophesy, give scandal, cast the stone' becomes harder to resist. Moreover, it is all too easy for such resistance to slide into a passive *entente* with the powers-that-be, especially if one has a comfortable position in life. On the other hand, the dramatisation of that inner struggle – and of the venerator's shambling along in scarf and waders, grotesque and useless in a world that demands that something be done – can also be a form of action. Such thought experimentation adds to the political weather in ways that allow others to envisage their struggle differently, and perhaps to find more imaginative forms of action than stone-throwing and car bombs. To refuse both of the proffered options – on the one hand, a be-glamoured alliance with the gunman, and, on the other, the blithe collaboration of the sheltered – is at least to set the stage for other possibilities, for words and actions that make a tangible difference in the struggle for justice.

Yet there is still more to it than that. By 'making strange' the things we take for granted (that is, the entirety of quotidian life, from the political to the commonplaces of 'the dailiness of life'), Heaney's poetry transforms everyday existence to such an extent that we recognise that it is the minute detail of the ordinary lives that we all live, day to day, that is most meaningful. What endures, in spite of the tanks and guns and tribal rhetoric, are the 'rights of way', 'wet slates, the greens and reds/ Of outhouse roofs'. Such a revelation is a socio-political force in its own right, because it contributes to a rejection of the glamorised and the illusory, of tribal righteousness and all the varieties of engineered consensus. To see the quotidian in its true light helps us to resist the synthetic experiences of a social system that perpetuates inequality, conflict and poverty. Admittedly, one poem is only a drop in the moral ocean, but a lifetime's work, especially an *oeuvre* that has become as much a part of the cultural fabric as Heaney's, becomes something more like a wave. To anyone reading Heaney the risible contention that poetry is politically ineffective is like saying that raising a child or planting a tree is a waste of time. It means nothing, because it gets the timescale wrong, and it ignores the law of unexpected consequences.

When Seamus Heaney died, in August 2013, he famously sent a text message to his wife, Marie, that said simply, *'Noli timere'* ('Do not be afraid'). Some weeks earlier, he had written 'In Time', a short but highly affecting addition to a lyrical tradition whose genus type is Juan Ramón Jiménez's 'El viaje definitivo', as noted above. In Heaney's case, the subject is a small child, who will continue to grow and develop after the poet is gone:

> Energy, balance, outbreak:
> Listening to Bach
> I saw you years from now
> (More years than I'll be allowed)
> Your toddler wobbles gone,
> A sure and grown woman.[11]

It is a beautiful and touching piece, but there is more to it than is obvious at first sight. The opening line, with its references to energy, balance and outbreak, expresses the basic ground of a philosophical tradition as old as Daoism, in which the *yin* and *yang* complementarities constantly seek to balance each other until a new shift, a new 'outbreak', renews the cycle once more; or, in European terms, it is comparable with the original vision of the dialectic, in which one energy brings into being its complement and they temporarily balance one another, before a new balancing act arises out of constant flux. This idea is basic to all our thinking about change, mortality and growth, but it is also fundamental to our understanding of how art works, an underlying current in works as diverse as *The Tempest* and a Mahler symphony. Energy, balance, outbreak: here is the endless pursuit of an order that is never altogether achieved (if it were, the result would be entropy). It is characteristic of Heaney's economy that he suggests this with what seems, in the context of the poem's subject matter, not much more than an aside. It is also a comfort – not an easy or sentimental matter, but something hard won in the face of mortality, the ultimate strangeness that is nevertheless, as the Spanish poets knew, the way in which we share the world with others.

THE POETS IN GHANA

I drive the interstate,
watch faces come and go on either
side. I am free to be sung to;
I am free to sing. This woman
can cross any line.[1]

Joy Harjo

OCTOBER 2016. IT WAS autumn three days ago, when I left Scotland, a geographical entity that, for reasons of memory and certain trace elements in the blood, remains my home-place, unelected and changed beyond recognition but still discernibly alive with the energy of the old gods for those of us who persist in the sentiment that, in spite of everything, we are more Pict or Celt than Christian or Brexiteer. As a Briton, I have become a veteran of seasonal change, attuned to every nuance of the national weather, not only to the rare beauty of a hot summer's day but also to the shifting rhythms of rain and new snowfall, laid down over decades like barcodes in my arthritic bones.

Today, however, I sit in the tropical heat of Singapore; or rather, I sit in air-conditioned comfort with the tropics at first hand for, on the far side of a single pane of glass in this third-floor office, a vast rain tree stands covered in profuse pink-and-white blossoms. This office is not mine (which is on the floor above); it belongs to the poet Kim Cheng Boey, my host for a month-long residency at

440

Nanyang Technological University. This is our first meeting, face to face, but we have corresponded off and on for some years; now, I am intrigued to meet a poet whose work I admire and, while the official purpose of this meeting is to familiarise me with the university's *modus operandi*, we have already catalogued a shared passion for jazz and a more than usual admiration for the work of William Matthews. It isn't autumn here (I assume it never is), but I feel just right with the world in a home-from-home kind of way.

Kim Cheng Boey was born in Singapore in 1965, but spent many years in Australia – a move that has had a direct impact on his writing. 'Displacement has always been there in my work,' he told the poet Desmond Kon in 2010, and he continued:

> The feeling of not-being-at-home. The quarrel with the self and where one is. In a sense, displacement is what makes writing possible and necessary. Moving from one place to another, adopting different positions of seeing and being. In hindsight, the move to Sydney was an inevitable step. It was like many other things I have done, a leap into the dark, a throw of the dice, but I couldn't bear to see the way the places I loved in Singapore disappear, the thoughtlessness, the carelessness with which the country discards its past.

This is not an uncommon sentiment in our age, especially among poets. When I think of Philip Larkin, for example, it is the writer of 'Going, Going' who comes to mind, watching helplessly as 'a cast of crooks and tarts' gradually dismantle the 'the meadows, the lanes, / The guildhalls, the carved choirs' that he loves, not so much from malice as from lack of thought and a seemingly inevitable avarice:

> Most things are never meant.
> This won't be, most likely; but greeds
> And garbage are too thick-strewn
> To be swept up now, or invent
> Excuses that make them all needs.
> I just think it will happen, soon.[2]

In Boey's work, however, the contained grief for what has been lost of the cityscape and values of his early years is matched by the sense of a poet going his own way, teasing out the elements of a modern *via negativa* from remembered moments, a particular set of cultural touchstones (the Tang Dynasty poets, certain recent masters, such as Mark Strand or William Matthews, jazz music) and a lived engagement with the spiritual traditions of Zen, Thomas Merton and Kierkegaard. 'We write because we don't know the answers', he says. 'And to paraphrase Rilke again, it is sometimes sufficient to be able to frame the right questions.' Framing those questions demands discipline and a certain engagement with solitude, which sets Boey apart, somewhat, from so many of his contemporaries, with their newly acquired skills in social media, networking and self-promotion:

> I have never been part of, active or visible in literary circles. When my [1989 collection] *Somewhere-Bound* came out, I turned down a few requests for interviews. At that time, poetry and spirituality were inextricable for me. I had to protect my solitude, and practise in poetry the self-renunciation that I admired in Hopkins, Merton.

Perhaps it is this independence of spirit that allows Boey to carry out such detailed explorations of his and his city's past without playing the nostalgia card. As he recalls and commemorates the Singapore of his youth ('Change Alley, the old Raffles Place, the unrenovated Chinatown'), what emerges is a preoccupation with some universal meaning of change and loss and the slow process by which, after years of distance, we come to terms with those we loved and those who hurt us in our early years. There is often an elegiac tone to his work, but it is not change, per se, that he opposes – only the thoughtlessness and the pointless waste, as beloved places and traditions disappear. Occasionally reading his work, we may be minded of the letter T. S. Eliot, Dorothy Sayers, Max Beerbohm and others sent to *The Times* in July 1941, in response to the loss of so many of the city's churches during the recent bombing: 'we have been improvident trustees of a beauty that we judged imperishable, it had been so long with us. But there is beauty still, and still unprotected.' What we find in Boey's work is a concern for what is being lost, not because it is somehow *his* (a native place, a locus of memory, a physical extension of the self) but because it is worth keeping for its own sake.

In the poem 'Clear Brightness' he summons up a long-ago memory of the Qingming, or Tomb Sweeping ceremony, when Chinese families come together to sweep the graves of their ancestors and offer them gifts of wine and sweetmeats.* It is a day of contemplation and commemoration, marked by the burning of incense and joss paper, or 'spirit money'. This memory of old Singapore's Chinese community is provoked by an event in the present, a bush fire in the suburbs of Sydney that threatens the speaker's home, so that he and his children are temporarily obliged to move to safety:

> The house and yard dressed in a skin of ash.
> It was raining embers, the night air thronged
> with giddy petals that swirled
> on the updraft, flared
> to incandescence before curling into papery
> ash.[3]

When that fire has died down, the family returns in due course to 'sweep the aftermath like penitents' – and it is this echo of a former time that brings back the memory of Qingming from the speaker's early years in Singapore:

> when families filed to the tombs with broom,
> rice wine, boiled whole chicken and fruits, and stacks
> of paper money, gold and silver currency

---

* *Qingming*, 清明 (meaning 'Pure Brightness'), is celebrated on 4 or 5 April of the Western calendar. In its mainland Chinese origins it marks the beginning of the ploughing and sowing season, as well as the occasion, as winter moves into spring, of honouring one's ancestors, an occasion that often involves picnicking at their graves in family groups.

valid only in afterlife.

Because the description of this special day is straightforward, even matter-of-fact, Boey allows no room for sentimentality or routine poeticising of the scene; in this way he avoids what one reviewer has called 'identity narrative, or [...] the Wordsworthian "egotistical sublime"'.[4] Instead, he handles the memory with the lightest of touches, allowing a hint of irony to creep in with the observation that the paper money the family are offering is intended to bolster the financial standing of the deceased in the otherworld:

> The dead were fed,
> their abodes swept, and the filial queue
> of joss offered. Then the money was given
> in fanned reams to the flames, transferred
> to replenish the ancestors' underworld credit.

In the lines that follow, however, the poem shifts, as the speaker recalls a visit to the cemetery with his grandmother (a recurring figure in Boey's work):

> I don't remember whose grave
> it was we were tending, or Grandma telling us
> to pray. Only a blurred oval photo of a man
> on the worn headstone, and the hundreds of fires
> around us, the air swimming
> with ash-drifts, the sun eclipsed in the smoke.

Unsurprisingly, the child is less concerned with a solemn observation of the rites for the dead than with the sense-data he is picking up from the world around him: the fires, the ash drifts, the smoke so thick that it blots out the sun. At this point the man whose grave he is sweeping is not important; what matters is the risk of bankruptcy hanging over the boy's father – and it is on this note that the memory ends, as the poem shifts into an almost journalistic report of how the ceremony, and the dead themselves, have been sacrificed to the ubiquitous god of development:

Now grave news from the living I have left;
the cemeteries are dug up, razed, the dead
expelled, their bones unhoused, ashed
and relocated to columbaria to make
room for progress. No more tomb-sweeping
and picnicking with the dead.*

The final note here is wistful, but not over-emotional; overall, the impression is more of stoical chronicle than righteous judgement. What this does is to suggest that the speaker is accustomed to seeing the things that matter to him swept away by 'progress'; the poem exists as testimony to the fact that this is neither justified nor logical, but is merely the inevitable outcome of greed and thoughtlessness. The poem ends with a return to the present day, in the aftermath of the Sydney bush fire, as the family sweeps away the ashes in an unconscious echo of Qingming; but, while they do all they can to clean up, they cannot dispel the ghosts that have now risen from this new fire:

The ash taste clings
to the house, even after hosing and sweeping.
It seeps into my dreams, into the new life
I have made, and on my sleep it is still raining
ash, flakes falling like memory, on my dead settling
like a snowdrift of forgetting.

---

*In Singapore, hundreds of thousands of bodies have already been hauled up from the ground to pave the way for malls, roads and apartment blocks. The entire city-state of Singapore covers a mere 71,830 hectares, less than half the size of Greater London, so land is always at a premium here – and the needs of the dead generally give way to those of the living. As the country marks 50 years since independence with a weekend of golden jubilee celebrations, however, questions are finally asked about how to preserve what little heritage Singapore has left. In a city where many buildings are brand new, cemeteries are a rare link to the past. What's more, as the exhumations continue, the custom of visiting and worshipping at an ancestor's tomb – once so integral to Chinese culture – is starting to become unfamiliar to Singapore's Chinese population.

Kirsten Han, *Guardian*, 7 August 2015

At the same time, even while 'Clear Brightness' touches on the power of memory and ponders the duties we owe to the dead (and how we carry those duties out), what it most forcefully brings to light for the reader is the realisation that all too often we do not fully understand, or begin to value, the fabric of the home-places that we have lost until long after they are consigned to the unrepeatable past. Everything here is held in check, the rhetoric stripped back, the observations of the rite at times ironic, the emotion contained – but this self-containment, this quietness, is what makes the poem so effective. As it ends, the ash settles, in memory and in the now, so that both past and present are consigned to oblivion, in a 'snowdrift of forgetting'. 'Clear Brightness' is a poem in the contemplative tradition of such classic Chinese masters as Li Bo and Du Fu: understated, matter-of-fact, it reveals the underlying loss not just of beloved ancestors and traditions but of all that flakes and falls away, like the 'papery ash' of ghost money, in the relentless current of time.*

In the 1959 poem 'The Day Lady Died' Frank O'Hara interrupts a meandering ramble through the streets of New York to buy the latest issue of an arts magazine:

> I walk up the muggy street beginning to sun
> and have a hamburger and a malted and buy
> an ugly NEW WORLD WRITING to see what the poets
> in Ghana are doing these days.[5]

As always with O'Hara, this quotidian detail is altogether accurate: *New World Writing*, edited by Stewart Richardson and Corlies M. Smith, did include a section entitled 'Voices of Ghana: Prose and Poetry' in the summer of 1959. However, the lead item in the

---

*Boey's prose works include the novel *Gull between Heaven and Earth*, a detailed account of the life of Du Fu (712–770), a minor Tang court official who passed his life in exile and political isolation but created some of the finest poems ever written.

issue to which the poem refers (no. 15) was a new story by Boris Pasternak; other highlights included a translation of 'Canto II' of Dante's *Purgatorio* by the American poet and critic John Ciardi, a photographic essay by the surrealist Deep South photographer Clarence John Laughlin and several poems by Robert Bly. That O'Hara bought it purely to 'to see what the poets/ in Ghana are doing these days' is, therefore, somewhat unlikely (though it adds a touch of tongue-in-cheek humour, as we picture the kind of person who might *say* something like this, a joke amplified by the term 'these days'). Does O'Hara really feel the need, or at least a duty, to catch up with developments in Ghanaian literature? Or is he interested in adding a suitably exotic, outsider note to a poem that also mentions the controversial Irish playwright Brendan Behan and Jean Genet's play *Les Nègres*?

It is hard not to think that the poets in Ghana have no specific role here, that they could just as easily have hailed from Ethiopia or Sierra Leone. They are there for the same reason that the African masks are there in paintings by Matisse or Picasso – because just knowing about them is *cool*. 'The Day Lady Died' is not just a poem about the city that has recently become the cultural and political centre of the world but is also, and more specifically, an arty, jazz insider's view of a happening, avant-garde New York shaped by hip musicians like Mal Waldron and Billie Holiday, by the inner circle of O'Hara's New York School painter friends – and, of course, by O'Hara himself. The reference says that he is one of the in-crowd: culturally internationalist, maverick, a nonconformist in what was, beyond the bounds of that inner circle, a hugely conformist society.

This is understandable. Poets can be as parochial as anyone else (and a sense that the world has its centre anywhere, whether it be New York or rural Shropshire, is by any standard parochial), and when everything seems to be happening on one's doorstep, it can seem that one's own culture is, if not the only, then certainly the best, game in town. Throughout the twentieth century poetry from out-groups, indigenous peoples or from the so-called 'Third World' was to some degree regarded as of mainly political (or to use Toni Morrison's term, 'sociological') interest, and worthy of the same more or less benign, more or less paternalistic support accorded by 'First World' entrepreneurs to, say, African musicians or Aboriginal 'X-Ray' painters. Yet if a poet like Frank O'Hara was happy to use the poets of Ghana as furniture for a poem that needed just the right touch of African-ness, what chance was there, in the US of the late 1950s, for the recognition of a genuine world culture? The more interesting question to ask, however – and this is worth asking for all our sakes, 'developed' and 'marginalised' artists alike – is what chance we have now of finally envisioning a genuine world culture, one that might exceed even Mandelstam's wildest expectations.

It may or may not be a useful exercise to imagine what a *New World Writing* issue based on a specific African country might feature today, but it might be instructive. The fact that, worldwide, people (especially those with an advanced education or 'transferable skills') are so much more mobile than they were back then might well be one factor in the selection: is Kwame Dawes, for example, a poet from Ghana (having been born there in 1962) or from Jamaica (where he lived from 1971 onwards)? The Zimbabwean poet Togara Muzanenhamo was born in Lusaka, Zambia, in 1975, but moved as a child to Zimbabwe. He was educated in Paris and The Hague, and has spent time in England, but now lives near Harare. Another factor might be language: for example, a poet from Chad whom I greatly admire, Nimrod Bena Djangrang, writes in French, which means he is less likely to be included in American anthologies (though, to be fair, many English-language poets from Africa and Asia are at a disadvantage if, unlike some of their peers, they have not spent time in the US or Europe – such is the power and the constriction of networking). At the same time, anthologists often look for what they think of as typical works – typical of a place or a culture, of a person of a specific background and gender or of a language community. When

I asked the Botswanan poet Tjawangwa Dema about a poem of hers that I admired, wanting to know about the background to the hunting scene in one of its sections, she said:

> I grew up in the city of Gaborone – not much hunting there but almost everyone has a village they 'come from' and where they keep a second home and possibly a cow / goat farm that they visit intermittently. My family was no exception and Christmas meant stories about who had legally or otherwise had a successful (subsistence or defensive but not trophy) hunt. Because of this I expect that these hunters are in an imagined Botswana […] I should say that as a woman and a black one at that I filter a lot of existence through violence. It is possible I identify here more with the hunted and those who clean up after the hunters than I do with the hunters themselves […] It may be all I know of the hunters is that they are male and are often silent except perhaps when it comes to singing songs about their exploits. That they visit violence upon the world just as it occasionally exacts a price for participating in the dance.

The poem, 'In the House of Mourning', is in four sections, the first of which confronts the reader with a stark challenge:

> We've practice enough at grieving.
>
> Perhaps fire is right,
> let us burn everything and be done with it.

The second section is a deft vignette, in which a widow's grief is poignantly dramatised:

> A boy of five or six twirls like a maple seed,
> making a whirlwind of the falling cloud
> inside his absent father's house –
>
> the dead resurrect
> in the faces of their young, ants
> fidgeting in the mind's underbrush.

And the theme of widowhood carries forward into the third section, as another echo is seen in the face of a grieving woman:

> the look of a lost child
> wanders across her face.
> Only the dead are relieved.
>
> We are left to recollect
> and gather
> what remains
>
> in the house of mourning.

If the first three sections have been spare, even minimal, skirting around narrative to offer stark, declarative phrases and observations that verge on the Imagist ideal, the final part, 'In the House of Mourning', teases us with the makings of a narrative, in which the limits of the available details only increase the sense of tragedy. Dema begins with another declarative that is at once beautifully expressed and chilling: 'Everyone rehearses death at nightfall. The rise and fall of breath taken or withheld'. Then the story unfolds, with deceptive simplicity:

> when the hunters return
> to the table, reeking of blood
> and tales, and one is not amongst them.
>
> The one who liked songs is gone.[6]

The economy of expression here is wonderful. It is an old storyteller's strategy, to leave the listener wanting more, and this stark passage takes that strategy to its logical limit. The only characterisation, the one poignant detail that might reveal something of this lost hunter, is his liking for songs. The poem says that this is all that anyone ever really noticed about him, and this fact only makes his loss all the more tragic. As with the unknown species in the forest that is crushed under the developer's bulldozer before it could even be catalogued or named, we feel the waste all the more keenly for never having attended to this young man, who is now lost for ever.

T. S. Eliot famously remarked that 'a tradition without intelligence is not worth having'. In saying this, it seems clear that he was critiquing a common misconception that confuses tradition with the dead letter of convention. In fact, as Eugenio Montale points out, tradition is the polar opposite of conventionality:

> Where tradition is understood not as a dead weight of forms, of extrinsic rules and customs, but as an inner spirit, a genius of the race, a consonance with the most enduring spirits that our country has produced, then it becomes somewhat difficult to suggest an external model for it or draw a precise lesson from it. Tradition is continued not by those who want to do so, but by those who can, sometimes by those who are least aware of doing so. Programs and good intentions are of little help in this regard.[7]

Here Montale is speaking about Italy, though his idea of tradition could easily be applied to many other European countries. Where it becomes more problematical, however, is where questions of 'race' and 'our country' have been points of issues for decades, or generations. For example, what happens when a tradition, and even a language, are imposed on a poet by those who colonised her ancestral home and eradicated much of her culture? 'I have forgotten my name in the language I was born to', says the Muscogee poet Joy Harjo, who writes in English because, having been educated in the language and traditions of those who displaced her forebears, she has no choice. As a poet, this led her to the Iowa Writers' Workshop and to academic positions, but the work she produced, though written in what she has called 'the enemy's language', remained true to that forgotten name. 'I have a responsibility to all the sources that I am,' she has said: 'To all past and future ancestors, to my home country, to all places that I touch down on and that are myself, to all voices, all women, all of my tribe, all people, all earth, and beyond that to all beginnings and endings.' In her poem 'How to Write a Poem in a Time of War', she tells the story of a people invaded by a nameless army:

> We tried to pretend war wasn't going to happen.
> Though they began building their houses all around us and
>   demanding more.
> They started teaching our children their god's story,
>   A story in which we'd always be slaves.

This could be a painfully succinct summary of what happened to the indigenous people of North America when whites arrived, but it could also be applied to any colonised culture. What Harjo sets up in opposition to this war, however, is a powerful expression of survivance, an act of indigenous self-validation that the Anishinaabe scholar and writer Gerald Vizenor defines as 'an active sense of presence, the continuance of native stories, not a mere reaction, or a survivable name. Native survivance stories are renunciations of dominance, tragedy, and victimry. Survivance means the right of succession or reversion of an estate, and in that sense, the estate of native survivancy.' As is so often the case in her work, Harjo emphasises the importance of narrative song and story to this process of reclaiming native presence:

> Someone has to make it out alive, sang a grandfather to his
>   grandson,
> His granddaughter, as he blew his most powerful song into
>   the hearts of the children.
> There it would be hidden from the soldiers,
> Who would take them miles, rivers, mountains from the navel
>   cord place
> Of the origin story.
> He knew one day, far day, the grandchildren would return,
>   generations later
> Over slick highways constructed over old trails

Through walls of laws meant to hamper or destroy, over the
    libraries of
The ancestors in the winds, born in stones.[8]

Harjo's pledge to 'to all voices, all women, all of my tribe, all
people' reveals the profound commitment that the project of
native survivance demands. A somewhat different approach can
be found in Terrance Hayes's extraordinary poem 'Snow for
Wallace Stevens', from his 2010 collection *Lighthead*:

No one living a snowed-in life
can sleep without a blindfold.[9]

The reference here, of course, is to the Wallace Stevens not only
of 'The Snow Man' but also of 'Like Decorations in a Nigger
Cemetery', a poem in which Stevens reveals a brand of casual
racism that has tainted his work for many readers. As an African-
American poet working in an American tradition, however, Hayes
cannot simply abandon a predecessor of Stevens's importance,
and so, as he seeks to find a way to avoid throwing the baby out
with the bathwater, as it were, he works the last line of 'Like Decorations' into what he calls his 'song':

This song is for the wise man who avenges
by building his city in snow.

From the first, Hayes identifies Stevens's snowed-in life as a
retreat, the whiteness blinding, his city predicated on vengeance.*

---

* It is difficult to read the last lines of 'Decorations' without thinking of John
Winthrop, whose famous 'city on a hill' speech was such an inspiration to the
early settlers, not to mention presidential candidates from John F. Kennedy
to Reagan. Winthrop was no model for a modern democracy, however, while
his attitude to the indigenous people he and his fellow settlers encountered
was altogether heartless. 'But for the natives in these parts,' he wrote to a
friend in England in 1634, 'God hath so pursued them, as for 300 miles space
the greatest part of them are swept away by smallpox which still continues
among them. So as God hath thereby cleared our title to this place, those

As for the 'song' he claims to be addressing to Stevens, he explained in an interview with the poet David Wojahn that 'the contradictory gesture of singing for a foe is meant to be ironic and sincere. It's maybe more complicated than ambivalent. It's another moment of trying to capture paradoxical impulses.' What is problematical here – what leads to those paradoxical impulses – is that Stevens, in spite of his racism and his retreat into the comforts of Hartford, remains a formidable poet and an essential figure in the tradition to which Hayes belongs. Stevens's genius as a poet is a source of wonder:

> How, with pipes of winter
> lining his cognition, does someone learn
> to bring a sentence to its knees?

And at the same time Hayes is obliged to recognise a poetic connection with a man whose routine prejudices he abhors, to the extent that, like Stevens:

> I too, having lost faith
> in language, have placed my faith in language.

It is here, in this recognition, that the surprising yet wonderfully elegant turning point of the poem comes as Hayes resorts not to anger, or hatred, but to the basic imperative that, officially at least, lies at the heart of white Christian morality:

> Thus, I have a capacity for love without
> forgiveness. This song is for my foe,
> the clean-shaven, gray-suited, gray patron
> of Hartford, the emperor of whiteness
> blue as a body made of snow.

Now the song is for a 'foe', which means that the love Hayes speaks of is love for an enemy. That love does not imply forgiveness,

---

who remain in these parts, being in all not 50, have put themselves under our protection.'

however; after all, Jesus may have instructed his followers to love their enemies, but he did not demand that they overlook the enemy's misdeeds. In fact, is it not a vital element of charitable love that we recognise others for what they are, and do not blind ourselves to their flaws? What Jesus was advocating was, as Hayes puts it here, a specific capacity, an ability to hold or contain the anger and disappointment that arises from recognition of an author's failures alongside the love one feels for the example of his work. That capacity – *love without forgiveness* – is born of hope, not optimism – and it is this that informs both its truth and its elegance. Where optimism (like pessimism, which is by no means its opposite) is frequently a mistake, hope is always an act of courage, even when it is contradicted by every rule of logic. As we have noted, optimism speaks of the individual or in-group, not for the species as whole. Optimism tries to engineer accord by setting up sociological standards by which to judge art; hope thrives on the idea that the fundamental measure of an art work – of anything at all – is its quality. Quality, first and last. The task remains to seek out quality work wherever it is being made, regardless of race, gender, sexual orientation and geography (i.e., social class), but we have to remember that 'regardless' – and, like Terrance Hayes, we need to exercise the great virtue of love without forgiveness, so that the tradition may continue, even while we take cognisance of, and then set aside, the uglier characteristics of its practitioners, and of the sometimes rapacious cultures to which, historically and geographically at least, they belonged. We do not overlook Pound's anti-Semitism, and we do not forgive Stevens his racism (an impossibility, according to Christian doctrine, in fact; for the sinner to be forgiven, he or she must first repent, and there is no persuasive evidence of such contrition in either case). We treasure the work, however, because it adds something to a 'live tradition'*

---

*The term 'live tradition' is, in fact, Pound's; see Canto LXXXI:

But to have done instead of not doing
    this is not vanity
To have, with decency, knocked

that is forever changing and adapting and, as Hayes so pertinently asks about us all: 'Who is not more than his limitations?'

A few days before I leave Nanyang, after weeks of solid heat, it rains on the streets and gardens of Singapore with little to no warning, the whole thing coming at once, headlong, all movement and drama and a strange, plashing music, like the opening act of a Chinese circus. Sheltering in the Li-Ho tea shop, I feel something more akin to joy than to ordinary pleasure, as I gaze out at the pouring rain, people running for cover, the construction work around the Chinese Heritage Centre suddenly coming to a halt. It is astonishing, to me at least, how suddenly the atmosphere changes. What I love most about this weather, though, is how the soundscape changes, from a contained quiet to fiercest downpour and back to near-silence again, everything around me still and taut, like a held breath in the gaps between rains. I have always been drawn to the machinery we construct to manage water. Ditches, mole drains, weirs, sluice gates, boreholes, wells. Most of all, I love the transient landscapes that result from decisions that are made when the drainage engineer is faced with an intractable natural contingency. The drains here on campus are fairly modest; elsewhere they become more elaborate and so more beautiful. In the Botanical Gardens, for example, there is a fine system of geometrically precise drains, carefully engineered to fit in with the garden itself so that at times they are scarcely noticeable, while at other times, when the burden of work is too much to conceal, they form part of the overall design, becoming, on such acquaintance, strangely beautiful in themselves, an elegant canal crossing a lawn here, a deep, almost guttural plainsong skirting a flowerbed elsewhere. Now, walking back to my apartment after the second

---

That a Blunt should open
> To have gathered from the air a live tradition
or from a fine old eye the unconquered flame
This is not vanity.

thunderstorm of the day, I am drawn to the sound of the rain water, pouring down the storm drains from the hillside, and I stop by the Heritage Centre, where a long, uninterrupted line flows from above to meet another, narrower run that crosses the lower campus. The water is silvery at its furthest reach, the shadows in the drains already a little eerie – and I remember that this is the time when day turns unfussily to night in Singapore, the hour when the rain trees fold their leaves against the darkness, regular as clockwork. It is cooler, now, than it has been since I first arrived, but not so cool as to be taken for granted: every touch of a breeze, every gust of wind, is a blessing, and even though I had a large mug of tea just twenty minutes ago, I am already thirsty. If this were the hillside path above Rilke's last resting place, I would get down on my knees and scoop ice-cold water from the *bisse*, letting the pure, cold liquid run down my throat and spill over my hands, but this is not that kind of water. It is warm and silty, charged with life, almost primordial.

I cannot say for sure why I am so attracted to the technology of water management – and clearly it could only be considered a fit subject for dinner-table small talk in the most exclusive company.* I suspect, however, that it is rooted in the same damp corner of my psyche where poetry takes hold. The thing about water is that, no matter what technology one has at one's disposal, it will still flow where it wants to flow, still find its own level, still dissolve some things and sweep others away to who knows where. All we can do, with our sluices and storm drains and catch basins, is slow or divert it for a while. With real ingenuity we can perform minor, and temporary, water management miracles, like the Alhambra's Acequia Real, an elegant system of channels and aqueducts created by the Moors to supply the whole place with water for its pools and fountains in a distinctly arid landscape. (When the

---

*Needless to say, like all the other boring subjects of conversation, like infrastructure, or maintenance, it is a vitally important issue – increasingly so considering current trends in climate change. It is not at all frivolous to ask what kind of world we would inhabit if we talked more about flood control and less about the latest celebrity scandal.

Christian forces drove the Moors out of Spain in 1492, the entire system fell into disrepair.) What we are working with, however, is a natural element, a force in its own right that is always, eventually, beyond our control. The skill of the water engineer is to calculate just how far we can intervene in that flow (and whether we should do so*), how far it can be shaped and when and how to let it go its own way – and this skill is the same wherever we go or, at least, wherever there is water. In general, analogies cannot bear too much weight for very long, but if there is an analogy for the work of the poet, when he or she is working alone in the instant of composition, it is that of the consummate ditch-digger.

'I, too, dislike it.'

Those words of Marianne Moore's linger in the mind, as does Alastair Reid's remark, made towards the end of his life, that he had come to see poetry as 'something of an artificial gesture, like wearing a tie'. Such reservations are not surprising when we take into account the abuses to which poetry has been subjected, from the feckless amateurism of unchecked 'self-expression' to the facile scheming of those contemporaries whose poetry has clear and palpable and all too often extraneous designs upon us, whether it be in the form of sociological 'relevance', prurient confession or the current practice of stating the obvious about 'the human condition'. Yet both Moore and Reid qualify their remarks in ways that illuminate the discipline they pretend so to disdain. In Reid's elaboration one finds all the hurt of a man who has seen the worst sins and excesses committed against the art he loves, not to mention that gift for grudging affection with which we Scots, in particular, are so happily blessed.

---

* Similarly with poetry: as Kwame Dawes points out, 'Some moments demand a sermon, or a speech, or fist, or a bowl of water, or a rose, not a poem.'

Yet, in spite of his reservations, Reid returned to poetry from time to time, partly for the pleasure of putting-well-into-words,* of good writing (he was also a wonderfully subtle translator and a fine critic), and partly for the never-ending mystery of the process itself, of which he said, in 'Poem without Ends':

> The process is continuous as wind,
> the bird observed, not rising, but in flight,
> unrealised, in motion of the mind.[10]

Marianne Moore has, perhaps, a more detailed argument to make, in the long version of her poem 'Poetry', but it comes in the end to this now famous statement:

> nor till the poets among us can be
>   'literalists of
>   the imagination' – above
>   insolence and triviality and can present
>
> for inspection, imaginary gardens with real toads in them,
>   shall we have
>   it.

It is one thing for me to present to you my imaginary garden and have you see it, as it were, in a literal sense; it is another thing still to populate it with toads that we both understand to be real – but this is the test. If we are to dream of a world culture, it is a test that must apply across cultures, and across traditions, a test for poets and translators alike, but it is more than anything a test for readers. Is it not a reasonable notion, then, to say that poetry is not 'about' the individual writing it, or the clique to which they belong, so much as a method of investigation that faces out to the world, curious, alert, open, unmediated by the societal as far as that is possible? That it is a lifelong discipline that trusts not to

---

* 'I feel that the fine attention one gives to words in poems can also be applied to prose,' he said. 'But it is from poetry more than anything that one learns to say well.'

favouritism or the steady attrition of social media but to quality? Che Guevara said that silence was argument carried out by other means. I believe quality has a similar role, but where silence can be heard by everyone quality is considered a personal matter – and it seems futile to insist that this is only true up to a point. There may be no absolutes in nature, but I do believe that (to take just one example) wherever English is spoken, no matter what else has happened in the culture, there will be some, hopefully many, who can appreciate a poem by Emily Dickinson, or John Donne, or Elizabeth Bishop. It can never be proven – it is, in fact, an entirely quixotic enterprise – but I find that it is essential to my sense of order that some things that human beings make will always offer nourishment to those who require it. The same is true of other languages – as Joy Harjo remarked during a radio interview at the Riddu Riddu festival in Manndalen, north Norway, in 2003: 'We also have classical forms, we also have integrity and a sense of aesthetics that are just as important and just as developed.' In some cases, however, it will take a fully realised world culture – including close scrutiny of the great traditions that we already treasure – for this to be generally acknowledged.

Like Mandelstam, I feel nostalgic for that world culture – and in some senses I already live there, in spite of the economic, political and geographical pressures that prevent its fullest flowering. Because of the pressures imposed by 'cultural totalitarianism', the members of Ferlinghetti's mainstream culture have – or ought to have – more in common with one another across borders than we have with those who create the divisions. However, this book is a plea not for passive acceptance of whatever goes on (in Ghana or anywhere else) as inherently interesting for its own sake but for a live critical culture in which poets and readers from many backgrounds might engage with one another, on as equal a basis as political systems and commercial-cultural trends allow. This requires us to remember what we mean by a 'world culture' in the first place and to work together to sustain it. It will call, no doubt, for love without forgiveness. It will call for improbable feats of memory and reconstruction. More than anything else, however, it will call for *la razón poética* to be placed on its proper footing as a method for investigating the given world as an equal and fully respected partner with logical method, so that human beings come to see that, in the overall scheme of things, the music of what happens is all one fabric, and what we think of as noise is part of that fabric's warp and weft. The obligation we have, as observers and venerators, is to become more attentive to that fabric and so learn how to stay attuned to the music we have been given, rather than trying to create a perfect harmony that can never exist.

NOTES

Introduction

1. 'Silentium' by Fyodor Tyutchev, in *Three Russian Poets: Selections from Pushkin, Lermontov and Tyutchev,* Vladimir Nabokov (ed. and trans.), (New York: New Directions Books, 1944).

2. Osip Mandelstam, *Komissarzhevskaya, The Noise of Time (San Francisco: North Point Press, 1986), ed. and* trans. Clarence Brown.

3. Anna Akhmatova, trans. Stephen Edgar, *Poetry Magazine* (April 2008).

4. Walter Benjamin, trans. Dennis Redmond, *On the Concept of History*, Global Rights ebook (https://www.globalrights.info/2016/09/28/).

5. Langston Hughes, 'Question', *The Collected Poems of Langston Hughes* (London: Vintage Classics, 1995). Copyright © 1994 by the Estate of Langston Hughes. Used by permission of Alfred A. Knopf, an imprint of the Knopf Doubleday Publishing Group, a division of Penguin Random House, LLC

6. Collected in Eugenio Montale, *Auto da fé: cronache in due tempi* (Milan: Il Saggiatore, 1966) (my translation).

7. Marianne Moore, 'The Hero', *New Collected Poems of Marianne Moore*, ed. Heather Cass White (London: Faber & Faber, 2017).

Ghostly Music in the Air

1. Archibald MacLeish, 'Ars Poetica', *Collected Poems 1917–1952* (Boston, MA: Houghton Mifflin Harcourt, 1952).

2. W. H. Auden, *Collected Poems* (London: Faber & Faber, 1994).

3. W. B. Yeats, *Collected Poems* (London: Macmillan, 1950).
4. William Meredith, 'Effort at Speech', *Effort at Speech: New and Selected Poems* (Evanston, IL: Northwestern University Press Books, 1998). Copyright William Meredith by kind permission of Northwestern University Press Books.
5. Jonathan Franzen, *How To Be Alone* (New York: HarperPerennial, 2004).
6. Robert Lowell, 'Waking Early Sunday Morning', *Collected Poems* (London: Faber & Faber, 2003).
7. Jonathan Bate, *Song of the Earth* (London: Picador, 2000).
8. William Matthews, 'The Buddy Bolden Cylinder', *Search Party: Collected Poems of William Matthews* (Boston, MA: Houghton Mifflin, 2005). Copyright William Matthews with kind permission from The William Matthews Estate.

Everyone Sang

1. Charles Hamilton Sorley, *Marlborough, and Other Poems* (Cambridge: Cambridge University Press, 2012).
2. Siegfried Sassoon, 'Does It Matter?', *Collected Poems,* new edn (London: Faber & Faber, 2002). Copyright Siegfried Sassoon by kind permission of the Estate of George Sassoon.
3. Wilfred Owen, 'Futility', Jon Silkin (ed.), *The Penguin Book of First World War Poetry* (Harmondsworth: Penguin Books, 1979).
4. Siegfried Sassoon, 'Base Details', *Collected Poems*, new edn. Copyright Siegfried Sassoon by kind permission of the Estate of George Sassoon.
5. Siegfried Sassoon, 'On Reading the War Diary of a Defunct Ambassador', *Collected Poems*, new edn. Copyright Siegfried Sassoon by kind permission of the Estate of George Sassoon.
6. Siegfried Sassoon, 'Glory of Women', *Collected Poems*, new edn. Copyright Siegfried Sassoon by kind permission of the Estate of George Sassoon.
7. e. e. cummings, 'my sweet old etcetera'. Copyright 1926, 1954 © 1991 by the Trustees for the E. E. Cummings Trust. Copyright © 1985 by George James Firmage, from *Complete Poems 1904–1962*

by E. E. Cummings, edited by George J. Firmage. Used by permission of Liveright Publishing Corporation.

8. Siegfried Sassoon, 'Everyone Sang', *Collected Poems*, new edn. Copyright Siegfried Sassoon by kind permission of the Estate of George Sassoon.

9. Siegfried Sassoon, 'Falling Asleep', *Collected Poems*, new edn. Copyright Siegfried Sassoon by kind permission of the Estate of George Sassoon.

10. Siegfried Sassoon, 'Reconciliation', *Collected Poems*, new edn. Copyright Siegfried Sassoon by kind permission of the Estate of George Sassoon.

11. Lois Shepherd, 'Face to Face: A Call for Radical Responsibility in Place of Compassion', *St. John's Law Review*, vol. 77, no. 3 (summer 2003).

12. Siegfried Sassoon, 'A Chord', *The Tasking* (Cambridge: Cambridge University Press, 1954). Copyright Siegfried Sassoon by kind permission of the Estate of George Sassoon.

L'infinito

1. Giacomo Leopardi, 'L'infinito', *Canti* (bilingual edn) (New York: Farrar, Straus and Giroux 2012).

2. William Matthews, 'Civilization and Its Discontents', *Search Party: Collected Poems of William Matthews* (Boston, MA: Houghton Mifflin, 2005). Copyright William Matthews by kind permission of The William Matthews Estate.

3. Rainer Maria Rilke, *Duino Elegies*, trans. A. S. Kline (2001); available online, at http://uploads.worldlibrary.net/uploads/ pdf/20121103015056rilkepdf_pdf.pdf. From *The Poetry of Rainer Maria Rilke* by A. S. Kline (Trans), copyright 2009.

4. Giacomo Leopardi, 'A Silvia', *Canti* (bilingual edn).

5. Giacomo Leopardi, 'L'infinito', *Canti* (bilingual edn).

6. Wallace Stevens, 'The Snow Man', *The Collected Poems of Wallace Stevens* (New York: Vintage Books, 2015).

7. Giuseppe Ungaretti, 'Mattina', *Selected Poems* (Manchester: Carcanet, 2003).

8. Stephen Crane: 'I was in the darkness', *The Poems of Stephen*

Crane: A Critical Edition, ed. Joseph Katz (New York: Cooper Square Press, 1976).

9. Eugenio Montale, 'Forse un mattino', *Ossi di seppia* (Milan: Mondadori, Milan, 2018).

Einen reinen Vorgang

1. Rainer Maria Rilke, *Selected Poems, Duino Elegies and The Fountain of Joy; A Commentary on the Elegies*, trans. A. S. Kline (Online publication: Poetry in Translation, 2009). From *The Poetry of Rainer Maria Rilke* by A. S. Kline (Trans), copyright 2009.

2. Rainer Maria Rilke, *Letters to a Young Woman (Briefe an eine junge Frau)*, trans. William Needham (Online publication: Project Gutenberg Australia, 2009).

3. William Gass, *Reading Rilke: Reflections on the Problems of Translation* (New York: Alfred A. Knopf, 1999).

4. Rainer Maria Rilke, 'Une rose seule', *Vergers, et autres poèmes français* (Paris: Gallimard, 1978).

5. 'Gedicht', published in the magazine *Deutsche Arbeit* in 1901.

6. Rainer Maria Rilke, *Letters to a Young Poet*, trans. Reginald Snell (London: Sidgwick & Jackson, 1945).

7. Rainer Maria Rilke, *Letters to a Young Woman*.

8. Rainer Maria Rilke, *Duineser Elegien/Die Sonette an Orpheus* (Leipzig: Insel Verlag, 1974).

9. Rainer Maria Rilke to Nanny Wunderly-Volkart, 15 July 1921; Fondation Rilke, Sierre.

10. Emily Dickinson, '"Nature" is what we see …', *The Complete Poems of Emily Dickinson*, ed. Thomas Herbert Johnson (Boston, MA: Little, Brown & Co., 1960).

11. The English version is from *Poetry, Language, Thought*, trans. Albert Hofstadter (Harper Colophon Books, New York, 1971).

The Grief That Does Not Speak

1. Rainer Maria Rilke, 'Nichts ist mir zu klein', *Poems from The Book of Hours*, ed. Babette Deutsch (New York: New Directions, 2018). Copyright © 1941 by New Directions Publishing Corp. Reprinted by permission of New Directions Publishing Corp.

2. Rainer Maria Rilke, 'Die Worte des Engels', *Die Gedichte* (Leipzig: Insel Verlag, 2006).

3. Rainer Maria Rilke, 'Elegie (an Marina Zwetajewa-Efron)', *Die Gedichte.*

4. Marina Tsvetaeva, *New Year's: An Elegy for Rilke*, trans. Mary Jane White (Easthampton, MA: Adastra Press, 2008).

5. Joseph Brodsky, *Less Than One: Selected Essays* (New York: Farrar, Straus and Giroux, 1986).

6. Marina Tsvetaeva, 'I Know the Truth', *Selected Poems*, trans. Elaine Feinstein (London: Penguin Books, 1994).

7. T. S. Eliot, 'Burnt Norton', *Four Quartets* (London: Faber & Faber, 2019).

8. Wallace Stevens, 'The Owl in the Sarcophagus', *The Collected Poems of Wallace Stevens* (London and New York: Vintage Books, 2015).

9. Judith Butler, *Precarious Life: The Powers of Mourning and Violence* (London: Verso, 2004).

10. *Numéro Cinq*, vol. VIII, no. 4 (April 2017); see: http://numerocinqmagazine.com/2017/04/14/hells-small-heaven-poems-marina-tsvetaeva-translated-mary-jane-white/

11. Marina Tsvetaeva, 'Bus', *Selected Poems*, trans. Elaine Feinstein.

12. Philip Larkin, 'Wants', *The Less Deceived* (London: Faber & Faber, 2012).

The Power of the Visible

1. Marianne Moore, 'The Steeple-Jack', *New Collected Poems of Marianne Moore*, ed. Heather Cass White (London: Faber & Faber, 2017). Copyright © 1935 by Marianne Moore, renewed 1963 by T. S. Eliot. Reprinted with the permission of Scribner, a division of Simon & Schuster, Inc.

2. Marianne Moore, 'The Steeple-Jack'. Copyright © 1935 by Marianne Moore, renewed 1963 by T. S. Eliot. Reprinted with the permission of Scribner, a division of Simon & Schuster, Inc.

3. Marianne Moore, 'He Digesteth Harde Yron', *New Collected Poems of Marianne Moore.*

4. Barry Lopez, *Crossing Open Ground* (New York: Scribner, 1988).

5. A. R. Ammons, 'Corson's Inlet', copyright © 1963 by A. R. Ammons from *The Complete Poems of A. R. Ammons*, ed. Robert West (New York: W.W. Norton & Co., 2017). Used by permission of W. W. Norton & Co, Inc.

A Very Young Policeman Exploding

1. Archibald MacLeish, 'Ars Poetica', *Collected Poems 1917–1952*.
2. Hart Crane, 'The Wine Menagerie', *Complete Poems of Hart Crane*, ed. Marc Simon (New York: Liveright, 2001).
3. Hart Crane, 'Legend', *Complete Poems of Hart Crane*.
4. Marianne Moore, 'Poetry', *New Collected Poems of Marianne Moore*.
5. Hart Crane to Harriet Monroe, repr. in *Poetry* (October 1926).
6. Dylan Thomas, 'Poem in October', *The Collected Poems of Dylan Thomas* (London: Weidenfeld & Nicolson, 2014). Copyright © 1945 by The Trustees for the Copyrights of Dylan Thomas, first published in *Poetry*. Reprinted by permission of New Directions Publishing Corp and The Dylan Thomas Trust.
7. John Arnott MacCulloch, *The Religion of the Ancient Celts* (Edinburgh: T. & T. Clark, 1911).
8. Dylan Thomas, 'Fern Hill', *Collected Poems*. Copyright The Dylan Thomas Trust.
9. Dylan Thomas, 'Refusal to Mourn the Death, by Fire, of a Child in London', *Collected Poems*. Copyright © 1945 by The Trustees for the Copyrights of Dylan Thomas. Reprinted by permission of New Directions Publishing Corp and The Dylan Thomas Trust.
10. Dylan Thomas, 'The Force That through the Green Fuse Drives the Flower', *Collected Poems*. Copyright © 1939 by New Directions Publishing Corp. Reprinted by permission of New Directions Publishing Corp and The Dylan Thomas Trust.

An Old Chaos of the Sun

1. Wallace Stevens, 'Final Soliloquy of the Interior Paramour', *The Collected Poems of Wallace Stevens* (New York: Vintage Books, 2015).

2. Wallace Stevens, 'Thirteen Ways of Looking at a Blackbird', *The Collected Poems*.

3. Wallace Stevens, 'Sunday Morning', *The Collected Poems*.

4. Wallace Stevens, 'Restatement of Romance', *The Collected Poems*. Copyright © 1954 by Wallace Stevens and copyright renewed 1982 by Holly Stevens. Used by permission of Alfred A. Knopf, an imprint of the Knopf Doubleday Publishing Group, a division of Penguin Random House, LLC.

Weltenton

1. All the quotations from Haushofer in this chapter come from *Moabiter Sonette* (Berlin: Union Verlag, 1975).

2. David Gascoyne, 'Snow in Europe', *Poems, 1937–1942* (London: Nicholson and Watson/PL Editions, 1943).

3. Juan Ramón Jiménez, 'El viaje definitivo', *Antología poética* (Madrid: Alianza Editorial, 1984).

La razón poética

1. Rafael Alberti, 'Balada de lo que el viento dijo', *Baladas y canciones del Paraná (1953–1954)* (Buenos Aires: Losada, 1999).

2. Miguel Hernández, 'Falta el espacio', *Poesías* (Madrid: Taurus, 1980).

3. Miguel Hernández, 'Si me muero, que me muera', *Poesías*.

4. All quotations from Guillén here are drawn from his book *Language and Poetry: Some Poets of Spain*, The Charles Eliot Norton Lectures (Cambridge, MA: Harvard University Press, 1961).

5. Federico García Lorca, 'Despedida', *Poesia completa* (New York: Vintage Español, 2012).

6. Maria Zambrano, 'Delirio del incrédulo', *El ángel del límite y el confín intermedio: tres poemas y un esquema de María Zambrano* (Madrid: Endymion, 1999).

7. Juan Ramón Jiménez, 'No era nadie', *Antología poética*.

8. *Alcibiades I*, trans. Benjamin Jowett; see http://www.gutenberg.org/files/1676/1676-h/1676-h.htm

Why Look at Animals?

1. Robert Frost, 'Two Look at Two', *The Poetry of Robert Frost: The Collected Poems* (New York: Henry Holt, 1979).
2. William Stafford, 'Traveling Through the Dark', *The Darkness Around Us Is Deep: Selected Poems of William Stafford* (New York: Harper Perennial, 1993).
3. Brigit Pegeen Kelly, 'Dead Doe', *Song* (New York: BOA Editions, 1995). With thanks to Michael Madonick.
4. D. H. Lawrence, 'Snake', *Selected Poems of D. H. Lawrence*, ed. James Fenton (London: Penguin, 2008).
5. Jefferson Airplane, 'Eskimo Blue Day', from the album *Volunteers* (1969).
6. W. S. Merwin, 'Witness', *The Rain in the Trees* (New York: Alfred A. Knopf, 2010). Reproduced by permission of Bloodaxe Books.
7. Sherman Alexie, 'The Powwow at the End of the World', *The Summer of Black Widows* (New York: Hanging Loose Press, 1998).
8. Lucie Brock-Broido, 'Self-Deliverance by Lion' and 'Self-Portrait on the Grassy Knoll' from *Trouble in Mind: Poems* (New York: Alfred A. Knopf, 2004). Copyright © 2004 by Lucie Brock-Broido. Used by permission of Alfred A. Knopf, an imprint of the Knopf Doubleday Publishing Group, a division of Penguin Random House, LLC

A Stony Invitation To Reflect

1. *The Cantos of Ezra Pound* (New York: New Directions, 1999).
2. Karl Marx, *Capital*, vol. III (London: Penguin Classics, 1992).
3. Anne Sexton, Excerpt from 'After Auschwitz', *The Complete Poems of Anne Sexton* (Boston, MA: Houghton Mifflin, 1999). Copyright © 1975 by Loring Conant Jr., executor of the Estate of Anne Sexton. Reprinted by permission of Houghton Mifflin Harcourt Publishing Company.
4. William Carlos Williams, *Paterson* (New York: New Directions, 1963). Copyright © 1946 by William Carlos Williams. Reprinted by permission of New Directions Publishing Corp and The Dylan Thomas Trust.

5. Interview in *Writers at Work, 2nd series*, ed. George Plimpton (London: Penguin, 1963).

A Golden Age of Poetry and Power

1. Robert Frost, 'The Gift Outright', *The Poetry of Robert Frost: The Collected Poems.*
2. Robert Frost, 'Dedication', *The Poetry of Robert Frost: The Collected Poems* (my italics).
3. Emma Lazarus, 'The New Colossus', *Selected Poems and Other Writings* (Peterborough, Ontario: Broadview Press, 2002).
4. Robert Frost, 'The Death of the Hired Man', *The Poetry of Robert Frost: The Collected Poems.*
5. Robert Frost, 'Mending Wall', *The Poetry of Robert Frost: The Collected Poems.*
6. F. D. Reeve, *Robert Frost in Russia* (Boston, MA: Little, Brown, 1963).
7. Stewart L. Udall, 'Robert Frost's Last Adventure', *New York Times* (11 June 1972).
8. Sigmund Freud, *An Autobiographical Study* (1925).
9. W. H. Auden, 'Elegy for J.F.K', *Words of Protest, Words of Freedom: Poetry of the American Civil Rights Movement and Era*, ed. Jeffrey Lamar Coleman (Durham, NC: Duke University Press, 2012).
10. Floyd Salas, 'Kaleidoscope of an Assassination in Black and White', *Eleven Eleven*, issue 13 (2012).

Where Turtles Win

1. Lawrence Ferlinghetti, 'Junkman's Obbligato', *A Coney Island of the Mind* (New York: New Directions 1968).
2. Robert Bly, 'The Great Society', *The Light Around the Body* (New York: Harper & Row, 1967).
3. Lawrence Ferlinghetti, 'Pity the Nation', *Pity the Nation (after Khalil Gibran)* (San Francisco: City Lights Bookstore, 2008).
4. Lawrence Ferlinghetti, 'I Am Waiting', *A Coney Island of the Mind.*
5. Lawrence Ferlinghetti, 'Baseball Canto', *San Francisco Poems,*

San Francisco Poet Laureate Series (San Francisco, CA: City Lights Bookstore, 2003).

6. James Agee, 'Lyric', *The Collected Poems of James Agee* (Boston, MA: Houghton Mifflin, 1968).

7. José Emilio Pacheco, 'Alta Traición', *Alta traición: antología poética* (Madrid: Alianza Editorial, 1985). 'Alta Traición', No me preguntes cómo pasa el tiempo © 1969, Heirs of José Emilio Pacheco.

Sólo tú, alma mía

1. Olga Orozco, 'Para Emilio en su cielo', *Relámpagos de lo invisible* (Buenos Aires: Fondo de Cultura Económica, 1998).

2. Olga Orozco, 'Olga Orozco', *Relámpagos de lo invisible*.

3. Olga Orozco, 'Balada de los lugares olvidados', *La noche a la deriva* (Córdoba: Alción, 1995).

Like a Stripèd Pair of Pants

1. Charles Wright, 'California Dreaming', *The World of the Ten Thousand Things* (New York: Noonday Press, 1990).

2. Emily Dickinson, 'I heard a Fly buzz – when I died', *The Complete Poems of Emily Dickinson*, ed. Thomas Herbert Johnson (Boston, MA: Little, Brown, 1960).

3. Charles Wright, *The World of the Ten Thousand Things*.

4. Emily Dickinson, 'I Dwell in Possibility', *The Complete Poems of Emily Dickinson*.

5. Weldon Kees, 'The Smiles of the Bathers Fade', *The Collected Poems of Weldon Kees* (Lincoln, NE: University of Nebraska Press, 2003).

Tantalus in Love

1. Louise Glück, 'Earthly Love', *Poems, 1962–2012* (New York: Farrar, Straus and Giroux, 2012). Reprinted by permission of Carcanet Press Ltd.

2. Philip Larkin, 'Annus Mirabilis', *High Windows* (London: Faber & Faber, 2015).

3. e. e. cummings, 'Epithalamion', *Collected Poems of E. E.*

Cummings. Copyright 1952 © 1980, 1981 by the Trustees for the E. E. Cummings Trust.

4. e. e. cummings, 'one's not half two', *Collected Poems of E. E. Cummings*. Copyright 1944 © 1972, 1991 by the Trustees for the E. E. Cummings Trust.

5. Robert Graves, 'At First Sight', *Complete Poems* (Manchester: Carcanet, 1997). With kind permission by The Robert Graves Copyright Trust.

6. Robert Graves, 'A Former Attachment', *Complete Poems*. With kind permission by The Robert Graves Copyright Trust.

7. Pablo Neruda, 'Poema 17' from *Veinte poemas de amor y una canción desesperada* (Barcelona: Ediciones Altaya, 1995). (Translation by Mark Eisner.) Copyright © Pablo Neruda 1924, and Fundacion Pablo Neruda.

8. W. H. Auden, 'Funeral Blues', *Collected Poems*.

9. W. H. Auden, 'As I Walked Out One Evening', *Collected Poems*.

10. William Carlos Williams, 'The Ivy Crown', from *The Collected Poems: Volume II, 1939–1962*. Copyright © 1953 by William Carlos Williams. Reprinted by permission of New Directions Publishing Corp.

11. Louise Glück, 'Mock Orange', *Poems, 1962–2012*. Copyright © 1968, 1971, 1972, 1973, 1974, 1975, 1976, 1977, 1978, 1980, 1985, 1995 by Louise Glück. Reprinted with permission of HarperCollins Publishers.

12. Emma Goldman, *Anarchism and Other Essays* (New York and London: Mother Earth Publishing, 1911).

13. Robert Lowell, 'Skunk Hour', *Collected Poems*.

14. See Kay Redfield Jamison, *Robert Lowell, Setting the River on Fire* (London: Vintage, 2018).

15. Alan Shapiro, 'Anger', *Tantalus in Love* (Boston, MA: Houghton Mifflin, 2006). With kind permission of Alan Shapiro.

16. Wallace Stevens, 'Notes towards a Supreme Fiction', *The Collected Poems of Wallace Stevens*.

17. Louise Glück, 'Earthly Love', *Vita Nova* (New York: Ecco Press, 2001). Copyright © 1968, 1971, 1972, 1973, 1974, 1975, 1976, 1977, 1978, 1980, 1985, 1995 by Louise Glück. Reprinted with permission of HarperCollins Publishers and Carcanet Press Ltd.

18. Charles Bukowski, 'Oh Yes', from *Love Is a Dog from* Hell: Poems 1974–1977 (New York: Ecco/HarperCollins, 2002). Copyright © 1977 by Charles Bukowski. Reprinted by permission of HarperCollins Publishers.

19. William Matthews, 'Care', *After All* (Boston, MA: Houghton Mifflin, 1998). With kind permission of The William Matthews Estate.

20. Robert Graves, 'Perfectionists', *Complete Poems*. With kind permission by The Robert Graves Copyright Trust.

A Gift to the Future

1. Jorge Guillén, 'Muerte a lo lejos', *Cántico* (Madrid: Diario Público, 2011). Copyright © Herederos de Jorge Guillén.

The Panic of the Adversary

1. This aesthetic draws partly on ideas expressed by the Yoruba Itutu ethic, in which calm and self-reliance inform not only that society's art works but also its day-to-day philosophy. See Robert Farris Thompson, 'An Aesthetic of the Cool', *African Arts*, vol. 7, no. 1 (autumn 1973), pp. 91–2.

2. Haki R. Madhubuti, 'But He Was Cool, or: he even stopped for green lights', *Liberation Narratives: New and Collected Poems, 1966–2009* (Chicago, IL: Third World Press, 2009).

3. Haki R. Madhubuti, 'the self-hatred of don l. lee', *Liberation Narratives*.

4. Amiri Baraka, 'Black Art', *SOS: Poems, 1961–2013* (New York: Grove Press, 2016).

5. Haki R. Madhubuti, 'One Sided Shoot-Out (for brothers fred hampton & mark clark, murdered 12/4/69 by Chicago police at 4:30 AM while they slept)', *Liberation Narratives*.

6. Translation by Richmond Lattimore, in *The Greek Tragedies*, vol. 1, ed. David Grene and Richmond Lattimore (Chicago, IL: The University of Chicago Press, 1960).

7. Haki R. Madhubuti, 'For the Consideration of Poets', *Liberation Narratives*.

The Bat-Poet

1. John Masefield, 'Cargoes', *The Collected Poems of John Masefield* (London: Heinemann, 1961). By kind pemission of The Society of Authors as the Literary Representative of the Estate of John Masefield.

2. Ogden Nash, 'The Hunter', *Versus* (Boston, MA: Little, Brown, 1949). Copyright 1949 by Ogden Nash, renewed. Reprinted by permission of Curtis Brown, Ltd.

3. Walter de la Mare, 'The Listeners', *The Complete Poems of Walter de la Mare* (London: Faber & Faber, 1969). With kind permission by The Literary Trustees of Walter de la Mare and the Society of authors as their representative.

4. Leo Zanderer, 'Randall Jarrell: About and for Children', *The Lion and the Unicorn*, vol. 2, no. 1, 1978, pp. 73–93.

5. Randall Jarrell, 'Well Water', *Complete Poems* (New York: Farrar, Straus and Giroux, 1969).

To Reclaim Lost Space

1. Philip Levine, 'Making It Work', *A Walk with Tom Jefferson* (New York: Alfred A. Knopf, 1988). With permission of Alfred A. Knopf, an imprint of the Knopf Doubleday Publishing Group, a division of Penguin Random House, LLC.

2. John Masefield, 'Autumn Ploughing', *The Collected Poems of John Masefield*. By kind permission of The Society of Authors as the Literary Representative of The Estate of John Masefield.

3. Edward Thomas, 'Adlestrop', *The Annotated Collected Poems of Edward Thomas,* ed. Edna Longley (Newcastle upon Tyne: Bloodaxe Books, 2008).

4. Edna St Vincent Millay, 'The Goose-Girl', *The Harp-Weaver and Other Poems* (New York: Harper & Brothers, 1923).

5. D. H. Lawrence, 'The Collier's Wife', *Selected Poems of D. H. Lawrence*.

6. Philip Levine, 'The Future', from *The Last Shift: Poems*, compilation copyright © 2016 by The Estate of Philip Levine. Used by permission of Alfred A. Knopf, an imprint of the

Knopf Doubleday Publishing Group, a division of Penguin Random House, LLC.

7. Philip Levine, 'Something Has Fallen', *Ashes: Poems New & Old* (New York: Atheneum, 1979).

A Towering Strangeness

1. Seamus Heaney, 'Making Strange', *Station Island* (London: Faber & Faber, 1984). Copyright Seamus Heaney, reproduced with kind permission of The Seamus Heaney Estate.

2. Seamus Heaney, 'The Forge', *Door into the Dark* (London: Faber & Faber, 1969). Copyright Seamus Heaney, reproduced with kind permission of The Seamus Heaney Estate.

3. Seamus Heaney, 'Sunlight', *North* (London: Faber & Faber, 1975). Copyright Seamus Heaney, reproduced with kind permission of The Seamus Heaney Estate.

4. Seamus Heaney, 'Death of a Naturalist', *Death of a Naturalist* (London: Faber & Faber, 1966). Copyright Seamus Heaney, reproduced with kind permission of The Seamus Heaney Estate.

5. Tim Lilburn, *Living in the World as if It Were Home* (Toronto: Cormorant Books, 1999).

6. Seamus Heaney, 'Tollund', *The Spirit Level* (London: Faber & Faber, 1996). Copyright Seamus Heaney, reproduced with kind permission of The Seamus Heaney Estate.

7. Seamus Heaney, 'Sandstone Keepsake', *Station Island* (London: Faber & Faber, 1984). Copyright Seamus Heaney, reproduced with kind permission of The Seamus Heaney Estate.

8. Seamus Heaney, 'Servant Boy', *Wintering Out* (London: Faber & Faber, 1972). Copyright Seamus Heaney, reproduced with kind permission of The Seamus Heaney Estate.

9. Dennis O'Driscoll, *Stepping Stones: Interviews with Seamus Heaney (London: Faber & Faber, 2009).*

10. Seamus Heaney, 'The Flight Path', *The Spirit Level*. Copyright Seamus Heaney, reproduced with kind permission of The Seamus Heaney Estate.

11. Seamus Heaney, 'In Time', *New Selected Poems, 1988–2013*

(London: Faber & Faber, 2014). Copyright Seamus Heaney, reproduced with kind permission of The Seamus Heaney Estate.

The Poets in Ghana

1. Joy Harjo, 'Alive'. Copyright © 1983 by Joy Harjo, from *She Had Some Horses* (New York: W. W. Norton & Co., 2008). Used by permission of W. W. Norton & Company, Inc.
2. Philip Larkin, 'Going, Going', *High Windows* (London: Faber & Faber, 2015).
3. Kim Cheng Boey, 'Clear Brightness', *Clear Brightness* (Singapore: Epigram Books, 2012). Reproduced by permission of Epigram Books.
4. Christopher Pollnitz, *Mascara*, November 2013.
5. Excerpt from Frank O'Hara, 'The Day Lady Died', from *Lunch Poems*. Copyright © 1964 by Frank O'Hara. Reprinted with permission of The Permissions Company, LLC on behalf of City Lights Books, www.citylights.com.
6. Tjawangwa Dema, 'In the House of Mourning', *The Careless Seamstress* (Lincoln, NE: University of Nebraska Press, 2019).
7. Eugenio Montale, 'Style and Tradition', in *The Second Life of Art: Selected Essays of Eugenio Montale*, trans. Jonathan Galassi (New York: Ecco Press, 1982).
8. Joy Harjo, 'How to Write a Poem in a Time of War', *Poetry* (September 2017). With kind permission of Joy Harjo.
9. Terrance Hayes, 'Snow for Wallace Stevens', *Lighthead* (New York: Penguin Poets, 2010). With kind permission to reproduce rfom Terrence Hayes.
10. Alastair Reid, 'Poem without Ends', *Inside Out: Selected Poetry and Translations* (Edinburgh: Polygon, 2008). With thanks to Alastair Reid and the *New Yorker*.

Also: Gwendolyn Brooks, 'We Real Cool: The Pool Players, Seven at the Golden Shovel', reprinted by consent of Brooks Permissions; Seamus Heaney, 'Weighing In', from *Human Chain*, (London: Faber & Faber, 2010). Copyright Seamus Heaney, reproduced with kind

SELECT BIBILIOGRAPHY

James Agee, *The Collected Poems of James Agee* (Boston, MA: Houghton Mifflin, 1968)

A. R. Ammons, *The Complete Poems of A. R. Ammons*, ed. Robert West (New York: W. W. Norton & Co., 2017)

W. H. Auden, *Collected Poems* (London: Faber & Faber, 1994)

James Baldwin, *Collected Essays* (New York: Penguin Random House, 1998)

Amiri Baraka, *SOS: Poems, 1961–2013* (New York: Grove Press, 2016)

Jonathan Bate, *The Song of the Earth* (London: Picador, 2000)

Walter Benjamin, trans. Dennis Redmond, *On the Concept of History*, Global Rights ebook (https://www.globalrights.info/2016/09/28/)

John Berger, *About Looking* (New York: Pantheon Books, 1980)

Robert Bly, *The Light Around the Body* (New York: Harper & Row, 1967)

Kim Cheng Boey, *Clear Brightness* (Singapore: Epigram Books, 2012)

Lucie Brock-Broido, *Trouble in Mind* (New York: Alfred A. Knopf, 2004)

Joseph Brodsky, *Less Than One: Selected Essays* (New York: Farrar, Straus and Giroux, 1986)

Judith Butler, *Precarious Life: The Powers of Mourning and Violence* (London: Verso, 2004)

James P. Carse, *Finite and Infinite Games* (New York: The Free Press, 1986)

Ernestina de Champourcín, *Poemas de exilio, de soledad y de oración: antología poética* (Madrid: Ediciones Encuentro, 2004)

Hart Crane, *Complete Poems of Hart Crane*, ed. Marc Simon (New York: Liveright, 2001)

e. e. cummings, *Collected Poems of E. E. Cummings* (New York: Harcourt, Brace & World, 1966)

Alex Danchev, 'The Angel of History', *International Affairs*, vol. 90, no. 2 (March 2014), pp. 367–77

Tjawangwa Dema, *The Careless Seamstress* (Lincoln, NE: University of Nebraska Press, 2019)

Emily Dickinson, *The Complete Poems of Emily Dickinson*, ed. Thomas Herbert Johnson (Boston, MA: Little, Brown & Co., 1960)

Arthur Stanley Eddington, *Science and the Unseen World* (London: Allen & Unwin, 1958)

T. S. Eliot, *Four Quartets* (London: Faber & Faber, 2019)

Lawrence Ferlinghetti, *A Coney Island of the Mind* (New York: New Directions 1968)

—, *Pity the Nation (after Khalil Gibran)* (San Francisco: City Lights Bookstore, 2008)

Robert Frost, *The Poetry of Robert Frost: The Collected Poems* (New York: Henry Holt, 1979)

Louise Glück, *Poems, 1962–2012* (New York: Farrar, Straus and Giroux, 2012)

Robert Graves, *Complete Poems* (Manchester: Carcanet, 1997)

Jorge Guillén, *Language and Poetry: Some Poets of Spain*, The Charles Eliot Norton Lectures (Cambridge, MA: Harvard University Press, 1961)

—, *Cántico* (Madrid: Diario Público, 2011)

Joy Harjo, *She Had Some Horses* (New York: W. W. Norton & Co., 2008)

Albrecht Haushofer, *Moabiter Sonette* (Berlin: Union Verlag, 1975)

Terrance Hayes *Lighthead* (London: Penguin Poets, 2010)

Seamus Heaney, *Death of a Naturalist* (London: Faber & Faber, 1966)

—, *Door into the Dark* (London: Faber & Faber, 1969)

—, *Wintering Out* (London: Faber & Faber, 1972)

—, *North* (London: Faber & Faber, 1975)

—, *Field Work* (London: Faber & Faber, 1979)

—, *Station Island* (London: Faber & Faber, 1984)

—, *The Spirit Level* (London: Faber & Faber, 1996)

—, *New Selected Poems, 1988–2013* (London: Faber & Faber, 2014)

Martin Heidegger, *Poetry, Language, Thought*, trans. and intro. Albert Hofstadter (New York: Harper & Row, 1971)

Miguel Hernández, *Poesías* (Madrid: Taurus, 1980)

Langston Hughes, *The Collected Poems of Langston Hughes* (London: Vintage Classics, 1995)

Robert Hughes, *The Spectacle of Skill* (New York: Random House, 2016)

Kay Redfield Jamison, *Night Falls Fast: Understanding Suicide* (London: Picador, 2012)

—, *Robert Lowell, Setting the River on Fire* (London: Vintage, 2018)

Randall Jarrell, *Complete Poems* (New York: Farrar, Straus and Giroux, 1969)

—, *Poetry and the Age* (New York: Ecco Press, 1985)

—, illus. Maurice Sendak, *The Bat-Poet* (New York: HarperCollins, 1992)

Juan Ramón Jiménez, *Antología poética* (Madrid: Alianza Editorial, 1984)

Brigit Pegeen Kelly, *Song* (New York: BOA Editions, 1995)

Philip Larkin, *The Less Deceived* (London: Faber & Faber, 2012)

—, *High Windows* (London: Faber & Faber, 2015)

D. H. Lawrence, *Selected Poems*, ed. James Fenton (London: Penguin, 2008)

—, *Life with a Capital L: Essays Chosen and Introduced by Geoff Dyer* (London: Penguin Modern Classics, 2019)

Giacomo Leopardi, *Canti* (bilingual edn) (New York: Farrar, Straus and Giroux 2012)

Philip Levine, *Ashes: Poems New & Old* (New York: Atheneum, 1979)

Federico García Lorca, *Poesia Completa* (New York: Vintage Español, 2012)

Robert Lowell, *Collected Poems* (London: Faber & Faber, 2003)

Archibald MacLeish, *Collected Poems 1917–1952* (Boston, MA: Houghton Mifflin Harcourt, 1952)

Haki R. Madhubuti, *Liberation Narratives: New and Collected Poems, 1966–2009* (Chicago, IL: Third World Press, 2009)

Karl Marx, *Capital*, vol. III (London: Penguin Classics, 1992)

William Matthews, *After All* (Boston, MA: Houghton Mifflin, 1998)

—, *Search Party: Collected Poems of William Matthews* (Boston, MA: Houghton Mifflin, 2005)

Eugenio Montale, *Le occasioni* (Turin: Einaudi, 1939)

—, *Auto da fé: cronache in due tempi* (Milan: Il Saggiatore, 1966)

—, *The Second Life of Art: Selected Essays of Eugenio Montale*, trans. Jonathan Galassi (New York: Ecco Press, 1982)

—, *Ossi di seppia* (Milan: Mondadori, Milan, 2018)

Marianne Moore, *New Collected Poems of Marianne Moore*, ed. Heather Cass White (London: Faber & Faber, 2017)

Pablo Neruda, *Veinte poemas de amor y una canción desesperada; cien sonetos de amor; cien sonetos* (Barcelona: Ediciones Altaya, 1995)

Olga Orozco, *La noche a la deriva* (Córdoba: Alción, 1995)

—, *Relámpagos de lo invisible* (Buenos Aires: Fondo de Cultura Económica, 1998)

José Emilio Pacheco, *Alta traición: antología poética* (Madrid: Alianza Editorial, 1985)

Ezra Pound, *The Cantos of Ezra Pound* (New York: New Directions, 1999)

Alastair Reid, *Inside Out: Selected Poetry and Translations* (Edinburgh: Polygon, 2008)

Rainer Maria Rilke, *Duineser Elegien / Die Sonette an Orpheus* (Leipzig: Insel Verlag, 1974)

—, *Vergers, et autres poèmes français* (Paris: Gallimard, 1978)

—, *Die Gedichte* (Leipzig: Insel Verlag, 2006)

Carne Ross, *The Leaderless Revolution: How Ordinary People will Take Power and Change Politics in the 21st Century* (London: Simon & Schuster, 2012)

—, *Independent Diplomat: Despatches From An Unaccountable Elite* (London: Hurst & Co., 2017)

Denis de Rougemont, *Love in the Western World* (Princeton, NJ: Princeton University Press, 1983)

Siegfried Sassoon, *Collected Poems*, new edn (London: Faber & Faber, 2002)

George Seferis, trans. Edmund Keeley and Philip Sherrard, *Collected Poems* (Princeton, NJ: Princeton University Press, 2016)

Alan Shapiro, *Tantalus in Love* (Boston, MA: Houghton Mifflin, 2006)

Lois Shepherd, 'Face to Face: A Call for Radical Responsibility in Place of Compassion', *St. John's Law Review*, vol. 77, no. 3 (summer 2003)

William Stafford, *The Darkness Around Us Is Deep: Selected Poems of William Stafford* (New York: Harper Perennial, 1993)

Wallace Stevens, *The Collected Poems of Wallace Stevens* (New York: Vintage Books, 2015)

Dylan Thomas, *Quite Early One Morning* (New York: New Directions, 1968)

—, *The Collected Poems of Dylan Thomas* (London: Weidenfeld & Nicolson, 2014)

Marina Tsvetaeva, *Selected Poems*, trans. Elaine Feinstein (London: Penguin Books, 1994)

—, *New Year's: An Elegy for Rilke,* trans. Mary Jane White (Easthampton, MA: Adastra Press, 2008)

Yi-Fu Tuan, *Space and Place: The Perspective of Experience* (Minneapolis, MN: University of Minnesota Press, 1977)

Wamsutta (Frank B.) James, 'Suppressed Speech on the 350th Anniversary of the Pilgrims' Landing at Plymouth Rock', in Howard Zinn and Anthony Arnove, *Voices of a People's History of the United States,* 10th anniversary edn (New York: Seven Stories Press, 2014)

William Carlos Williams, *Journey to Love* (New York: Random House, 1955)

—, *Paterson* (New York: New Directions, 1963)

Ludwig Wittgenstein, *Tractatus Logico-Philosophicus*, trans. D. F. Pears and B. F. McGuines (London: Routledge, 2004)

Charles Wright, *The World of the Ten Thousand Things* (New York: Noonday Press, 1990)

—, *A Short History of the Shadow* (New York: Farrar, Straus and Giroux, 2014)

W. B. Yeats, *Collected Poems* (London: Macmillan, 1950)

Maria Zambrano, *Obras Completas I (Libros 1930–1939)* (Barcelona: Galaxia Gutenberg, 2015)

ACKNOWLEDGEMENTS

Thanks to Mike Jones who got me started, and to Robert Wrigley, whose example lit the way. Huge thanks to everyone at Profile who helped shape this book, and particularly to Cecily Gayford, without whom it might never have been completed. Finally, thanks to all who encouraged, supported, critiqued and generally took an interest in a book that, in its modest claim that poetry is as necessary today as it was in Shelley's time, has at times seemed too quixotic for words.

INDEX